THE
SCHOOL
MATHEMATICS
PROJECT
New Book 1: Part 2

CAMBRIDGE
UNIVERSITY PRESS

Published by the Press Syndicate of the University of Cambridge
The Pitt Building, Trumpington Street, Cambridge CB2 1RP
40 West 20th Street, New York, NY 10011–4211, USA
10 Stamford Road, Oakleigh, Victoria 3166, Australia

© Cambridge University Press 1987

First published 1987
Third printing 1992

Printed in Great Britain at
the University Press, Cambridge

British Library cataloguing in publication data
The School Mathematics Project.
New bk. 1
Pt. 2
1. Mathematics – 1961–
I. School Mathematics Project
510   QA39.2

ISBN 0 521 31118 7

Contents

	Preface	*page*	v
17	Negative numbers		1
18	Symmetry		21
19	Calculations and approximations		40
	Quickies 6		55
	Revision exercises 6A, 6B		57
20	Brackets in formulae		59
21	Let's look at number		66
	Try this 4: 'Yes, grandpa, we do know how lucky we are'		81
22	Area		82
	Quickies 7		101
	Revision exercises 7A, 7B		103
23	Angles		105
24	Formulae using squares		132
25	Factors		143
	Quickies 8		155
	Revision exercises 8A, 8B		157
26	Volume		159
	Try this 5: Constructions		172
27	Through the centre of enlargement		173
28	Fractions		194
	Quickies 9		208
	Revision exercises 9A, 9B		210
29	Percentages		212
30	Conversion and travel graphs		219
31	Illustrating data		229
	Quickies 10		250
	Revision exercises 10A, 10B		252
	Try this 6: A paper chase		254
	Puzzle corner 2		255
	Answers		257
	Index		265

The School Mathematics Project

When the SMP was founded in 1961, its main objective was to devise radically new secondary school mathematics courses to reflect, more adequately than did the traditional syllabuses, the up-to-date nature and usages of mathematics. The first texts produced embodied new courses for O-level and A-level, and SMP GCE examinations were set up, available to schools through any of the GCE examining boards.

Since its beginning the SMP has continued to develop new materials and approaches to the teaching of mathematics. Further series of texts have been produced to meet new needs, and the original books are revised or replaced in the light of changing circumstances and experience in the classroom.

The SMP A-level course is now covered by *Revised Advanced Mathematics Books 1, 2 and 3*. Five shorter texts cover the material of the various sections of the A-level examination SMP Further Mathematics. The SMP Additional Mathematics syllabus has been revised and a new text replaces the original two books at this level.

There is now a range of materials for the eleven to sixteen age-range. *SMP 11–16*, the newest of these, is designed to cater for about the top 85% of the ability range, and offers a rich variety of materials which facilitate the provision of a differentiated curriculum to match the varying abilities of pupils. For the purposes of examination, it has been designated a National Curriculum Project, with its own GCSE examination. Publication of the course began in 1983 and will be completed in 1988.

The original SMP O-level course has been revised and modernised in *New Books 1 to 5*, and these together with *Books A–H, X, Y, Z* and the *SMP Calculator series* provide a range of textbooks suitable for other GCSE examinations.

The six units of *SMP 7–13*, designed for pupils in that age-range, provide a course which is widely used in primary schools, middle schools and the first two years of secondary schools. A useful preliminary to Unit 1 of *SMP 7–13* is *Pointers*, a booklet for teachers which offers suggestions for mathematical activities with young children.

Teacher's Guides accompany all these series.

The SMP has produced many other texts, and teachers are encouraged to obtain each year from Cambridge University Press, The Edinburgh Building, Shaftesbury Road, Cambridge CB2 2RU, the full list of SMP publications currently available. In the same way, help and advice may always be sought by teachers from The School Mathematics Project, The University of Southampton, Southampton SO9 5NH. SMP syllabuses and other information may be obtained from the same address.

The SMP is continually evaluating old work and preparing for new. The effectiveness of the SMP's work depends, as it always has done, on the comments and reactions received from a wide variety of teachers – and also from pupils – using the SMP materials. Readers of the texts and materials can, therefore, send their comments to the SMP in the knowledge that they will be valued and carefully studied.

Preface

SMP Books 1–5 were published in the early sixties and remained as the basic SMP O-level course, unchanged except for metrication, until the publication, starting in 1981, of *SMP New Books 3, 4 and 5*. The success of these has prompted further work, the revision of *Books 1* and *2*. The complete series of *SMP New Books 1–5* draws on the experience of teaching with the original texts and incorporates other material developed by the SMP during the intervening years. While the mathematical content remains fundamentally unchanged, the order of presentation of the material has been modified; the TEC Level I mathematics objectives have been borne in mind throughout the writing of the later books. The aim has been to make the texts accessible to a wider range of pupils, with clearer explanations and more carefully graded exercises, giving attention both to the practice of the necessary technical skills and to the use of the concepts in a wide variety of contexts.

The electronic calculator is seen as the primary calculating aid throughout the books. Suggestions for ways in which pupils can use computers as an aid to learning mathematics are made at appropriate points in the latter half of the course.

With one or two exceptions each chapter concludes with a summary exercise and a miscellaneous exercise. *SMP New Books 1 and 2* also contains some 'Try this' investigations, 'Quickies' and 'Puzzle corners'. The investigations should be seen as an integral part of the course, providing much of interest and extension value. 'Quickies' are designed to help develop the ability to do mental mathematics of all kinds, including simple calculations, to complement the increasing use of the calculator. 'Closed book quickies' contain questions to be read out by the teacher, with pupils given a few seconds to write down the answer, all working being done in the head. 'Open book quickies' should be done by the pupil working from the book in a set time. Again all working should be done in the head. Answers to some of the questions in exercises in the chapters (marked by an asterisk) are given at the back of each book. Other answers together with answers to summary, miscellaneous and revision exercises, 'Quickies', 'Puzzle corners' and 'Try this' investigations are to be found in the *Teacher's Guides*.

The new books, like their predecessors, provide opportunities to develop topics beyond the SMP examination syllabuses.

The 'two books per year' arrangement of the 'lettered books' has proved convenient and economical. By presenting the current revision in the same format it is hoped to give schools the flexibility to allow for the different paces at which pupils work through the course, *SMP New Books 1 and 2* lead into *New Book 3*, but the latter contains sufficient material for pupils who transfer to the SMP course at this stage.

The authors of the original books, on whose contributions this series is based, are named in *The School Mathematics Project: The First Ten Years*, published by Cambridge University Press.

SMP New Books 1 and 2 have been produced by

David Atherton	Keith Jupp
Neil Bibby	Charles Parker
Rick Finch	Heather Pilton
John Harcourt	James Pullen
Gwen Hersee	Jane Southern
John Hersee	Nigel Webb

and edited by Charles Parker.

Many others have helped with advice and criticism, particularly Alan Tammadge and the teachers and pupils who have tested the material in draft form.

17

Negative numbers

1. SOME NEW NUMBERS

The first numbers we meet as children are the counting numbers.

Figure 1

But we soon discover that not all problems can be solved using counting numbers.
   Try dividing nine chocolate bars between 4 friends. See Figure 2.

Figure 2

How many bars does each person get?

The answer is neither 2 nor 3 but something in between. So we have to find numbers to fill the gap. In this case we say that each person gets $2\frac{1}{4}$ bars (or 2.25 bars).

In terms of arithmetic $\frac{9}{4} = 2.25$ or $9 \div 4 = 2.25$.

Now suppose you start with nine chocolate bars and decide to give your four friends one bar each. How many bars have you left? It's easy to work out that $9 - 4 = 5$.

If you give them two bars each you will have $9 - 8 = 1$ bar left.

If you give them three bars each you will have $9 - 12 = ?$ bars left. You will have difficulty in giving your friends 3 bars each! You will also find difficulty in working out $9 - 12$ with only counting numbers to use. However, you are probably used to statements like the following:

(a) The temperature in Aylesbury is 6 °C; the temperature in Elgin is -3 °C.
(b) Berkhamsted is 12 km east of Wendover; Haddenham is 11 km west of Wendover.
(c) The London train arrived at ten past nine; the Edinburgh train arrived at five to nine.

In each of these examples we are making a measurement from a chosen point and the two values stated are on opposite sides of this chosen point. They are illustrated in Figure 3.

Some new numbers 3

(a)

(b) Haddenham — Wendover — Berkhamsted
11 km W   Fixed point   12 km E

(c)

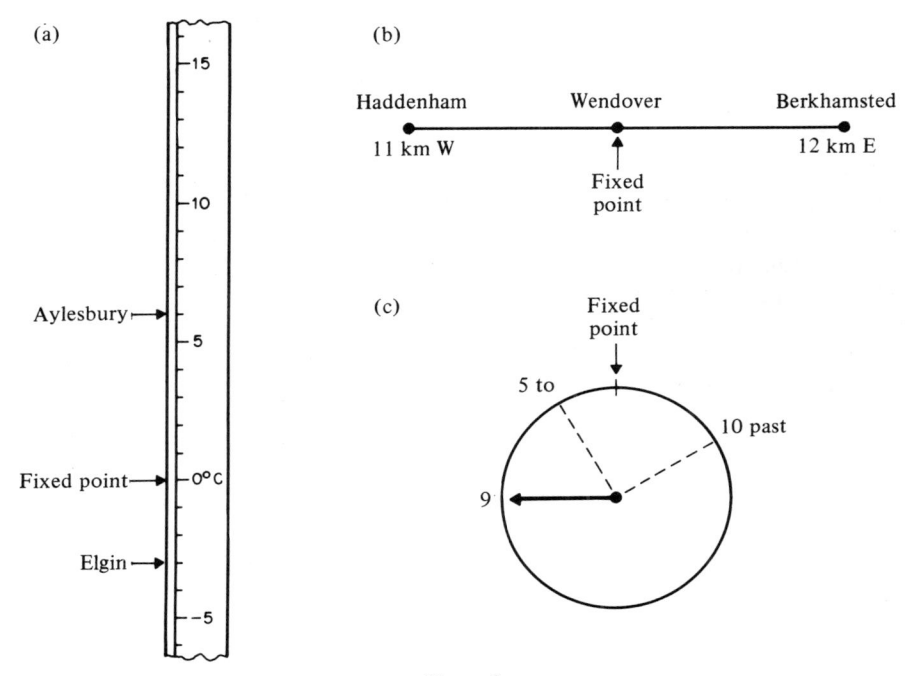

Figure 3

In each of the examples above we have a different way of saying on which side of the chosen point the measurements are. In mathematics we can illustrate numbers on a number line; we choose one point as zero. Figure 4 illustrates this; we have met the idea before, of course, in coordinates.

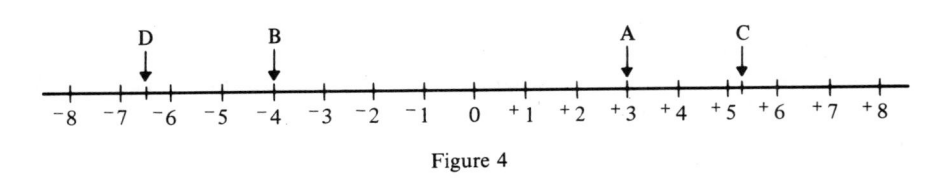

Figure 4

Numbers to the right of zero are greater than 0 and are called positive; numbers to the left of zero are less than 0 and are called negative.

For positive 5 we write $^+5$; for negative 7 we write $^-7$. Hence A is at $^+3$; B at $^-4$; C at $^+5.3$; D at $^-6.5$ (see Figure 4).

We write the + and − signs in a high position to avoid muddling with + and − signs in the usual position meaning add and subtract. If we don't attach a sign to a number we take that number to be positive. So we often write 5.3 instead of $^+5.3$. In this chapter, however, we shall usually put in + and − signs. Zero is neither positive nor negative.

Negative numbers Ch. 17

Example 1

John and his friends live in a tall block of flats. See Figure 5.

John thinks that all floors should be numbered *relative to his floor*, that is by counting from his floor. He has chosen his floor as zero. So Alan who lives three floors above him is on floor $^+3$ while Neil who lives five floors below him is on floor $^-5$.

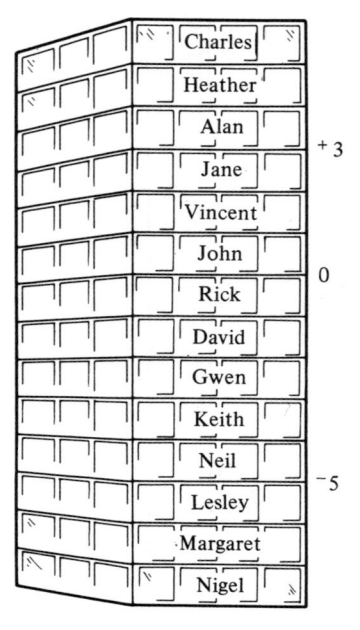

Figure 5

Exercise A

*1 All these questions refer to the block of flats shown in Figure 5.
    (a) How does John number the floors on which the following live?
        (i) Gwen; (ii) Charles; (iii) Margaret; (iv) Nigel; (v) Rick; (vi) Jane
    (b) Jane numbers the floors on which her friends live in a similar way but chooses her own floor to be zero. What number does she give to the floors on which the following live?
        (i) John; (ii) Alan; (iii) Neil; (iv) Heather; (v) Gwen.
    (c) Use the same system to number the floors lived on by the following, relative to David's floor.
        (i) Jane; (ii) Neil; (iii) Margaret; (iv) Vincent; (v) Keith.

*2 The ground floor of Richard's house is 300 m above sea level. Describe the positions of the following objects in numbers of metres relative to the ground floor of Richard's house (the answer to (a) is given as an example):
    (a) a church 374 m above sea level (answer $^+74$);
    (b) a boat at sea level;
    (c) a school 73 m above sea level;
    (d) a submarine 10 m below sea level;
    (e) the top of a TV mast 423 m above sea level;
    (f) a sub-aqua diver 7 m below the submarine.

Some new numbers 5

*3 Suppose 8.50 a.m. is zero time for arrival at school, otherwise you are late!
   (a) Express the following arrival times, in numbers of minutes, relative to zero time.
   For example 8.45 a.m. is ⁻5.
   (i) 8.37 a.m.; (ii) 9.01 a.m.; (iii) 9.15 a.m.;
   (iv) 8.27 a.m.; (v) 8,39 a.m.
   (b) What arrival times correspond to the following?
   (i) ⁻7; (ii) ⁺9; (iii) ⁻23; (iv) ⁻17.

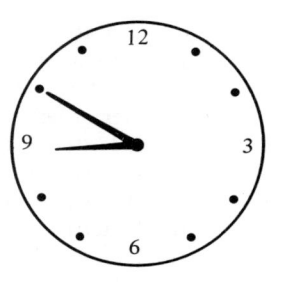

Figure 6

*4 On January 4th 1985 the following mid-day temperatures, in °C, were reported: Athens 12; Birmingham 2; Bristol 4; Cairo 21; Edinburgh 4; Gibraltar 15; Melbourne 25; Perth 32; Venice ⁻3; Warsaw ⁻10.
   (a) Make a copy of the thermometer drawn in Figure 7.
   Write the name of each of the ten places at the correct point on the scale, e.g. mark 'Athens' at 12 and so on.
   (b) Write down the difference in temperature (in numbers of °C) between:
   (i) Athens and Perth; (ii) Cairo and Venice; (iii) Warsaw and Edinburgh; (iv) Venice and Warsaw.

5 (This question uses the data of question 4.)
   (a) The temperature in London was 3 °C. Athens was therefore 9°C warmer, so relative to London its temperature in numbers of °C was ⁺9.
   Relative to London the temperature in numbers of °C in Birmingham was ⁻1.
   In a similar way write down the temperature in °C of the following places relative to London:
   (i) Perth; (ii) Venice; (iii) Gibraltar; (iv) Warsaw.
   (b) The temperature in Tenerife was 19 °C. Use a positive or negative number to write down the temperature of each of the following places relative to Tenerife:
   (i) Melbourne; (ii) Bristol; (iii) Warsaw; (iv) Cairo.

6 The average age of a class is 12 years, 3 months.
   (a) Judith is 12 years, Joan is 11 years, 10 months, Jack is 12 years, 7 months and Jim is 11 years, 8 months.
   Use positive and negative numbers to express the number of months each child is above or below the average age.
   (b) Using the same system for the same class Barbara's age is given as ⁺3, Ben's as 0 and Bernard's as ⁻5. What are their actual ages?

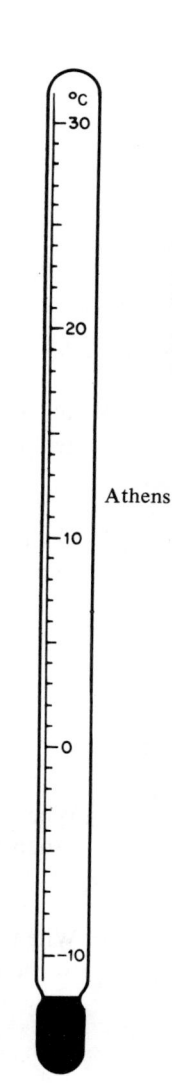

Figure 7

*7 Queen Elizabeth II was crowned in 1953. John was born in 1945, David in 1973. Their years of birth relative to the Coronation year are ⁻8 and ⁺20 respectively.
   Use positive and negative numbers to express the following dates as numbers of years after or before the Coronation year.
   (a) 1937 (the first helicopter flight);
   (b) 1928 (the first 'talkie' movie);
   (c) 1969 (the first man on the moon);
   (d) 1906 (the world's first radio broadcast);
   (e) 1914 (the opening of the Panama Canal);
   (f) 1966 (England's World Cup victory).

8 The temperature is 8 °C.
   (a) What will the temperature be after it has fallen by 13 degrees?
   (b) If it falls a further 4 degrees what will the temperature then be?
   (c) What rise will then be necessary for the temperature to reach 6 °C?

*9 Write down the next four numbers in each of the following sequences:
   (a) ⁺9, ⁺7, ⁺5, ⁺3, ...;
   (b) ⁺7, ⁺2, ⁻3, ...;
   (c) ⁻10, ⁻8, ⁻6, ...;
   (d) 23, 16, 9, ...

2. ADDITION

Adding positive numbers

We can add counting numbers, for example $4 + 3 = 7$. The counting numbers are positive whole numbers and we can emphasise this by writing

$$^{+}4 + {^{+}3} = {^{+}7}.$$

On a number line we can see this as starting at ⁺4 and then moving 3 units to the right along this line.

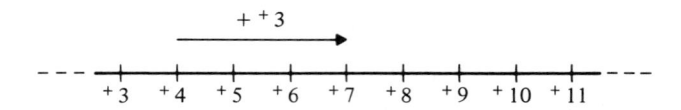

When we add ⁺3 we shift three units to the right from the starting number. When we add ⁺5 we shift five units to the right from the starting number. So

$$(^{+}2) + (^{+}5) = (^{+}7).$$

When we work out $(^{-}2) + (^{+}5)$ the addition of ⁺5 still means a shift of five units to the right so we have

Addition

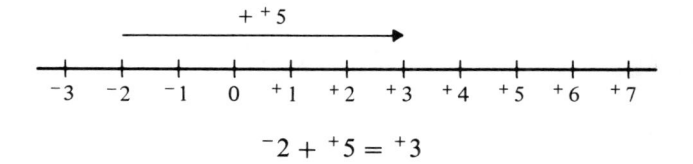

$$^-2 + {}^+5 = {}^+3$$

Adding negative numbers

How can we add $^-4$? Notice first that the shift we apply in adding $^+5$ is the same as the shift that takes us from 0 to $^+5$.

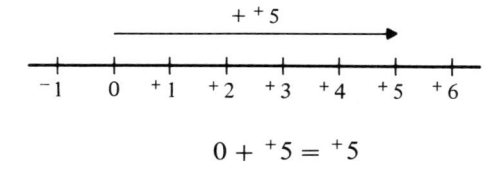

$$0 + {}^+5 = {}^+5$$

So, using a similar idea, the shift that we apply to add $^-4$ is the same as the shift that takes us from 0 to $^-4$.

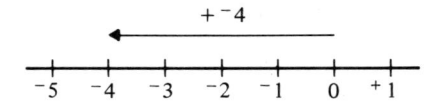

In other words, to add $^-4$ we apply a shift of 4 units to the *left*.

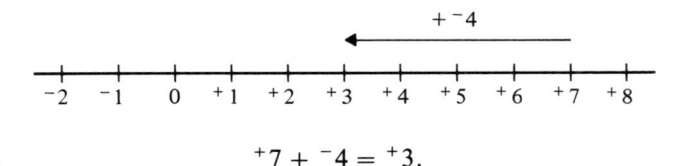

Therefore
$$^+7 + {}^-4 = {}^+3.$$

Negative numbers

Also $^+3 + {}^-4 = {}^-1,$

and $^-2 + {}^-3 = {}^-5.$ (See below.)

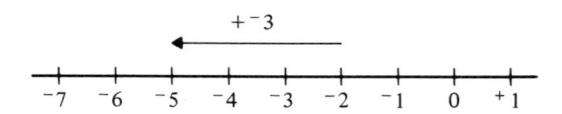

When we add positive numbers we shift to the right along the number line. When we add negative numbers we shift to the left along the number line.

Example 2

Draw a number line to illustrate $^+5 + {}^-2.7$ and write down the answer.

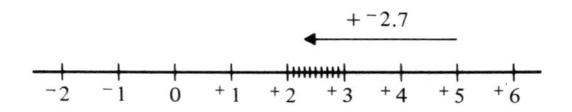

From the number line it can be seen that the answer is $^+2.3$. (Compare this with $5 - 2.7 = 2.3$.)

Example 3

Draw a number line to illustrate $^-2.4 + {}^+3.7$ and write down the answer.

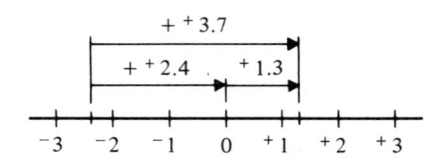

From the number line it can be seen that the answer is $^+1.3$. Extra care must be taken because the shift takes us across zero; we have to work out $3.7 - 2.4$.

Addition

Exercise B

Calculators should not be used.

Draw one number line for each of questions 1–3. Work out the answers to the additions, illustrating these on your number line.

*1   (a) $^+3 + {^+2}$;   (b) $^+3 + {^-4}$;   (c) $^+3 + {^-2}$.
2   (a) $^-2 + {^+3}$;   (b) $^-2 + {^-5}$;   (c) $^-2 + {^+2}$.
3   (a) $^+2.4 + {^+3.6}$;   (b) $^+2.4 + {^-6.0}$;   (c) $^+2.4 + {^-2.4}$.

In questions 4–17 write down the answers.

*4 $^+3 + {^+9}$.   5 $^+3 + {^-5}$.   6 $^+17 + {^-5}$.
*7 $^-7 + {^-5}$.   8 $^+23 + {^-17}$.   9 $^-5 + {^+10}$.
*10 $^-20 + {^-30}$.   11 $^+17 + {^-17}$.   12 $0 + {^-91}$.
13   $^-13 + {^+7}$.   14 $^-7 + {^+12}$.   15 $^+17 + {^+12}$.
16   $^-7 + {^-3}$ 17 $^+6 + {^-10}$.

In questions 18–23 try to write down the answers by first thinking of a number line with appropriate numbers and shifts marked. Only draw the number line as a last resort.

18   $^+1.1 + {^+2.3}$.   19 $^-3 + {^-2.7}$.   20 $^+2.3 + {^-3}$.
21   $^+6.3 + {^-3.3}$.   22 $^+5 + {^+2.4}$.   23 $^-2.4 + {^+5}$.

Use of calculator

It is now time to see how this type of calculation can be done with a calculator. You will always take a number without a sign to be positive. Your calculator does the same. If you wish to enter a negative number, first enter the digits in the usual way *and then* enter the negative sign. This is generally done by pressing the button marked $\boxed{+/-}$, but this depends on the calculator. If necessary you should check the calculator's instruction booklet, or ask your teacher.

Example 4

Use your calculator to work out $^+3 + {^-4}$.

With your calculator, work through the following steps:
   Enter $^+3$. (Enter 3, the sign is automatically positive.)
   $+$
   Enter $^-4$. (Enter 4 followed by $\boxed{+/-}$.)
   $=$
(Ask for help if you do not get the correct answer of $^-1$.)

Before starting the next exercise you should work through the following questions with your calculator using the same method as for Example 4. Ask for help if you do not get the correct answers.

  (a) Work out $^-12 + {^-7}$.   Answer $^-19$.
  (b) Work out $^-5.1 + {^+3.2} + {^-7.8}$.   Answer $^-9.7$.

10 Negative numbers Ch. 17

Example 5
Find the output from the following flow chart.

$$^-12 \longrightarrow \boxed{+ {}^+7} \longrightarrow ?$$

We start with $^-12$ and add $^+7$. In other words we work out

$$^-12 + {}^+7.$$

The answer, obtained by calculator or number line or mental arithmetic, is $^-5$. The output from the flow chart is $^-5$.

Exercise C Calculator Exercise

Evaluate
- *1 $^+17 + {}^+21$
- *2 $^-33 + {}^-22$
- 3 $^-5 + {}^+1.3$
- 4 $^+7.1 + {}^-2.3$
- 5 $^-321 + {}^+179$
- *6 $^-3 + {}^-9 + {}^+21$
- *7 $^-2.7 + {}^+3.8 + {}^+7.1$
- 8 $^+180 + {}^-63 + {}^-72$
- 9 $^+2.8 + {}^-12.7 + {}^+3.2$
- 10 $^-3.7 + {}^-4.2 + {}^+7.7$

Find the output of the flow charts in questions 11–15.

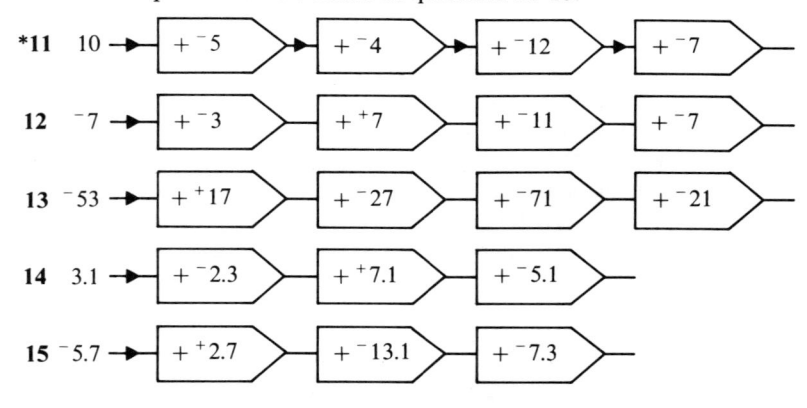

*11 $10 \to \boxed{+ {}^-5} \to \boxed{+ {}^-4} \to \boxed{+ {}^-12} \to \boxed{+ {}^-7}$

12 $^-7 \to \boxed{+ {}^-3} \to \boxed{+ {}^+7} \to \boxed{+ {}^-11} \to \boxed{+ {}^-7}$

13 $^-53 \to \boxed{+ {}^+17} \to \boxed{+ {}^-27} \to \boxed{+ {}^-71} \to \boxed{+ {}^-21}$

14 $3.1 \to \boxed{+ {}^-2.3} \to \boxed{+ {}^+7.1} \to \boxed{+ {}^-5.1}$

15 $^-5.7 \to \boxed{+ {}^+2.7} \to \boxed{+ {}^-13.1} \to \boxed{+ {}^-7.3}$

3. SUBTRACTION

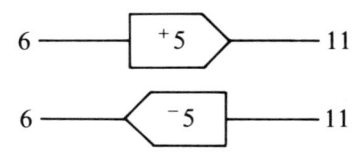

$$6 \longrightarrow \boxed{{}^+5} \longrightarrow 11$$

$$6 \longrightarrow \boxed{{}^-5} \longrightarrow 11$$

The flow chart reminds us that subtraction is the reverse process to addition. Working on a number line

we shift 5 to the *right* when we *add* $^+5$.

Subtraction 11

To reverse this

we shift 5 to the *left* when we *subtract* $^+5$.

See below.

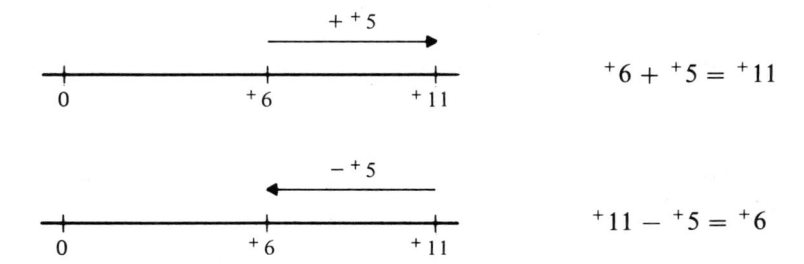

$$^+6 + {}^+5 = {}^+11$$

$$^+11 - {}^+5 = {}^+6$$

Extending this idea,

we shift 4 to the *left* when we *add* $^-4$,

so

we shift 4 to the *right* when we *subtract* $^-4$.

See below.

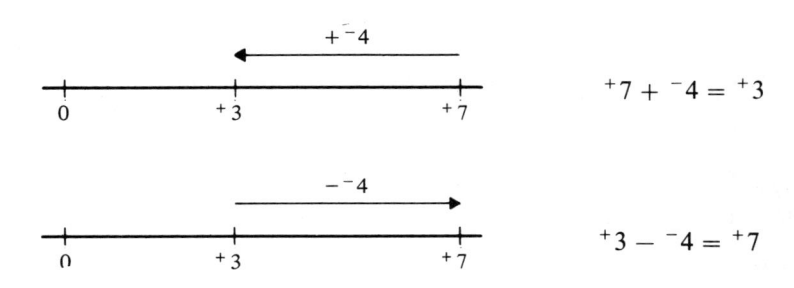

$$^+7 + {}^-4 = {}^+3$$

$$^+3 - {}^-4 = {}^+7$$

Use the following steps (as a guide) for checking this final result on your calculator:

Enter $^+3$

$-$

Enter $^-4$ (i.e. 4 followed by $+/-$)

$=$

Negative numbers

To summarise (with starting numbers omitted):

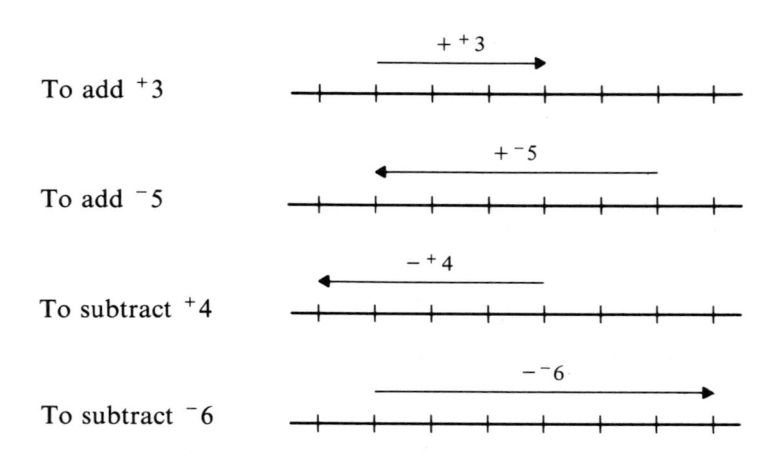

To add $^+3$

To add $^-5$

To subtract $^+4$

To subtract $^-6$

Example 6

Use a diagram of a number line to evaluate (work out) $^-2.5 - {}^+4.5$.

We start at $^-2.5$ and shift 4.5 to the left.

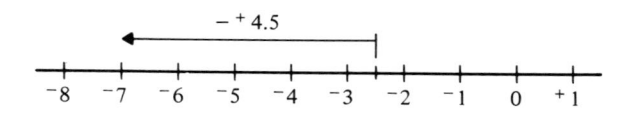

The answer is $^-7$ and should be checked with your calculator.

Example 7

Use a number line to evaluate $^+2.7 - {}^-3.2$.

We start at $^+2.7$ and shift 3.2 to the right.

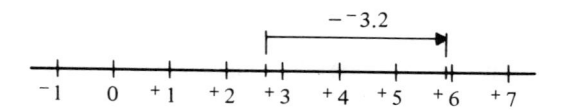

The answers is $^+5.9$ and should be checked with your calculator.

Subtraction

Difference

By the *difference* between two numbers we mean the number giving their distance apart on the number line. Thus, for example, the difference between 7 and 12 is 5 and this is the same as the difference between 12 and 7.

Example 7
  Find the difference between ⁻3.8 and ⁺2.3.

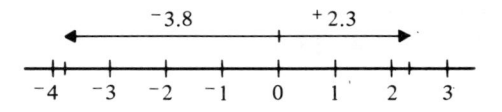

As can be seen from the number line the required answer is

$$3.8 + 2.3 = 6.1.$$

The difference between ⁺2.3 and ⁻3.8 is also 6.1.

Exercise D

Draw one number line for each of questions 1–3. Work out the answers to the subtractions, illustrating them on your number line. (Do not use a calculator.)
*1 (a) ⁺5 − ⁺2;   (b) ⁺5 − ⁻3;   (c) ⁺5 − ⁺7.
2 (a) ⁻4 − ⁺2;   (b) ⁻4 − ⁻3;   (c) ⁻4 − ⁻7.
3 (a) ⁻2.4 − ⁺1.6;   (b) ⁻2.4 − ⁻2.4;   (c) ⁻2.4 − ⁻4.8.

Write down the answers to questions 4–13. Check your answers with a calculator.
*4 ⁺3 − ⁺7.   5 ⁺2 − ⁺3.   6 ⁻3 − ⁻7.
*7 ⁻8 − ⁺2.   8 ⁻3 − ⁻5.   9 3 − ⁻4.
*10 ⁻1.3 − 7.   11 ⁺3.7 − ⁺9.7.   12 ⁻5.7 − 4.5.
13 ⁻5.3 − ⁻5.7.
14 Calculate the following:
    (a) ⁺3 + ⁻4;   ⁺3 − ⁺4.
    (b) ⁻2 + ⁻3;   ⁻2 − ⁺3.
    (c) ⁺7 + ⁻3;   ⁺7 − ⁺3.
    (d) ⁺5 + ⁻2;   ⁺5 − ⁺2.
  Copy and complete the sentence 'Adding the negative number ⁻n has the same effect as ...'
15 Calculate the following:
    (a) ⁺3 − ⁻2;   ⁺3 + ⁺2.
    (b) ⁻7 − ⁻3;   ⁻7 + ⁺3.
    (c) ⁻2 − ⁻5;   ⁻2 + ⁺5.
    (d) ⁺10 − ⁻12;   ⁺10 + ⁺12.
  Copy and complete the sentence 'Subtracting the negative number ⁻n has the same effect as ...'

*16 Find the difference between:
(a) $^+6$ and $^+2$; (b) $^+5$ and $^-3$; (c) $^-5$ and $^+11$; (d) $^-13$ and $^-9$;
(e) 8 and 0; (f) 0 and $^-6$; (g) $^-2.6$ and $^+4.5$; (h) $^-8.7$ and $^-13.2$.

4. SPEEDING THINGS UP

Once you thoroughly understand how addition and subtraction work on a number line you can use your answers to questions 14 and 15 in Exercise D to speed things up. This is illustrated below.

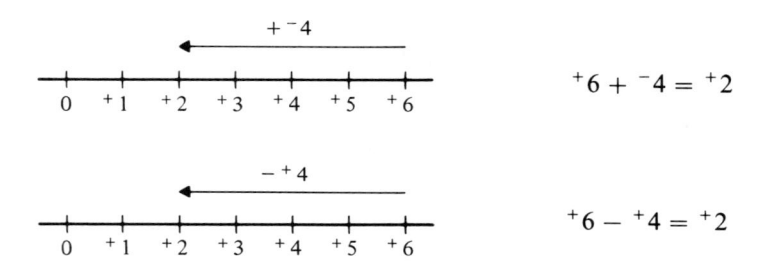

$$^+6 + {^-4} = {^+2}$$

$$^+6 - {^+4} = {^+2}$$

Adding $^-4$ is the same as subtracting $^+4$.

$$^-3 - {^-5} = {^+2}$$

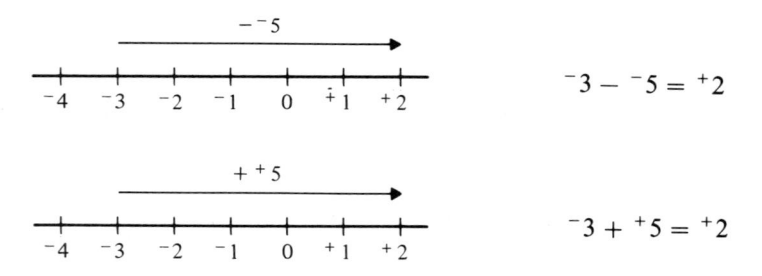

$$^-3 + {^+5} = {^+2}$$

Subtracting $^-5$ is the same as adding $^+5$.

Calculations involving positive numbers may be easier to 'see in your head' and, in any case, are easier to enter into a calculator. The following examples illustrate:

Example 8
   Evaluate $^+5 - {^-7}$.

$$^+5 - {^-7} = {^+5} + {^+7} \quad (5 + 7 \text{ on calculator})$$
$$= {^+12}.$$

Example 9
   Evaluate $^-3.8 + {}^-4.1$.

$$^-3.8 + {}^-4.1 = {}^-3.8 - {}^+4.1 \quad (^-3.8 - 4.1 \text{ on calculator})$$
$$= {}^-7.9.$$

Applications

Negative numbers are often met with in daily life. The following example shows one situation; others are explored in the exercise which follows.

Example 10
We can consider heights above sea level to be positive altitudes and depths below sea level to be negative altitudes. The following altitudes are given (in numbers of metres).

Top of cliff	50
Top of lighthouse	62
Helicopter	217
Shark	$^-5$
Submarine	$^-125$
Diver	$^-12$
Climber on cliff	37

This data can be used to answer various questions. For example the difference in altitude of the shark and the diver is 7 metres (given by $12 - 5 = 7$).
   Find the following:
   (a) the difference in altitude between the climber and the shark;
   (b) the height of the lighthouse;
   (c) the vertical distance between the submarine and the helicopter;
   (d) the distance the climber has to go to reach the top of the cliff.

The answers are:

   (a) $37 - {}^-5 = 42$ (or $37 + 5$)   42 metres
   (b) $62 - 50 = 12$ 12 metres
   (c) $217 - {}^-125 = 342$ (or $217 + 125$)   342 metres
   (d) $50 - 37 = 13$ 13 metres

Exercise E

*1 The temperatures around the world at lunchtime on January 18th 1985 were as follows (all in °C)

Algiers	17	Edinburgh	3	Montreal	⁻18
Barbados	27	Frankfurt	⁻5	Perth	24
Cardiff	⁻1	London	2	Warsaw	⁻10

(a) Find the difference in temperature between the following:
    (i) Algiers and Frankfurt; (ii) Frankfurt and Perth; (iii) Montreal and Warsaw; (iv) Barbados and Cardiff; (v) Cardiff and Montreal.

(b) Name two places where the difference in temperature in °C is
    (i) 10; (ii) 35; (iii) 13; (iv) 5; (v) 12; (vi) 20; (vii) 28; (viii) 45.

*2 In a test at school, ⁺4 is scored for each correct answer but ⁻1 for an incorrect one.

(a) Write down the final score of each of the following:
    (i) Alan   6 correct, 4 incorrect
    (ii) Brian   3 correct, 7 incorrect
    (iii) Clyde   8 correct, 2 incorrect
    (iv) Elizabeth   5 correct, 5 incorrect
    (v) Jane   1 correct, 9 incorrect
    (vi) Karen   7 correct, 3 incorrect

(b) Write down the difference in marks between:
    (i) Karen and Brian;
    (ii) Jane and Clyde;
    (iii) Elizabeth and Alan.

(c) What were the total marks for:
    (i) the girls;
    (ii) the boys?

(d) Which two candidates had the biggest difference between their scores, and what was it?

3 In a Space Wars game you score ⁺10 points for hitting a Hawk spy rocket, ⁺20 points for a Vulcan offensive rocket, ⁺50 for an Albatross base station. For each miss you score ⁻5 and if you hit one of your own Vixen spy rockets you score ⁻35.

Write down the scores after each shot in this game. (You start with zero points.)

1 Miss	6 Hawk	11 Hawk
2 Hawk	7 Vixen	12 Albatross
3 Vulcan	8 Vixen	13 Vulcan
4 Vixen	9 Miss	14 Vixen
5 Albatross	10 Vulcan	15 Albatross

4 When I pay £20 into my bank, ⁺20 is added to the number of pounds in my account. When my account is debited by £30 then ⁻30 is added. In one week the following happens:

Starting value in number of £'s	200		
Credits	6	Debits	30
(Payments in)	10	(payments out)	70
	7		94

What is the value of my account at the end of the week?
What have I left if there is a further debit of £40?

5 During a single day the tide rises up a sea wall to 2.5 m above a certain mark. What figure must be *added* to 2.5 to get the low tide position which is 1.3 m below that mark?

6 In France the floors in a block of flats are often given positive numbers $^+1, ^+2, \ldots$ if above ground level and negative numbers $^-1, ^-2, \ldots$ if below ground level. The latter are often floors in the car park. Write down the shift in floors in going from
(a) 0 to $^+5$; (b) $^+5$ to $^-2$; (c) $^-2$ to $^-3$; (d) $^-3$ to $^+10$.

SUMMARY

We can extend our number line to include numbers either side of zero.

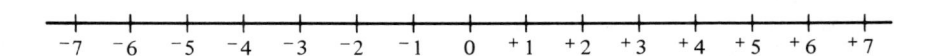

$$-7 \quad ^-6 \quad ^-5 \quad ^-4 \quad ^-3 \quad ^-2 \quad ^-1 \quad 0 \quad ^+1 \quad ^+2 \quad ^+3 \quad ^+4 \quad ^+5 \quad ^+6 \quad ^+7$$

Numbers greater than zero (to the right of zero) are called positive numbers. Numbers less than zero (to the left of zero) are called negative numbers.

For example $^+5$ is 'positive 5'; $^-3$ is negative 3'. Numbers written with no sign are taken to be positive.

When we add a number we can think of this as a shift along the number line. The direction of the shift depends on the sign of the number. For example we shift 4 units to the right to add $^+4$.

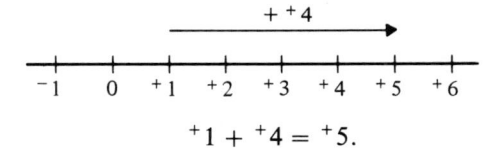

So $\qquad ^+1 + ^+4 = ^+5.$

We shift 7 units to the left to add $^-7$.

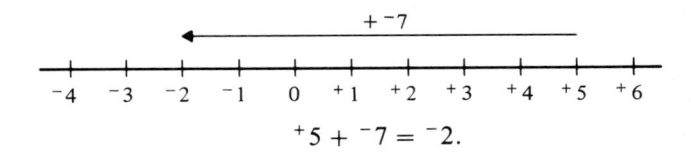

So $\qquad ^+5 + ^-7 = ^-2.$

Subtraction is the reverse of addition. When we subtract a number, therefore, the shift must be applied in the reverse directions. For example we shift 4 units to the left to subtract $^+4$.

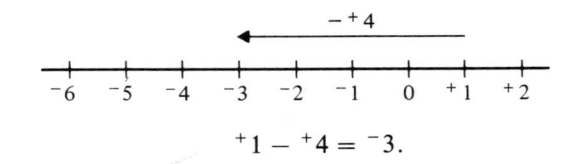

So $^+1 - {^+4} = {^-3}$.

We shift 7 units to the right to subtract $^-7$.

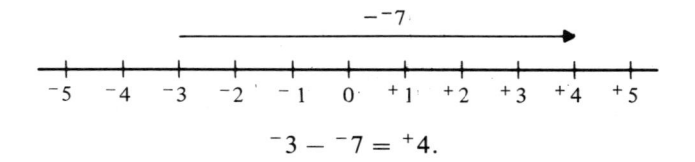

So $^-3 - {^-7} = {^+4}$.

Examples:

$$^+5 + {^+3} = {^+8}; \quad {^+5} + {^-3} = {^+2};$$
$$^+5 - {^+3} = {^+2}; \quad {^+5} - {^-3} = {^+8}.$$

Remember that (a) subtracting $^+3$ has the same effect as adding $^-3$; and (b) subtracting $^-3$ has the same effect as adding $^+3$.

Summary exercise (non calculator)

Calculate the following:
1. $^+3 + {^+5}$.
2. $^+3 + {^-7}$.
3. $^-2 + {^+3}$.
4. $^-7 + {^-5}$.
5. $^+5 - {^+7}$.
6. $^+5 - {^-7}$.
7. $^-3 - {^-4}$.
8. $^-9 - {^+5}$.
9. $^+1.7 + {^-3.2}$.
10. $^-3.9 + {^-5.2}$.
11. $^+5.3 + {^+11.1}$.
12. $^-7.3 - {^+3.2}$.

13 The time of sunset in London on February 2nd 1986 was 5.04 p.m. Use positive and negative numbers to express the following sunset times in minutes relative to London (i.e. taking 5.04 p.m. as the zero time).

Belfast 5.11 p.m.
Nottingham 5.02 p.m.
Birmingham 5.06 p.m.
Newcastle 4.52 p.m.
Bristol 5.14 p.m.
Manchester 5.03 p.m.
Glasgow 4.57 p.m.

Miscellaneous exercise

1. What must be added to (a) $^+7$ to get $^+13$;
   (b) $^-5$ to get $^+13$;
   (c) $^-1.7$ to get $^-3.5$;
   (d) $^+13$ to get $^-3.7$?

2. What must be subtracted from (a) $^+7$ to get $^+2$;
   (b) $^+3$ to get $^+8$;
   (c) $^-5$ to get $^-13$;
   (d) $^-12$ to get $^-7$?

3. A dice game. David and Anne are playing a game with two dice. The score on the blue die is counted as positive, the score on the red die as negative. David and Anne throw the dice three times and the results are as follows:

		Blue	Red
1st throws	Anne	5	1
	David	1	2
2nd throws	Anne	3	5
	David	5	6
3rd throws	Anne	4	2
	David	3	4

   (a) Find their scores for each throw.
   (b) The winner is the one with the highest score over three throws. Who won and by how many points?
   (c) If you have some dice, play this game with a friend.

4. Another dice game. Two dice are thrown, the score for each die is considered to be negative if it is even, positive if odd. So if the first die shows 3, the second 4, then the combined score is $^+3 + {^-4} = {^-1}$. David's and Anne's scores were as follows:

1st throws	David	5	3
	Anne	4	1
2nd throws	David	3	6
	Anne	6	3
3rd throws	David	6	3
	Anne	4	4

   Calculate the total score for (a) David, (b) Anne.
   Try the game for yourself.

5. Selina is much better at darts than Wayne. They play a game where each starts with a total of 301 points and at each round they subtract their score from their total. To even the game up, Selina agrees to subtract 30 from the number of points she scores before subtracting it from her total. Complete the following table to find her points total after 8 throws.

	Points scored	Points to be deducted	Total left
Round 1	47	17	284
2	27	⁻3	287
3	101		
4	53		
5	19		
6	2		
7	96		
8	2		

6 In each case, say which pair of coordinates is the odd one out.
   (a) (⁺3, ⁻2), (⁻5, ⁺6), (⁻1, ⁺2), (⁺2, ⁻3).
   (b) (⁻2, ⁺2), (⁺1, ⁺5), (⁻5, ⁻1), (⁻6, ⁺2).
   (c) (⁺7, ⁻2), (⁻3, ⁻2), (⁺3, ⁺2), (⁻3, ⁺8).
   (d) (5, ⁻7), (⁻2, 0), (⁻4, ⁻2), (⁻1, 1).

7 Find the connection between the x- and y-coordinates in each of the following. Part (a) is done for you as an example.
   (a) (7, 4), (1, ⁻2), (0, ⁻3), (⁻3, ⁻6). $x - y = 3$.
   (b) (⁻2, ⁻4), (⁻1, ⁻3), (0, ⁻2), (⁺2, 0).
   (c) (⁻5, ⁺3), (⁻3, ⁺1), (0, ⁻2), (⁺3, ⁻5).
   (d) (⁻5, ⁺3), (⁻2, ⁺6), (⁺1, ⁺9), (⁺4, ⁺12).

18

Symmetry

1. INTRODUCTION

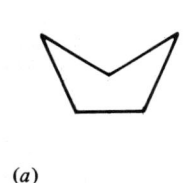

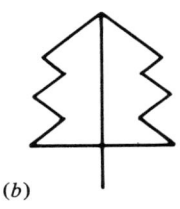

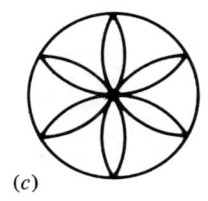

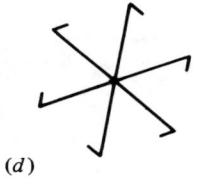

Figure 1

If you compare the drawings in Figure 1 with those in Figure 2 you will recognise that there is a fundamental difference between the two groups. The drawings in Figure 1 have a kind of 'balance', a regular pattern which is not present in Figure 2. We call this property *symmetry*.

Figure 2

There are two types of symmetry to discuss and we look at these separately.

22   Symmetry   Ch. 18

2. LINE SYMMETRY

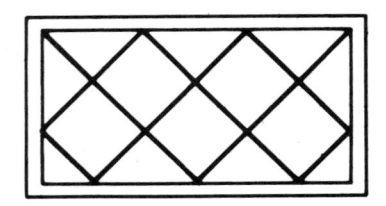

Figure 3

The ornamental gate and the window with 'leaded lights' shown in Figure 3 are both examples of shapes which have *line symmetry*. This means that it is possible to draw a line somewhere on each that divides the shape exactly into two matching parts. The line we draw is called the *line of symmetry*.

Figure 4

Figure 4 shows each drawing of Figure 3 with the line of symmetry indicated by a broken line.

A shape may have more than one line of symmetry; Figure 5(*a*) shows a 'letter box' with two lines of symmetry. How many lines of symmetry are there in the star in Figure 5(*b*)? How many lines of symmetry are there in Figure 1(*a*), (*b*) and (*c*)?

Figure 5

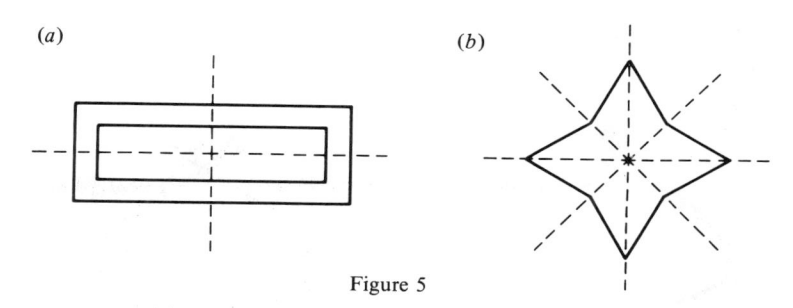

Many shapes have no lines of symmetry at all, for example the drawings of the pencil sharpener blade and paper clip shown in Figure 6.

Figure 6

3. TESTING FOR LINE SYMMETRY

1. Paper folding

We can make use of the fact that a line of symmetry divides a shape exactly into two matching parts to check for symmetry. Fold a drawing or tracing of the shape along what is thought to be a line of symmetry. If one part fits exactly over the other part then the fold line is a line of symmetry. See Figure 7.

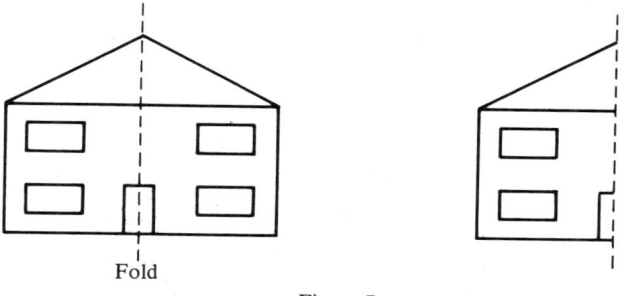

Figure 7

This can also be used to make patterns which have a line of symmetry. Fold a piece of paper in half, open it out and put a small quantity of ink on the paper; using the same fold, press the paper over quickly and firmly. After a short time open out the paper and you should have an 'ink devil'.

24   Symmetry   **Ch. 18**

The lines in Figure 8(a) made the pattern in Figure 8(b).

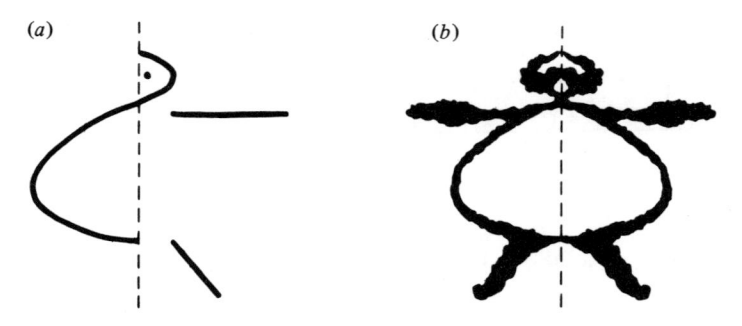

Figure 8

Look at any point on an ink devil. Measure its distance (it must be the perpendicular distance – why?) from the fold line. Now measure the distance from the fold line to the matching point on the other side of the smudge. (A geo-liner makes this easy.) What do you notice? Check with other pairs of points that they are on opposite sides at equal distances from the fold line. Is there any other line which divides the pattern equally like this?

2. Using a mirror

By placing a small rectangular mirror along what is thought to be a line of symmetry, the image in the mirror of one part of the shape should be identical to the other part of the shape. If it is, you have found a line of symmetry; if it isn't, try again! [Of course, there may not be a line of symmetry...]

Figure 9 shows a line of symmetry of a shape and two points A and A' which are in corresponding positions. If you place (or imagine) a mirror along the broken line you will see that A' is the image of A in the mirror. We say that A' is the image of A in m and also that A is the image of A'.

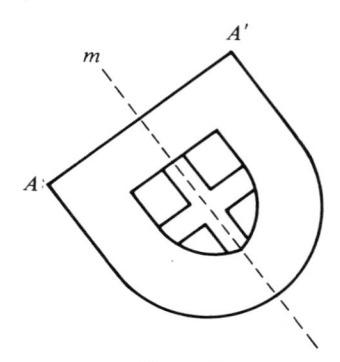

Figure 9

3. Using a geoliner

Figure 10 shows a geoliner being used to check that AB is a line of symmetry of the diagram shown. Note that the two points that correspond to each other are equal distances from O and that the line of symmetry runs from O to the right-angle of the geoliner.

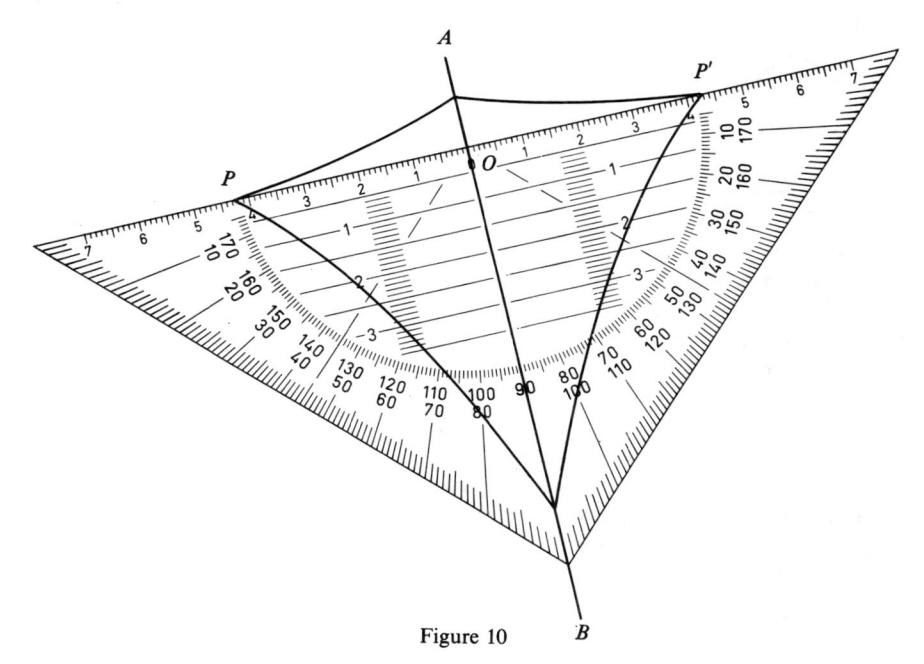

Figure 10

Exercise A

You will need tracing paper and a geoliner.

1. Which of the diagrams in Figure 11 have line symmetry? Which have more than one line of symmetry? Copy those which have line symmetry and mark the line(s) of symmetry in different colours.

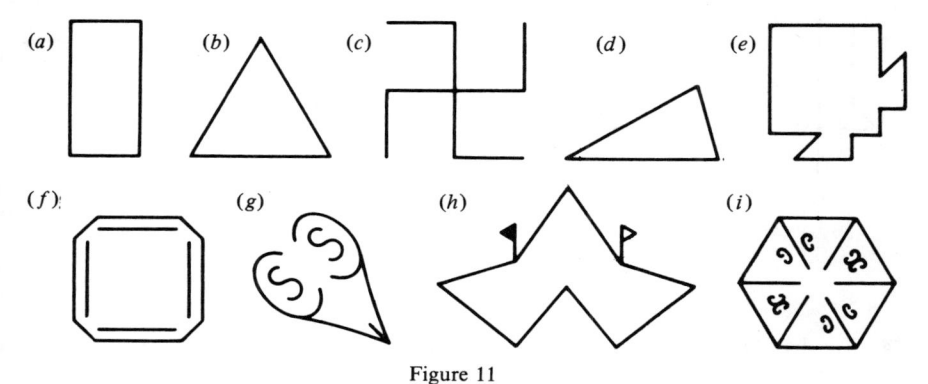

Figure 11

26　Symmetry　　　　　　　　　　　　　　　　　　　　　　　　Ch. 18

*2　How many lines of symmetry, if any, have the diagrams in Figure 12?

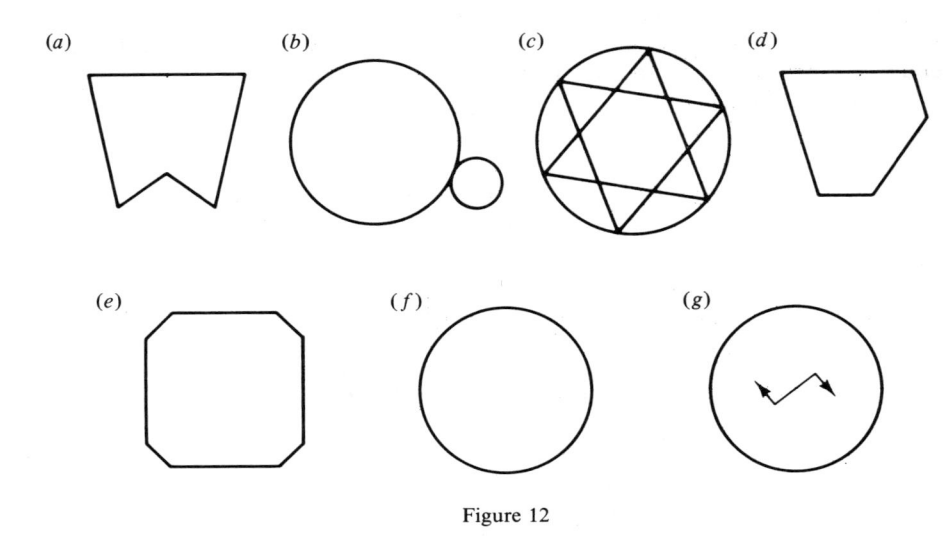

(a)　　　　　　(b)　　　　　　(c)　　　　　　(d)

(e)　　　　　　(f)　　　　　　(g)

Figure 12

3　Each of the unfinished diagrams in Figure 13 has a line of symmetry marked with the letter *m*. Use tracing paper to make a copy of the diagrams. Then turn the tracing paper over and complete them.

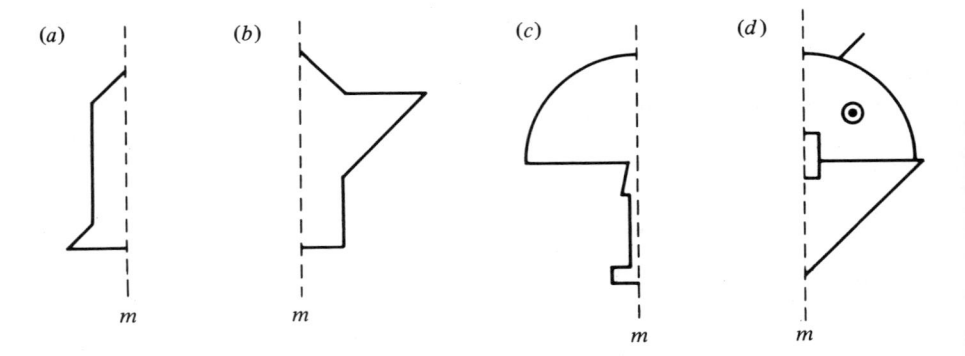

(a)　　　　　　(b)　　　　　　(c)　　　　　　(d)

m　　　　　　*m*　　　　　　*m*　　　　　　*m*

Figure 13

*4　The half-finished figures in Figure 14 have a line of symmetry marked *m*. Copy them and use tracing paper or a geoliner to complete them.

Testing for line symmetry

Figure 14

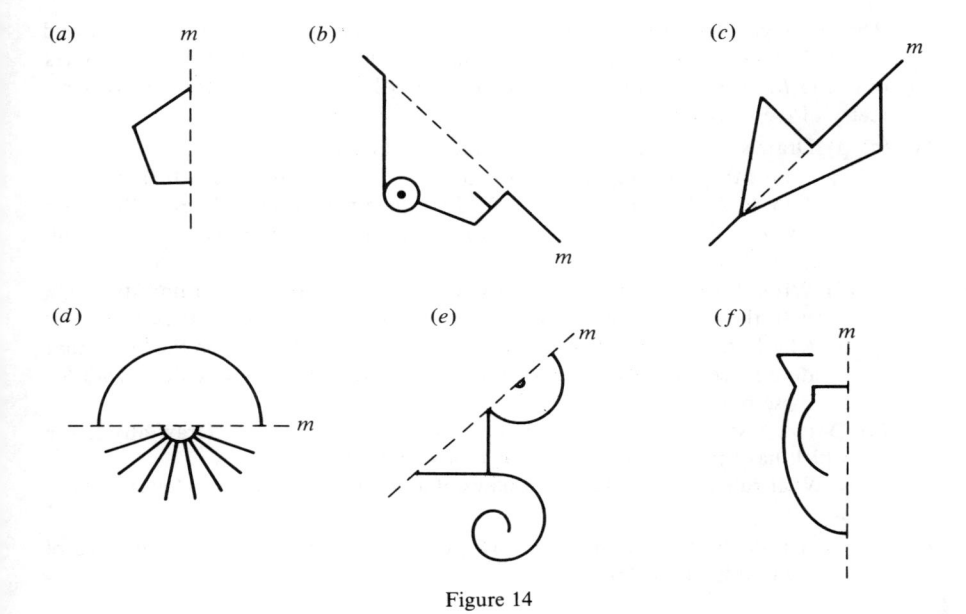

5 Draw a shape which has exactly 2 lines of symmetry. Mark the lines of symmetry with broken lines.
6 Repeat question 5 for shapes which have (a) 0; (b) 1; (c) 3 and (d) 4 lines of symmetry.
*7 A rectangle has the x-axis as a line of symmetry. Two of its vertices have coordinates (4, 1) and (¯3, 1). Show this on a diagram, giving the coordinates of the other vertices and draw the rectangle.
8 A pentagon has the y-axis as a line of symmetry. The points (3, 2), (1, ¯1) and (0, 1) are vertices of the figure. Show this on a diagram, giving the coordinates of the other vertices and draw the pentagon.
9 Copy Figure 15 which shows two lines marked *l* and *m*. P (4, 2) is the vertex of a polygon with *l* and *m* as lines of symmetry. Mark two points Q and R which are the images of P in *l* and *m*. Mark also the images of Q and R in *l* and *m*. What do you find? What sort of polygon is formed with these points as vertices?

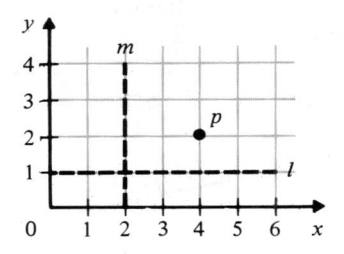

Figure 15

28   Symmetry   Ch. 18

10 The rectangle *ABCD* has a line of symmetry which passes through (⁻2, 2) and (2, ⁻2). If *A* has coordinates (0, 2) and *B* has coordinates (3, ⁻1) find the coordinates of *C* and *D*. Give the coordinates of two points which lie on the other line of symmetry of the rectangle.

11 (*a*) (i) Draw axes marking values of *x* and *y* from ⁻8 to ⁺8.
  Plot the following points *A* (⁻5, 0), *B* (⁻4, 1), *C* (0, 1), *D* (3, 7), *E* (4, 7), *F* (5, 1), *G* (7, 1), *H* (8, 2), *I* (8, 0). Join them with straight lines in the given order. If the *x*-axis is a line of symmetry for the figure draw the other half. What figure is produced?
  (ii) Write down the coordinates of one of the above points and find its image with the *x*-axis as line of symmetry. What rule connects their coordinates? Check that it works for other points. There are two points on the figure that do not seem to follow this rule. Explain why, in fact, the rule does work for these points.
  (*b*) Draw axes marking values of both *x* and *y* from ⁻6 to ⁺6. Draw any figure which has the *y*-axis as the only line of symmetry.
  What rule connects the coordinates of a point and its image? Does it always work?

12 Draw each of the figures on your SMP polygon stencil. Draw in all the lines of symmetry in different colours.

4. ANGLE BISECTORS AND MEDIATORS

A line of symmetry bisects a figure (cuts it exactly in two equal parts) and hence also bisects any angle of the figure through which it passes.

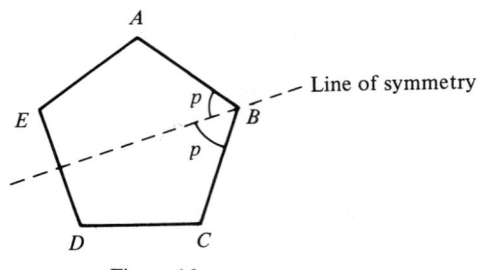

Figure 16

The line of symmetry shown is the *angle bisector* of ∠*ABC* in Figure 16, a regular pentagon. From the earlier chapter on polygons we can show that ∠*ABC* = 108° and hence *p* = 108° ÷ 2 = 54°.

A line *KL* is drawn 4 cm long (Figure 17); has it got any lines of symmetry? (We call a line of definite length a *line segment*.)

Figure 17

Angle bisectors and mediators

The point K can be folded onto L as shown in Figure 18.

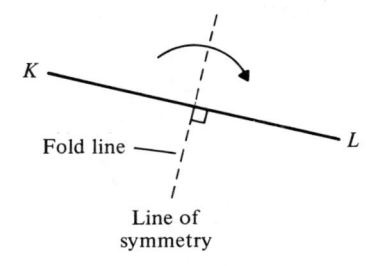

Figure 18

Every line segment has a line of symmetry, which bisects it at 90°.

This line of symmetry is called the *mediator* of the points K and L. The mediator of the points K and L bisects the line segment KL at right angles; it is also called the *perpendicular bisector* of KL.

Exercise B

Tracing paper and SMP polygon stencil are required.

1. Draw each of the figures on the SMP polygon stencil. Using coloured pen draw in all the lines which bisect the interior angles. Some of these lines are not lines of symmetry; suggest a rule that might tell you if an angle bisector will be a line of symmetry.

*2 Trace the diagrams in Figure 19 and draw the lines of symmetry which are also bisectors of the sides. Indicate, by colouring, those which are also angle bisectors.

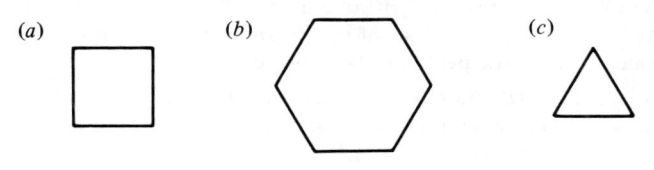

(a) (b) (c)

Figure 19

*3 For each diagram in Figure 20, draw a figure in such a way that the given lines bisect some of its angles.

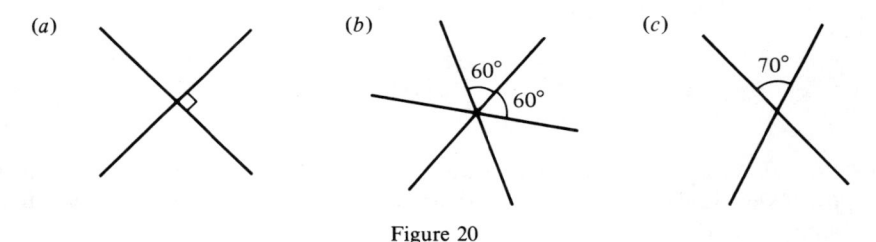

(a) (b) 60°, 60° (c) 70°

Figure 20

In which cases can you draw a figure which has line symmetry?

30 Symmetry Ch. 18

4 Repeat question 3 but with the given lines as mediators of sides.

*5 Copy the regular hexagon *ABCDEF* shown in Figure 21.

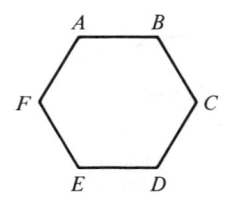

Figure 21

Draw in one colour any lines of symmetry which bisect interior angles. Draw in another colour any lines of symmetry which are perpendicular bisectors of sides. What is the angle between:
   (a) any adjacent pair of lines of the same colour;
   (b) any adjacent pair of lines of different colours?

6 *P* is the point with coordinates $(^-1, 4)$, *Q* is $(^-1, 0)$ and *R* is $(3, 0)$. Draw the triangle *PQR*.
   (a) Mark on it the bisector of $\angle PQR$. Is this a line of symmetry of triangle *PQR*?
   (b) Mark on the triangle the mediator of *Q* and *R*. Is this a line of symmetry? Write down the coordinates of three points which lie on this line; what do you notice about these coordinates?

7 Draw a pair of parallel lines of different lengths such that
   (a) they have the same perpendicular bisector;
   (b) they have different perpendicular bisectors.

If the parallel lines in (a) were part of a figure what could you say about the perpendicular bisector. [Join the ends of the parallel lines if it helps!]
Is the same true for the perpendicular bisectors in (b)?

8 Draw any two lines *AB* and *CD* (not at right-angles) and let *P* be the point where they meet. See, for example, Figure 22. Draw the angle bisectors of:
   (a) $\angle DPB$;   (b) $\angle APC$;   (c) $\angle APD$;   (d) $\angle BPC$.

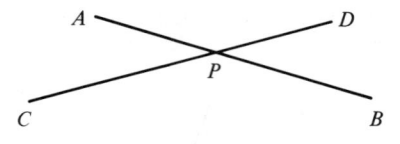

Figure 22

What do you notice about your answers to (a) and (b)? Is the same true for (c) and (d)? What is the angle between the angle bisectors of any pair of intersecting straight lines?

9 Use the fact that angles on a straight line add up to 180° to show why the result in question 8 is always true.

5 ROTATIONAL SYMMETRY

Copy each shape of Figure 23 onto tracing paper.

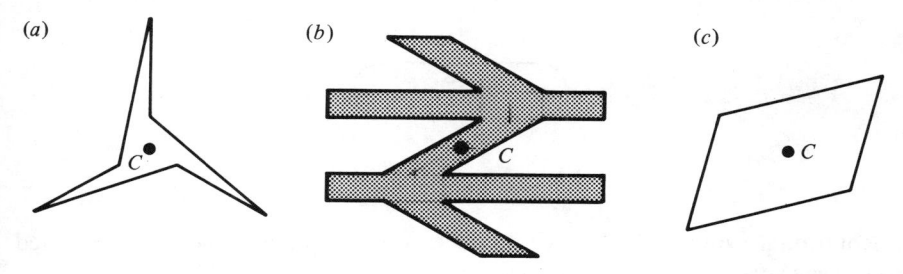

(a)   (b)   (c)

Figure 23

Using either paper folding, or a mirror, test these shapes for line symmetry. Although they look 'balanced' there are no lines of symmetry to be found ... if you found any for the parallelogram check again!

Now rotate each tracing about the point marked *C*. Can you get your tracing to map onto the original drawing exactly? How many times will each tracing map onto the original during a complete turn?

These shapes have *rotational symmetry*. The shape maps onto itself at least once during a complete turn by rotation. In each case the point marked *C* is the *centre of rotational symmetry*.

The number of times during a complete turn that the shape maps onto itself is called the *order* of rotational symmetry. The orders of rotational symmetry for the shapes in Figure 23 are (*a*) 3, (*b*) 2, (*c*) 2. The result for Figure 23(*a*) is shown in Figure 24.

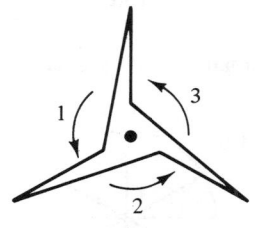

Figure 24

A shape that can be mapped onto itself only by a rotation of 360° (a whole turn) could be said to have rotational symmetry of order 1. But it is more usual to say that it has *no* rotational symmetry. See Figure 25.

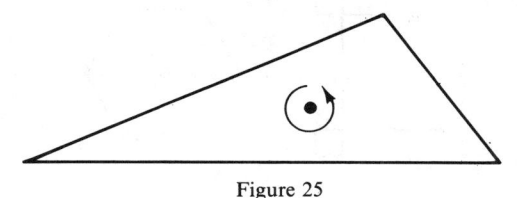

Figure 25

32   Symmetry   Ch. 18

It is quite possible for a shape to have both line and rotational symmetry; for example the shape in Figure 26 has 2 lines of symmetry and rotational symmetry of order 2 about S.

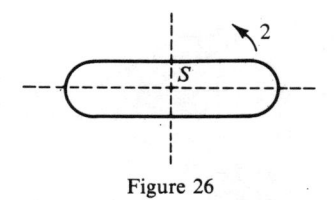

Figure 26

Rotational symmetry of order 2 occurs very frequently and is often called *point symmetry* or *half-turn symmetry*.

Exercise C

Tracing paper is required.

*1 Which of the diagrams in Figure 27 have rotational symmetry and of what order?

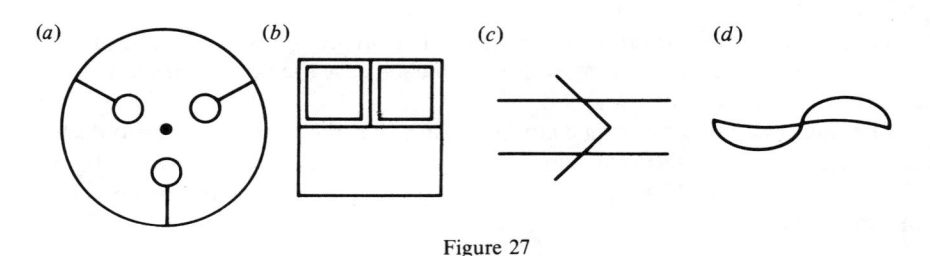

(a)   (b)   (c)   (d)

Figure 27

*2 What is the order of rotational symmetry of each diagram in Figure 28?

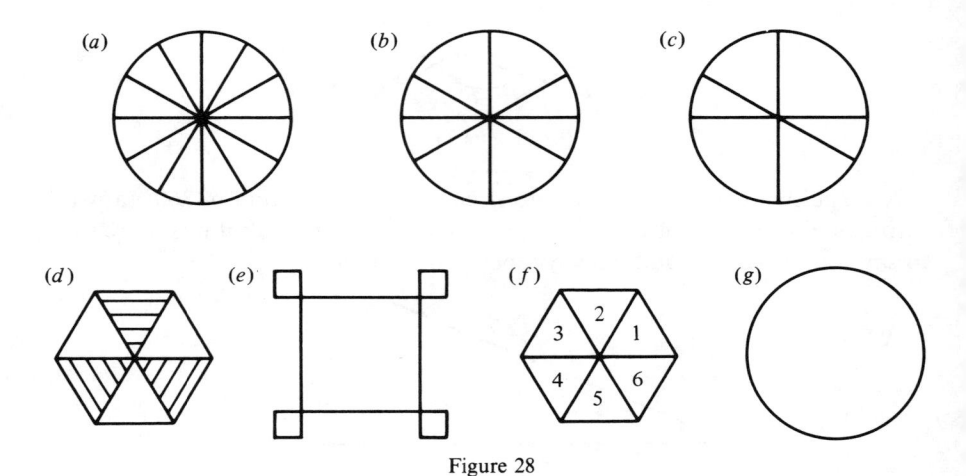

(a)   (b)   (c)

(d)   (e)   (f)   (g)

Figure 28

Rotational symmetry 33

3 Make a copy on tracing paper of the flag in Figure 29.

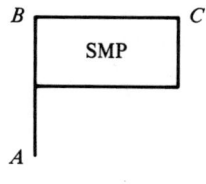

Figure 29

Use the point A as centre of rotation for the flag and draw a figure which has rotational symmetry of order 4.

Make a separate drawing with rotational symmetry of order 4 using B as centre and a third drawing using C as centre.

*4 Consider the capital letters of the alphabet printed as follows:
  A B C D E F G H I J K L M N O P Q R S T U V W X Y Z
  (a) Which letters have line symmetry?
  (b) Which letters have rotational symmetry of order 2?
  (c) Which letters appear in your answers to both (a) and (b)?

5 In Figure 30, the lines m and n are two lines of symmetry of a polygon. Three of its vertices are (3, 4), (5, 2) and (0, 1).

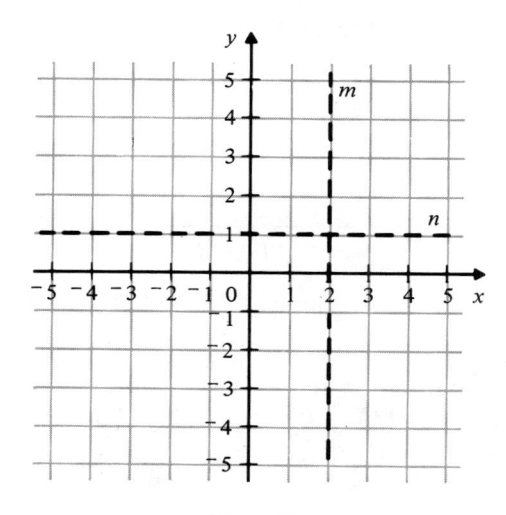

Figure 30

Find the coordinates of the other vertices and draw the complete polygon. How many sides has it? What is its order of rotational symmetry and what are the coordinates of the centre of rotation?

34 Symmetry Ch. 18

6 List the symmetries of the diagrams in Figure 31. Show your results in a copy of Table 1.

Figure 31

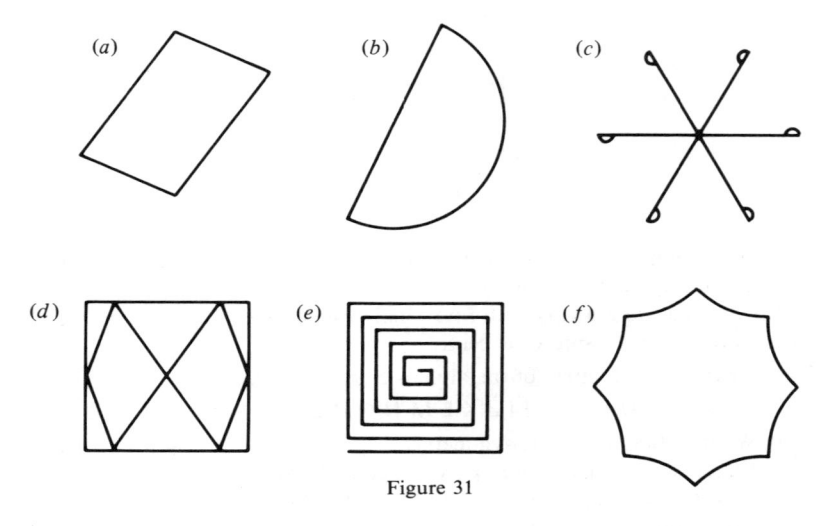

Figure	Lines of symmetry	Order of rotational symmetry
a	0	2
b		
c		
d		
e		
f		

Table 1

7 List the symmetries of the eight diagrams in Figure 32. Tabulate your answers as in question 7.

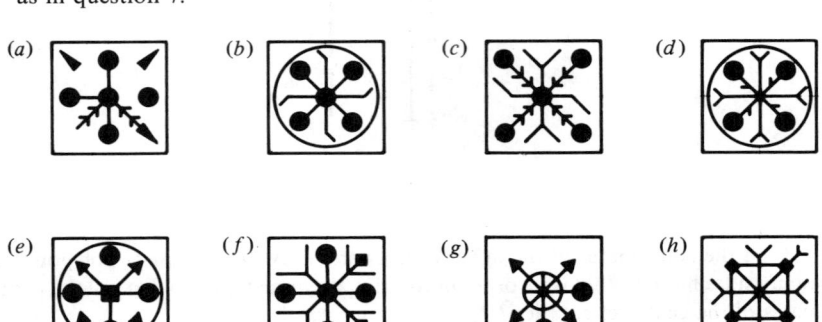

Figure 32

8 Design patterns if possible with the following symmetries:

	a	b	c	d	e	f	g
Number of lines	4	1	3	2	0	1	6
Order of rotation	4	1	0	2	5	2	6

9 A polygon has rotational symmetry of order 4. What is the smallest angle of rotation that could be used to map the polygon onto itself?

What are the smallest angles in the case of polygons with rotational symmetry of order (a) 2; (b) 3; (c) n?

Use your calculator to find these angles when n = 4, 5, ..., 10. Which of the polygons could be used to make a tessellation?

SUMMARY

A figure has line symmetry if there is a line along which it may be folded so that one part exactly maps on to the other part. A line of symmetry bisects at 90° the line joining a point P and its corresponding point P' and is thus the *mediator* of the points P and P'. The points P and P' are images of each other.

A figure has rotational symmetry if it is mapped onto itself by rotation about a point. The number of times this happens in a whole turn is the order of rotational symmetry of the figure.

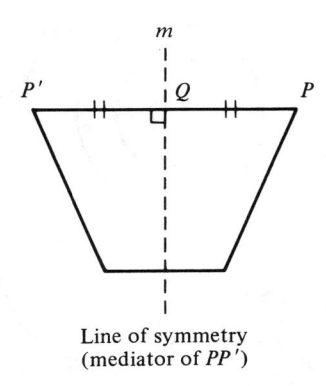

Line of symmetry
(mediator of PP')

Rotational symmetry
of order 3

Figure 33

Summary exercise

1 Which of the diagrams in Figure 34 have line symmetry? Draw those figures which have line symmetry and show the lines of symmetry in a different colour. In which figures is the line of symmetry a mediator of a side?

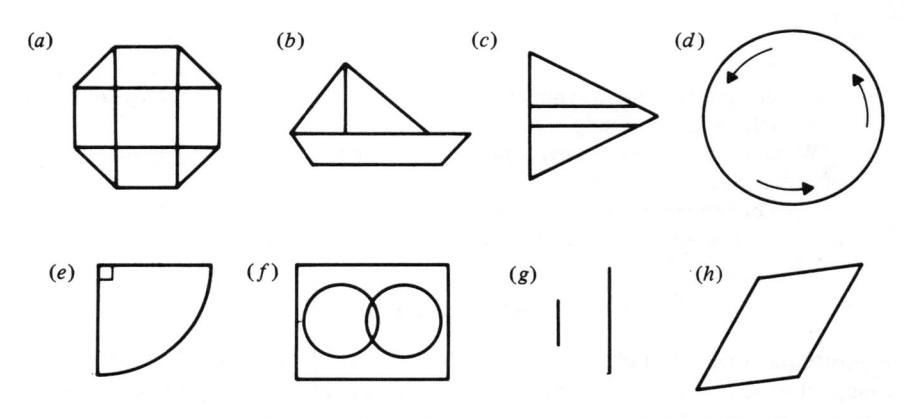

Figure 34

2 Which of the diagrams in Figure 35 have rotational symmetry? What is the order of rotational symmetry in each case?

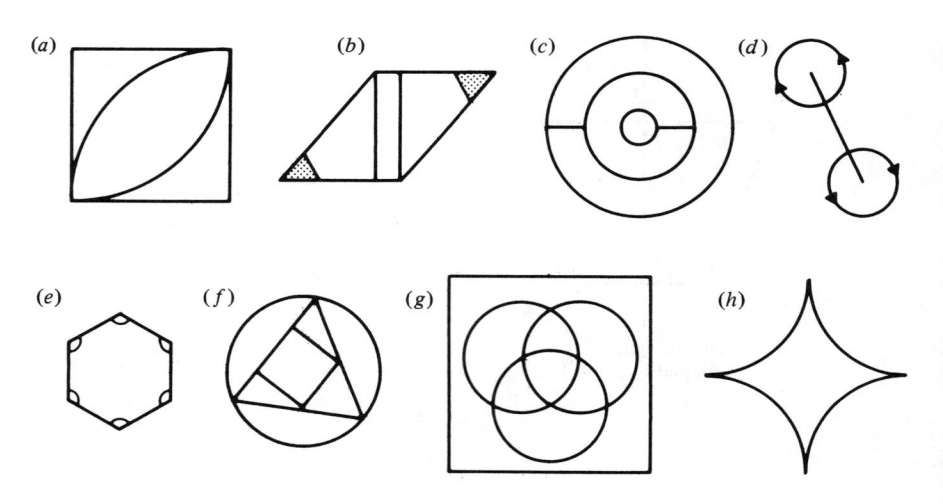

Figure 35

3 The quadrilateral *PQRS* has the *x*- and *y*-axes as lines of symmetry. If *P* has coordinates (5, ⁻4), what are the coordinates of the other 3 vertices? What shape is *PQRS* and what is its order of rotational symmetry?

4 A figure has a line of symmetry which passes through (⁻1, ⁻1) and (4, 4). Four points which are part of the figure are (5, 5), (4, 5), (0, 1) and (⁻2, 1). Illustrate with a diagram. Write down the coordinates of the points which correspond to those given and then complete the figure.

5 Draw the following polygons, marking any lines of symmetry and giving the order of rotational symmetry.
  (*a*) square;   (*b*) rectangle;   (*c*) rhombus;   (*d*) kite;
  (*e*) concave pentagon with equal sides;   (*f*) arrowhead;   (*g*) parallelogram.

Miscellaneous exercise

1 Figure 36 shows four half finished diagrams each with a line of symmetry marked *m*. Copy (by tracing) and complete each of them, but first describe what you *think* the result will be.

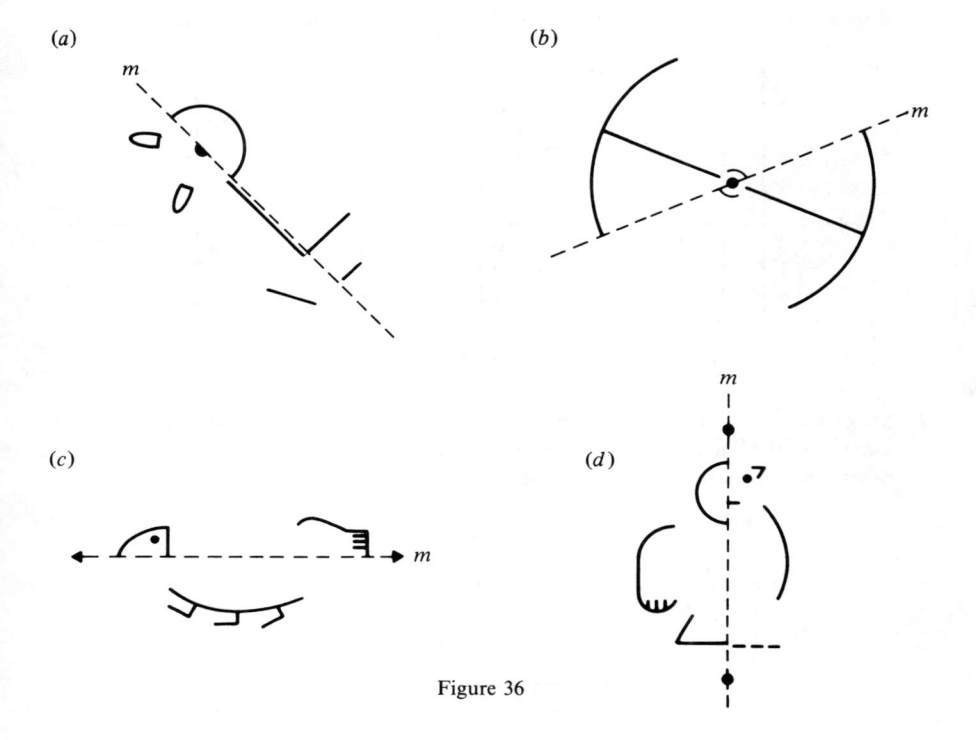

(*a*)

(*b*)

(*c*)

(*d*)

Figure 36

38 Symmetry   Ch. 18

2 Copy Figure 37 onto squared paper. Draw any figure which has the line *m* as a line of symmetry. Find a rule which connects the coordinates of a point with those of its image (the point that it maps onto).

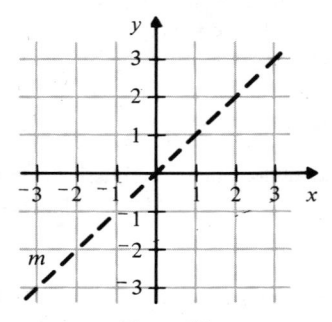

Figure 37

3 Repeat question 2 for the three lines of symmetry shown in Figure 38.

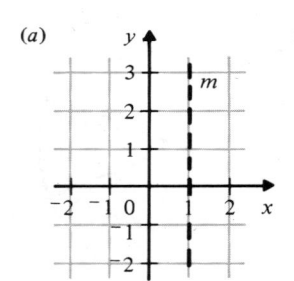

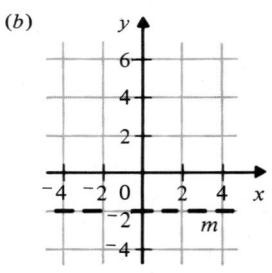

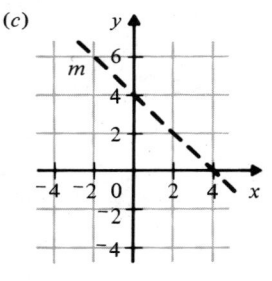

(a)   (b)   (c)

Figure 38

4 Make a copy of Figure 39 in which points *P* and *Q* are vertices of a polygon. The *x*-axis and the line *l* are lines of symmetry of the polygon. Find the coordinates of the other vertices marking them on your diagram.

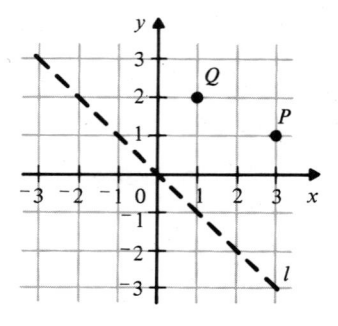

Figure 39

Draw in any other lines of symmetry of the polygon.

5 (a) Draw axes marking values of both x and y from ⁻8 to 8.
      Plot and label the points $O(0, 0)$, $P(1, 1)$, $Q(3, 3)$ and $R(6, 6)$. Join the points O and R to form a straight line. Construct a figure which has O as centre of rotational symmetry of order 2 and which contains the points P, Q and R.
   (b) Mark on your figure the images of P, Q and R after rotating through 180° and label them P', Q' and R'. What are their coordinates? How can these coordinates be obtained from the coordinates of P, Q and R? Does this also work with other points on the line OR?
   (c) Using the same drawing repeat (a) but with the points O, $S(^-1, 1)$, $T(^-3, 3)$, $U(^-6, 6)$. Then mark the images S', T' and U' and compare their coordinates with S, T and U.
      Does the same rule apply as you found in (b)?
6 Draw axes marking values of both x and y from ⁻8 to 8.
      Plot and label the points $A(2, 4)$, $B(3, 6)$ and $C(4, 8)$. Construct a figure which has the origin as centre of rotational symmetry of order 4 and which contains the points A, B and C. Write down the coordinates of the three images of A after rotating through 90°, 180° and 270° in an anticlockwise direction about O. What connection is there between each of these and the coordinates of A? Use this connection to predict the coordinates of the three images of B and C. Check your results on your diagram.
7 Copy and complete Table 2.

Name of triangle	No. of equal sides	No. of equal angles	No. of lines of symmetry	Order of rotational symmetry
equilateral	3			
isosceles	2			
scalene				

Table 2

   Write down a connection between the results. Make a similar table for quadrilaterals and investigate your results.
8 Use hole 1 on your polygon stencil, and some of the polygons, to create a pattern which has rotational symmetry of order 3.
      Use different shapes and/or holes to create patterns which have order of rotational symmetry of at least 4.

19
Calculations and approximations

Figure 1

1 INTRODUCTION

We can use simple arithmetic to work out, mentally, calculations which involve very large or very small numbers.

Example 1
  Work out 0.05×90.

    First, we know that $5 \times 9 = 45$; that gives us the figures to write down.
    Second, we know (*a*) $0.05 = 5 \div 100$ and (*b*) $90 = 9 \times 10$.
    So the first result, 45, must be

    (*a*) divided by 100   and   (*b*) multiplied by 10.

This gives   45 —[÷ 100]—[× 10]— 4.5.

So $0.05 \times 90 = 4.5$.

Notice how the last line of working follows the order of thinking.

Example 2
Find 0.6×0.03.

Again we think in two steps:
first: $6 \times 3 = 18$;
second: $0.6 = 6 \div 10$ and $0.03 = 3 \div 100$.

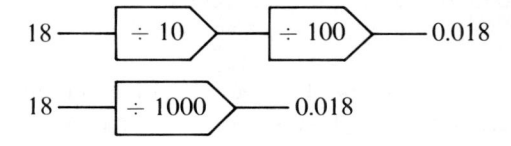

This gives   18 —[÷ 10]—[÷ 100]— 0.018

or   18 —[÷ 1000]— 0.018

So $0.6 \times 0.03 = 0.018$.

Exercise A

Do not use a calculator. Most of these questions may be done orally.
Work out:
- *1 7×5
- 2 7×0.5
- 3 7×0.05
- *4 70×0.5
- 5 700×0.5
- 6 7000×0.5
- *7 0.7×0.5
- 8 0.07×5
- 9 0.7×50
- *10 90×0.6
- 11 900×0.6
- 12 900×0.006
- *13 4×0.05
- 14 4×0.005
- 15 0.1×12
- *16 0.1×0.1
- 17 0.1×0.7
- 18 0.2×0.4
- *19 3000×0.2
- 20 150×0.02
- 21 0.04×300
- *22 0.04×5000
- 23 400×500
- 24 4000×0.02
- 25 Which of the following is (*a*) the largest; (*b*) the smallest?
    (i) 0.5×7; (ii) 0.05×7; (iii) 70×0.05; (iv) 700×0.5.
- 26 Which of the following is (*a*) the largest; (*b*) the smallest?
    (i) 0.3×8; (ii) 90×0.09; (iii) 0.06×8; (iv) 0.9×0.9; (v) 11×0.03.
- 27 Copy and complete the following using the fact that $9 \times 60 = 540$:
    (*a*) $0.9 \times \Box = 540$; (*b*) $90 \times \Box = 540$; (*c*) $\Box \times 0.6 = 540$;
    (*d*) $\Box \times 6000 = 540$; (*e*) $9000 \times \Box = 540$.

Calculations and approximations — Ch. 19

*28 Complete the following so that each has an answer of 72.
   (a) 8 × ▢;   (b) ▢ × 90;   (c) ▢ × 0.9;   (d) 0.08 × ▢;   (e) 8000 × ▢;
   (f) 800 × ▢.

*29 Complete the following so that each has an answer of 24.
   (a) 6 × ▢;   (b) 3 × ▢;   (c) ▢ × 0.4;   (d) ▢ × 0.8;   (e) 0.6 × ▢;
   (f) 0.3 × ▢;   (g) ▢ × 400;   (h) ▢ × 800;   (i) 24 × ▢;   (j) 2.4 × ▢.

*30 Complete the following so that each has an answer of 3600.
   (a) 600 × ▢;   (b) 6000 × ▢;   (c) 60 000 × ▢;   (d) 1800 × ▢;   (e) 18 × ▢;
   (f) 1.8 × ▢;   (g) ▢ × 9000;   (h) ▢ × 90 000;   (i) ▢ × 0.3;   (j) ▢ × 300.

*31 Which of the following give the answer 120?
   (a) 30 × 40;   (b) 0.3 × 400;   (c) 300 × 0.4;   (d) 300 × 4;   (e) 3000 × 0.4;
   (f) 3000 × 0.04;   (g) 60 × 20;   (h) 600 × 0.2;   (i) 0.6 × 2000;   (j) 0.6 × 200;
   (k) 1200 × 0.1;   (l) 0.12 × 100.

2. APPLICATIONS

We can use these methods in many different ways.

Example 3

In an avenue there are 40 poplar trees. Carl reckons that there are 60 000 leaves on each tree. How many leaves does he estimate there are in the avenue?

Figure 2

Each tree is assumed to have the same number of leaves. So Carl's estimate will be 40 × 60 000 leaves altogether;

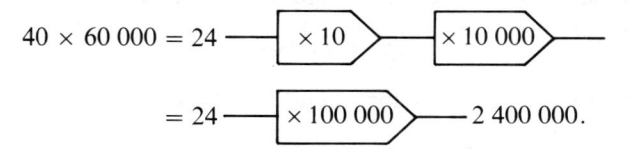

$$40 \times 60\,000 = 24 \longrightarrow \boxed{\times 10} \longrightarrow \boxed{\times 10\,000}$$

$$= 24 \longrightarrow \boxed{\times 100\,000} \longrightarrow 2\,400\,000.$$

Carl estimates 2 400 000 leaves altogether.

Example 4

If each leaf in Example 4 was 0.02 cm thick, how tall would a pile of 30 000 leaves be (assuming that they could be piled)?

We must work out 30 000 × 0.02. We know that 3 × 2 = 6 so we have

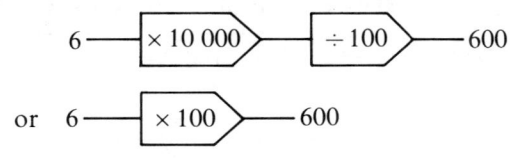

$$6 \longrightarrow \boxed{\times 10\,000} \longrightarrow \boxed{\div 100} \longrightarrow 600$$

$$\text{or} \quad 6 \longrightarrow \boxed{\times 100} \longrightarrow 600$$

The pile would be 600 cm high.

Exercise B

Do not use a calculator in this exercise.

*1 The thickness of a piece of paper is 0.04 mm. Calculate, in cm, the thickness of a pile of (*a*) 500 sheets, (*b*) 2000 sheets.

2 One sweet has a mass of 1.2 g. Find the mass of the sweets in a packet containing forty sweets.

3 A computer does one type of calculation in 0.0003 seconds. How long does it take to do 500 similar calculations?

4 If each member of a school of 1200 pupils decides to give £0.15 to charity how much money will be given in all?

*5 In completing one lap of a circuit a racing car travels 3000 metres. Find the distance travelled, in kilometres, by a car in a 120 lap race.

6 If a car travels 50 metres every second, calculate how far, in metres, it will travel in one hour.

7 People queue up in a single file for a ride on the Space Twister at the SMP Leisure Park. Estimate in cm, to the nearest 10 cm, the length of space required for an average person standing in this queue. Use your estimate to calculate the length of the queue when 600 people are waiting.

8 If one man works for 50 hours he has worked 50 man hours. If two men each work for 25 hours, together they have worked 50 man hours. If 3500 men each work for 40 hours in one week, how many man hours will they have worked in all?

9 A telephone directory contains 700 pages and each page contains about 16 000 characters. Estimate how many characters there are in the directory.

10 A computer disk system has 9 surfaces which are used for storing data. If each surface contains 400 tracks, and each track contains approximately 10 000 characters, calculate how many characters are stored in the system.

3. DIVISION

We can use a similar approach for mental calculation here, but a little more care is necessary.

Example 5
  Work out $2400 \div 60$.

  We think in two steps:

first $24 \div 6 = 4$;
second $2400 = 24 \times 100$ and $60 = 6 \times 10$,

but while we multiply by 100 we must *divide* by 10 (since we are dividing by 60).

So $2400 \div 60 = 4 \longrightarrow \boxed{\times 100} \longrightarrow \boxed{\div 10} \longrightarrow$

         $= 4 \longrightarrow \boxed{\times 10} \longrightarrow 40.$

So $2400 \div 60 = 40.$

Example 6
  Find $0.56 \div 0.0008$.

We think in the two steps:

first $56 \div 8 = 7$;
second $0.56 = 56 \div 100$ and $0.008 = 8 \div 10\,000$

So $0.56 \div 0.008 = 7 \longrightarrow \boxed{\div 100} \longrightarrow \boxed{\times 10\,000} \longrightarrow 700$

or $= 7 \longrightarrow \boxed{\times 100} \longrightarrow 700.$

So $0.56 \div 0.0008 = 700.$

(While we divide by 100 we must *multiply* by 10 000, since we are dividing by a number less than one.)

As a quick check we notice that since we are dividing by a number less than 1 we expect a larger answer than the number we are dividing into.

Exercise C

Do not use a calculator in this exercise. Many questions may be done orally. Work out the answers to questions 1 to 24.

*1 (a) $3.6 \div 4$; (b) $0.36 \div 4$; (c) $0.036 \div 4$; (d) $360 \div 4$; (e) $360 \div 400$.
 2 (a) $27 \div 0.9$; (b) $270 \div 9$; (c) $2700 \div 9$; (d) $270 \div 90$; (e) $270 \div 0.9$.

*3 (a) 5.6 ÷ 8;   (b) 56 ÷ 0.8;   (c) 56 ÷ 80;   (d) 5.6 ÷ 0.8;   (e) 5600 ÷ 80.
 4 (a) 39 ÷ 0.3;   (b) 0.39 ÷ 3;   (c) 3.9 ÷ 0.3; (d) 390 ÷ 0.3;   (e) 0.39 ÷ 300.
*5   60 ÷ 3.   6 6000 ÷ 30.   7 6 ÷ 30.
*8   0.6 ÷ 0.3.   9 2.4 ÷ 4.   10 2.4 ÷ 0.4.
*11 48 ÷ 0.1.   12 480 ÷ 20.   13 1400 ÷ 0.2.
*14 14 ÷ 200.   15 0.14 ÷ 0.2.   16 3600 ÷ 0.9.
*17 0.36 ÷ 90.   18 3.2 ÷ 400.   19 320 ÷ 0.4.
 20 The mass of 60 sweets in a packet is 0.9 kg. Find the mass of each sweet in kg.
*21 Fred travels 7000 miles in his car and the petrol costs him £420. Find the petrol cost per mile, in £.
 22 Janet pays £240 for 6000 units of electricity. What is the cost of each unit, in £?
 23 A line printer on a computer prints out 2000 lines in one minutes. How many seconds does it take to produce one line?
*24 A pile of 500 sheets of paper is 3 cm high. What is the thickness, in mm, of each sheet of paper?
*25 (a) Is 27 ÷ 0.3 greater or less than 27?
     (b) Is 2.7 ÷ 3 greater or less than 2.7?
     (c) Is 0.27 ÷ 0.03 greater or less than 0.27?
     (d) Is 2700 ÷ 30 000 greater or less than 2700?

In Questions 26 to 35 predict the size of the answer compared to the first number. (For example the answer to 17 ÷ 0.5 is 'greater than 17'.)

*26 24 ÷ 6.   27 24 ÷ 0.6.   28 24 ÷ 60.
 29 240 ÷ 6.   30 240 ÷ 0.6.   *31 240 ÷ 60.
 32 2.4 ÷ 6.   33 2.4 ÷ 0.6.   34 2.4 ÷ 60.
 35 2400 ÷ 6.

4. CHECKING!

I used my calculator to work out 71.6 ÷ 0.003 12 and the display showed 54 242.424. This is a large number, as I would expect, since I had divided by a very small number. But are the figures correct?

Figure 3

I can say that the calculation is *approximately* 70 ÷ 0.003.

Then I can use the two step approach. First I need 7 ÷ 3. Since I am working approximately, I need only work out the first figure of this calculation, which is 2.

We have   2 —[× 10]—[× 1000]— 20 000

or   2 —[× 10 000]— 20 000.

Obviously I have made an error in using the calculator!

Quick checks like this are always valuable. We check the *size* of the result and the *first figure*.

Example 7
  Give an approximate value for 4.9 × 8.1.

You might say that this is approximately 4 × 8 = 32.
But 4.9 is much closer to 5 than to 4, so a better approximation is 5 × 8 = 40. If you use a calculator you will see that this is a better approximation than 32.

Example 8
  Estimate 124 ÷ 35.

We notice that 35 is mid way between 30 and 40. We also notice that 120, which is an approximation for 124, is divisible by both 30 and 40. So there are two equally good ways of estimating this:

$$124 \div 35 \approx 120 \div 30 = 4$$
or $$124 \div 35 \approx 120 \div 40 = 3$$

($\approx$ means 'is approximately equal to'.) Either 3 or 4 is acceptable and can be used to check a calculator result. We could also use 100, instead of 120, as an approximation to 124.

Exercise D

  Work these questions without using a calculator. Use the methods of Examples 7 and 8, writing out your working in a similar way.
  *1 Estimate (a) 8.7 × 3.2;   (b) 10.3 × 4.7.
   2 Estimate (a) 12.6 × 3.7;   (b) 83.1 × 2.2.
  *3 Estimate (a) 0.93 × 0.37; (b) 0.41 × 0.75.
   4 Estimate (a) 0.61 × 0.09; (b) 0.07 × 0.28.
  *5 William goes to Germany and spends DM44.6 on presents to bring back. The rate of exchange is DM1 = £0.23. Estimate the value of his presents in £.
   6 There are approximately 2.5 cm in one inch. Estimate the number of centimetres in 78 inches.
  *7 Croydon is 42 miles from Brighton. 1 mile is approximately 1.609 km. Estimate the distance from Croydon to Brighton in kilometres.

8   In Zambania the unit of mass is 1 dirham. Given that 1 dirham is approximately 3.68 kg estimate the mass in kg of a Zambanian cooking pot of mass 2.2 dirham.
9   In Cherrapunji it rains for an average of 5.2 days per week. Estimate how many days it rains during a year.
*10 Estimate   (a) 29.4 ÷ 5.2;   (b) 51.8 ÷ 9.2.
11   Estimate   (a) 123 ÷ 20.6;   (b) 18.4 ÷ 0.91.
*12 Estimate   (a) 0.71 ÷ 0.14; (b) 191 ÷ 0.41.
13   Estimate   (a) 0.87 ÷ 0.03; (b) 0.077 ÷ 0.036.
*14 A local council has counted the number of flowers planted in 19 identical flower-beds. If there were 968 plants estimate the number in each bed.
15   A British tourist in France sees a signpost reading 'Le Havre 34.5 km'. He knows that 1 mile ≈ 1.6 km. Estimate his distance from Le Havre in miles.
16   (a) Georgina wanted to measure the length of her back garden. She counted 156 'pigeon steps' from the back door to the end of the garden. Each 'pigeon step' was about 21 cm. Estimate the length of the garden. Give your answer in sensible units.
     (b) Georgina's mother said that she did not understand centimetres and asked her daughter to work out this length in feet. Georginia knew that 1 inch ≈ 2.54 cm and that there are 12 inches in 1 foot. Estimate the answer Georgina should give her mother.
17   During a drought a reservoir contained about half a million gallons of water. The water engineers calculated that each day another 35 000 gallons would be used. In how many days would the reservoir be empty assuming it didn't rain in the meantime?

5. REASONABLE ACCURACY

Figure 4

Evelyn has a cookery book in which the quantities of ingredients in the recipes are given in Imperial units, but her new kitchen scales only measure in grams.

She knows that 454 grams are very nearly the same as 16 ounces (oz.) and uses her calculator to find that 1 oz. = 28.375 g.

The recipe for Eve's pudding requires 3 oz. of demerara sugar. Evelyn converts this to

$$3 \times 28.375 \text{ g} = 85.125 \text{ g}.$$

Kitchen scales do not measure as accurately as this and quantities in recipes are not very precise since the weight of some ingredients such as eggs can vary. So she weighs out 85 g of demerara sugar. This is sufficiently accurate, and for future uses she can record the weight as 85 g in the cookery book.

Converting the 5 oz. of flour required gives $5 \times 28.375 = 141.875$ g. Once again, it is reasonable to *work to the nearest gram*, but since 141.875 is nearer to 142 g than 141 g, this is what Evelyn weighs out and writes in her recipe book.

Example 9

A cricket pitch is 22 yards long. There are 36 inches in a yard and each inch is approximately 2.54 cm. What is the length of a cricket pitch in cm?

Using a calculator we find that $22 \times 36 \times 2.54 = 2011.68$. So we might say that the length of a cricket pitch is 2011.68 cm. However, it is not reasonable to give so much apparent accuracy in the result. In the first place we are only told that 1 inch is approximately 2.54 cm, so we should not rely on the last two figures (which are, in fact, millimetres and tenths of millimetres). We should also think of the actual situation, as we did with the recipe. A cricket pitch on a playing field could not be measured to such accuracy. Perhaps the accuracy possible would be *to the nearest 10 cm*, so we would give the result as 2010 cm (to the nearest 10 cm).

Notice that, to check the calculator work we might work out either $20 \times 30 \times 2 = 1200$, or $20 \times 40 \times 3 = 2400$. Either of these gives us the correct number of digits, or *order of magnitude* and it is easy to see why the first gives a first digit which is too small.

In any calculation where measurements are involved it is always important to give results carefully, bearing in mind the actual situation and what would be a reasonable degree of accuracy.

Exercise E

*1 Use the fact that 454 g $\approx$ 16 oz to convert all the quantities in the recipe shown in Figure 5 to grams, giving all your answers to the nearest gram.

Figure 5

*2 A door is 6 feet 4 inches high. There are 12 inches in a foot and one inch is approximately 2.54 cm. Give the height of the door to the nearest cm.

*3 The average height of a man is about 5 feet 9 inches; the average height of a woman is about 5 feet 7 inches. Convert these to cm to the nearest cm.

4 On average my car travels 7.7 miles on a litre of petrol. How many litres of petrol will I use in travelling 120 miles? Give your answer to a reasonable degree of accuracy.
   Petrol costs 41.7 p per litre. What will be the cost of the petrol for the journey?

5 A landscape gardener is going to plant a straight row of trees 100 metres long. There are 38 trees and they are to be equally spaced. How far apart should the trees be planted? (Hint: How many spaces will there be?)

6 On a milk bottle I read that 1 pint is 568 ml. Using this information convert the following quantities from recipes into millilitres (ml). Give your results to a reasonable accuracy.
   (a) $\frac{1}{2}$ pint;   (b) $\frac{1}{4}$ pint;   (c) $\frac{1}{8}$ pint;   (d) $\frac{1}{3}$ point.

7 Jason buys a new carpet which needs binding on all four edges. The carpet is rectangular and measures 2.93 m by 3.12 m. How much binding should Jason buy?

8 A farmer has a field which is approximately rectangular with sides 52 m and 43.5 m long. Calculate the perimeter of the field. (The perimeter is the total distance round the field.)
   The farmer intends to plant a hedge of small trees all round the field and will need to plant 25 trees every 10 metres on average. How many trees should he buy?

9 My hand-span measures about 238 mm. Give the measurements, in suitable units, of the following things, measured in hand-spans:
   (a) a table, $4\frac{3}{4}$ by $3\frac{1}{2}$;   (b) a window sill, 5 wide;   (c) a wall, 11 high.

10 The frequency of the note A is 440.0 hertz. In the 'just intonation' scale used before the time of Bach, the frequency of the note C#, a major third above A, was obtained by multiplying the frequency of A by 1.250, and the frequency of E, a perfect fifth above A, by multiplying by 1.422.

In the 'well-tempered' scale these multipliers are changed to 1.260 and 1.498 respectively. Copy and complete the table below.

	'Just Intonation' frequency	'Well-tempered' frequency
C#	550 hertz	
E		

6. ROUNDING UP . . . OR DOWN

We have worked a number of calculations where, instead of using all the digits in a number, we have *approximated*, using only one or two digits. Sometimes we have ignored some of the digits in the result of a calculation too.

Suppose we need to estimate 3.1 × 4.8.

We would probably work out 3 × 5 = 45. In this case we say that 3.1 has been *rounded down.* to 3, but 4.8 has been *rounded up* to 5 because 4.8 is nearer to 5 than it is to 4.

We have no difficulty in rounding *up* 4.9, 4.8, 4.7, 4.6 to 5, nor in rounding *down* 4.1, 4.2, 4.3, 4.4 to 4. What should we do with a number like 4.5, which is exactly half-way between 4 and 5?

There is no simple answer. In the case of a calculation, where we have the numbers and no other information, we always follow the same rule: round *up* when the given number is halfway between two numbers. Using this rule, 4.5 will be rounded up to 5, 75 would be rounded up to 80. However, if we know the situation, things may be different. If I want to find an approximate cost for the item in my shopping trolley, so that I am sure that I have enough to pay, then it would be better to round *up* 35p to 40p for safety. But if I am making shelves and I know that a piece of wood is about 3.5 metres long, it is better to think of that as 3 metres, rounding *down*, to be sure that it will be long enough for what I need.

Rounding rules work for numbers of all sizes and for numbers with two or more digits in them. The rules can be summarised:

if the unwanted part begins with a 4 or less round down;

if the unwanted part begins with a 5 or more, round up.

Example 10

Round 367 to the nearest hundred.

Since 367 is nearer to 400 than to 300 it is rounded to 400. So 367 ≈ 400.

Example 11

Round 4.3751 to the nearest hundredth (the nearest 0.01).

Here we need to leave two digits after the decimal point to record tenths and hundredths. The 5 is the first unwanted digit and according to the rule we round up. Hence 4.3751 is 4.38 to the nearest hundredth. So $4.3751 \approx 4.38$. (Notice that the rule is strengthened here by the fact that the 5 is not the final figure; the number is in fact larger than 4.375.)

Example 12
Use rounding rules to give an approximate value for 367×845.

There is no point in rounding to the nearest ten since this will give a multiplication which is still difficult. So we round to the nearest hundred, which gives us numbers with only one digit to use.

$$367 \times 845 \approx 400 \times 800.$$

Now $4 \times 8 = 32$ so we have

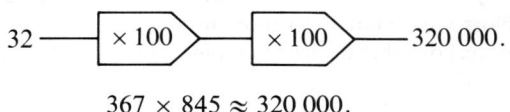

$$32 \longrightarrow \boxed{\times 100} \longrightarrow \boxed{\times 100} \longrightarrow 320\,000.$$

Hence $$367 \times 845 \approx 320\,000.$$

Exercise F

Questions 1 to 5 may be done orally.
In each of questions 1 to 5 use the rounding rules to give estimates of each number to the accuracy required.

*1 To the nearest whole number: 7.7, 1.3, 4.9, 11.6, 7.5, 19.1, 6.09.
2 To the nearest ten: 31, 56, 45, 26.4, 78.6, 90.5, 14.398.
*3 To the nearest hundred: 85, 126, 224, 751, 749, 750, 483.65, 975.
4 To the nearest tenth: 0.93, 0.777, 5.55, 8.44, 35.95, 3.7482, 0.97.
5 To the nearest hundredth: 0.387, 0.192, 0.131, 7.564, 13.1313, 8.467.

In the remainder of the exercise use the rounding rules to help you give approximations to the required answers. Write down sufficient working to make clear what you are doing. Do not use a calculator.

*6 Estimate
    (a) 7.6×1.3;   (b) 4.9×11.6;   (c) 7.5×19.1;   (d) $56 \div 6.09$;
    (e) $204 \div 36.9$;   (f) $89.1 \div 28.3$;   (g) 22.3×7.2;   (h) 9.5×3.5;
    (i) 45×95;   (j) $176.1 \div 57.3$;   (k) $244.2 \div 27.4$;   (l) $356 \div 45.3$;
    (m) $\dfrac{3.94 \times 14.5}{5.96}$;   (n) $\dfrac{12.5 \times 6.34}{8.07}$;   (o) $\dfrac{231 \times 22.1}{365.3}$.

7 A boy had a calculator for Christmas and did the following calculations with it:
    (a) 863×2.4;   (b) 237×19.6;   (c) 87.5×78.5;   (d) 26.5×0.97;
    (e) $327 \div 26.1$;   (f) $973 \div 21.9$.
His answers were: (a) 20 712, (b) 4645.2, (c) 686.875, (d) 25.705, (e) 12.56705, (f) 444.29224.
Use rounding rules to see how many answers must be wrong.

52 Calculations and approximations Ch. 19

*8 An Inter City express uses 1 gallon of fuel every 2.3 miles. How many gallons does it use going from London to Peterborough and back, a distance of 76.5 miles each way?

9 Each lap of a running track is 400 m. Mary takes 57.2 sec to go round once. What is her average speed in metres per second?

10 A family buys 19 pints of milk each week. If each pint holds about 568.3 ml, estimate how many litres they buy in
  (a) one week; (b) one year.

*11 A packet of 24 fish fingers weighs 705 g. Estimate the mass of each fish finger.

12 Alice has a board book which is 2.9 cm thick. If there are 86 pages in the book how thick is each page
  (a) in cm; (b) in mm?

13 The Earth rotates every 24 hours. During each rotation all points on the Equator move 40 600 km. At what speed are these points moving in km per hour?

14 (a) 50 g of hair are needed to make a wig; if each hair has a mass of 0.023 g, how many hairs are required to make one wig?
  (b) If a man reckons that his hair has a mass of 32.6 g, how many hairs has he got on his head?

SUMMARY

Calculations such as (a) 700 × 0.003 and (b) 0.12 ÷ 30 000 can be worked out mentally thinking like this:

 (a) 700 × 0.003. We know 7 × 3 = 21, so we have

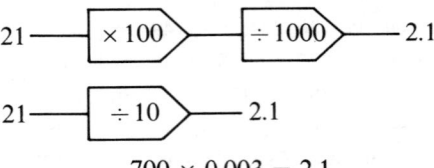

$$21 \to \boxed{\times 100} \to \boxed{\div 1000} \to 2.1$$

or

$$21 \to \boxed{\div 10} \to 2.1$$

Hence   700 × 0.003 = 2.1

 (b) 0.12 ÷ 30 000. We know 12 ÷ 3 = 4, so we have

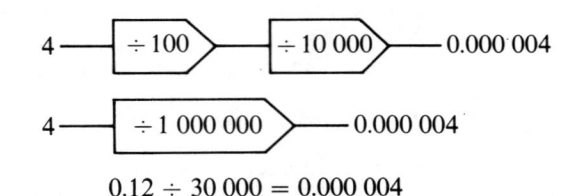

$$4 \to \boxed{\div 100} \to \boxed{\div 10\,000} \to 0.000\,004$$

or

$$4 \to \boxed{\div 1\,000\,000} \to 0.000\,004$$

Hence   0.12 ÷ 30 000 = 0.000 004

The rounding rules are:
 if the unwanted part begins with a 4 or less round down;
 if the unwanted part begins with a 5 or more, round up.

Summary

These rules can be used, with the methods above, to estimate results. For example:

Estimate (c) 36.7 × 0.089 and (d) 273.1 ÷ 0.176.
   (c) 36.7 × 0.089 ≈ 40 × 0.09.   We know 4 × 9 = 36, so we have

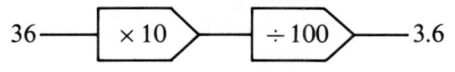

$$36 \longrightarrow \boxed{\times 10} \longrightarrow \boxed{\div 100} \longrightarrow 3.6$$

Hence   36.7 × 0.089 ≈ 3.6

   (d) 273.1 ÷ 0.176 ≈ 300 ÷ 0.2.   We know 3 ÷ 2 = 1.5, so we have

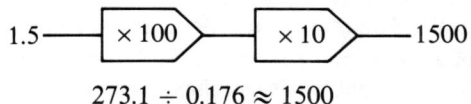

$$1.5 \longrightarrow \boxed{\times 100} \longrightarrow \boxed{\times 10} \longrightarrow 1500$$

Hence   273.1 ÷ 0.176 ≈ 1500

Summary exercise

Calculators must not be used in this exercise.

1 Complete the following so that each has an answer of 30.
    (a) 30 × □; (b) 3 × □ ; (c) 0.3 × □; (d) 300 × □;
    (e) □ × 60; (f) □ × 600; (g) □ × 0.6; (h)   □ × 6;
    (i) 2 × □; (j) 0.2 × □ ; (k) 20 × □; (l) 200 × □.

2 Insert decimal points and any necessary zeros to make each of the following equal 400. (Make each answer different!)
    (a)   4 × 1; (b)   4 × 1; (c)   4 × 1; (d) 8 × 5; (e)   8 × 5; (f) 8 × 5;
    (g) 36 ÷ 9; (h) 36 ÷ 9; (i) 36 ÷ 9.

3 Work out
    (a) 70 × 0.3; (b) 0.8 × 400; (c) 0.6 × 0.9; (d) 20 × 90; (e) 900 × 0.7;
    (f) 18 ÷ 0.3; (g) 1.8 ÷ 0.3; (h) 0.18 ÷ 0.3.

4 Estimate
    (a) 7.86 × 4.358; (b) 16.72 × 3.551; (c) 29.34 × 6.45;
    (d) 78.6 ÷ 4.358; (e) 167.2 ÷ 3.551; (f) 293.4 ÷ 6.45.

5 There are roughly 11.3 French francs to the pound. What is the approximate cost of a holiday
    (a) in francs of a holiday in Britain costing £324;
    (b) in £ of a holiday in France costing 1628 francs?

6 There are 2240 lb in 1 ton (old British units). A coal mine produces 568 tons of coal per day. Approximately how many pounds is that
    (a) in one day; (b) in a working week of 5 days?
If a train wagon can carry 69 tons how many wagons will be needed to move 1 week's production?

54 Calculations and approximations Ch. 19

Miscellaneous exercise

1 (*a*) Use your calculator to find 2 ÷ 13. Use the rounding rules so that your answer has (i) one; (ii) three; (iii) six figures after the decimal point.

(There are many occasions when answers are too accurate and need rounding as above. For example if I were to use 2 kg of sugar to make 13 identical cakes, each cake should contain 0.153 846 1... kg of sugar. Needless to say, you could not weigh sugar so accurately!)

(*b*) My old kitchen scales can only weigh accurately to one figure after the decimal point. My new kitchen scales are accurate to three figures after the point, and a chemical balance accurate to six figures. If 47 g of currants were to be put into the 13 cakes, what readings would I get on (i) my old scales; (ii) my new scales; (iii) a chemical balance for the mass of currants contained in each cake?

2 Perhaps you can think of some people who need to use all the figures shown on a calculator. One example might be a space flight planner. If he set a course on an angle of 45.743 948 degrees for 500 000 km, what kind of error might there be if he rounded the angle to 2 figures after the decimal point? Would this be an important error if you were in a spaceship?

Make a list of other people who might need very accurate answers.

3 A magnetic tape on a computer holds 50 million characters and costs £10. What is the cost of storing one character? (Work out your answer in pence, without a calculator.)

4 A magnetic disk on a computer holds 100 million characters and costs £400. What is the cost in pence of storing one character? What reason can you find for the very large difference in price?

5 A computer can process 3 500 000 instructions in one second. How long will it take to process 7000 instructions?

Quickies 6

CLOSED BOOK

Calculators must not be used
1. Which number, when squared, gives 49?
2. Which of these would be a reasonable estimate of the length of a bus: 1 metre, 3 metres, 5 metres?
3. Work out $^+4 + {}^-3$.
4. What is the cost of 6 train tickets at £5.95 each?
5. Estimate the value of 29×41 to the nearest hundred.
6. A regular polygon has exterior angles of 45°. How many sides has it?
7. Neil walks at $4\frac{1}{2}$ m.p.h. How far does he walk in 6 hours?
8. I think of a number, double it and subtract 4. The result is 10. What number did I first think of?
9. What is the total mass, in kilograms, of 6 pots of jam each of mass 450 g?
10. £24 is shared between two people so that the first receives £8 more than the second. How much does the first receive?

OPEN BOOK

Calculators must not be used.
1. How many lines of symmetry has the regular pentagon shown in Figure 1?

Figure 1

2. What must be added to $^-5$ to get $^+12$?
3. Estimate the value of 18.1×9.8 to the nearest ten.
4. If $p = 3$ and $q = 2$ write down the value of $(p + q)^2$.
5. Write down the two missing numbers in the following sequence:
$$27, 9, 3, \ldots, \ldots, \tfrac{1}{9}.$$
6. How much change would you get from £10 if you brought four items each costing £1.95?
7. A piece of string 4.5 m in length is cut into two pieces. One piece is 2.75 m long. How long is the other piece?

Quickies 6

8 A book has pages numbered 1 to 26. What are the numbers of the middle two pages?

9 Find the value of x in the triangle shown in Figure 2.

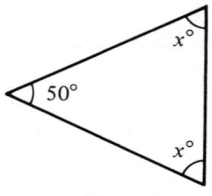

Figure 2

10 A water lily doubles its size every day and completely covers a pond in 21 days. After how many days will it cover half the pond?

Revision exercises 6A, 6B

REVISION EXERCISE 6A

1 Make a sketch copy of the diagrams in Figure 1. Add broken lines to show any lines of symmetry.

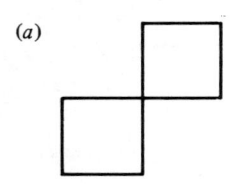

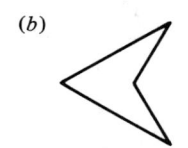

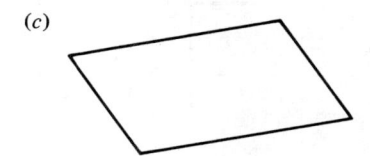

(a) (b) (c)

Figure 1

2 Which of the diagrams in Figure 2 have rotational symmetry, and of what order?

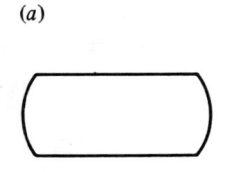

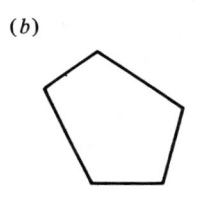

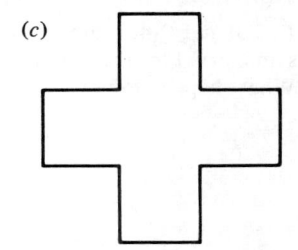

(a) (b) (c)

Figure 2

3 Write down the next three numbers in each of the following sequences stating the 'rules' you have used.
  (a) 10, 7, 4, 1, ...;   (b) 10, 4, ⁻2, ...;   (c) ⁻9, ⁻6, ⁻3, ...

4 Write down the answers to each of the following:
  (a) ⁺5 + ⁺8;   (b) ⁺5 + ⁻8;   (c) ⁺23 + ⁻23;   (d) ⁺19 + ⁻17;   (e) ⁻8 + ⁻3;
  (f) ⁻9 + ⁺4.

5 (a) A pile of 400 sheets of paper is 2.8 cm high. What is the thickness, in mm, of each sheet of paper?
  (b) Without using a calculator, write down estimates of the following:
      (i) 8.3×14.7;   (ii) $43.7 \div 8.4$;   (iii) 249×0.37.

REVISION EXERCISE 6B

1 Use your calculator to work out:
  (a) ⁺9.3 + ⁻7.8;   (b) ⁻10.7 + ⁻2.6;   (c) ⁺8.6 − ⁻5.8;
  (d) ⁻15.6 − ⁺12.5;   (e) ⁻17.3 − ⁻5.6;   (f) ⁻3.7 + ⁻14.4.

2 The pupils of form 1Z were set a target of £2.00 each to collect on a sponsored silence. Use positive and negative numbers to express the following amounts, in pence, relative to the target:
  Dawn £3.27;   Kate £2.14;   Marti £1.10;   Valerine 85p;   Dami 8p;
  Ronke £6.29.

3 Copy the diagrams in Figure 3 onto squared paper. Complete each so that it has rotational symmetry of the order shown. Use the dots as centres of symmetry.

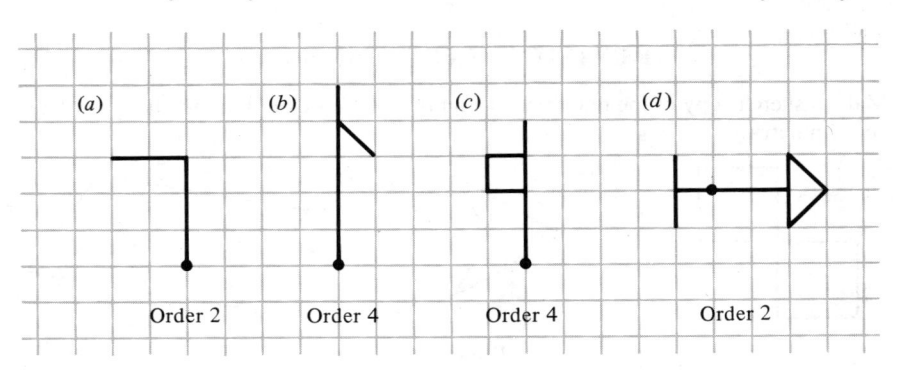

(a) Order 2 (b) Order 4 (c) Order 4 (d) Order 2

4 Round each of the following numbers to the nearest hundredth:
(a) 1.745; (b) 0.8375; (c) 0.333 33; (d) 0.666 66.

5 $P(1, 3)$ and $Q(4, 2)$ are two points of a figure $PQRS$ which has the x-axis as a line of symmetry. Plot these points on squared paper and find the coordinates of R and S. What shape is $PQRS$?

20

Brackets in formulae

1. A NEED FOR BRACKETS

Janice paints her own Christmas cards. She makes a different card each year and it takes her a little while to achieve the right colour and design. The first half dozen cards she does are 'practice' cards. The special pieces of card she uses cost 2p each and she needs 25 cards to send to friends.

We can work out the cost of the card she must buy like this.

Cards needed for friends	Practice cards		Cost per card 2p		Total cost in pence
25	+6	25 + 6 = 31	×2	31 × 2 = 62	62

60 Brackets in formulae — Ch. 20

Janice's sister Stephanie wants 12 of the cards so Janice agrees to make 25 + 12 = 37 good cards.

The flow chart now gives the total cost in pence as:

$$37 \longrightarrow \boxed{+6} \xrightarrow{43} \boxed{\times 2} \xrightarrow{86} 86$$

Other members of the family are now becoming interested too, so Janice decides she needs a formula for the cost, where the total number of cards is n:

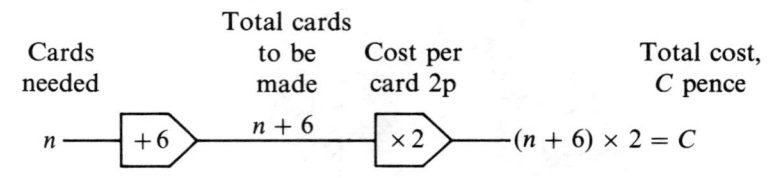

$$\begin{array}{cccc} \text{Cards} & \text{Total cards} & \text{Cost per} & \text{Total cost,} \\ \text{needed} & \text{to be made} & \text{card 2p} & C \text{ pence} \end{array}$$

$$n \longrightarrow \boxed{+6} \xrightarrow{n+6} \boxed{\times 2} \longrightarrow (n+6) \times 2 = C$$

So she could write $C = (n + 6) \times 2$.

Notice that the $n + 6$ must be in brackets because if we wrote $n + 6 \times 2$ that would mean that the multiplication should be worked out first. For instance for 25 cards, $n + 6 \times 2$ would give $25 + 6 \times 2 = 25 + 12 = 37$, which is wrong. We need $(25 + 6) \times 2 = 31 \times 2 = 62$.

Instead of writing $C = (n + 6) \times 2$, we always write $C = 2(n + 6)$.

If the whole family want to use Janice's Christmas cards (her father agrees to pay for the card needed!), they will need 65 cards. How much will the card for this cost?

The cost, in pence, is given by $C = 2(65 + 6) = 2 \times 71 = 142$.
The cost is £1.42.

Sometimes formulae involve division and use of brackets.

Example 1

Write down the formula represented by the following flow chart:

$$n \longrightarrow \boxed{-5} \xrightarrow{n-5} \boxed{\div 3} \longrightarrow (n-5) \div 3 = C$$

We write the results of putting n through this flow chart as

$$C = (n-5)/3$$

or
$$C = \frac{(n-5)}{3}$$

or
$$C = \tfrac{1}{3}(n-5)$$

since dividing by 3 has the same effect as multiplying by $\tfrac{1}{3}$.

These are all acceptable answers but we do not write the formula as
$$C = (n - 5) \div 3.$$

Example 2

Give the formula that corresponds to the following flow chart, and find the value of q when $p = 3$:

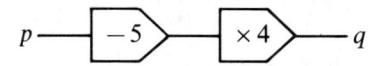

$$p \longrightarrow \boxed{-5} \longrightarrow \boxed{\times 4} \longrightarrow q$$

First we subtract 5, obtaining $p - 5$, and then multiply the whole of this by 4. We use brackets:
$$q = (p - 5) \times 4$$
and write this as
$$q = 4(p - 5).$$
Substituting $p = 3$ into the formula we have
$$q = 4(3 - 5)$$
$$= 4 \times {}^{-}2$$
$$= {}^{-}8.$$

Exercise A

*1 In each part of this question begin by writing a formula equivalent to the given flow chart.

(a) $x \longrightarrow \boxed{+3} \longrightarrow \boxed{\times 4} \longrightarrow y$ What is the value of y if $x = 2$?

(b) $x \longrightarrow \boxed{\times 4} \longrightarrow \boxed{+3} \longrightarrow y$ Why are no brackets needed here?

    What is the value of y if $x = 2$?

(c) $p \longrightarrow \boxed{+8} \longrightarrow \boxed{\div 4} \longrightarrow q$ What is the value of q when $p = 16$?

(d) $p \longrightarrow \boxed{\div 4} \longrightarrow \boxed{+8} \longrightarrow q$ What is the value of q when $p = 16$?

*2 Give the flow charts for the following formulae:
  (a) $a = 2x + 7$; (b) $b = 2(x + 7)$; (c) $c = 3x - 5$; (d) $d = 3(x - 5)$;
  (e) $e = \frac{1}{4}x + 2$; (f) $f = \frac{1}{3}(x + 7)$; (g) $g = \frac{x}{4} - 5$; (h) $h = \frac{x - 5}{4}$.

Find the values of a, b, c, d, e, f, g, h, when $x = 2$.

3   From selling home-made cakes on a market stall in aid of charity, Karen, Cynthia and Andrew take £26. After they have paid £5 for the hire of the stall, how much is left? If they divide this equally between the three of them (because they each have their favourite charity), how much does each charity receive?

Give a flow chart and a formula for calculating the amount, £A, that each charity receives if they sell £P worth of cakes. Calculate A if $P = 47$.

How much money would they have to take in order to be able to give £20 to each charity?

2. REMOVING BRACKETS

A box of 'tweeties' contains g green sweets, r red sweets and y yellow sweets. In the 'small' box $g = 20$, $r = 30$ and $y = 25$. We want to work out how many sweets there will be in 10 boxes.

Method 1   In one box there are $20 + 30 + 25$ sweets, so in 10 boxes there are $10 \times (20 + 30 + 25)$ or $10(20 + 30 + 25)$ sweets. This can be worked out as $10 \times 75 = 750$ sweets.

Method 2   In 10 boxes there will be:

$10 \times g$ green ones, so $10 \times 20 = 200$ green ones;
$10 \times r$ red ones, so $10 \times 30 = 300$ red ones;
$10 \times y$ yellow ones, so $10 \times 25 = 250$ yellow ones.

Thus the total is $200 + 300 + 250 = 750$.
In method 1 we worked out $10(20 + 30 + 25)$ or $10(g + r + y)$.
In method 2 we worked out $10 \times 20 + 10 \times 30 + 10 \times 25$ or $10g + 10r + 10y$. The answers are the same.
We have $10(g + r + y) = 10g + 10r + 10y$.

You do calculations like this in ordinary everyday life. Here is another example:

Removing brackets

Example 3

The total cost of 8 stamps at 17p (first class postage in 1985) and of another 12 stamps at 17p can be worked out, in pence, in four different ways:

(1) $8 \times 17 + 12 \times 17 = 136 + 204 = 340$;
(2) $(8 + 12) \times 17 = 20 \times 17 = 340$;
(3) $17 \times 8 + 17 \times 12 = 136 + 204 = 340$;
(4) $17 \times (8 + 12) = 17(8 + 12) = 17 \times 20 = 340$.

The total cost is £3.40.

This example illustrates that

$$(8 + 12) \times 17 = 8 \times 17 + 12 \times 17$$

and that

$$17 \times (8 + 12) = 17 \times 8 + 17 \times 12$$

and that all of these come to the same total.

If there had been x stamps bought at 17p followed by a further y stamps at 17p, the total cost, in pence, could have been written in any of these equivalent ways:

(1) $(x + y) \times 17$;
(2) $x \times 17 + y \times 17$;
(3) $17 \times (x + y)$, which we shorten to $17(x + y)$;
(4) $17 \times x + 17 \times y$, which we shorten to $17x + 17y$.

The process of going from $(x + y) \times 17$ to $x \times 17 + y \times 17$ or from $17(x + y)$ to $17x + 17y$ is known as *removing the brackets*. The following examples illustrate this further.

Example 4

Remove the brackets from $3(x + y)$.

$$3(x + y) = 3 \times (x + y)$$
$$= 3 \times x + 3 \times y = 3x + 3y$$

Example 5

Remove the brackets from $2(3p - 5q)$.

$$2(3p - 5q) = 2 \times (3 \times p - 5 \times q) = 2 \times 3 \times p - 2 \times 5 \times q$$
$$= 6p - 10q$$

Notice that $(3p - 5q) \times 2 = 3p \times 2 - 5q \times 2 = 6p - 10q$ also.

After a little practice, we write down the answers to examples like this without any in-between working.

Exercise B

*1 Remove the brackets from
(a) $2(x + y)$; (b) $5(a - b)$; (c) $7(p + q + r)$; (d) $8(f + g)$; (e) $(a + b) \times 4$; (f) $(a - b) \times 3$.

2 Remove the brackets from
(a) $5(x - y)$; (b) $3(a + b)$; (c) $4(p - q + r)$; (d) $6(s + t - u)$; (e) $(m + n) \times 7$; (f) $(d + e - f) \times 10$.

*3 Remove the brackets from
(a) $3(5x - 2y)$; (b) $\frac{1}{2}(4a + 2b)$; (c) $2(2p + 3q)$; (d) $5(p - 2q)$; (e) $5(3y - 4z)$; (f) $(2p + 3q - 4r) \times 2$.

4 Remove the brackets from
(a) $2(3x + 4y)$; (b) $2.1(a - 3.2b + 8.6c)$; (c) $\frac{1}{4}(8a - c)$; (d) $\frac{1}{3}(6q - 2r)$; (e) $(2m - 4n) \times 3$; (f) $(0.6x + y - 2.1z) \times 7$.

*5 Use the methods of Section 2 and Example 3 to work out, in two ways, each of the following:
(a) The total mass of 12 tins full of coffee. The empty tins are each of mass 30 grams and each contains 250 grams of coffee.
(b) The total cost of 7 records in a sale each marked £3.99 but all in a rack labelled '£1.50 off all prices'.
(c) The total value of 25 books of stamps each of which contains 3 stamps at 13p, 2 stamps at 4p and 3 stamps at 1p.

SUMMARY

The flow chart

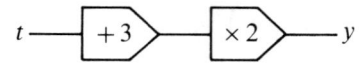

$$t \longrightarrow \boxed{+3} \longrightarrow \boxed{\times 2} \longrightarrow y$$

is equivalent to the formula

$$y = (t + 3) \times 2$$

which is written as

$$y = 2(t + 3).$$

The flow chart

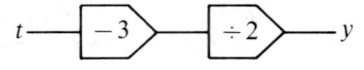

$$t \longrightarrow \boxed{-3} \longrightarrow \boxed{\div 2} \longrightarrow y$$

is equivalent to the formula $y = (t - 3) \div 2$ which is correctly written as

$$y = (t - 3)/2 \quad \text{or} \quad y = \tfrac{1}{2}(t - 3) \quad \text{or} \quad y = \frac{t - 3}{2}.$$

Brackets may be removed so that, for instance, $2(a + b) = 2a + 2b$ and $(a + b) \times 2 = a \times 2 + b \times 2 = 2a + 2b$, also.

Summary

Summary exercise

1. In each part of this question begin by writing a formula equivalent to the given flow chart.

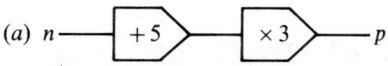

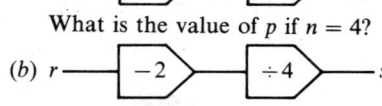

   (a) $n \longrightarrow \boxed{+5} \longrightarrow \boxed{\times 3} \longrightarrow p$

   What is the value of p if $n = 4$?

   (b) $r \longrightarrow \boxed{-2} \longrightarrow \boxed{\div 4} \longrightarrow s$

   What is the value of s if $r = 14$?
   What is the value of r if $s = 0$?

2. In each part of this question begin by writing a flow chart equivalent to the given formula.

   (a) $v = (t - 2)/5$.
   What is the value of v if $t = 27$?

   (b) $p = \frac{1}{4}(n - 1)$.
   What is the value of p if $n = 13$?

   (c) $q = \dfrac{r + 2.4}{5}$.
   What is the value of q if $r = 2.6$?

3. Remove the brackets from:
   (a) $4(p + q)$; (b) $9(a - b + c)$; (c) $(x - y) \times 5$; (d) $3(2a - 4b)$;
   (e) $(m - 2n) + 2$; (f) $(2x + 4y - 3z) \times 5$.

Miscellaneous exercise

1. Using a calculator, work out the value of:
   $2.57 \times 4.29 + 2.57 \times 3.61 - 2.57 \times 2.98$.
   Can you find another way of working this out which involves less key-pressing?
   If you did not use brackets, and your calculator has bracket keys find a method of evaluating the result using the bracket keys.
   Which method involves the least amount of key-pressing?

2. If $y = (1.6x + 3.5)/2.5$, calculate the value of y when $x = 3$ and when $x = 4$.
   Find the value of x for which $y = 3$, showing your method clearly.

3. If $4(a + 3b) = 2(24 + 2a)$, where a and b are unknown numbers, what can you say about b?

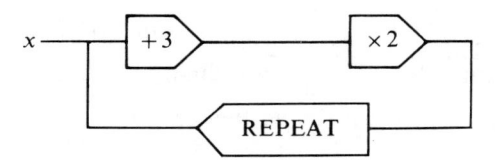

4.
   $x \longrightarrow \boxed{+3} \longrightarrow \boxed{\times 2} \longrightarrow$

   $\boxed{\text{REPEAT}}$

   Show that, after one repeat (that is, after you have gone through the top line of the flow chart twice), the expression obtained is equivalent to $4x + 18$.
   After one more repeat, the expression obtained is equivalent to $px + q$ when p and q are unknown numbers. Find the values of p and q.
   What would be the value of p after five repeats?

21

Let's look at number

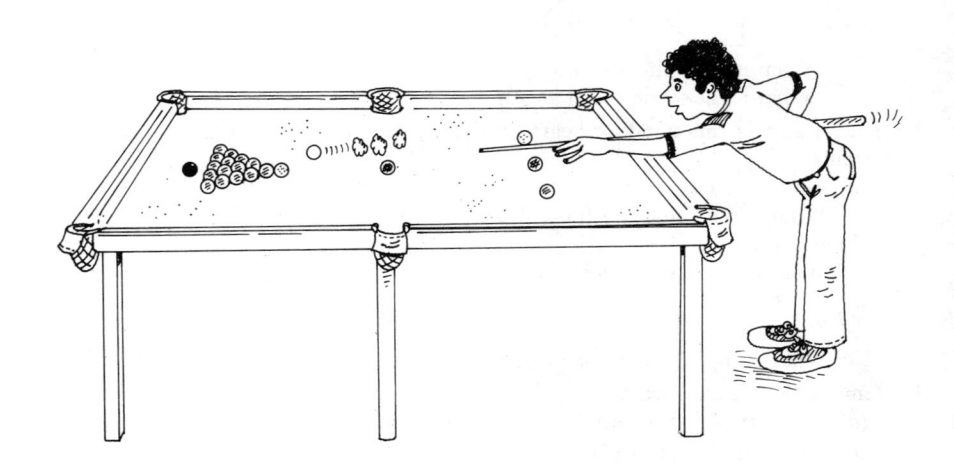

1. FLOW CHARTS

We have already met flow charts which have involved simple operators such as $\boxed{+5}$ and $\boxed{\times 8}$. We shall need to be able to put more complicated instructions into the boxes. We have previously used letters to stand for numbers and we do the same here.

The instruction LET $N = 7$ means that the numerical value of N is to be taken as 7. We shall use instructions like this in flow charts, so we enclose them in an arrow box to show the direction of flow:

$$\boxed{\text{LET } N = 7}$$

In the same way $\boxed{\text{LET } P = 2 \times N}$ means that the numerical value of P is to be twice the current value of N. As in ordinary algebra it is usual to omit the multiplication sign. This is usually written as $\boxed{\text{LET } P = 2N}$.

Example 1
Find the output from the following flow chart:

$$\longrightarrow \boxed{\text{LET } N = 7} \longrightarrow \boxed{\text{LET } P = 2N} \longrightarrow \boxed{\text{Output } P}$$

The value of N is 7, $P = 2N$ which is 14. The output is 14.

Flow charts

Example 2
Find the output from the following flow chart:

→ LET $A = 5$ → LET $B = 2$ → LET $C = 3A - B$ → Output C

The value of C is $3 \times 5 - 2 = 13$ (remember multiplication first). The output is 13.

Using the same letter again

If we had a very long flow chart we might run out of letters to use. So we invent a new notation in order that we can re-use letters.

LET NEW $N = N + 2$

means that we add 2 to the present value of N and this then becomes the new value of N. The old value of N is then *lost*.

The following examples make this clear.

(a) LET $N = 4$ → LET NEW $N = N + 7$ → Output N
results in an output of 11, and the original value, 4, of N is lost.

(b) LET $N = 9$ → LET NEW $N = 3N - 5$ → Output N
results in output 22, and the original value 9, of N, is lost.

(c) LET $C = 3$ → LET $N = 12$ → LET NEW $N = N/C$ → Output N
results in output 4. In this example note that the sloping dash / is used to show division. This is usual in all flowchart and computing work.

Exercise A (Oral)

Find the output from each of the flow charts in questions 1 to 8.

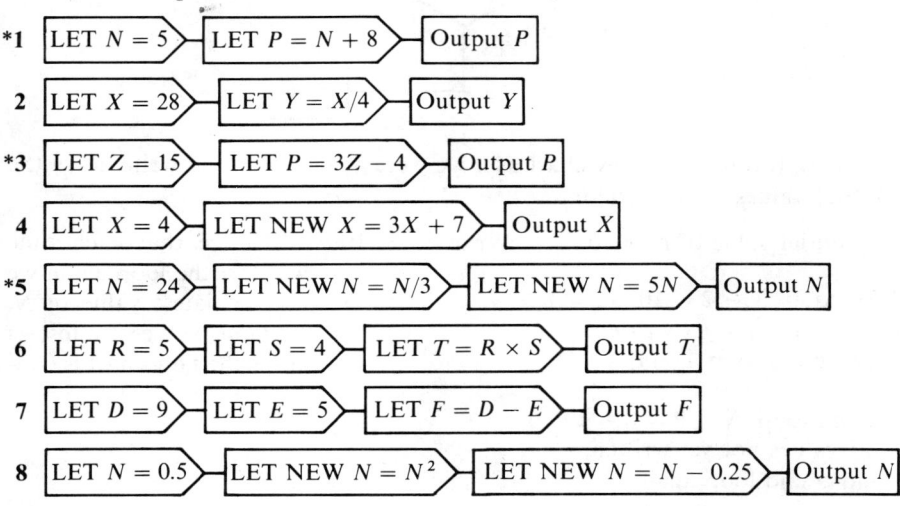

*1 LET $N = 5$ → LET $P = N + 8$ → Output P

2 LET $X = 28$ → LET $Y = X/4$ → Output Y

*3 LET $Z = 15$ → LET $P = 3Z - 4$ → Output P

4 LET $X = 4$ → LET NEW $X = 3X + 7$ → Output X

*5 LET $N = 24$ → LET NEW $N = N/3$ → LET NEW $N = 5N$ → Output N

6 LET $R = 5$ → LET $S = 4$ → LET $T = R \times S$ → Output T

7 LET $D = 9$ → LET $E = 5$ → LET $F = D - E$ → Output F

8 LET $N = 0.5$ → LET NEW $N = N^2$ → LET NEW $N = N - 0.25$ → Output N

2. DECISION BOXES

Sometimes in a flow chart we have to decide what to do, and we need to be able to show this in the chart. Here is part of an 'everyday' flow chart to show you:

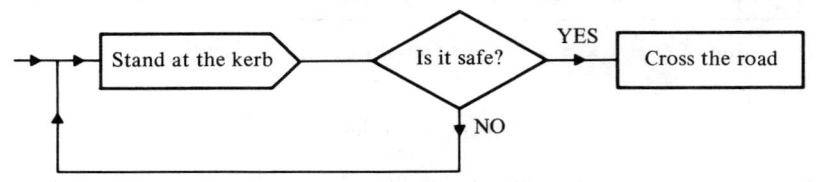

```
         ┌─────────────────┐      ╱╲  YES  ┌──────────────┐
    ────▶│ Stand at the kerb├────▶ Is it safe?├──────▶│ Cross the road│
         └─────────────────┘      ╲╱       └──────────────┘
                  ▲                 │ NO
                  └─────────────────┘
```

If it is not safe to cross then you would stand at the kerb until it was safe. This is shown by the line from the diamond shaped *decision box* back to the instruction 'Stand at the kerb'. Such a line creates a *loop* in the flow chart. A question in a decision box must be written in such a way that the only possible answers to it are 'Yes' or 'No'. In a numerical case the 'Output' instruction may be inside the loop in which case several values of the output have to be recorded. The following flowchart shows this. In such cases we use an arrow box for Output because the flow of numbers continues.

Example 1
   Find the output of the following flow chart:

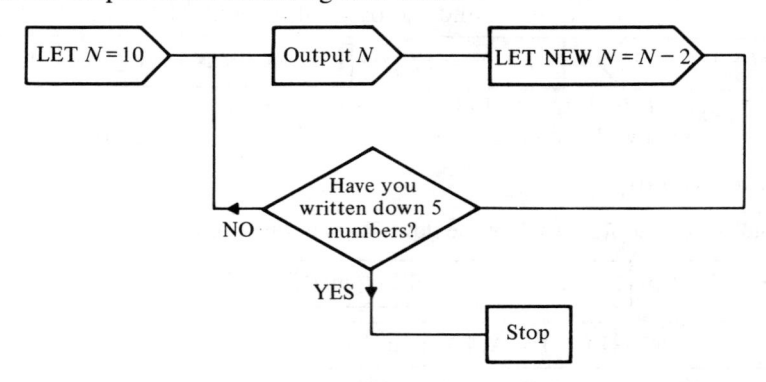

```
   ┌─────────┐   ┌─────────┐   ┌────────────────┐
   │ LET N=10├──▶│ Output N├──▶│ LET NEW N = N−2├──┐
   └─────────┘   └─────────┘   └────────────────┘  │
                      ▲              ╱╲            │
                      │   NO        ╱  ╲           │
                      └────────────Have you ◀──────┘
                                   written down 5
                                    numbers?
                                     ╲  ╱
                                      ╲╱
                                       │ YES
                                       ▼
                                    ┌──────┐
                                    │ Stop │
                                    └──────┘
```

We work through the flow chart as if we were a computer and write down the Output values of *N* as follows:

The initial value of *N* is 10	Write down 10	(Notice that each time we start the loop again we use the latest value of *N*. Previous values are lost as far as the flow chart is concerned)
First loop. $N - 2 = 10 - 2 = 8$ (5 values not yet written, go round loop again)	8	
Second loop. $N - 2 = 8 - 2 = 6$ (5 values not yet written, go round loop again)	6	
. . . . .		

Fourth loop. $N - 2 = 4 - 2 = 2$ 2
(5 values now written down,
so stop)

The output is 10, 8, 6, 4, 2.

Exercise B

Write down the outputs of the following flow charts.

*1

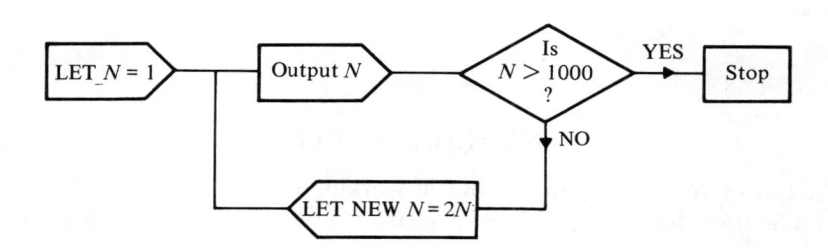

LET $N = 1$ → Output N → Is $N > 1000$? —YES→ Stop
                                         ↓ NO
            ←——————————— LET NEW $N = 2N$ ←

2

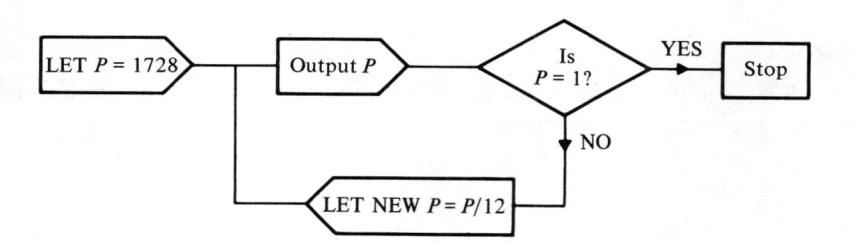

LET $P = 1728$ → Output P → Is $P = 1$? —YES→ Stop
                                         ↓ NO
            ←——————————— LET NEW $P = P/12$ ←

*3

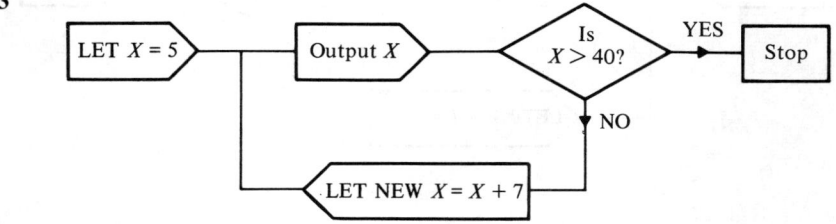

LET $X = 5$ → Output X → Is $X > 40$? —YES→ Stop
                                         ↓ NO
            ←——————————— LET NEW $X = X + 7$ ←

4

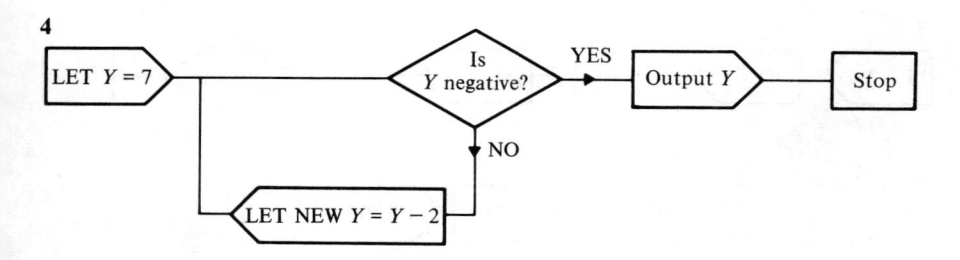

LET $Y = 7$ → Is Y negative? —YES→ Output Y → Stop
                   ↓ NO
            ←—— LET NEW $Y = Y - 2$ ←

*5

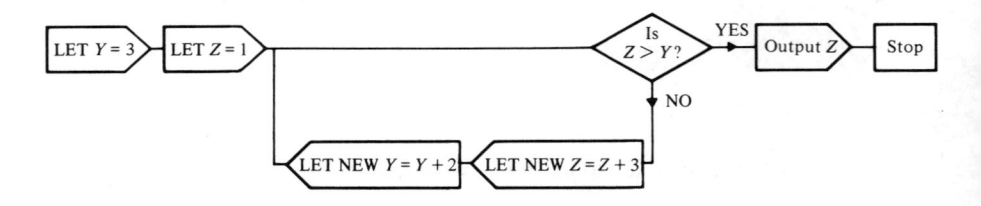

```
LET Y = 3 → LET Z = 1 ─────────────→ Is Z > Y? ──YES→ Output Z → Stop
                          │                    │NO
                          │                    ↓
                          └─ LET NEW Y = Y + 2 ← LET NEW Z = Z + 3
```

3. NUMBER PATTERNS

The last exercise gave you practice in working through flow charts. The next exercise uses the skills you have gained to produce some interesting number patterns.

Exerise C

Work through the following flow charts; it is important to attempt all five questions. Remember to write down the outputs.

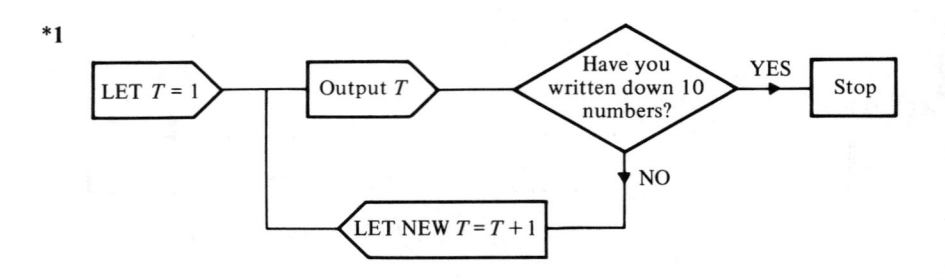

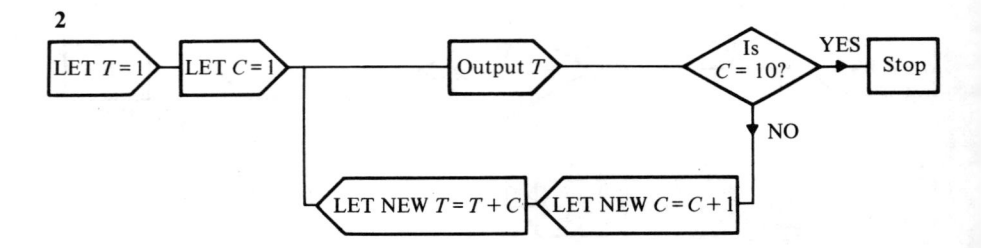

*1

```
LET T = 1 → Output T → Have you written down 10 numbers? ──YES→ Stop
                 │                                    │NO
                 └──────── LET NEW T = T + 1 ←────────┘
```

2

```
LET T = 1 → LET C = 1 ─────→ Output T → Is C = 10? ──YES→ Stop
                       │                          │NO
                       └──── LET NEW T = T + C ← LET NEW C = C + 1
```

Number patterns 71

*3

```
LET T=1 → LET C=1 → Output T → Is C=10? —YES→ Stop
                                      ↓NO
         ← LET NEW T=2C−1 ← LET NEW C=C+1 ←
```

4

```
LET T=0 → LET C=1 → LET D=(C−1)(C+1) → LET T=D+1
         ← LET NEW C=C+1 ←NO— Is C=10? ← Output T
                              YES↓
                              Stop
```

*5

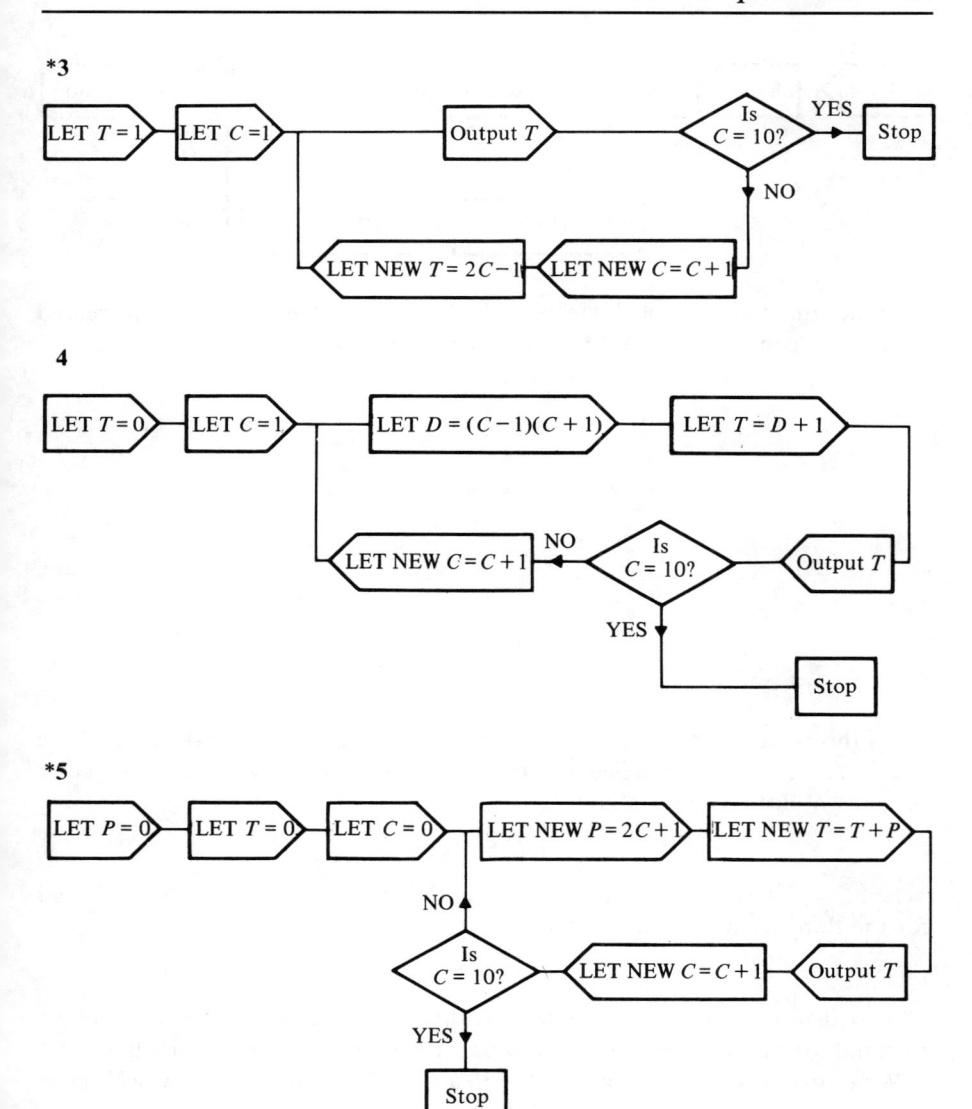

```
LET P=0 → LET T=0 → LET C=0 → LET NEW P=2C+1 → LET NEW T=T+P
                    NO↑
                    Is C=10? ← LET NEW C=C+1 ← Output T
                    YES↓
                    Stop
```

Triangle numbers

You may have recognised some of the number patterns produced in Exercise C. For instance question 1 gave the counting numbers and question 3 the odd numbers. In this section we look at the pattern produced by question 2 and in the next section we look at the pattern given by questions 4 and 5.

Here again is the flow chart for question 2 of Exercise C.

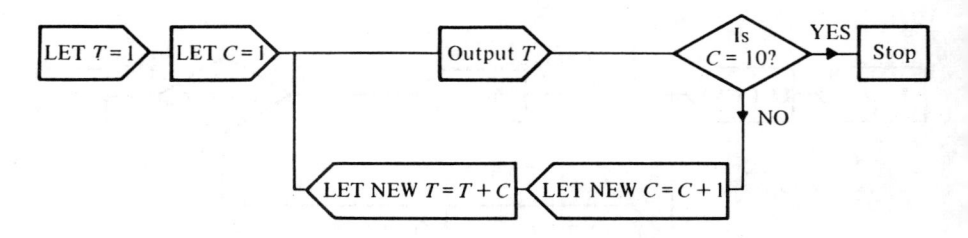

Let's look at number Ch. 21

```
LET T = 1 — LET C = 1 ──────── Output T ──── Is C = 10? ──YES── Stop
                    │                           │
                    │                           NO
                    └─ LET NEW T = T + C ◁ LET NEW C = C + 1 ┘
```

Notice that the value of C is increased by 1 and then the value of T is increased by C. This can be illustrated by a pattern of dots:

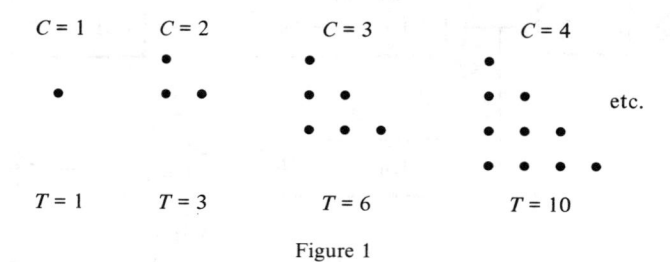

$C = 1$ $C = 2$ $C = 3$ $C = 4$

(dot patterns forming triangles)   etc.

$T = 1$ $T = 3$ $T = 6$ $T = 10$

Figure 1

Copy this pattern into your book and extend it up to $C = 10$. Make a list of the values of T. These are called the *triangle numbers* because of the triangular patterns of dots. The list starts:

$$1, 3, 6, 10, \ldots$$

When $C = 3$ we have the third triangle number, 6. We can write t_3 as shorthand for the third triangular number.

So $$t_3 = 6.$$

(We used, as is usual, a capital letter T within the flow chart. When using letters to stand for numbers in ordinary algebra it is more usual to use small letters.)

What are the values of t_4 and t_5? Is 35 a triangle number? If so, which one is it?

Square numbers

Questions 4 and 5 of Exercise C should both have produced the sequence

$$1, 4, 9, 16, \ldots$$

which you will recognise as the square numbers.

$$1^2 = 1, \; 2^2 = 4, \; 3^2 = 9, \; 4^2 = 16, \ldots.$$

Here, again, is the flow chart for question 5.

Number patterns 73

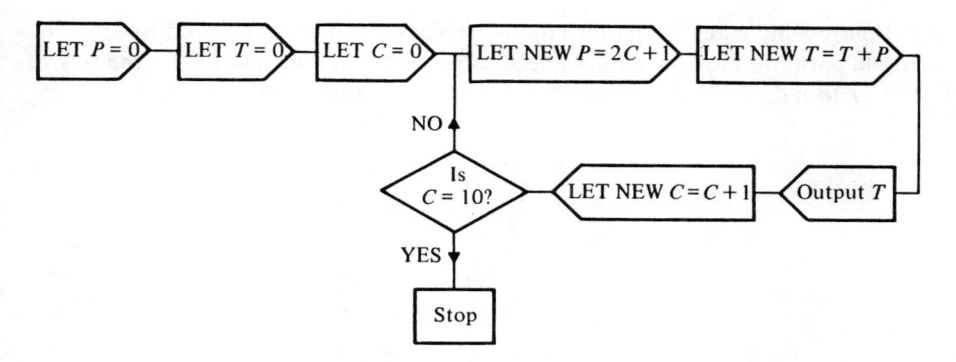

```
LET P = 0 → LET T = 0 → LET C = 0 → LET NEW P = 2C + 1 → LET NEW T = T + P
                              ↑                                    ↓
                              NO
                              Is C = 10? → LET NEW C = C + 1 → Output T
                              YES ↓
                              Stop
```

In question 5 the first value of T to be output was 1. This increased each time by the addition of the odd numbers 3, 5, 7 and so on. As with triangle numbers we can illustrate by a pattern of dots, this time drawn in squares (hence square numbers). As before we can use a shorthand of s_3 for the third square number, etc.

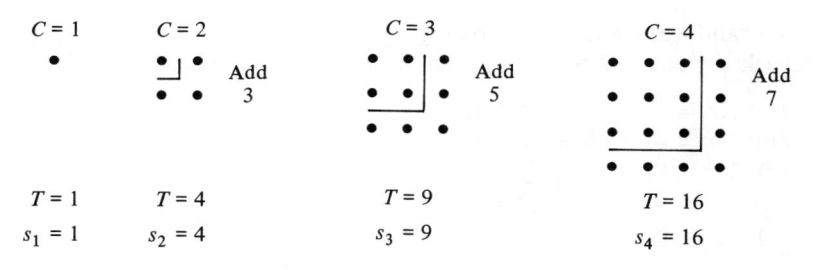

$C = 1$ $C = 2$ Add 3 $C = 3$ Add 5 $C = 4$ Add 7

$T = 1$ $T = 4$ $T = 9$ $T = 16$
$s_1 = 1$ $s_2 = 4$ $s_3 = 9$ $s_4 = 16$

Figure 2

We continue with two investigations.

Investigation 1
(a) Think of a number – square it – add twice the original number – add 1. (For example 3 gives $3^2 + 2 \times 3 + 1 = 9 + 6 + 1 = 16$.) Repeat a few times. What do you notice?
(b) Draw a square pattern of dots to show 36, the sixth square number. Add a 'backwards ∟' array of dots, like the ones shown in Figure 2, to show the seventh square number.
(c) Work part (a), again, starting with the number 6. This asks you to work out
$$6^2 + 2 \times 6 + 1.$$
What is the answer? What is the connection with part (b)?

Figure 3 indicates the pattern for 17^2. (Notice that we don't need to draw the whole pattern.) How many dots need to be added in the column and the row of the ⌐ to help make 18^2? Do not forget the extra one in the corner.

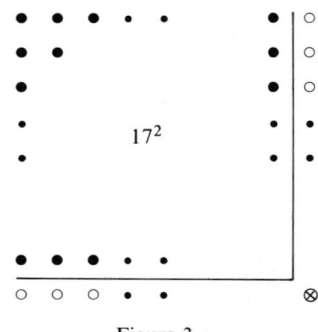

Figure 3

Explain why $18^2 = 17^2 + 2 \times 17 + 1$. Check with your calculator.

Copy and complete the following by writing correct numbers in the boxes. Check the answers to parts (a) to (d) with your calculator.

(a) $10^2 = \square^2 + 2 \times \square + 1$.
(b) $\square^2 = 41^2 + 2 \times 41 + 1$.
(c) $36^2 = \square^2 + 2 \times \square + 1$.
(d) $\square^2 = 98^2 + 2 \times \square + 1$.
(e) $\square^2 = n^2 + 2n + 1$.

Investigation 2
(a) We take two *consecutive* triangle numbers, say t_3 and t_4. Remember that
$$t_3 = 1 + 2 + 3 = 6 \quad \text{and} \quad t_4 = 1 + 2 + 3 + 4 = 10.$$

Notice that $t_3 + t_4 = 16$ and that s_4, the fourth square number, is also 16.
We have:
$$s_4 = t_3 + t_4$$

Draw the square pattern of dots to illustrate s_4. Investigate whether it is possible to divide the square pattern (by a single straight line) to show the two triangle numbers t_3 and t_4.
(b) What connection between square and consecutive triangle numbers is shown in Figure 4? Write your answer using the shorthand notation for square and triangle numbers as in part (a).

Figure 4

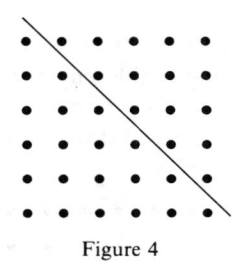

(c) Draw patterns of dots as in part (a) to investigate whether
  (i) $t_8 + t_9 = s_9$;
  (ii) $t_6 + t_7 = s_7$;
  (iii) $t_{20} + t_{21} = s_{21}$. (Take the hint from Figure 3 and do not draw all the dots.)

A Which two triangle numbers should add together to give the twelfth square number s_{12}?

B $s_{12} = 12^2 = 144$. Work out the values of the two triangle numbers you gave in part A and check that they add up to 144.

4. CLASSIFYING NUMBERS

Some numbers are triangle numbers, for example 6.

Some numbers are square numbers, for example 9.

Figure 5

Most numbers are neither triangle nor square numbers. For example, 7 can only be represented by a row (or column) of dots.

7 • • • • • • •

Figure 6

However 12 can be represented by a rectangle of dots in two ways (apart from a row or column of dots, which is not a proper rectangle). One of them is shown in Figure 7.

Figure 7

In what other way can 12 be shown by a rectangle of dots? (We do not count turning Figure 7 on end as being a different way.)

15 can also be shown as a rectangle of dots – but only in one way.

$$15 \begin{matrix} \bullet & \bullet & \bullet & \bullet & \bullet \\ \bullet & \bullet & \bullet & \bullet & \bullet \\ \bullet & \bullet & \bullet & \bullet & \bullet \end{matrix}$$

Figure 8

These patterns illustrate the facts that

$12 = 4 \times 3$ (or 3×4);
$12 = 6 \times 2$ (or 2×6); Did you get that one?
$15 = 5 \times 3$ (or 3×5)

but that 7 can only be written as 7×1 (or 1×7).

Numbers that can be shown by a rectangular pattern of dots are known as *rectangle numbers*. So 12 and 15 are rectangle numbers. But the pattern for 7 doesn't look like a proper rectangle and we do not consider 7 to be a rectangle number.

In fact there is a very special name for numbers that can only be represented by a single row (or column) of dots. They are called *prime numbers*.

As a square is a special case of a rectangle, however, we consider 9 and 16 to be rectangle numbers as well as square numbers.

Looking at the first few numbers, we have:

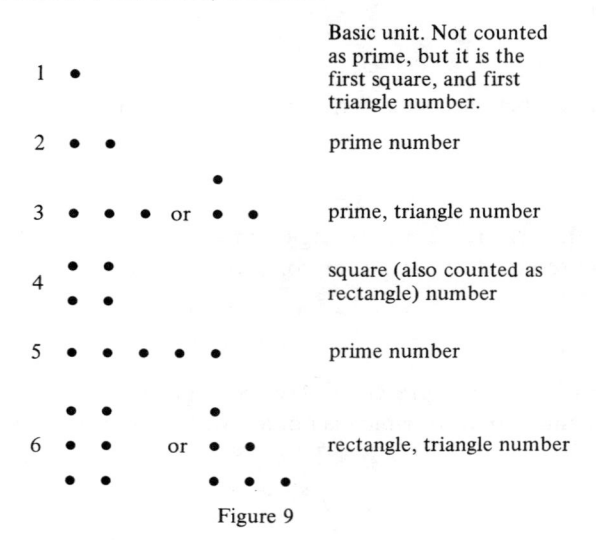

1	●	Basic unit. Not counted as prime, but it is the first square, and first triangle number.
2	● ●	prime number
3	● ● ● or ● / ● ●	prime, triangle number
4	● ● / ● ●	square (also counted as rectangle) number
5	● ● ● ● ●	prime number
6	● ● / ● ● / ● ● or ● ● ● / ● ● ●	rectangle, triangle number

Figure 9

Continue this classification of numbers up to 20. Remember that there are two ways of showing 12.

Factors

```
      • • • •
   3  • • • •
      • • • •
        4
```

Figure 10

Figure 10 shows the rectangle number 12 as the *product* of 3 and 4. (When two numbers are multiplied together the answer is referred to as the product of the numbers.)

We also call 3 and 4 *factors* of 12. A factor of a number is one that divides into it without remainder. The complete list of factors of 12 is therefore

1, 2, 3, 4, 6, 12.

Each of them will appear in one of the possible dot patterns:

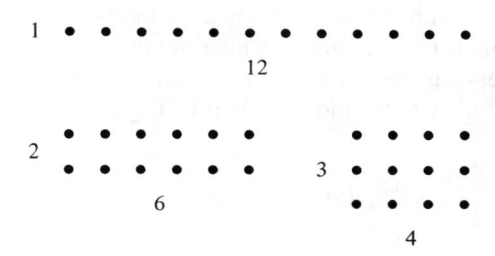

```
1  • • • • • • • • • • • •
              12

   • • • • • •          • • • •
2  • • • • • •       3  • • • •
        6               • • • •
                           4
```

Figure 11

If we know one factor of a rectangle number we can work out another one and then illustrate the number by a dot pattern. For example 3 is a factor of 24 and 3 × 8 = 24. This gives the pattern:

```
      • • • • • • • •
   3  • • • • • • • •
      • • • • • • • •
             8
```

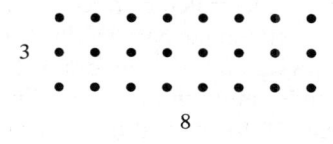

Figure 12

In the case of a prime number the only factors are 1 and the number itself. For example 5 = 1 × 5.

```
   1  • • • • •
         5
```

Figure 13

Exercise D

*1 Are the following prime, triangle, rectangle or square numbers?
    (a) 18;   (b) 20;   (c) 29.

2 Which is the next number after 66 which is both a rectangle and a triangle number?

*3 Which is the next square number after 49?

4 Which is the square number before 121?

5 Draw rectangular patterns of dots for each of 6, 10, 15, 21. These are all triangle numbers. Is it true to say that all triangle numbers are also rectangle numbers?

6 Write down the next 20 prime numbers after 2, 3, 5, 7, ...

*7 List *all* the factors of
    (a) 8;   (b) 14;   (c) 30;   (d) 36.

8 What is the smallest number that has as factors
    (a) both 4 and 5;   (b) both 3 and 6;   (c) both 6 and 15?

9 Is there a largest number that has both 4 and 5 as factors?

SUMMARY

Triangle numbers can be represented by a triangular pattern of dots. t_3 may be used as a shorthand for the third triangle number, 6.

Square numbers can be represented by a square pattern: for example s_4, the fourth square number is 16 and is shown in Figure 14(a).

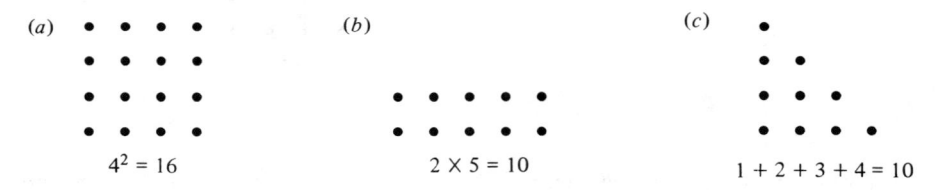

(a) $4^2 = 16$ (b) $2 \times 5 = 10$ (c) $1 + 2 + 3 + 4 = 10$

Figure 14

Rectangle numbers can be illustrated by a rectangular pattern of dots, some in more than one way. The rectangular pattern illustrates a pair of factors of the number. Figure 14(b) shows 2 and 5 as factors of 10.

Some numbers come under more than one heading. Figure 14(c) shows 10 as a triangle number whereas 14(b) showed it as a rectangle number.

Numbers such as 7 which cannot be represented by a rectangle of dots have only two factors, in this case 1 and 7. A number such as 7 is a prime number.

Summary exercise

1 Write down the output of the flow chart:

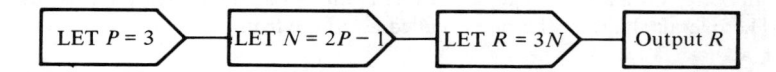

LET $P = 3$ → LET $N = 2P - 1$ → LET $R = 3N$ → Output R

2 Write down the output of the flow chart:

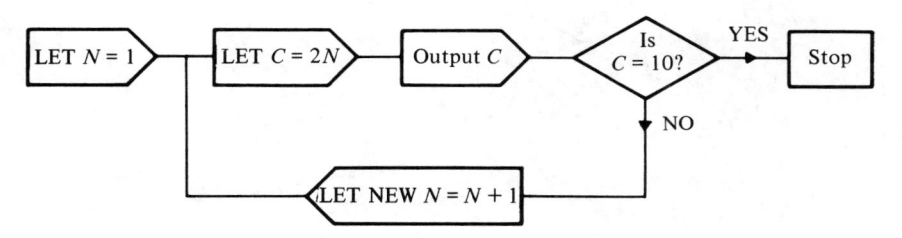

LET $N = 1$ → LET $C = 2N$ → Output C → Is $C = 10$? —YES→ Stop
↑   ↓ NO
└─────────── LET NEW $N = N + 1$ ←──────────────────┘

3 Draw a pattern of dots to find the 7th triangle number, t_7.

4 Draw a pattern of dots to show s_8, the eighth square number. Show by a line how to split s_8 up into the sum of two triangle numbers. Which are they?

5 Find (*a*) two prime numbers which add together to give a square number;
(*b*) two prime numbers which add together to give a rectangle number (one which is not also square).
(*c*) two rectangle numbers (not square) which add together to give a prime number.

Miscellaneous exercise

1 Draw a dot pattern to show 20, as the product of 4 and 5. Draw a line on your rectangular pattern to show, twice over, the triangle number 10. This shows that $t_4 = \frac{1}{2} \times 4 \times 5$.

Draw another dot pattern to show 56 as the product of 7 and 8. Draw a line to show 56 as being twice a certain triangle number. Which is this? Find a result similar to $t_4 = \frac{1}{2} \times 4 \times 5$.

Find a quick method of working out t_{10}.
Work out, painlessly, t_{100}.

2 Greengrocers often pile up fruit in the shape of a triangular based pyramid as shown in the diagram. Any one orange (for example) sits in the space formed by the three below it, these three sit in the spaces formed by the six below them. The total number of oranges in a pile of 4 layers is known as the fourth tetrahedron number. (The overall shape of the pile is called a tetrahedron).

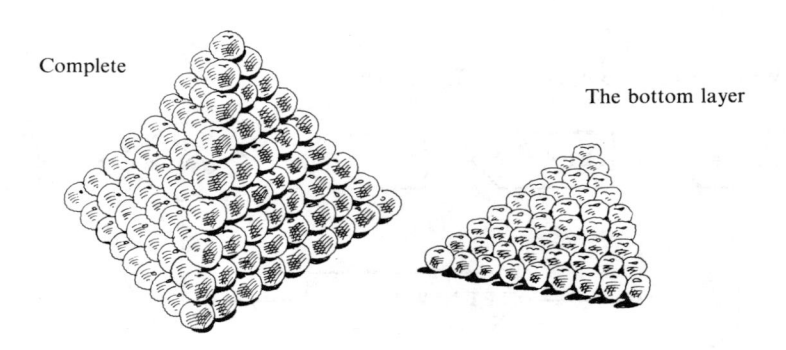

Complete

The bottom layer

If there is 1 layer there is 1 orange.
If two layers there are $1 + 3 = 4$ oranges.
In 3 layers there are $1 + 3 + 6 = 10$ oranges. The third tetrahedral number is 10.
(a) Find the 4th, 5th and 6th tetrahedral numbers.
(b) If the greengrocer has exactly 35 oranges in the pile, how many layers are there?
(c) Repeat part (b) for a pile containing 120 oranges.

3 Other greengrocers pile up their fruit in a different manner. They support the top piece with a square of 4 below it and these rest in the spaces formed by a square of 9 below them. The overall shape is of a pyramid (Egyptian type) and the number of pieces of fruit in a pile of 6 layers is called the 6th pyramid number.
In 1 layer there is one piece of fruit. In two layers there are 5 pieces $(1 + 4)$.
In 3 layers there are 14 pieces $(1 + 4 + 9)$, and 14 is the third pyramid number.
(a) Find the 4th, 5th and 6th pyramid numbers.
(b) If the greengrocer has exactly 140 pieces of fruit in a pyramid pile, how many layers are there?

4 A certain greengrocer has 204 grapefruit in a pile. Is he using the tetrahedron shaped pile or the pyramid shaped pile?

5 Another greengrocer has a very neat pile of fruit containing 149 apples. Describe one possible way in which the pile is arranged.

6 The 'maximum break' in snooker is 147. This can be put in the form
$$nt_a + t_b - 1$$
where n is a number and t_a and t_b are two triangle numbers.
Find n, t_a and t_b.
(This can be done by trial but is really for snooker addicts who know how the game is scored.)

Try this 4:

'Yes, grandpa, we do know how lucky we are.'

Try your hand at some of the sort of arithmetic your grandfather had to do at school.

A British currency used to consist of a pound (£1), divided into 20 shillings (20s), with each shilling divided into 12 pence (12d – the d stood for the Roman coin, denarius).
So £12 15s 11d meant twelve pounds, 15 shillings and 11 pence.
  (*a*) Add £12 15s 11d and £3 12s 4d.
  (*b*) Subtract £5 18s 6d from £8 12s 4d.
  (*c*) Multiply £2 7s 10d by 8.
  (*d*) Divide £18 13s 11d by 7.

B The old British measures of length are
  12 inches (12″)   making 1 foot (1′)
  3 feet   making 1 yard
  22 yards   making 1 chain
  10 chains   making 1 furlong
  8 furlongs   making 1 mile
  (*a*) If I cut 2 yards 1 foot 10 inches off a piece of material originally 10 yards 4 inches long, how long is the bit left?
  (*b*) How many yards are there in a mile?
  (*c*) How many fence posts, 10 ft apart, will be needed for one side of a field of length $1\frac{1}{4}$ furlongs?

C We used to weigh in these ('Avoirdupois') units:
  16 drams (dr)   make 1 ounce (1 oz)
  16 ounces   make 1 pound (1 lb)
  28 pounds   make 1 quarter (1 qr)
  4 quarters   make 1 hundredweight (1 cwt)
  20 hundredweight   make 1 ton
  (*a*) Multiply 5 cwt 1 qr 3 lb 11 oz by 9.
  (*b*) Divide 6 cwt 3 qr 1 lb 5 oz by 7.
  (*c*) How many drams in a quarter of a pound?
  (*d*) What is the literal meaning of the word 'avoirdupois'?

D A British unit not mentioned in part C is the stone. 1 stone = 14 lb. Daniel Lambert, born in 1773, weighed 52 stone 11 lb shortly before he died. What was his mass in pounds? Given that 1 kg = 2 lb 3 oz. find his mass in kg to the nearest kg. How many times heavier than you was he?

E (*a*) Calculate the price of 12 tons 17 cwt 30 lb of coal at the 1930 price of £2 6s 8d per ton.
  (*b*) Calculate the price of 32 yards 1 foot 7 inches of cloth at the 1930 price of 6s 11d per yard.

22
Area

1. A REMINDER ABOUT TESSELLATIONS

Look around in your home, or in the High Street in town, at the patterns produced by tiles, pavement slabs, bricks in a wall, etc. In 1891 a Russian named Fedorov showed that there are only 17 ways in which a basic pattern or shape can be repeated so that there are no gaps. These, you will remember, are called tessellations. Two such patterns are shown in Figure 1.

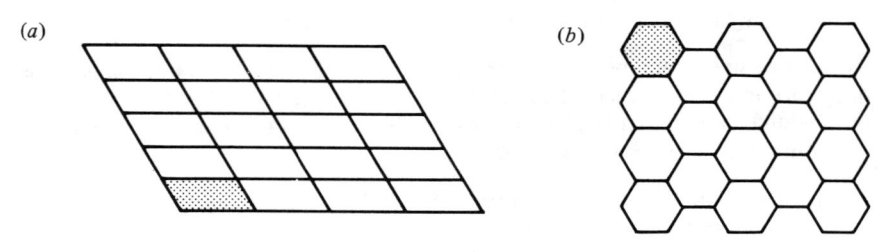

Figure 1

2. AREA

The area of a plane (flat) object is a measure of its size, the amount of plane space it takes up.

(a) (b)

Figure 2

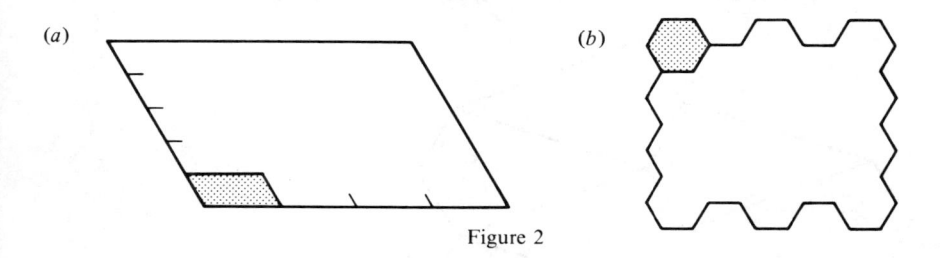

Figure 2 shows the outlines of Figure 1. Figure 2(a) is made up of 20 of the basic parallelograms used in Figure 1(a). We could say that the area of Figure 2(a) is 20 parallelogram units. This means that the amount of plane space occupied is twenty times that of the basic unit.

How many small hexagons are there in Figure 1(b). What is the area of Figure 2(b) if one small hexagon is taken as a unit?

Exercise A

*1 Figure 3 shows the outline of Figure 1(a) and part of a tessellation based on triangles.
    (a) How many triangles can be fitted into the outline?
    (b) What is the area of Figure 3, measured in these triangular units?

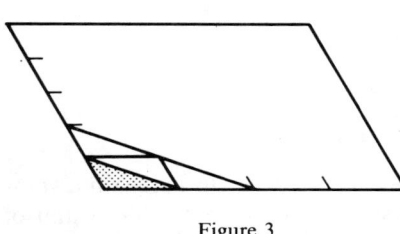

Figure 3

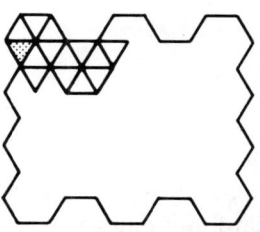

Figure 4

*2 Figure 4 shows the outline of Figure 1(b) and part of a tessellation based on equilateral triangles. What is the area of Figure 4 measured in these triangular units?

84 Area   Ch. 22

*3 (a) Figure 5(a) shows a tessellation based on a kite. What is the area of the figure measured in terms of a kite as a unit?
(b) Figure 5(b) shows the same outline but based on a triangular tessellation. What is the area of the figure in terms of this triangle as a unit?
(c) Figure 5(c) shows the same outline but made up from two different triangles. Why is it awkward to use this tessellation to give the area?

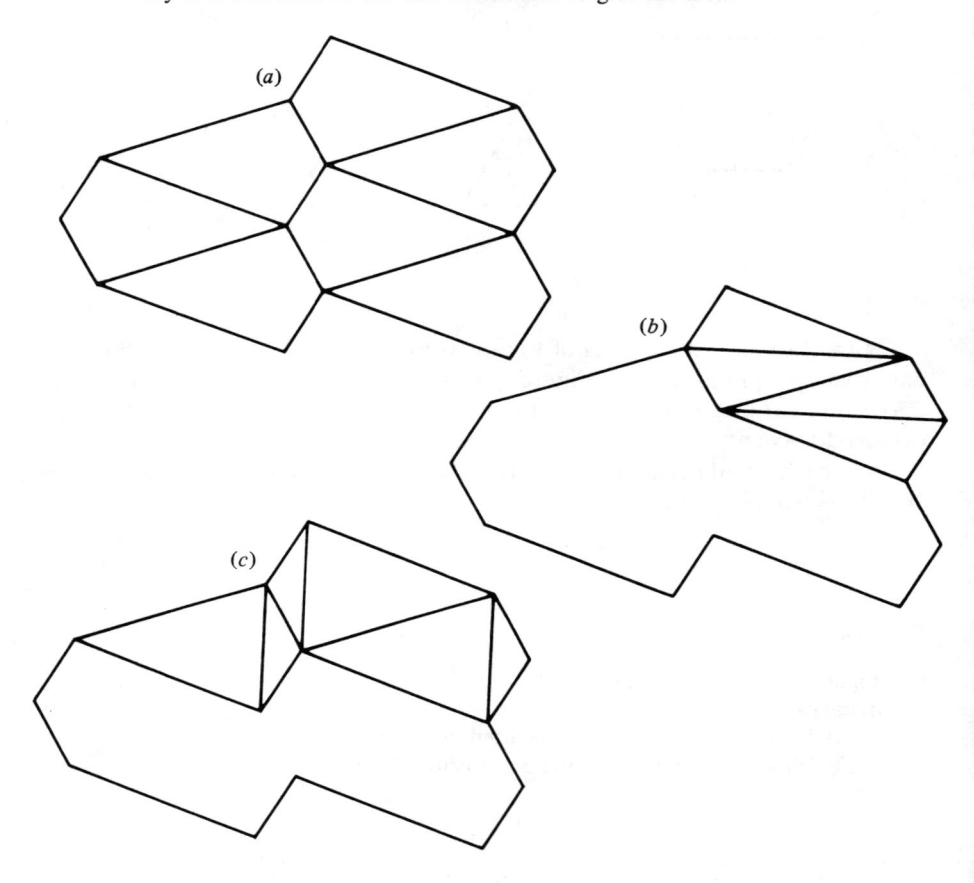

Figure 5

3. COMPARING AREAS

In order to compare the areas of two figures it is necessary to agree on a standard unit of area. We use a square that has sides 1 cm in length as our unit of area.

This unit of area is known as 1 *square centimetre* and is written 1 cm². See Figure 6(a). (Sometimes you may see it called 1 centimetre squared and written 1 sq cm.) Figure 6(b) consists of three of the squares we use as units, we say 3 unit squares, and therefore it has an area of 3 cm².

Comparing areas   85

(a) (b) (c) (d)

Figure 6

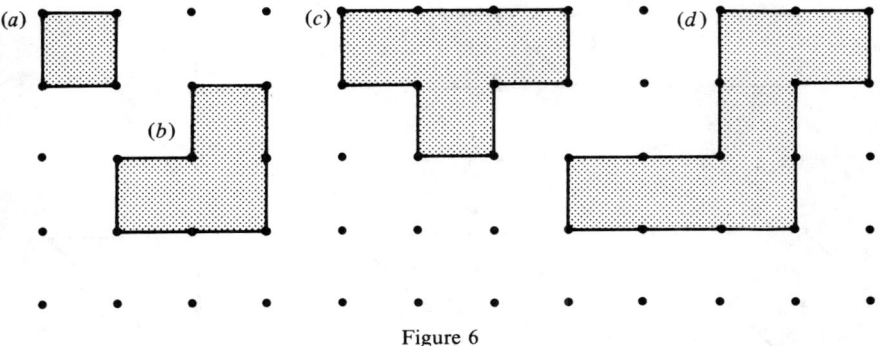

What are the areas of Figures 6(c) and (d)?

Example 1
What are the areas of the shapes in Figure 7, drawn on 1 cm spotty paper?

(a) (b) (c)

Figure 7

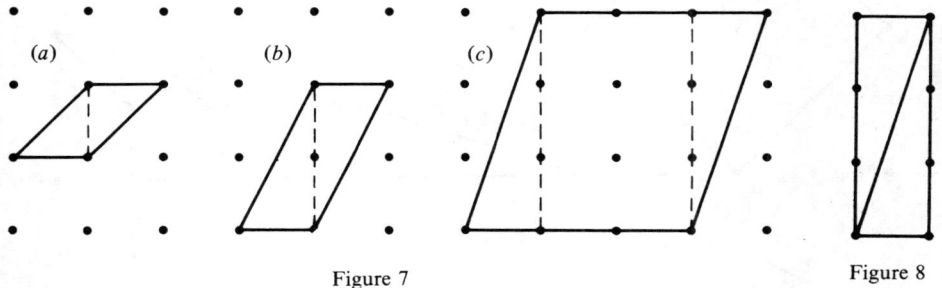

Figure 8

In (a) the broken line shows that the shape is made up of two triangles. Each triangle has an area of half a unit square therefore the total area is 1 cm².

In (b) the shape is also made up of two triangles. Each triangle has an area of one unit square (half of 2). Therefore the total area is 2 cm².

In (c) two broken lines have been added to help us. There are 6 unit squares in the central rectangle. If the triangles at each end were placed together as in Figure 8 then their total area can be seen to be 3 cm². So the area of Figure 7(c) is

$$6 \text{ cm}^2 + 3 \text{ cm}^2 = 9 \text{ cm}^2.$$

Exercise B

For questions 1–10 lay tracing paper over the page or copy the ten shapes in Figure 9 onto 1 cm square or spotty paper. Put in broken lines to help you work out how many unit squares there are in each. Write down the area of each.

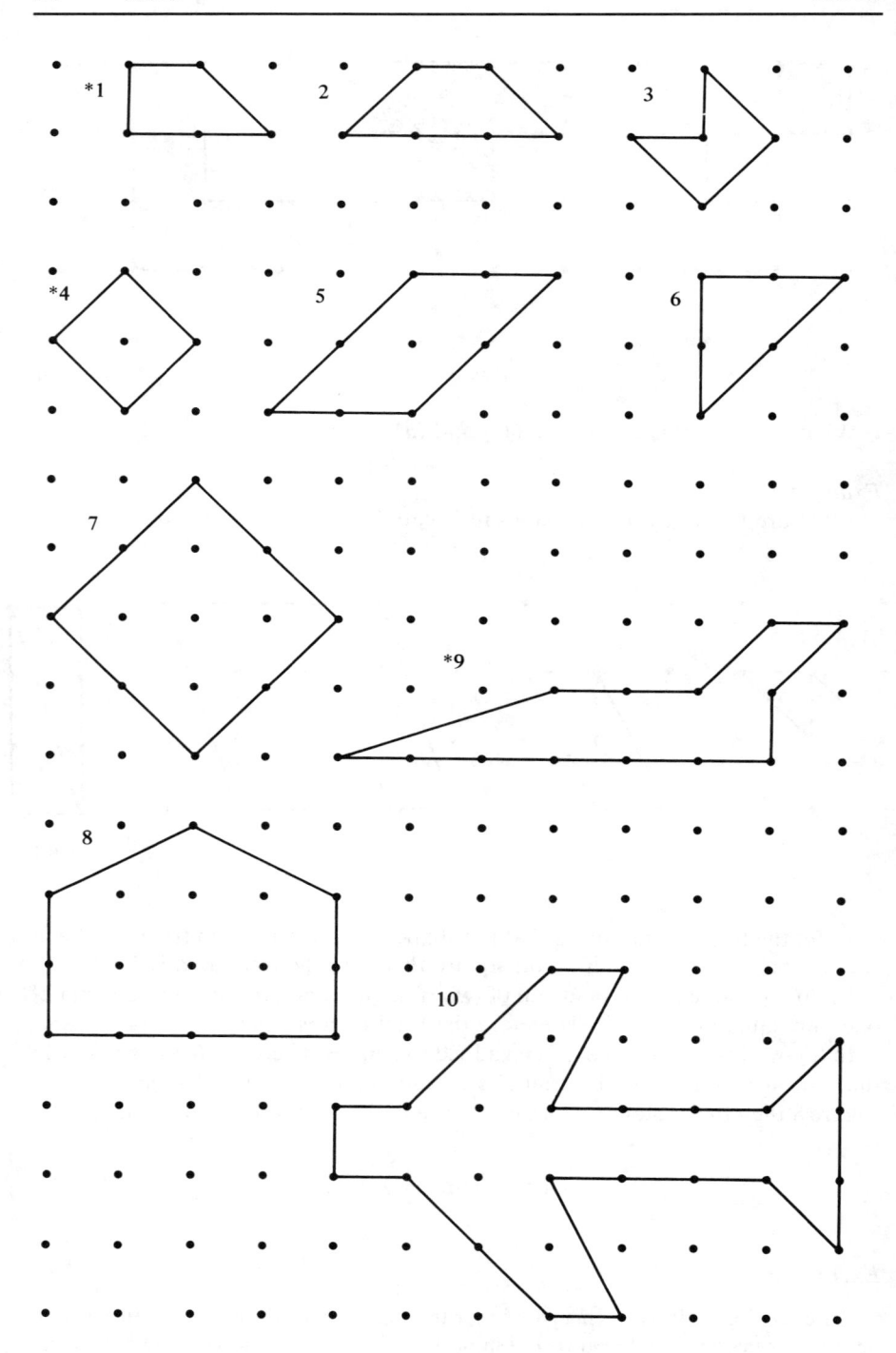

Figure 9

Other units of area 87

*11 The two shapes in Figure 10 are drawn on 1 cm spotty paper. The broken lines are added to help you. Calculate their areas.

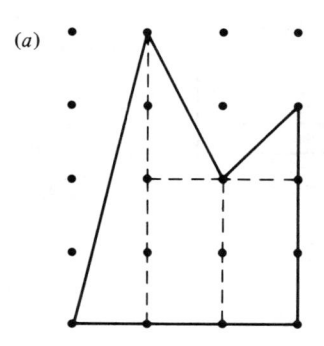

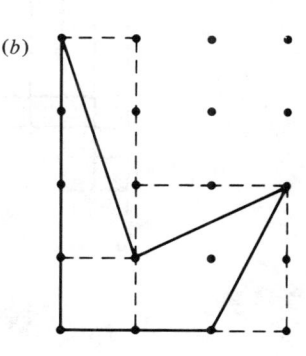

(a)   (b)

Figure 10

12 The two shapes in Figure 11 are also drawn on 1 cm spotty paper, but have no broken lines to help you. Copy them, insert suitable broken lines and calculate their areas.

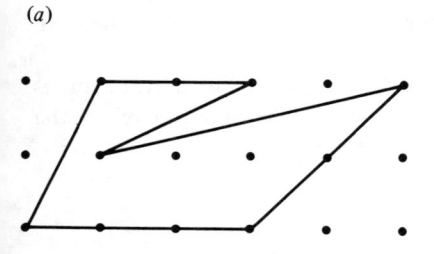

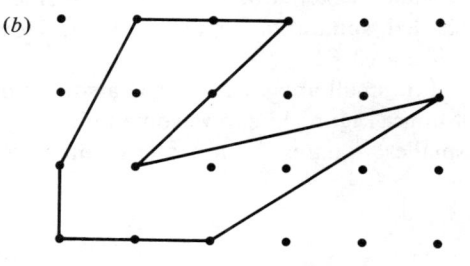

(a)   (b)

Figure 11

4. OTHER UNITS OF AREA

The unit of area used up to now has been 1 cm^2 but this is rather small if you are finding the area of your classroom. In cases like this we use a unit of 1 m^2; this is the area of a square whose sides are 1 m in length. Figure 12 illustrates this but is *not* to scale! The small shaded square represents 1 cm^2.

Area

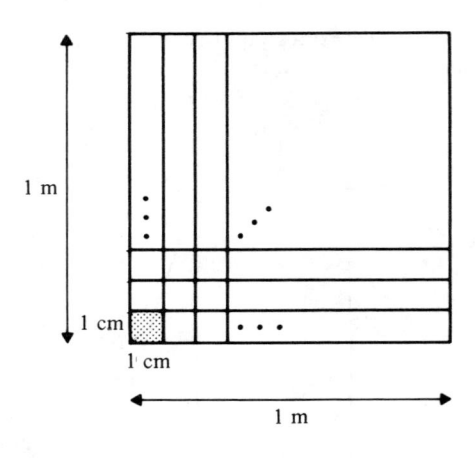

Figure 12

How many 1 cm² units can be fitted into the bottom row of Figure 12? How many rows can be fitted into the square? How many 1 cm² units can be fitted into the large square? The answers to these questions show that 1 m² = 10 000 cm².

For even larger areas, such as a sports ground or a farmer's land, the *hectare* is used. 1 ha (hectare) is the area of a square with sides 100 m in length. (Think of a square with a side equal in length to a 100 m sprint track.)

Make a sketch of Figure 12 with sides to represent 100 m and use the small shaded square to represent 1 m². How many square metres are there in 1 hectare?

For small areas we can use a square of side 1 millimetre. The area of this is 1 mm². Figure 13 shows some millimetre graph paper. The area of each of the smallest squares is 1 mm². How many mm² make up 1 cm²?

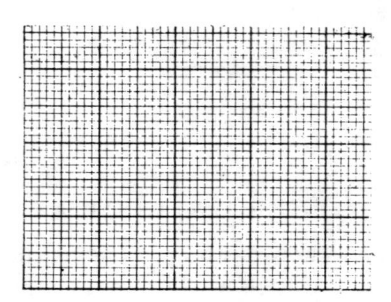

Figure 13

Other units of area

Exercise C

*1 In what units would you give the area of the following
   (a) the wall of your classroom;
   (b) the North Sea;
   (c) a page from this book;
   (d) an elephant's footprint;
   (e) a tennis court;
   (f) a postage stamp;
   (g) an airfield;
   (h) your little finger nail;
   (i) a garden pond;
   (j) a mouse's footprint?

2 Figure 14 shows various shapes and the lengths of their sides. Work out their areas, being careful to give the correct units in your answers. It will help to lay tracing paper over the page or to make copies on spotty paper, adding dotted lines as shown in part (a).

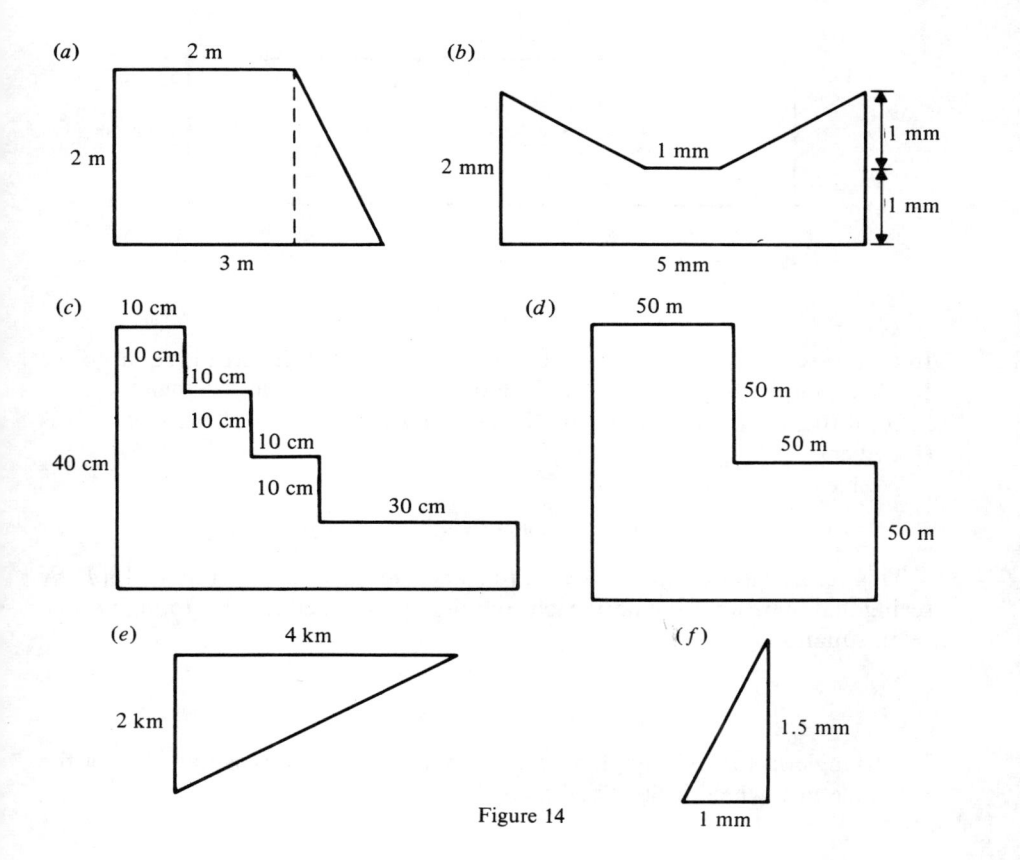

Figure 14

5. TWO RESULTS

Area of a rectangle

We often refer to the sides of a rectangle as the *length* and *breadth* taking the breadth to be the shorter side. The rectangles in Figure 15 are drawn on 1 cm spotty paper. For each rectangle:

(*a*) work out the area;
(*b*) multiply together the length and the breadth.

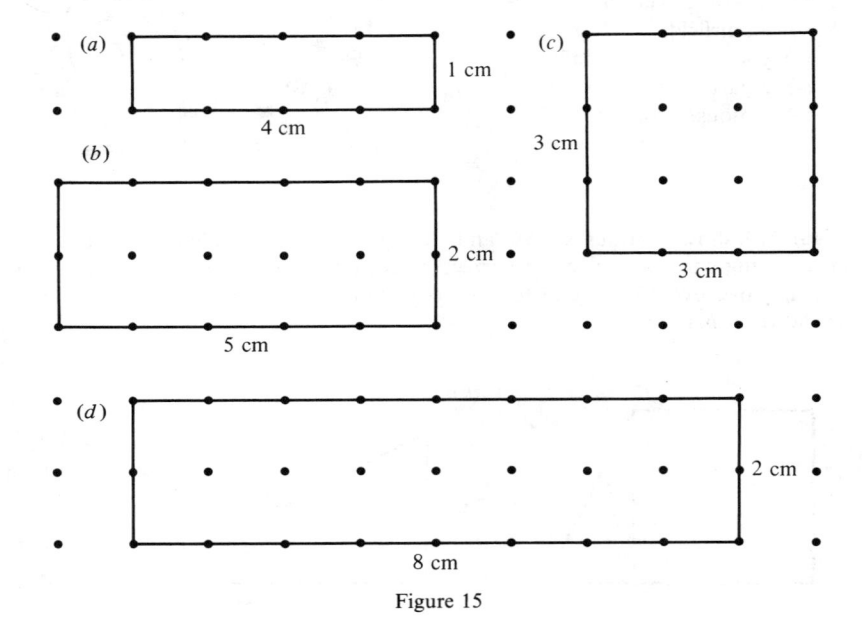

Figure 15

In each case you should see that the numerical value of the area is equal to the result of multiplying together the length and breadth of the rectangle.

So, if the length is l cm and the breadth is b cm the area of the rectangle is $(l \times b)$ cm^2.

We have:

$$\text{Area of rectangle} = \text{length} \times \text{breadth (or } A = lb\text{)}$$

This result can be explained with reference, for example, to Figure 15(*d*) by seeing that there are 8 columns each containing 2 squares giving a total of $8 \times 2 = 16$ squares.

Area of a triangle

If a triangle has a right angle it is easy to see that its area is half that of the rectangle into which it fits. See Figure 16.

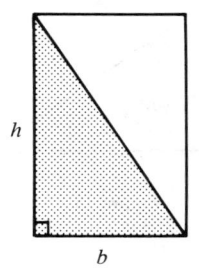

Figure 16

We call one side of the triangle its *base* and it is natural to call the other its *height*, so we can write for this triangle

$$\text{area} = \tfrac{1}{2} \text{ (base} \times \text{height)}$$
$$= \tfrac{1}{2}bh$$

If we have a triangle that is not right angled it is still possible to enclose it in a rectangle as shown in Figure 17. Notice that this triangle has been divided into two right-angled triangles and the surrounding rectangle into two rectangles. Each triangle has area equal to half of one of the rectangles. So the area of the whole triangle is half that of the rectangles put together. This is the same as half of the area of the large rectangle. Hence

$$\text{area of triangle} = \tfrac{1}{2} \text{ (base} \times \text{height)}.$$

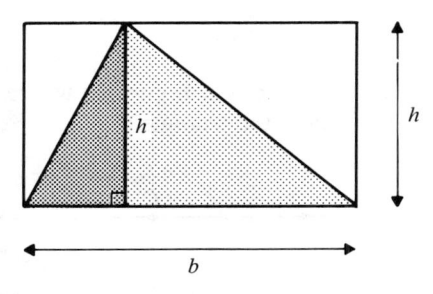

Figure 17

In Figure 17, b is the base and h is the *perpendicular* distance from the opposite vertex to the base. We can take any side of the triangle as the base, but there is a different height in each case. See Figure 18.

92 Area Ch. 22

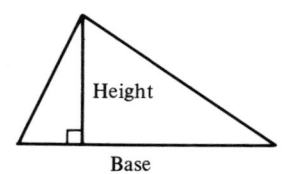

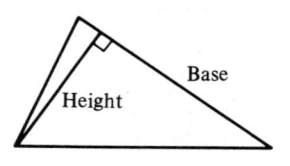

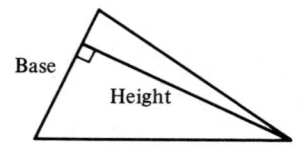

Figure 18

However we need to be sure that we shall get the same value for the area whichever base and height we use. In Figure 19 the area of the triangle is

$$\tfrac{1}{2} \times 7 \times 4 \text{ cm}^2 = 14 \text{ cm}^2.$$

Copy Figure 19 onto square spotty paper. Draw the height if *BC* is taken as the base. Measure the base and height in this case and check that they give 14 cm² as the area once again. (You may not get *exactly* 14 cm². Why not?)

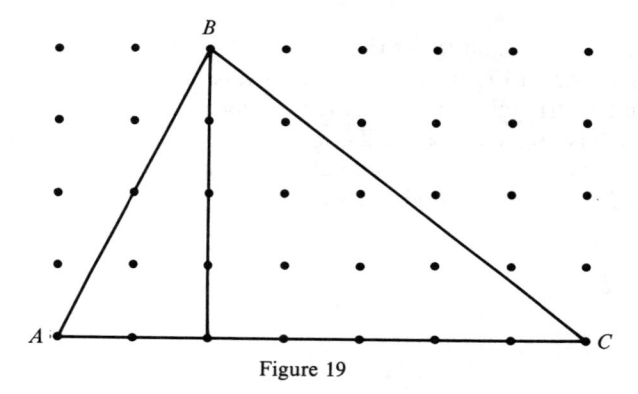

Figure 19

The situation is more complicated in Figure 20 where, if *OA* is taken as the base, the height *CB* falls outside the triangle.

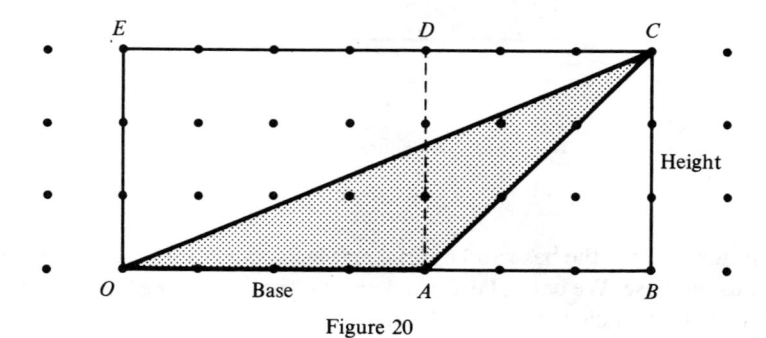

Figure 20

In this case we have:

area of shaded triangle = area of triangle OBC − area of triangle ABC
= half of area of rectangle $OBCE$ − half of square $ABCD$
= half of area of rectangle $OADE$
= $\frac{1}{2}$ (base) × (perpendicular height).

We have, therefore, a general formula for the area of a triangle.

Area of a triangle = $\frac{1}{2}$ (base) × (perpendicular height)   (or $A = \frac{1}{2}bh$)

Example 2

A photograph measuring 5 cm by 3 cm is mounted on a card which measures 6 cm by 4 cm. Calculate the area of the border surrounding the print.

The problem is illustrated in Figure 21.

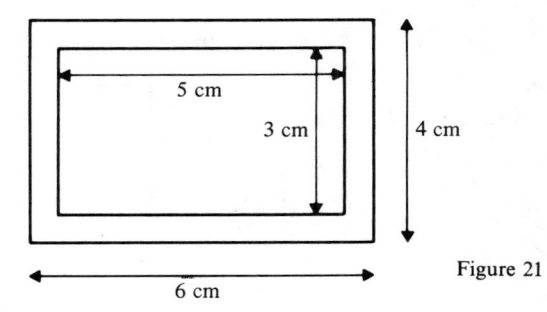

Figure 21

The easiest way is to find the area of the card and from this subtract the area of the print.

So, area of border in cm² = 6 × 4 − 5 × 3
= 24 − 15

Hence area = 9 cm².

(Notice that the print does not have to be mounted in the centre of the card.)

Exercise D

In questions 1–12 calculate the areas of the shapes given in Figure 22. Be careful to use the correct units. The drawings are not to scale.

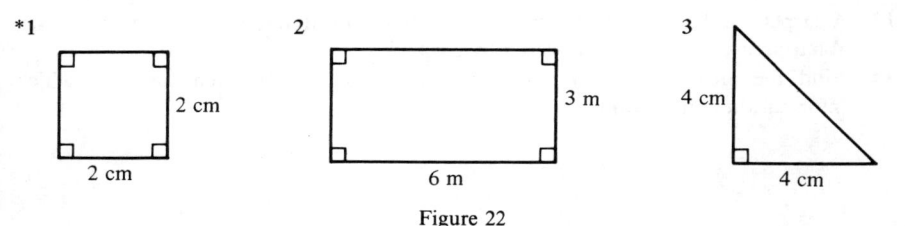

*1   2 cm × 2 cm square

2   6 m × 3 m rectangle

3   right triangle with legs 4 cm and 4 cm

Figure 22

Area　　　　　　　　　　　　　　　　　　　　　　　　　Ch. 22

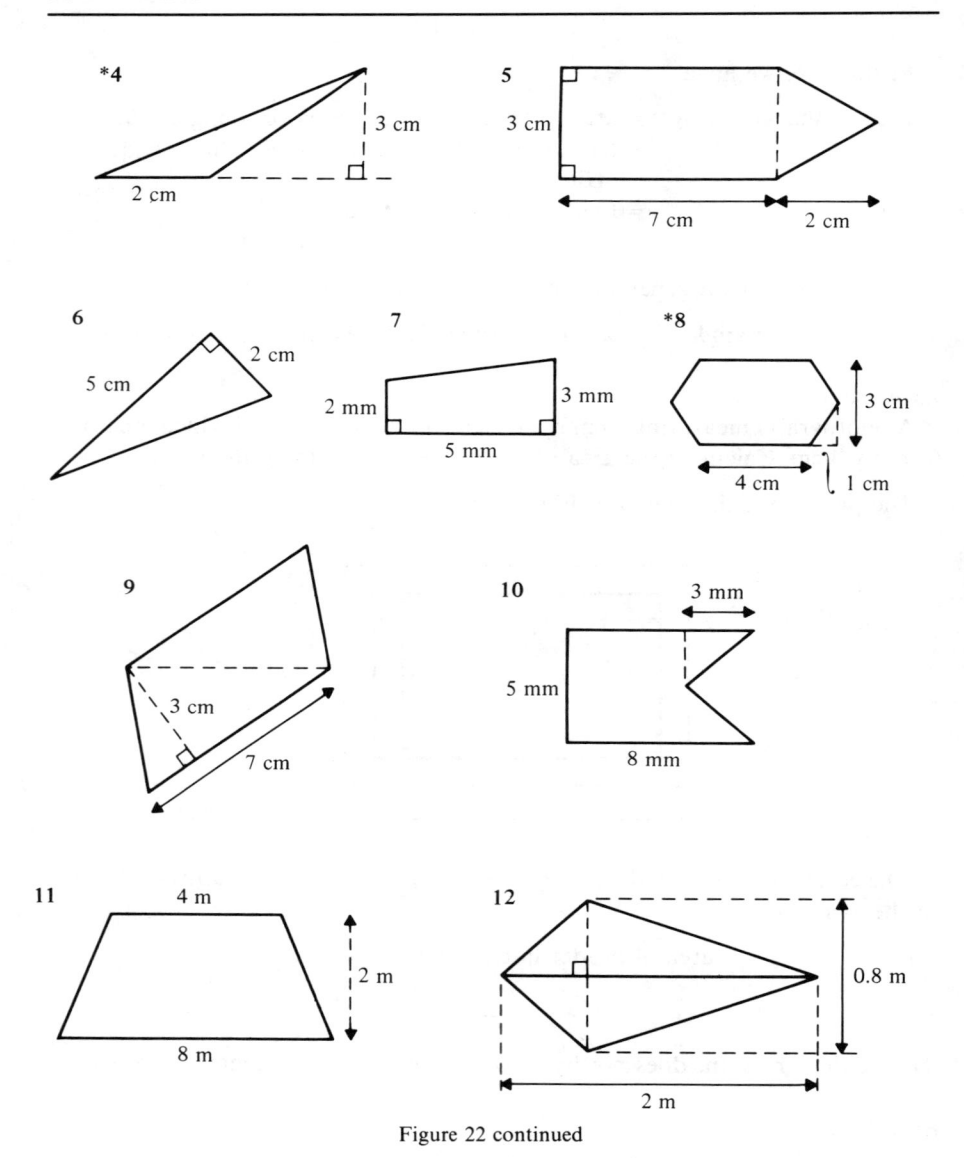

*4 (triangle with 2 cm base extension and 3 cm height)

5 (shape with 3 cm height, 7 cm and 2 cm lengths)

6 (right triangle with sides 5 cm and 2 cm)

7 (trapezium with 2 mm, 3 mm, 5 mm)

*8 (hexagon with 4 cm, 3 cm, 1 cm)

9 (parallelogram with 3 cm height and 7 cm base)

10 (arrow shape with 5 mm, 8 mm, 3 mm)

11 (trapezium with parallel sides 4 m and 8 m, height 2 m)

12 (kite with 2 m and 0.8 m)

Figure 22 continued

13 A carpet that has an area of 6 m² is laid onto a floor that is 5 m long and 3 m wide. What area of floor is not covered by carpet?

14 Find the areas of the shapes shown in Figure 23. In each case say which information is irrelevant.

(a)   4 m
3 m
7 m

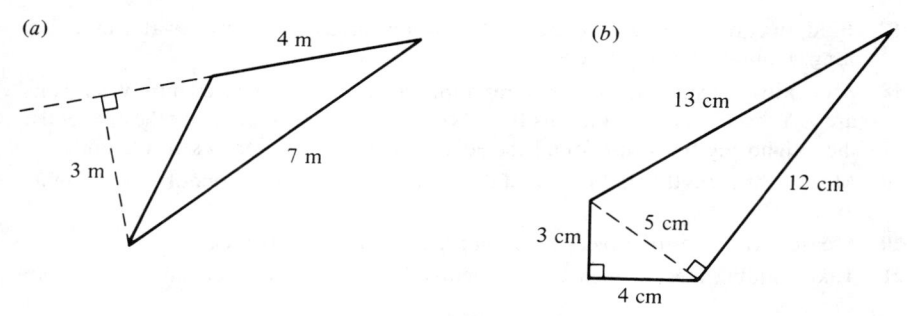

(b)   13 cm
12 cm
3 cm   5 cm
4 cm

Figure 23

15 Linda has made a very nice jewellery box for her mother. (See Figure 24.) She wants to cover the top and sides with velvet, but not the bottom. What is the total area of material she requires? Make a sketch of the single piece of material required to cover the sides. On your sketch mark the lengths of the sides.

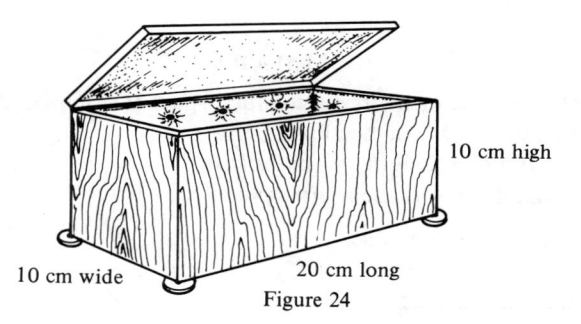

10 cm high
10 cm wide   20 cm long
Figure 24

16 A man decides to pave a patio at the back of his house. The area measures 7 m by 5 m but he leaves a rectangular plot of soil in the middle, for a tree and some flowers, measuring 2 m by 1 m. Calculate the area to be paved. If the area of a paving stone is 0.5 m^2, how many stones will be needed?

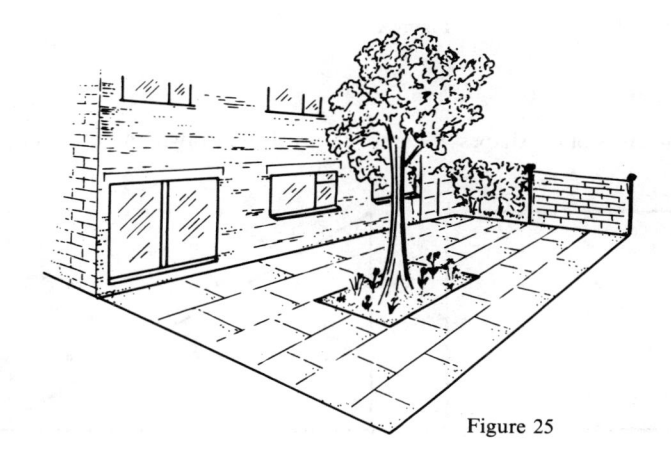

Figure 25

17 Find, in square metres, the area of the inside surface of an open water tank 3 m long, 1.5 m wide and 1 m deep.

18 A definitive postage stamp measures approximately 24 mm by 20 mm. What is its area? A sheet of stamps contains 10 rows each of 10 stamps. Estimate the area of the sheet (ignoring the strips round the edge). Give your answer in sensible units.

19 Measure the length and breadth of the front cover of your text book. Calculate its area.

20 Measure the sides of a piece of A4 paper and calculate its area.

21 Take suitable measurements and calculate the area of the regular pentagon in Figure 26.

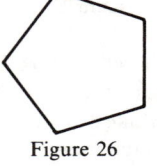

Figure 26

SUMMARY

The area of a plane shape measures how much space it occupies. Area is usually measured in cm², m², mm², or hectares.

Area of a rectangle = (length) × (breadth)
Area of a triangle = $\frac{1}{2}$ (base) × (perpendicular height)

Any side can be taken as the base.

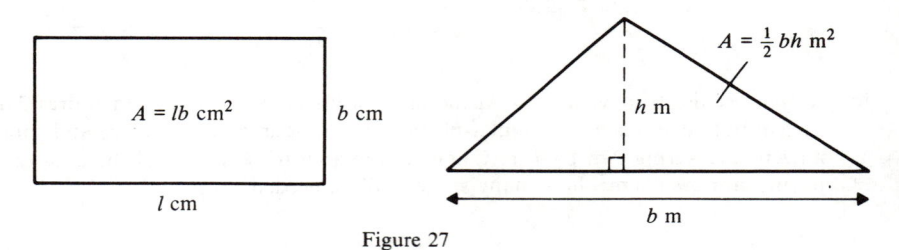

$A = lb$ cm² b cm l cm

$A = \frac{1}{2} bh$ m² h m b m

Figure 27

Summary exercise

1 Calculate the areas of the shapes in Figure 28 which are drawn on 1 cm spotty paper.

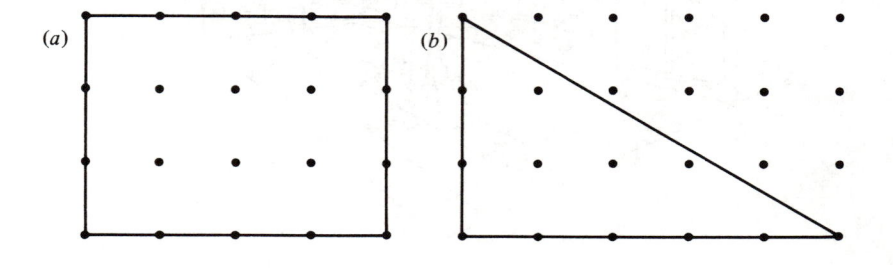

(a)

(b)

Figure 28

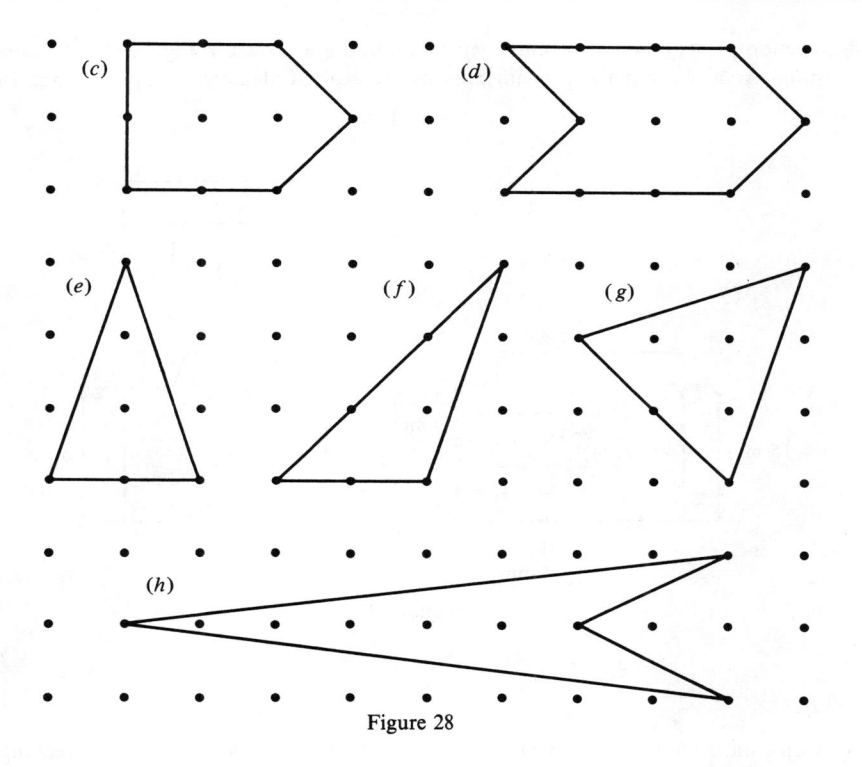

2 Which two of the shapes in Figure 29 have the same area, and what is that area? Take the dots as being 1 cm apart.

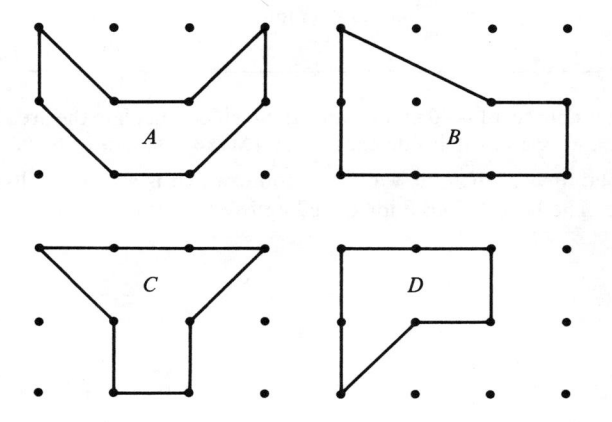

Figure 29

3 The footprints of a very strange pair of animals are shown in Figure 30. The dimensions are given, but the drawings are not to scale. Calculate the area of each footprint.

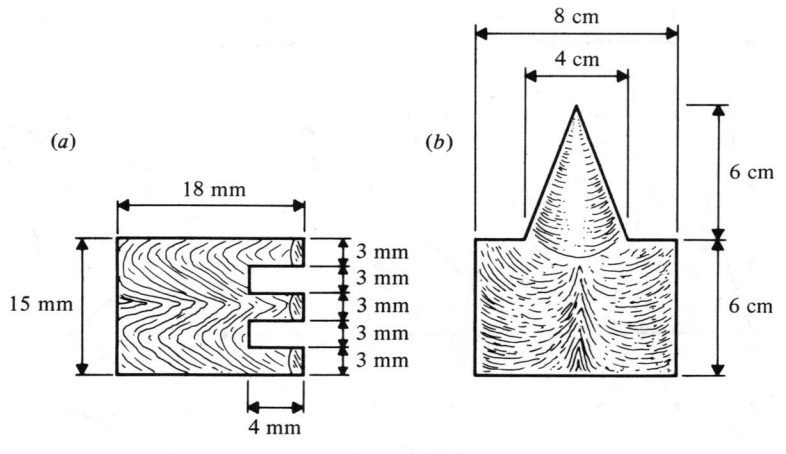

Figure 30

4 Copy and complete the table to show length, breadth and area for various rectangles:

Length	Breadth	Area
3 cm	4 cm	12 cm^2
7 cm	3 cm	
	4 cm	28 cm^2
12 m		12 m^2
2 mm	3.5 mm	
500 m		15 ha

5 A rectangular courtyard is 40 m long and 28 m wide. Calculate the area of a path 1 m wide which runs round the inside edges of it. (Make a sketch to help.)

6 Find the total area of the four walls of a room which is six metres long, and three metres wide. The height from floor to ceiling is two and a half metres.

Summary

Miscellaneous exercise

1 Work out the areas of the marine shapes shown in Figure 31. They are drawn on 1 cm spotty paper.

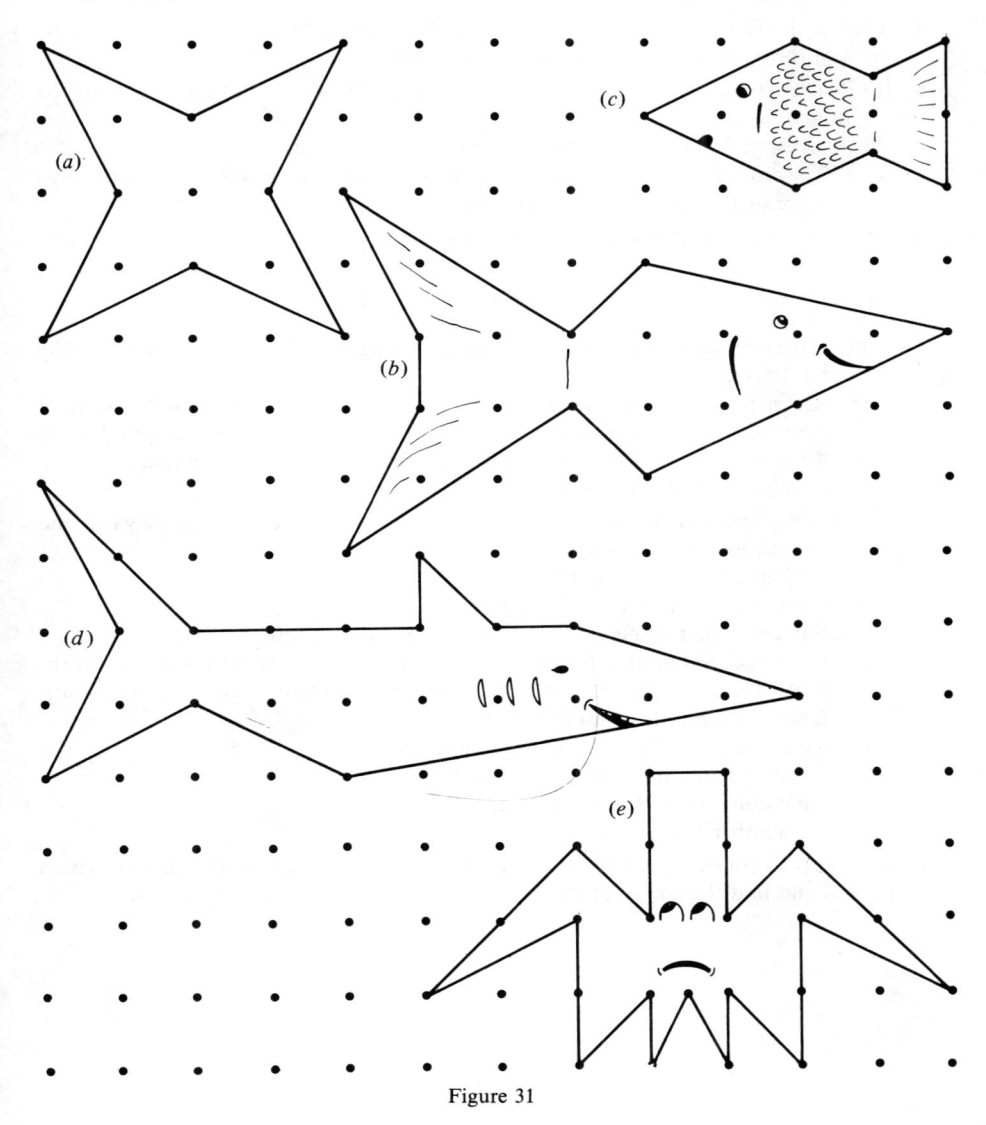

Figure 31

2 The area of a rectangular field is 60 000 m². If the width is 150 m what is the length of the field? What would be the length of fencing required to go round the outside of this field? What is the area of the field in hectares?

 The field is planted partly with sugarbeet and partly with cabbages. The cabbages occupy a rectangle 86 m by 100 m. What is the area occupied by sugarbeet?

3 Calculate
  (a) the number of mm² in 1 m²;
  (b) the number of cm² in 1 km²;
  (c) the number of ha in 1 km².
4 The length of a straight stretch of canal is 2.6 km and the width is 15 m. Calculate the area of the water surface in this stretch of canal.
5 (a) The length of a roll of adhesive tape is 10 m and the width is 1.8 cm. Calculate the total area of tape.
  (b) Another roll of tape is of length 5 m and width 3.5 cm.
        The cost of a roll of tape depends only on its area. Say whether this roll of tape is more or less expensive than that in part (a).
6 The inside measurements of a jewellery box are:
    length   18 cm,
    breadth   12 cm,
    depth   7.5 cm.
  (a) Calculate the cost of lining the box, including the lid, with velvet costing 50p for 100 cm².
  (b) All the pieces of velvet required for the box have to be cut from *one* rectangular piece which is charged at the same rate of 50p for 100 cm². Investigate how to do this as cheaply as possible. Give a drawing to show the rectangular piece of velvet and how it will be cut.
7 In pre-metric days, area was measured in square inches, square feet, square yards and acres. You should already know
    12 inches = 1 foot or 12″ = 1′
    3 feet   = 1 yard or 3′ = 1 yd.
  (a) Calculate the number of square inches in a square foot.
  (b) Calculate the number of square feet in a square yard. An *acre* is defined as the area of a rectangle measuring 220 yards by 22 yards. (220 yards sprint distance × length of a cricket pitch.)
  (c) How many square yards are there in an acre?
        Given that 1 m = 39.37″ calculate;
  (d) the number of hectares in 1 acre;
  (e) the number of acres in 1 hectare.
8 Joe wants to cut out a regular hexagon whose area is 24 cm². Discuss how he could do this and find the length of the side of the hexagon as accurately as you can.

Quickies 7

CLOSED BOOK

Calculators must not be used.
1. Work out $18 \div 0.6$.
2. Work out $^+7 - {}^-2$.
3. Find the area of a rectangle 12 m by 2.5 m.
4. What is the value of $6 \times 5 \times 4 \times 3 \times 2 \times 1 \times 0$?
5. I think of a number and call it n. I add 3 and then multiply by 7. Write down an expression for the result.
6. How long does it take to drive 12 km at 60 km/h?
7. Estimate the value of 390×2.1 to the nearest hundred.
8. £40 is shared between two people so that the second receives £10 more than the first. How much does the first receive?
9. 3.6 kg of honey is poured equally into 8 jars. How many grams of honey will each jar contain?
10. Two circles have centres 17 cm apart. The circles have radii 3 cm and 5 cm. How close together are the nearest points of the circles?

OPEN BOOK

Calculators must not be used.
1. Estimate, to the nearest hundred, the value of $641 \div 0.32$.
2. Calculate the area of the shape given in Figure 1.

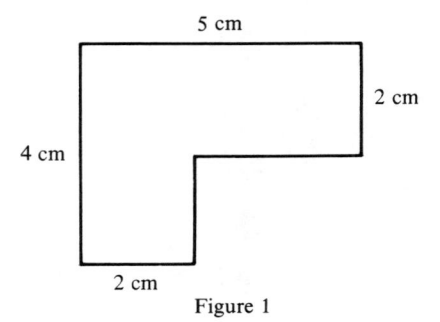

Figure 1

3. What number must be subtracted from $^-5$ to give $^-1$?
4. Find x if $\dfrac{x}{1000} = \dfrac{11}{125}$.

Quickies 7

5 Give the formula represented by the flow chart:

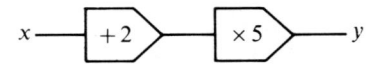

$$x \longrightarrow \boxed{+2} \longrightarrow \boxed{\times 5} \longrightarrow y$$

6 How many lines of symmetry has a square?
7 $q = (p - 7)/3$. Find the value of q if $p = 106$.
8 Write down the two missing numbers in the following sequence:
$$48, 35, 22, \ldots, \ldots, {}^{-}17.$$
9 Make a list of all the prime numbers which are factors of 60.
10 Two angles add up to 135° and one is half the size of the other. What is the size of the larger angle?

Revision exercises 7A, 7B

REVISION EXERCISE 7A

1. Use tracing paper to copy the diagrams in Figure 1. Complete them using the lines marked m as lines of symmetry.

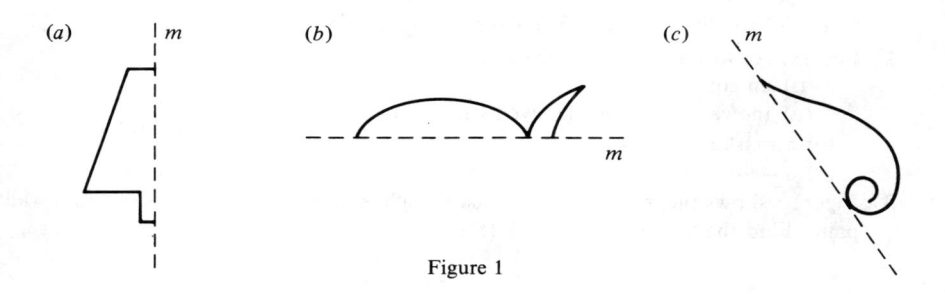

Figure 1

2. For each of flow charts (a) and (b) give
   (i) a formula which is equivalent;
   (ii) the output for the given input value.

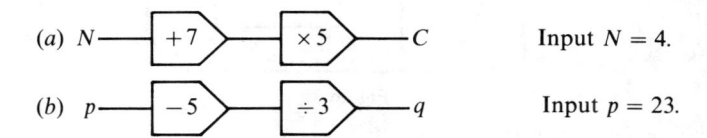

   (a) $N \longrightarrow [+7] \longrightarrow [\times 5] \longrightarrow C$ Input $N = 4$.

   (b) $p \longrightarrow [-5] \longrightarrow [\div 3] \longrightarrow q$ Input $p = 23$.

3. Find the areas of the shapes given in Figure 2. All lengths are in cm.

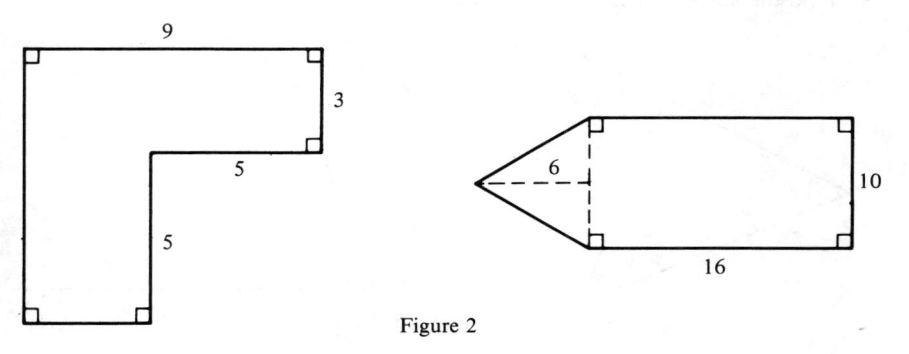

Figure 2

103

4 Find the total mass of 18 tins of MOGGINOSH cat food if each tin has mass 80 grams and contains 420 grams of food.
5 Work through the following flow chart with four different inputs of $N = 1, 2, 3, 4$. Comment on your results.

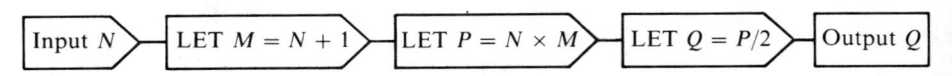

Input N → LET $M = N + 1$ → LET $P = N \times M$ → LET $Q = P/2$ → Output Q

REVISION EXERCISE 7B

1 Remove the brackets from the following:
 (a) $5(p + q)$;   (b) $8(p - r + 2)$;   (c) $(m + t) \times 9$;
 (d) $4(3a + 2b)$;   (e) $(c - 3d) \times 6$;   (f) $4(3u - 2v + 5w)$.
2 For each of formulae (a) and (b) give
   (i) an equivalent flow chart;
   (ii) the value of s for the given value of t.
 (a) $s = \frac{1}{2}(t + 5)$ $t = 9$;
 (b) $s = 4(t - 3)$ $t = 8$.
3 Figure 3 shows the front wall of a house which is to be painted with SNOGLO wall paint. Find the area to be painted. (Measurements are in m.)

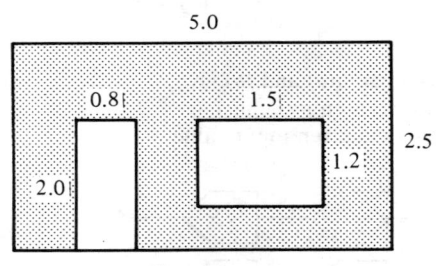

Figure 3

4 Without using a calculator, work out:
 (a) 0.4×0.07;   (b) $120 \div 0.6$;   (c) $\dfrac{3.2 \times 1.5}{0.02}$;   (d) $1\,000\,000 \times 0.0001$.
5 Find the angles indicated by letters in the diagrams in Figure 4.

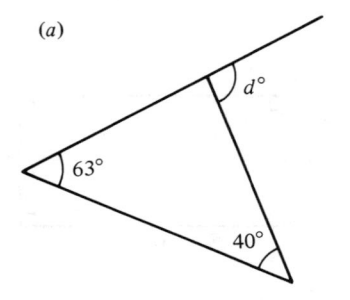

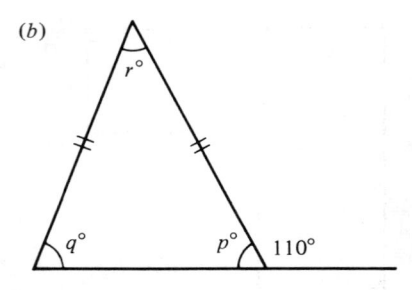

Figure 4

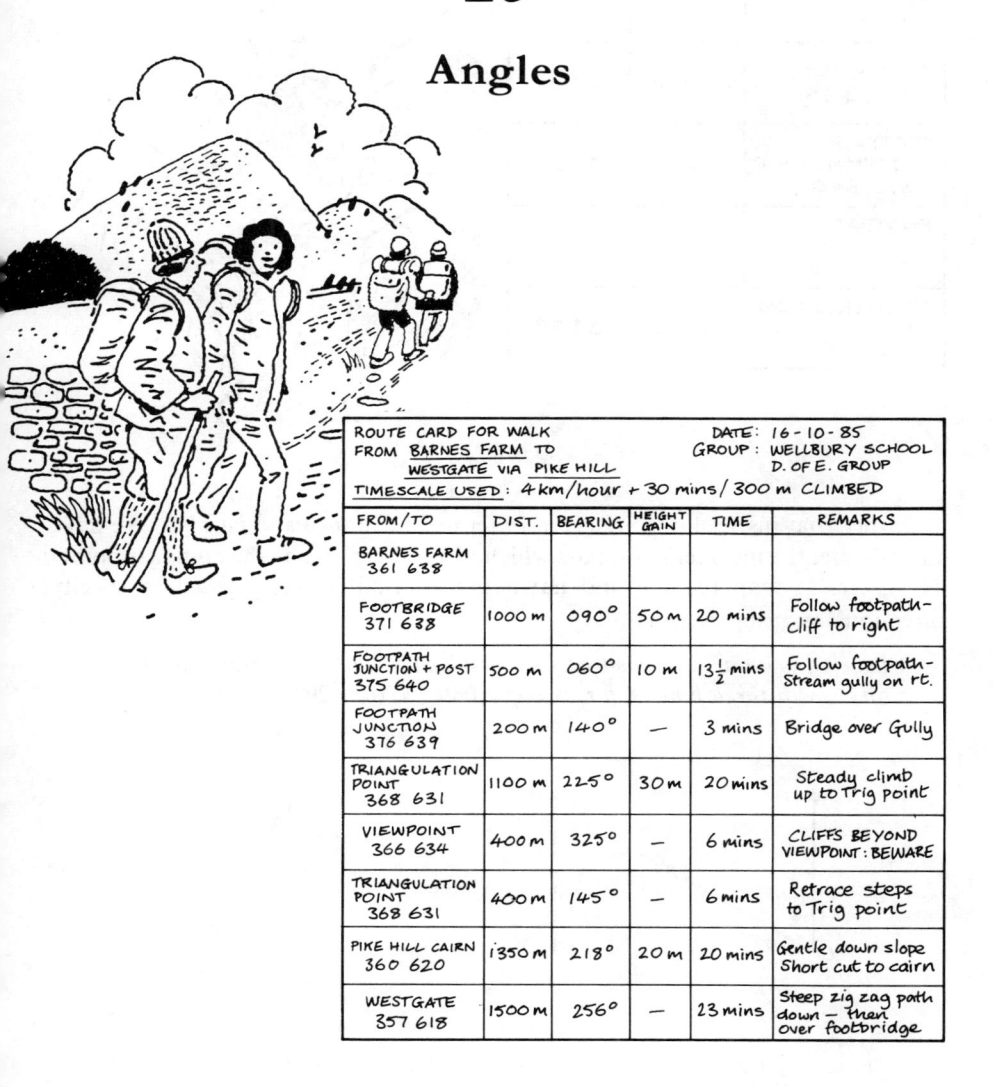

23

Angles

ROUTE CARD FOR WALK FROM **BARNES FARM** TO **WESTGATE** VIA **PIKE HILL**			DATE: 16-10-85 GROUP: WELLBURY SCHOOL D. OF E. GROUP		
TIMESCALE USED: 4 km/hour + 30 mins / 300 m CLIMBED					
FROM/TO	DIST.	BEARING	HEIGHT GAIN	TIME	REMARKS
BARNES FARM 361 638					
FOOTBRIDGE 371 638	1000 m	090°	50 m	20 mins	Follow footpath - cliff to right
FOOTPATH JUNCTION + POST 375 640	500 m	060°	10 m	13½ mins	Follow footpath - Stream gully on rt.
FOOTPATH JUNCTION 376 639	200 m	140°	—	3 mins	Bridge over Gully
TRIANGULATION POINT 368 631	1100 m	225°	30 m	20 mins	Steady climb up to Trig point
VIEWPOINT 366 634	400 m	325°	—	6 mins	CLIFFS BEYOND VIEWPOINT: BEWARE
TRIANGULATION POINT 368 631	400 m	145°	—	6 mins	Retrace steps to Trig point
PIKE HILL CAIRN 360 620	1350 m	218°	20 m	20 mins	Gentle down slope Short cut to cairn
WESTGATE 357 618	1500 m	256°	—	23 mins	Steep zig zag path down - then over footbridge

1. THREE FIGURE BEARINGS

The leader of a group planning a hill walking expedition is responsible for the safety of the group. One of the most important things to do is to leave a *route card* with a suitable person, or possibly with the police, giving details of the group's intentions. If the group encounters difficulties then the route card helps to trace them. The opening illustration shows part of a route card. Figure 1 shows some of this in more detail.

105

Angles Ch. 23

FROM/TO	DIST.	BEARING
BARNES FARM 361 638		
FOOTBRIDGE 371 638	1000 m	090°
FOOTPATH JUNCTION + POST 375 640	500 m	060°
FOOTPATH JUNCTION 376 639	200 m	140°
TRIANGULATION POINT 368 631	1100 m	225°

Figure 1

Notice that instructions are given in terms of distance and *bearing*. We have already met the mariner's compass which gives directions by the compass points N, S, etc. In map reading and navigation work it is more usual to specify directions by using bearings.

A bearing is an angle measured from north in a clockwise direction. A bearing is given with three figures, for example 060°, 120°, 329°.

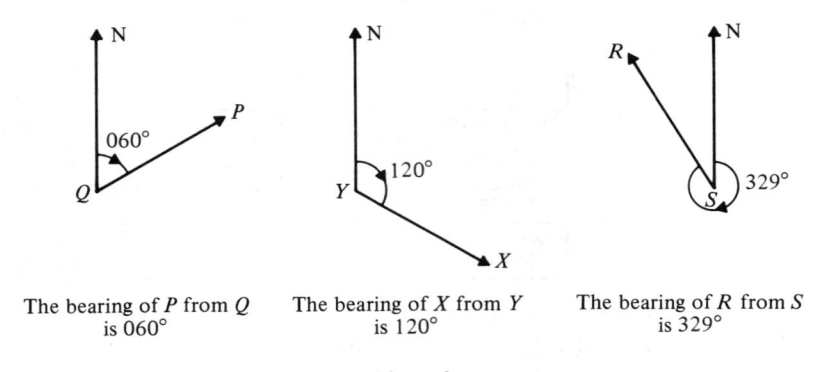

The bearing of P from Q is 060°   The bearing of X from Y is 120°   The bearing of R from S is 329°

Figure 2

In what follows you will need to refer to the route card in Figure 1 and the map in Figure 3.

Three figure bearings 107

Figure 3

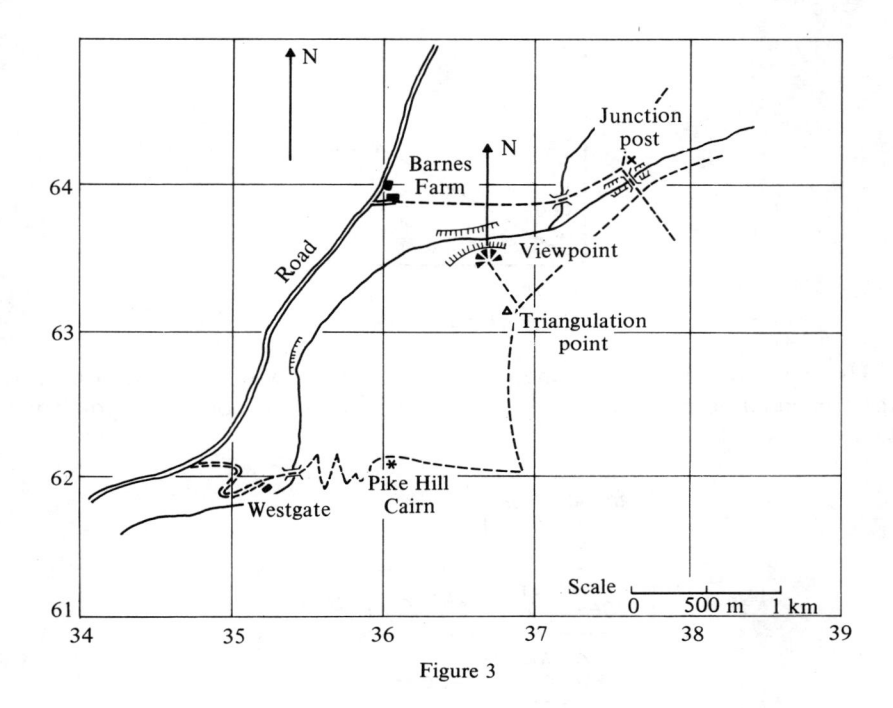

The first stage on the route card is to leave Barnes Farm and to walk 1000 m on a bearing of 090° to the footbridge. Find the farm on the map, using the grid reference if necessary. Imagine that you are standing at the farm and facing north. The bearing of 090° means that you are to turn clockwise through 90°. You will then be facing east. Now you can walk for 1000 m to the footbridge. Follow this on the map.

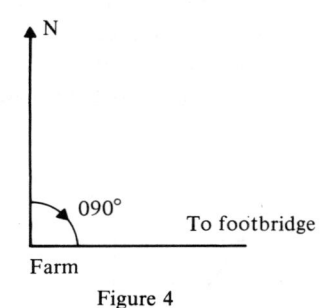

Figure 4

The second stage is to leave the footbridge on a bearing of 060° and to walk for 500 m. Imagine now that you are standing at the footbridge, facing north. You then turn through 60° clockwise until you are looking along the path to the post at the next junction.

108 Angles Ch. 23

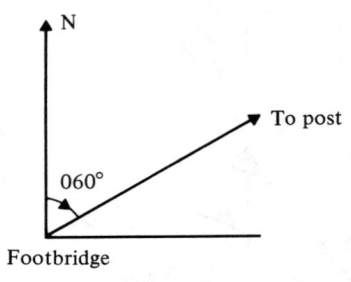

Figure 5 (Footbridge, bearing 060° to post)

Figure 5

Use the route card and the map to follow the next two instructions to get to the triangulation point. (Find out what a triangulation point is, if you don't know.)

TRIANGULATION POINT 368 631		
VIEWPOINT 366 634	400 m	325°
TRIANGULATION POINT 368 631	400 m	145°
PIKE HILL CAIRN 360 620	1350 m	218°

Figure 6

Drawing bearings

Figure 6 picks out another part of the route. In order to draw a bearing of 325° we can either use an SMP angle measurer or do a calculation before using a geoliner. As angles at a point add up to 360° we see that a clockwise rotation of 325° gives the same direction as an anti-clockwise rotation of 35°. Figure 7 illustrates.

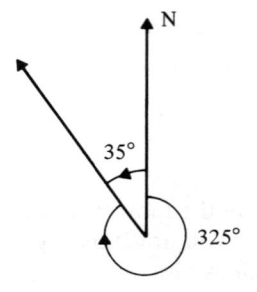

Figure 7

Three figure bearings 109

Note here that the bearing of the viewpoint from the triangulation point is 325° but the bearing of the triangulation point from the viewpoint is 145°. This is shown in Figure 8.

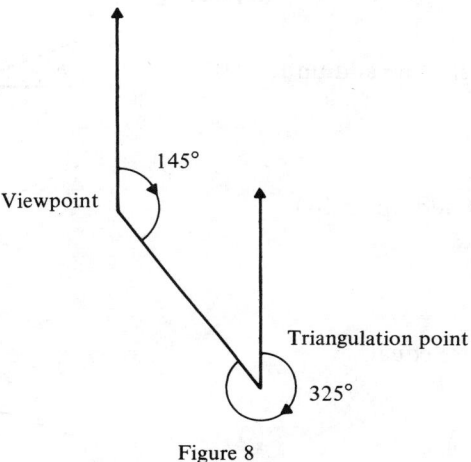

Figure 8

The final stage on the portion of route card in Figure 6 requires a bearing of 218°. This can be done in either of two ways as indicated in Figure 9.

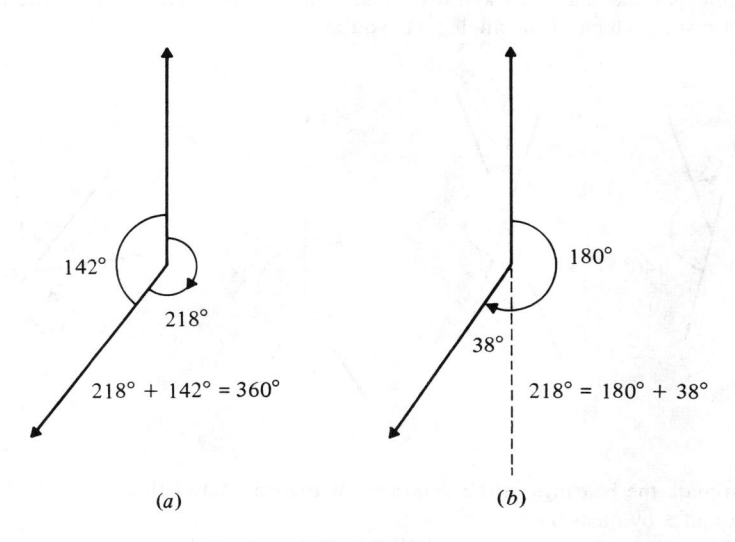

(a) 142°, 218°, 218° + 142° = 360°

(b) 180°, 38°, 218° = 180° + 38°

Figure 9

Angles Ch. 23

For the calculations it is necessary to remember some angle facts and, later, to develop some that are new.

Reminder

Angles on a straight line add up to 180°;

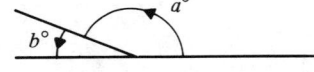

$a + b = 180$.

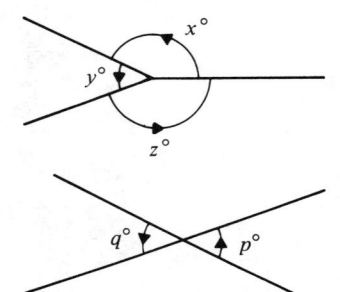

Angles at a point add up to 360;

$x + y + z = 360$.

Opposite angles are equal;

$p = q$.

Figure 10

Exercise A

*1 Calculate the angles marked with small letters in the diagrams in Figure 11. In each case state which of the angle facts you are using.

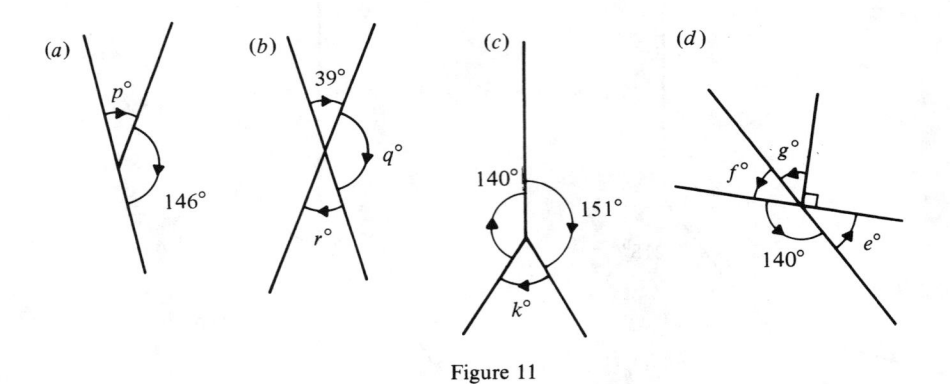

Figure 11

2 Estimate the bearings in the diagrams in Figure 12 and then check each of your estimates by measurement.
Set your work out as shown in Table 1. Part (a) is done for you.

Scale drawing 111

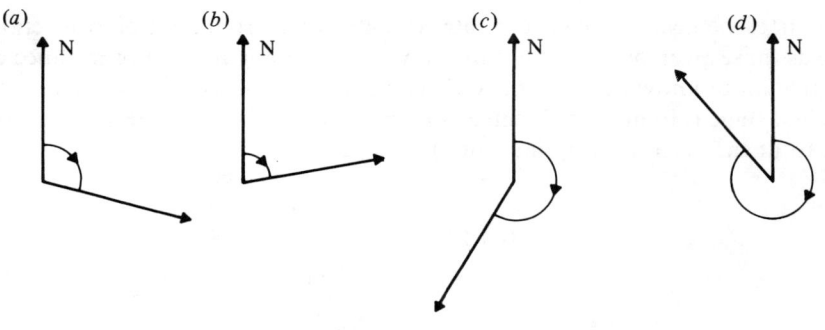

(a) (b) (c) (d)

Figure 12

	Between compass points N, E, S, W	Between degrees	Estimated bearing	Measured bearing
(a)	E and S	090° and 180°	100°	105°
(b)				
(c)				
(d)				

Table 1

3 Make drawings to show the following bearings, making any necessary calculations and showing your working for them.
(a) 075°; (b) 164°; (c) 246°; (d) 307°; (e) 270°.

*4 Hina was walking on a bearing of 140°. She stopped, turned round and walked in the direction from which she had come. On what bearing was she then walking?

5 Suppose that in the directions for an orienteering competition, you were told to run on a bearing of 076°. If instead of measuring clockwise from north, you measured 76° anticlockwise from north, on which bearing would you in fact be running?

*6 On the map in Figure 3 Barnes farm, Pike Hill Cairn, Westgate and the junction post are all visible from the viewpoint. Find the bearing of each of these places from the viewpoint.

2. SCALE DRAWING

Figure 13

112 Angles   Ch. 23

Sometimes we need to make accurate scale drawings from a set of instructions such as those given on the route card shown again in Figure 13. For instance we might want to know how far the walkers will be from *A* when they arrive at *C*. The first stage is to make a sketch as shown in Figure 14. This helps us see how best to fit the accurate diagram onto the page.

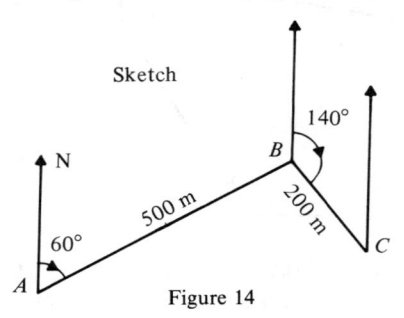

Sketch

Figure 14

Work through the following steps to make your own accurate scale drawing from the route card in Figure 13. This is best done on squared paper. (The steps for the accurate diagram are shown separately but you should make only one drawing.)

(1) Choose a scale. 1 cm to 100 m would be suitable.
(2) Mark a point *A* and draw a north line from *A*.

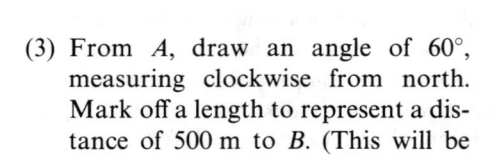

(3) From *A*, draw an angle of 60°, measuring clockwise from north. Mark off a length to represent a distance of 500 m to *B*. (This will be 5 cm on your drawing.)

(4) Draw a north line at *B*. It must be parallel to the north line at *A*! (This is easy on squared paper.)

(5) From *B*, draw an angle of 140°, measuring clockwise from north. Mark off a length to represent a distance of 200 m to *C*.

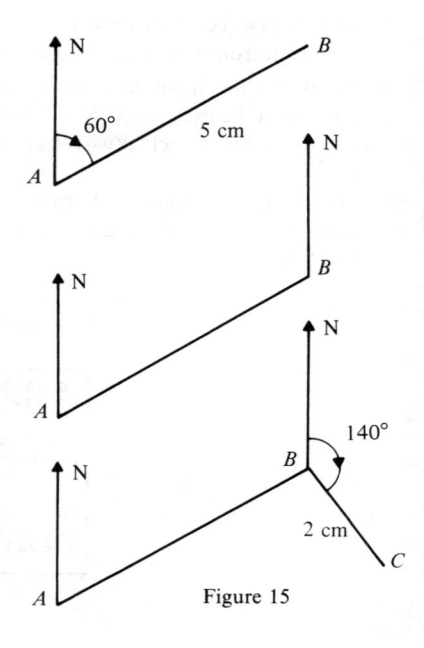

Figure 15

Scale drawing

(*Notice that whenever there is a change of direction we put in another north line.*)

From the final drawing we can answer various questions, including the one at the beginning of this section. For example:

(a) Having arrived at C how far are the walkers from A?

Measure the length of the line AC. On your diagram AC measures 5.7 cm, so the walkers are 5.7 × 100 = 570 m from A.

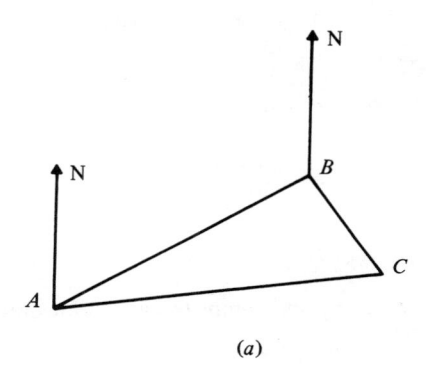

(b) What is the bearing of A from C?

Draw the north line at C.

Imagine yourself standing at C and facing north. Measure the clockwise angle through which you would turn from north to face A.

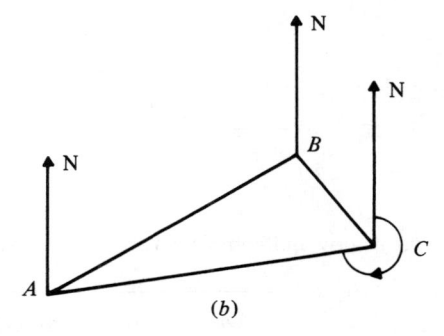

You may need to make a calculation. Since the angles at a point add up to 360 degrees, measure the angle marked $p°$ and then calculate the bearing.

In fact $p = 100$ so the bearing of A from C is 360° − 100° = 260°.

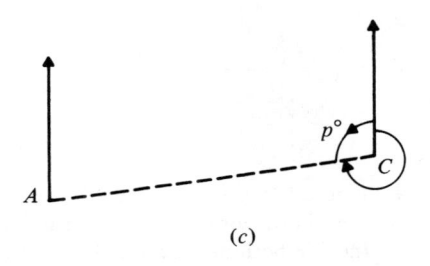

Figure 16

Angles

Exercise B

*1 Copy and complete Table 2 for drawings made to a scale of 1 cm to 100 m

Distances on the ground	Lengths on the drawing
560 m	
	2.8 cm
	13 cm
1 km	
	0.4 cm

Table 2

2 Copy and complete Table 3 for drawings made to a scale of 1 cm to 10 m

Distances on the ground	Lengths on the drawing
23 m	
	3.1 cm
	20 cm
4 m	
110 m	

Table 3

*3 Copy and complete Table 4 for drawings made to a scale of 2 cm to 1 km

Distances on the ground	Lengths on the drawing
6 km	
	4 cm
7 km	
	2.8 cm
4.5 km	

Table 4

4 Figure 17 represents a map drawn on a scale of 1 cm to 50 km. Give a set of instructions in the form of a route card, for the journey from *P* to *Q* to *R* and back to *P*. Include both distances and bearings.

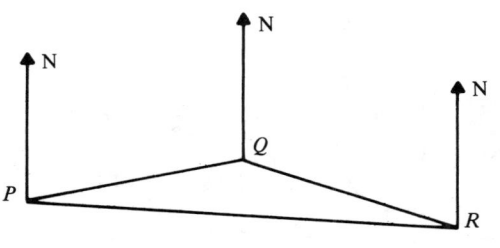

Figure 17

*5 By measuring suitable angles in Figure 18 state the bearing of Seaport from Pudley and the bearing of Pudley from Seaport. Given that the scale is 1 cm to 5 km, estimate the distance from Seaport to Pudley.

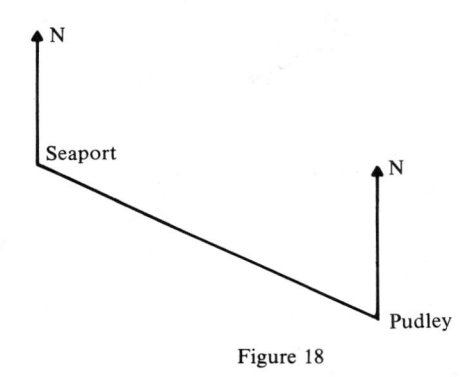

Figure 18

6 Peter is at Jake's farm and Kate is at the village shop. Peter is standing 800 m due west of Kate. The bearing of the church spire from Peter is 050° and from Kate it is 310°.

Make a rough sketch to illustrate this. Choose a suitable scale and then draw an accurate figure to show the church, Peter at the farm and Kate at the village shop.

How far are Peter and Kate from the church? What are the bearings of Peter and Kate from the church?

7 As in the previous question Peter is standing 800 m due west of Kate. There is a horse trough on the village green. Its bearing from Peter is 120°, and its bearing from Kate is 220°.

Draw a rough sketch and, using the same scale as in question 6, draw an accurate figure to show the positions of Peter, Kate and the trough. How far are Peter and Kate from the trough and what are their bearings from it?

116   Angles   Ch. 23

Figure 19

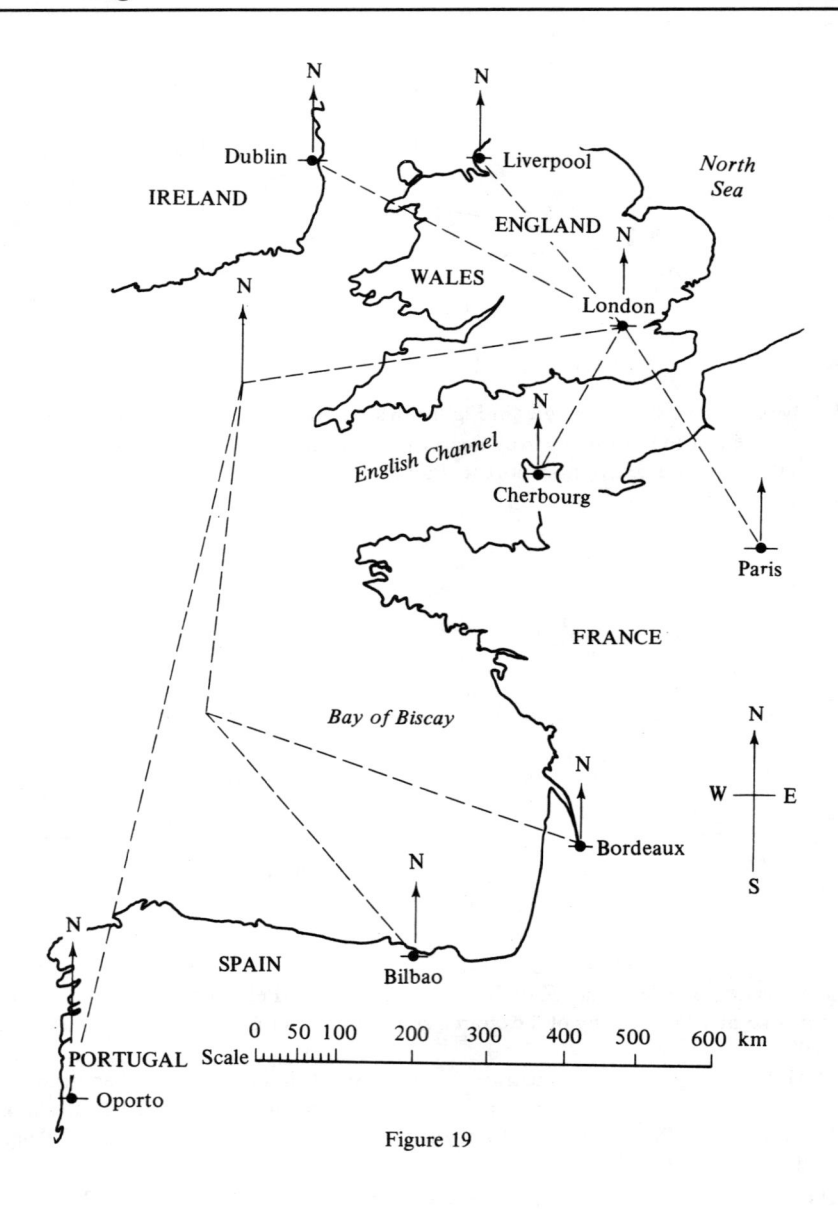

To avoid accidents aircraft keep to certain routes or airways. The broken lines on this map show some of the airways between London Airport and other towns and cities.

*8 You will find it helpful to make a copy on tracing paper of the *scale* of the map in Figure 19. Use the plan of airways to work out flight plans (along the given routes) for journeys:
(a) London to Paris;   (b) London to Dublin;   (c) Cherbourg to London;
(d) London to Oporto; (e) London to Bordeaux; (f) Bilbao to London;
(g) Oporto to London.

9 There are three buoys, A, B and C, marking a sandbank in a fishing area. B is 5 km due south of A. The bearing of C from A is 125°, and the bearing of C from B is 045°. Make a scale drawing and find the distances AC and BC. What are the bearings of A and B from C?

*10 A ship leaves a port, Avonhampton, and sails 60 km due west to Bixmouth. It then sails 45 km NW (315°) to Charford. Make a scale drawing to show the ship's journey. What are the bearings of Bixmouth from Avonhampton and of Bixmouth from Charford? Find the distance and bearing of Charford from Avonhampton.

3. PARALLEL LINES

A pair of parallel lines lie in the same direction. They are always the same distance apart. We usually mark them with arrows. The north lines which we have used are an example of parallel lines.

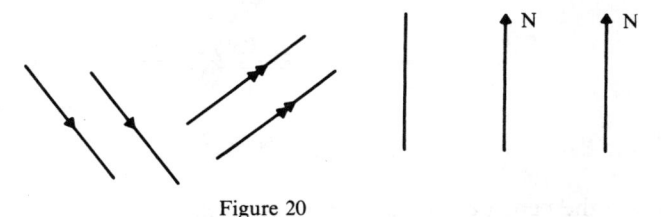

Figure 20

Draw a line in any direction on your page. Rest the longest side of a geoliner along it and draw a line along one of the shorter sides as shown in Figure 21. Move your geoliner along the first line and then repeat the instruction. Do this a number of times and you will have drawn a set of parallel lines.

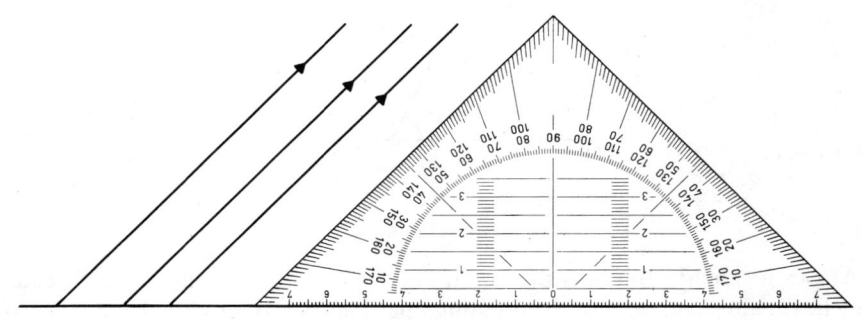

Figure 21

Alternate angles

On squared paper draw a pair of parallel lines about 4 cm apart and a line to cross them as shown in Figure 22.

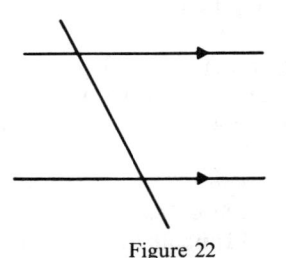

Figure 22

On your drawing place a pencil with its point in the direction of the arrow, in position 1 as shown in Figure 23.

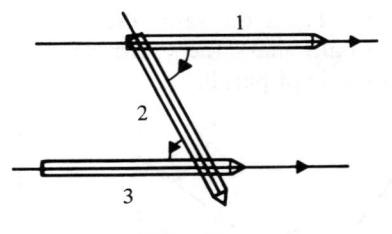

Figure 23

Rotate the pencil *clockwise* until it is in position 2 along the crossing line. Finally rotate the pencil *anticlockwise* until it is in position 3.

Notice that the initial and final directions in which the pencil points are the same. This shows that the angles marked $s°$ in Figure 24 are the same size even though the rotations were in opposite directions.

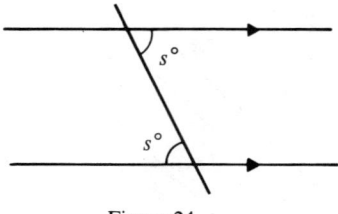

Figure 24

Angles formed in this way are equal and known as *alternate angles* because they lie on alternate sides of the crossing line. They are often called **Z** angles, for obvious reasons. Figure 25 shows some examples.

Parallel lines   119

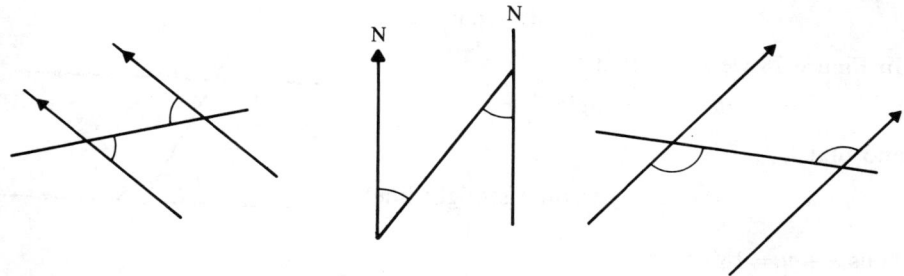

Figure 25 Alternate angles are equal.

Corresponding angles

Figure 26 shows a pair of parallel lines and two angles marked $a°$ and $b°$ which are called *corresponding angles* because they are in corresponding positions relative to the parallel lines.

(a)

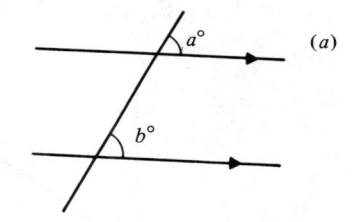

Figure 26(b) is a repeat of Figure 26(a) with another angle marked $x°$.
We know that $a = x$ (opposite angles) and that $b = x$ (alternate angles).
It follows that $a = b$.

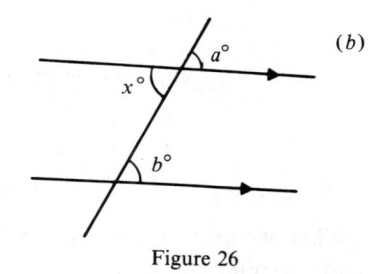

(b)

Figure 26

This result can be checked by direct measurement on the diagram you drew for the previous section. Figure 27 shows some further examples.

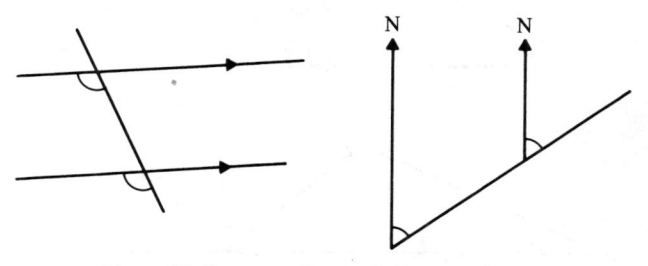

Figure 27 Corresponding angles are equal.

Interior angles

In Figure 28 we know that

$s = t$ (alternate angles)

and that

$u + t = 180$ (angles on a straight line).

Thus $s + u = 180$.

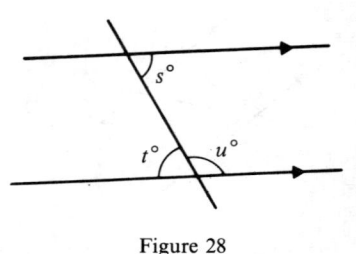

Figure 28

s and u are called interior angles because they are contained within the parallel lines. Figure 29 shows some further examples.

$p + q = 180$

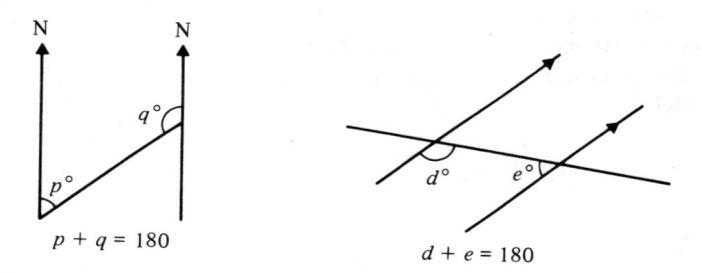

$d + e = 180$

Figure 29 Interior angles add up to 180°.

Calculations with angles

When we are working out angles by calculation from a diagram we need to be able to put together what we know. Look again at the list at the end of Section 1 and the facts just mentioned. Do not forget what you know about triangles from your previous work. Figure 30 reminds you.

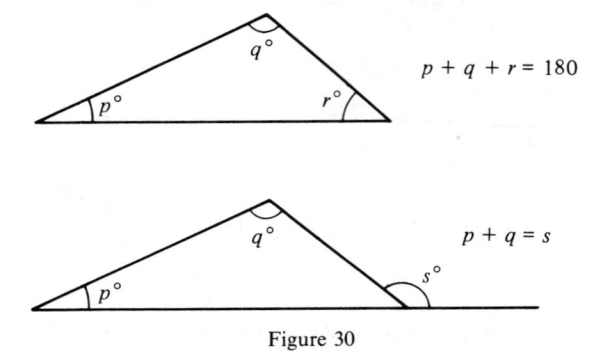

$p + q + r = 180$

$p + q = s$

Figure 30

Parallel lines 121

The following examples illustrate the use of these facts.

Example 1
Calculate the values of *a* and *b* in Figure 31.

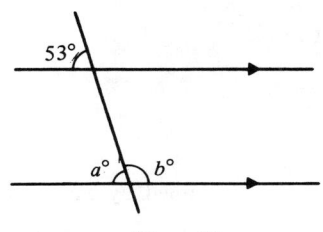

Figure 31

$a = 53$ (corresponding angles)
$b = 180 - 53$ (angles on a straight line)
so $b = 127$.

Example 2
Find *c* in Figure 32(*a*).

In order to do this we need to work out another angle first. One possible way is shown in Figure 32(*b*).

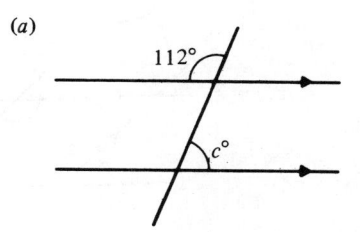

(a)

We can now say:

(b)

$y = 180 - 112$ (angles on a
$\quad = 68$ straight line)
so $\quad c = 68$ (alternate angles).

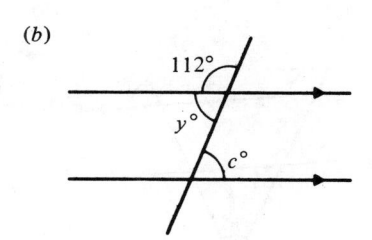

Figure 32

122   Angles   Ch. 23

Example 3
Find p and q in Figure 33.

There are several ways of doing this question. For instance:

$$p + 40 = 180 \quad \text{(interior angles)}$$
so $\quad p = 140.$

Also $\quad q + 60 = p \quad$ (exterior angle of a triangle)

so $\quad q = 80.$

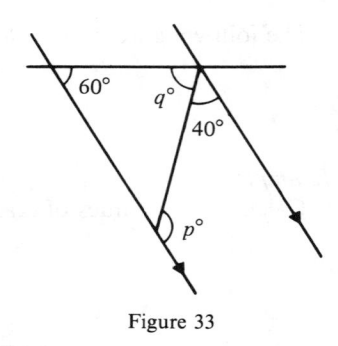

Figure 33

Exercise C

In this exercise answers must be obtained by calculation; the diagrams are intentionally not accurate.

*1   Calculate the angles indicated by letters in the diagrams of Figure 34.

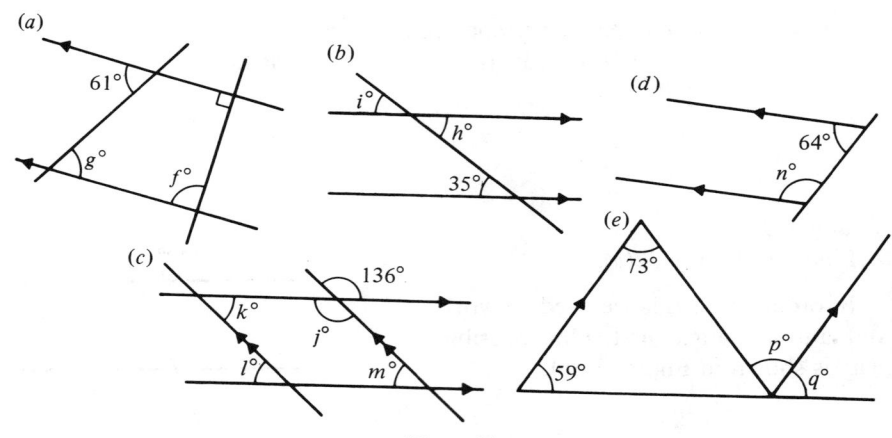

Figure 34

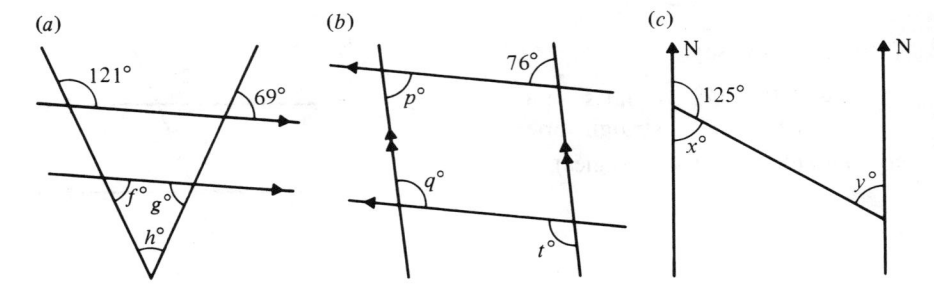

Figure 35

Parallel lines   123

2   Make a sketch copy of each of the diagrams in Figure 35. Work out the angles marked by letters. (If you need to find some unmarked angles give them letters of your choice.) Write out your answer in such a way that your method is clear.

*3 In each of the diagrams in Figure 36 imagine yourself standing at *A*. Find the bearing of *B* from *A*. (Begin by making sketch copies and marking in a north line at *A*.)

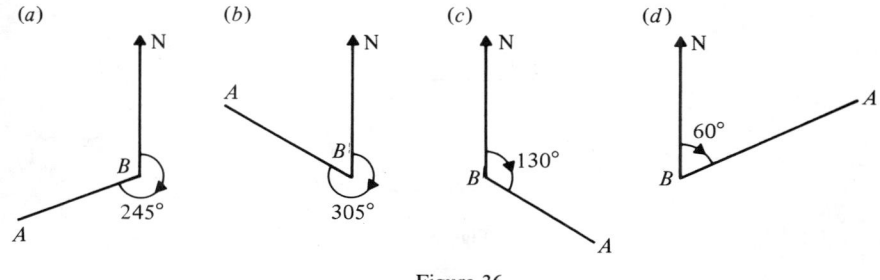

(a)   (b)   (c)   (d)

Figure 36

4   The bearing of Fort William from Ben Nevis is 290°. Make a sketch to illustrate this and find the bearing of Ben Nevis from Fort William.

*5 Make a sketch copy of each of the diagrams in Figure 37 and calculate the angles indicated by letters. Give reasons for the steps you take as in Examples 1–3 above.

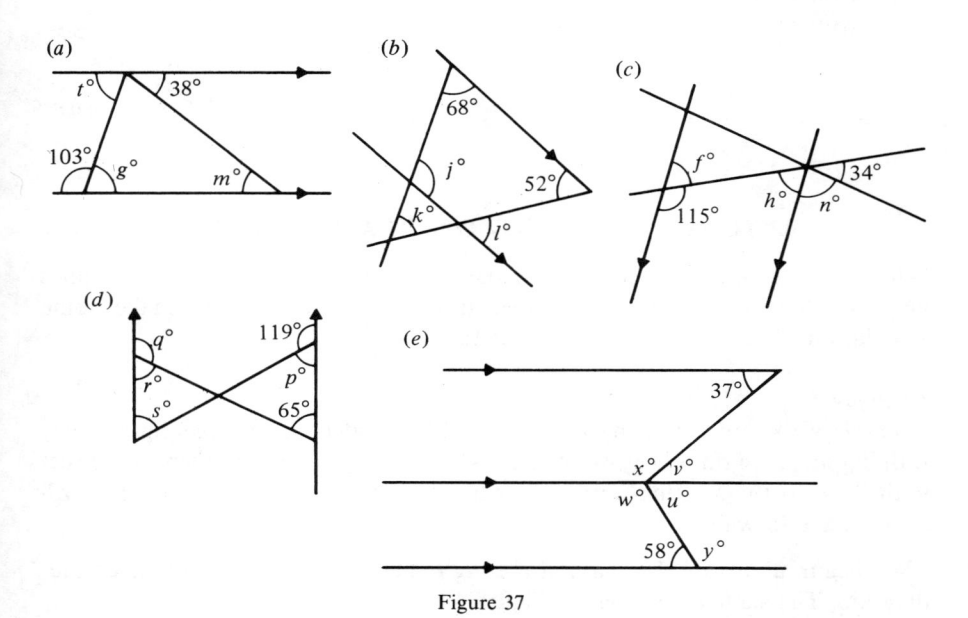

Figure 37

6 By calculation, find and name all pairs of parallel lines in Figure 38.

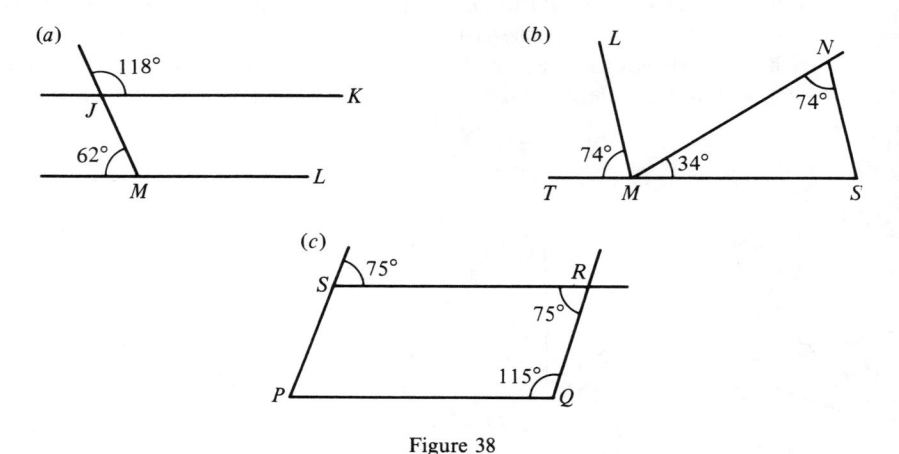

(a) [diagram with angles 118°, 62° at J, M and line to K, L]

(b) [diagram with L, T, M, N, S and angles 74°, 74°, 34°]

(c) [diagram with S, R, P, Q and angles 75°, 75°, 115°]

Figure 38

*7 On a triangular village green, a telephone kiosk, K, is due South of the church, C. F shows the position of the drinking fountain. The angles KCF and CKF are as shown in Figure 39.

Find (a) the bearing of C from F;
  (b) the bearing of K from F.

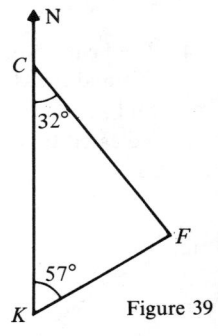

Figure 39

4. SCALE DRAWING ON PLAIN PAPER

When making drawings on squared paper it is very easy to put in the lines pointing due north. On plain paper it may be necessary to make some calculations first. Example 4 illustrates this.

Example 4

Jennie walks on a bearing of 110° for 3 km and then turns along a valley walking for 2 km on a bearing of 220°. At the end of the valley there is a direct path back to the starting point. On what bearing and for what distance will Jennie have to walk?

We begin, as before, by making a rough sketch to help plan the accurate diagram. The sketch is shown in Figure 40.

Scale drawing on plain paper

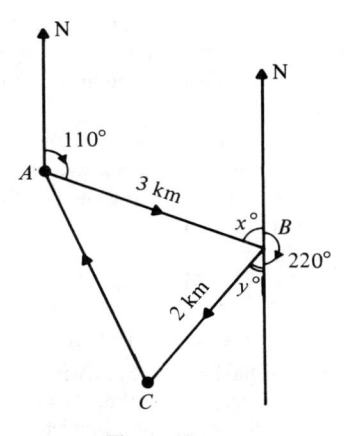

Figure 40

It is important to make the two north lines parallel. We use the fact that interior angles add to 180° to work out that the angle $x°$ on the rough sketch is, in fact, 70°.

We must also be careful to get BC in the correct direction. As 220° is 40° more than 180° the angle $y°$ in the rough sketch is to be 40°.

It is then possible to choose a suitable scale and complete the drawing. You should do this and find the answers to the question.

Exercise D

In this exercise all accurate drawings should be done on plain paper.

*1 Calculate the angles indicated by letters in the diagrams of Figure 41.

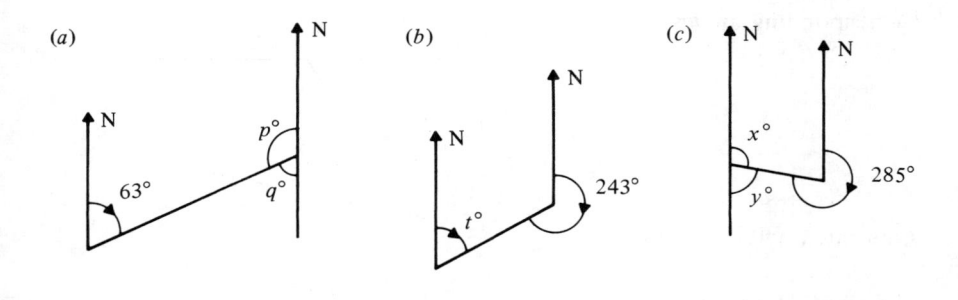

Figure 41

2 An aeroplane leaves airport A and flies on a bearing of 320° for 400 km to airport B. It then flies on a bearing of 260° for 350 km, landing at airport C. After refuelling it returns directly to A. Make a scale drawing and find the distance and bearing of its return flight.

*3 From the top of a hill three church spires can be seen. The first, A, is 6 km away on a bearing of 330°; the second, B, is 4 km away on a bearing of 070°; and the third, C, is 2 km due south. Draw a plan showing the positions of the three spires and the top of the hill, using a scale of 1 cm to 1 km.
    (a) Find the distances from:
        (i) A to B;   (ii) B to C;   (iii) C to A.
    (b) Find the bearings of:
        (i) A from B;   (ii) B from C;   (iii) C from A.

4 A ship sailed from Seatown harbour to Sandwind island 30 km away on a bearing of 080° and then on to Westferry, a further 25 km, on a bearing of 050°. Make a scale drawing of the route. What bearing must the ship take to sail directly back to Seatown from Westferry?

*5 A plane leaves an airport A and travels 350 km on a bearing of 070°. It then receives a radio instruction to alter course and fly on a bearing of 305° until it is due north of A. How far from A will it be then? (*Think* before making any accurate drawing!)

6 A crow, which has been sitting on a telegraph pole, flies straight for 50 m on a bearing 055° and lands in a tree. It then flies back to its nest, which is 30 m away, on a bearing 150°. Find the distance and bearing of the nest from the pole.

7 A small boat sets out from a harbour and has travelled 4 km on a bearing 140° when its engine fails. It then drifts with the current until it sticks on a sandbank at a point which is 2.5 km from the harbour on a bearing 205°. What is the direction of the current?

SUMMARY

In addition to what follows you need to know the facts about angles meeting at a point, adjacent angles on a straight line and the interior and exterior angles of a triangle.

Angle facts involving parallel lines:

Corresponding angles are equal.

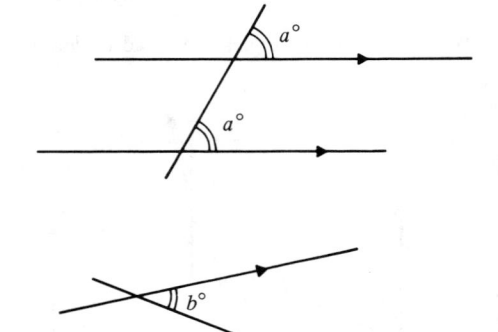

Alternate angles are equal.

Summary 127

Interior angles add up to 180°.

$p + q = 180$.

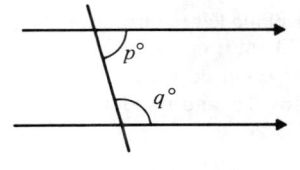

Figure 42

Bearings are measured in degrees, clockwise from the north, and are written with three digits. For example the direction NE is on a bearing of 045°.

Summary exercise

These questions may be answered on squared paper.
1. Calculate the angles indicated by letters in the diagrams of Figure 43. Give some indication of your method.

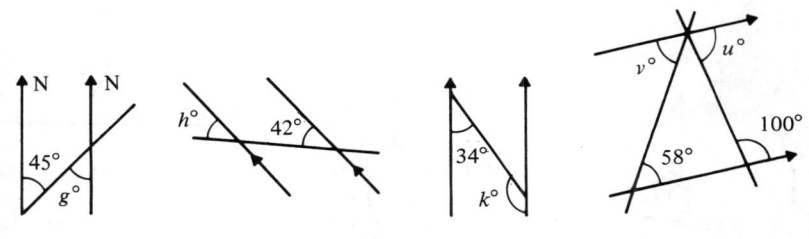

Figure 43

2. By measuring suitable angles in Figure 44, give the bearings of
   (a) A from B; (b) B from C; (c) C from A.

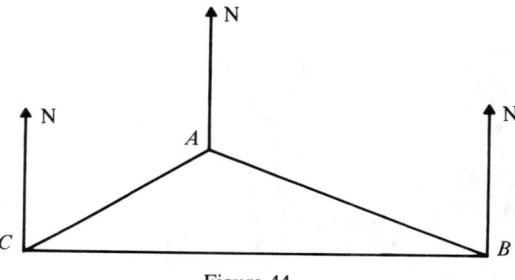

Figure 44

3. On the coast Weston Regis is 10 km due east of Middlehampton. An oil rig is being towed out to sea but has been temporarily anchored. Its bearing from Weston Regis is 205° and its bearing from Middlehampton is 130°. Make a scale drawing to show the position of the rig. How far is it from Weston Regis?

128   Angles   Ch. 23

4 A plane left Churn airport and set course on a bearing of 310°. After it had travelled 250 km it developed engine trouble and had to divert to Anster by flying a distance of 50 km on a bearing of 170°. Spare parts had to be flown from Churn to Anster. How far and in what direction does the relief aircraft have to fly?

Miscellaneous exercise

In questions involving maps it will help to make a copy of the *scale* on tracing paper.

1 In order to find his position on a map a walker took two bearings. A water tower was on a bearing of 035° and a church spire was on a bearing of 330°. From the map he worked out that the water tower was 12 km due east of the church.
   Make a sketch and use it to calculate:
   (a) the bearing of the walker from the water tower;
   (b) his bearing from the church.
   Use these answers to help you draw an accurate diagram to find how far he is away from the church.

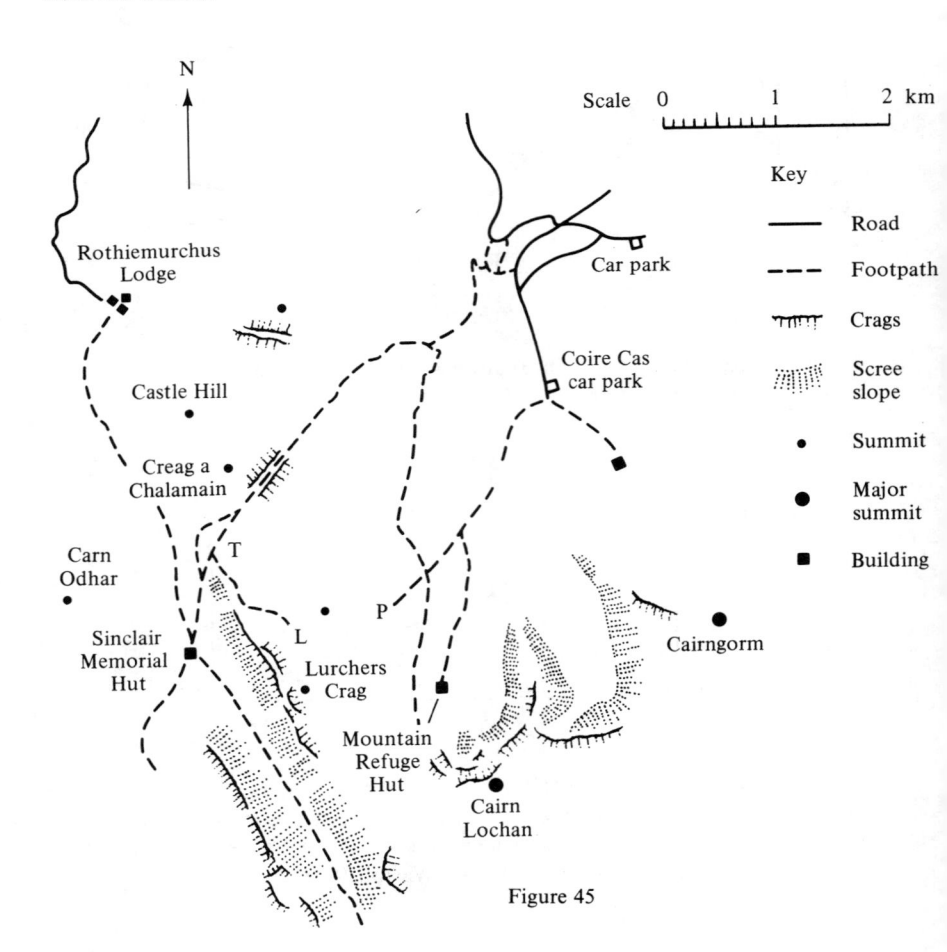

Figure 45

2   Peter sets out from the farm to meet Kate who is visiting a friend in the nearest village. His route, which is over country footpaths, takes him for 2 km on a bearing 037°, then 5 km on a bearing 082°. What is the distance and bearing of the village from the farm? They decide to walk back by road. If their return route and Peter's outward journey form a parallelogram, show this on your diagram and give instructions for the return journey.

3   The map in Figure 45 shows an area of the Cairngorms in Scotland. Make out a set of instructions for a walk starting at Sinclair Memorial Hut and passing the points T, L (near Lurchers Crag), P, to end at the Coire Cas car park. (You need not detail the small bends in the route, but be careful to get your answers correct because this can be very dangerous country in bad weather!)

4   Figure 46 is a simplified map of Southampton water.

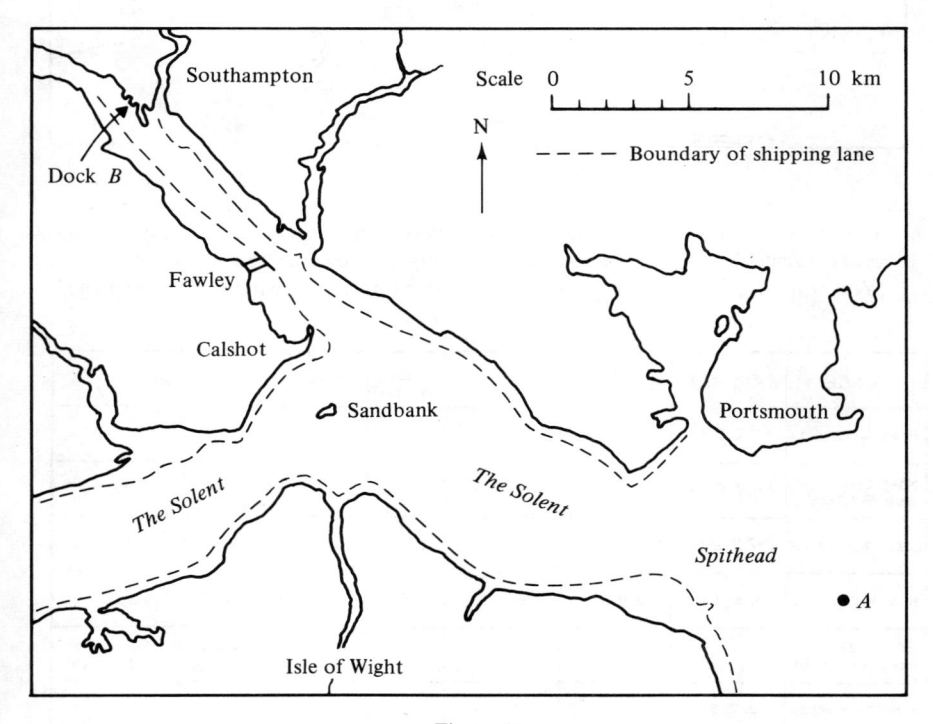

Figure 46

The Solent pilot comes on board a liner at the point marked A between Portsmouth and the Isle of Wight. His job is to ensure a safe passage to the dock B at Southampton. Give an appropriate set of instructions for this task.

130   Angles   Ch. 23

5   Figure 47 shows a practice course for orienteering. Make a set of instructions giving distances and bearings for the course.

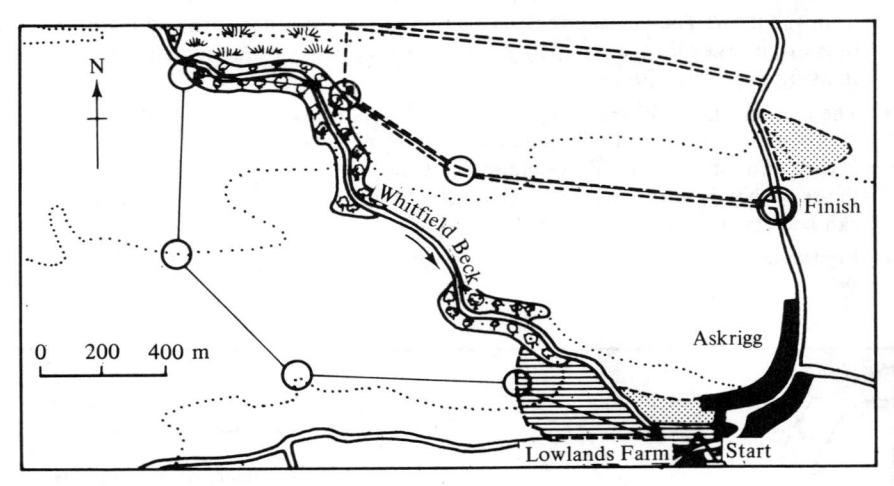

Figure 47

6   The route card in Figure 48 was made for a walk from Hope Church to Edale Station. Make a scale drawing of the walk as accurately as you can, choosing a suitable scale. (You will have to do some planning in order to fit the drawing onto your page.)

PLACE	GRID REF	GRID BEARING	DISTANCE (m)	HEIGHT GAIN(M)	TIME	REMARKS
HOPE CHURCH	172 834					
ROAD JUNCTION AND BRIDGE	168 845	338°	1150			ROAD RIVER JUST ON EAST SIDE
LOSE HILL SUMMIT	153 853	300°	1700	300		TRACK 200 m THEN FOOTPATH CLIMBING
HOLLINS CROSS	135 845	244°	1900	50		ALONG RIDGE
FOOTPATH ROAD JUNCTION	129 852	316°	1000	—		CONCAVE SLOPE DESCENDING BRIDGE
EDALE STATION	122 853	280°	700	—		
TIME SCALE	5 km/h and	300 m ↑/½ hr.				

Figure 48

(a) How far is it from Edale Station back to Hope Church 'as the crow flies'?
(b) Notice that there is a time scale shown on the route card. Decide what this means and calculate the length of time the walk from Hope Church to Edale Station would take.

Summary

7 Enid sets off across the fields, in a fog, to walk 2 km to Alma's house on a bearing of 027°. Unfortunately she walks on a bearing of 030°. Estimate by drawing the nearest she comes to Alma's house.

8 The instructions in this chapter have not distinguished between true north and magnetic north. Find out about magnetic north and how much difference there is at the moment between magnetic north and true north.

9 The markings on the map in Figure 49 are rather different from those in Ordnance Survey maps.

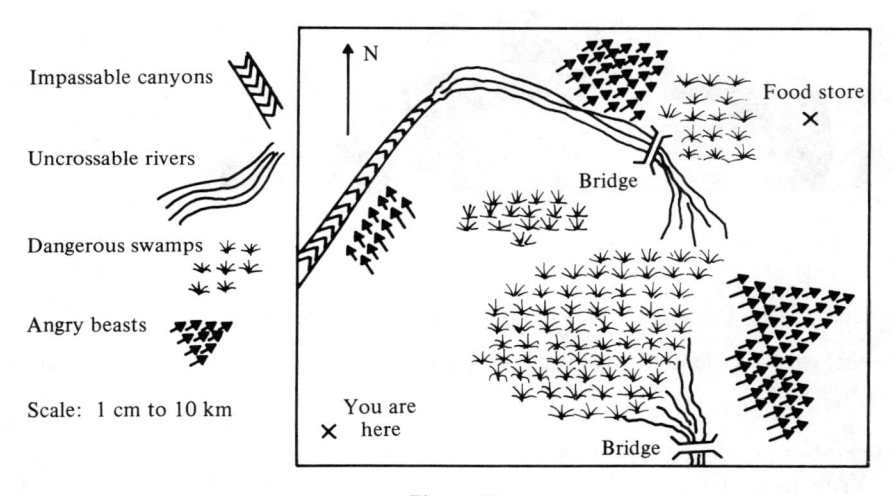

Figure 49

Plan, in your head, moves to enable you to reach your store of food. Test each one out to see if you have made a possible move. If you take more than 10 moves in all, you die of starvation! (You may not go beyond the area indicated on the map.)

24

Formulae using squares

1. A REMINDER ABOUT FORMULAE

So far, we have dealt with several types of formulae as shown in the following examples.

Example 1 (*Formulae using multiplication and division*)
Write down the formula represented by the following flow chart; calculate q if $p = 3$.

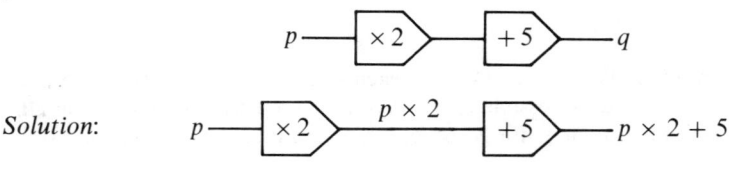

$$p \longrightarrow \boxed{\times 2} \longrightarrow \boxed{+5} \longrightarrow q$$

Solution:

$$p \longrightarrow \boxed{\times 2} \xrightarrow{p \times 2} \boxed{+5} \longrightarrow p \times 2 + 5$$

so we write

$$q = 2p + 5.$$

If $p = 3$,
$$q = 2 \times 3 + 5 = 6 + 5 = 11.$$

Example 2
Give a flow chart to represent the formula $m = \frac{1}{2}n - 5$. Also find the value of m when $n = 12.6$.

Solution: Looking at the formula we see that n has to be multiplied by $\frac{1}{2}$ and 5 subtracted from the result. The flow chart follows.

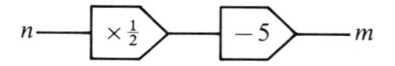

$$n \longrightarrow \boxed{\times \tfrac{1}{2}} \longrightarrow \boxed{-5} \longrightarrow m$$

A reminder about formulae

As multiplying by $\frac{1}{2}$ is the same as dividing by 2 there is an alternative answer.

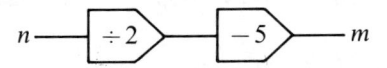

$$n \longrightarrow \boxed{\div 2} \longrightarrow \boxed{-5} \longrightarrow m$$

The value of m can be found by putting $n = 12.6$ into either flow chart. Alternatively we can work with the formula as follows:

$$m = \tfrac{1}{2}n - 5 \quad \text{and} \quad n = 12.6$$
so
$$m = \tfrac{1}{2} \times 12.6 - 5$$
$$= 6.3 - 5$$
$$= 1.3.$$
Hence $m = 1.3$ when $n = 12.6$.

Example 3 (Formulae using brackets)

Write down the formula represented by the following flow chart; calculate b if $a = 2$.

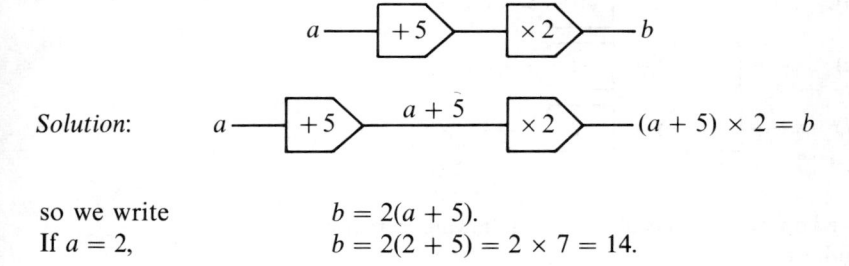

$$a \longrightarrow \boxed{+5} \longrightarrow \boxed{\times 2} \longrightarrow b$$

Solution: $a \longrightarrow \boxed{+5} \xrightarrow{a+5} \boxed{\times 2} \longrightarrow (a+5) \times 2 = b$

so we write $\quad b = 2(a + 5).$
If $a = 2$, $\quad b = 2(2 + 5) = 2 \times 7 = 14.$

Example 4

Write down the formula represented by the following flow chart; calculate d if $c = 11$:

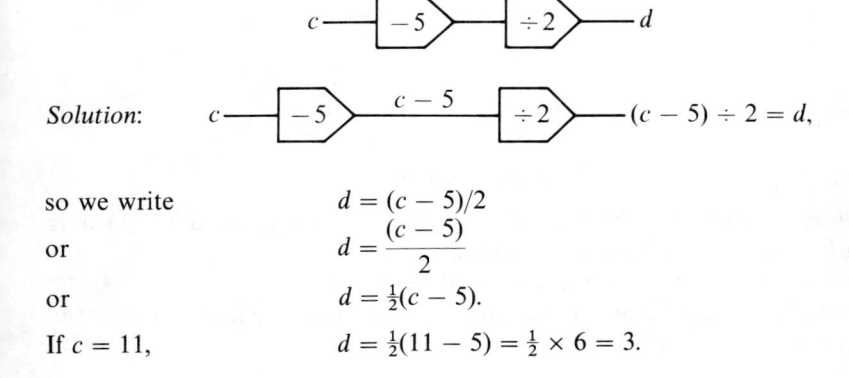

$$c \longrightarrow \boxed{-5} \longrightarrow \boxed{\div 2} \longrightarrow d$$

Solution: $c \longrightarrow \boxed{-5} \xrightarrow{c-5} \boxed{\div 2} \longrightarrow (c-5) \div 2 = d,$

so we write $\quad d = (c - 5)/2$
or $\quad d = \dfrac{(c-5)}{2}$
or $\quad d = \tfrac{1}{2}(c - 5).$
If $c = 11$, $\quad d = \tfrac{1}{2}(11 - 5) = \tfrac{1}{2} \times 6 = 3.$

134 Formulae using squares   Ch. 24

Exercise A (Revision)

*1 In each part of this question start by writing a formula equivalent to the given flow chart.

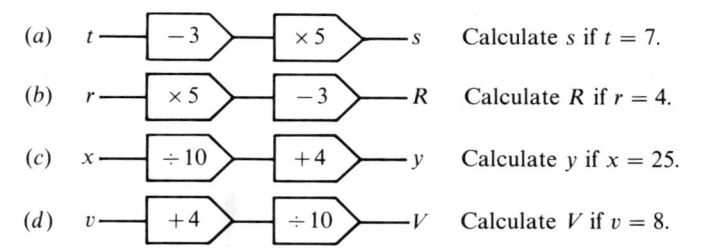

(a) $t \longrightarrow \boxed{-3} \longrightarrow \boxed{\times 5} \longrightarrow s$ Calculate s if $t = 7$.

(b) $r \longrightarrow \boxed{\times 5} \longrightarrow \boxed{-3} \longrightarrow R$ Calculate R if $r = 4$.

(c) $x \longrightarrow \boxed{\div 10} \longrightarrow \boxed{+4} \longrightarrow y$ Calculate y if $x = 25$.

(d) $v \longrightarrow \boxed{+4} \longrightarrow \boxed{\div 10} \longrightarrow V$ Calculate V if $v = 8$.

*2 Write down formulae represented by the following flow charts and, in each case, use your calculator to help you find y if $x = 9.8$.

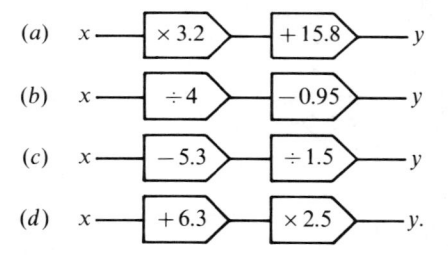

(a) $x \longrightarrow \boxed{\times 3.2} \longrightarrow \boxed{+15.8} \longrightarrow y$

(b) $x \longrightarrow \boxed{\div 4} \longrightarrow \boxed{-0.95} \longrightarrow y$

(c) $x \longrightarrow \boxed{-5.3} \longrightarrow \boxed{\div 1.5} \longrightarrow y$

(d) $x \longrightarrow \boxed{+6.3} \longrightarrow \boxed{\times 2.5} \longrightarrow y$.

*3 Give flow charts equivalent to the following formulae.
   (a) $s = 2.5t + 1.5$;
   (b) $s = 2.5(t + 1.5)$;
   (c) $s = \dfrac{t}{2.5} - 1.5$;
   (d) $s = \dfrac{(t - 1.5)}{2.5}$.

For each flow chart, use your calculator to help you find the value of s if $t = 9$.

2. SQUARES

You will remember that the area of a square measuring 3 cm by 3 cm is 3×3 cm^2 = 9 cm^2 (nine square centimetres).

We can write 3×3 as 3^2 (pronounced 'three-squared').

If the lengths of the sides of a square are x cm, an expression for the area of the square is $x \times x$ cm^2 or x^2 cm^2.

Squares   135

Example 5
The Seemee Glass Co. makes square mirrors of different sizes. If the length of side of a mirror is 10 cm and the cost of the glass is 2p per cm² the total cost is worked out like this:

| Side length in cm | Work out area | Find cost of glass | Add cost of 'Seemee' sticker | Cost in pence |

$10 \longrightarrow \boxed{\text{square}} \xrightarrow{10^2 = 100} \boxed{\times 2} \xrightarrow{200} \boxed{+50} \longrightarrow 250$

So the cost of a Seemee mirror 10 cm by 10 cm is £2.50.

A big wall mirror for a bathroom measures 80 cm by 80 cm. The cost is given by:

Cost in pence

$80 \longrightarrow \boxed{\text{square}} \xrightarrow{80^2 = 6400} \boxed{\times 2} \xrightarrow{12\,800} \boxed{+50} \longrightarrow 12\,850$

So the cost is £128.50.
The cost of a mirror measuring x cm by x cm is therefore found like this:

Cost in pence

$x \longrightarrow \boxed{\text{square}} \xrightarrow{x^2} \boxed{\times 2} \xrightarrow{2x^2} \boxed{+50} \longrightarrow 2x^2 + 50 = C$

So we write $C = 2x^2 + 50.$

Formulae using squares

Example 6

Give the formula equivalent to this flow chart:

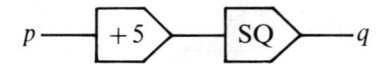

$$p \longrightarrow \boxed{+5} \longrightarrow \boxed{SQ} \longrightarrow q$$

Find the value of q when $p = 2$.

(Notice that we have used an obvious shorthand of 'SQ' for 'square' in the flow chart box.)

Solution:

$$p \longrightarrow \boxed{+5} \xrightarrow{p+5} \boxed{SQ} \longrightarrow (p+5)^2 = q$$

So the formula is $q = (p + 5)^2$.

Notice that it is the sum of 5 and p that is squared: we need the brackets to show this.

When $p = 2$, the flow chart gives q like this:

$$2 \longrightarrow \boxed{+5} \xrightarrow{7} \boxed{SQ} \longrightarrow 7^2 = 49$$

Similarly from the formula:

$$q = (p + 5)^2 = (2 + 5)^2 = 7^2 = 49.$$

Example 7

Give the formulae equivalent to these flow charts:

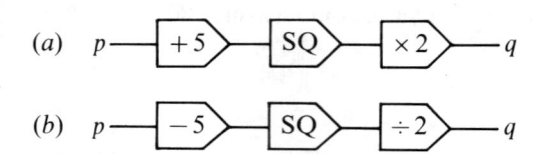

(a) $p \longrightarrow \boxed{+5} \longrightarrow \boxed{SQ} \longrightarrow \boxed{\times 2} \longrightarrow q$

(b) $p \longrightarrow \boxed{-5} \longrightarrow \boxed{SQ} \longrightarrow \boxed{\div 2} \longrightarrow q$

Solution:

(a) $p \longrightarrow \boxed{+5} \xrightarrow{p+5} \boxed{SQ} \xrightarrow{(p+5)^2} \boxed{\times 2} \longrightarrow (p+5)^2 \times 2 = q$

so $q = 2(p + 5)^2$.

(b) $p \longrightarrow \boxed{-5} \xrightarrow{p-5} \boxed{SQ} \xrightarrow{(p-5)^2} \boxed{\div 2} \longrightarrow (p-5)^2 \div 2 = q$

so $q = (p - 5)^2/2$ or $q = \dfrac{(p-5)^2}{2}$ or $q = \tfrac{1}{2}(p - 5)^2$.

Squares   137

Exercise B

*1 Nipper is not the postman's favourite dog. The number of WUFFCHOCS Nipper has to be given to stop him biting the postman's ankle depends on how long it is since Nipper was last fed.

If Nipper was last fed 3 hours ago, the number of WUFFCHOCS he has to be given is worked out like this:

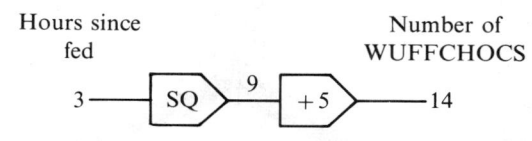

Hours since fed   Number of WUFFCHOCS

3 ──[SQ]── 9 ──[+5]── 14

(a) Draw a flow chart for calculating the number of WUFFCHOCS Nipper requires if he has not been fed for 5 hours. How many must the postman give him to preserve his ankles?
(b) If it is t hours since Nipper was fed, give a formula for N, the number of WUFFCHOCS the postman needs to give him.
(c) By putting $t = 8$ in your formula, calculate how many WUFFCHOCS the postman must give him if he has not been fed for 8 hours.
(d) If the postman only has 50 WUFFCHOCS and Nipper has been left for 7 hours without food, will the postman be nipped?

*2 Write down the formulae represented by the following flow charts.

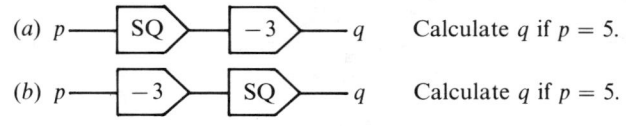

(a) p──[SQ]──[−3]── q Calculate q if $p = 5$.

(b) p──[−3]──[SQ]── q Calculate q if $p = 5$.

3 Write down the formulae represented by the following flow-charts.

(a) x──[SQ]──[−7]── y Calculate y if $x = 6$.

(b) x──[−7]──[SQ]── y Calculate y if $x = 6$.

*4 Give flow charts for the formulae below. In each case find the value of s when $t = 2$.
(a) $s = t^2 + 10$;   (b) $s = (t + 10)^2$;   (c) $s = 2(t + 10)^2$;
(d) $s = 2t^2 + 10$;   (e) $s = \dfrac{(t + 10)^2}{2}$.

138   Formulae using squares   Ch. 24

5 Give flow charts for the formulae below. In each case find the value of m when $n = 8$.
 (a) $m = n^2 - 5$;
 (b) $m = (n - 5)^2$;
 (c) $m = 3(n - 5)^2$;
 (d) $m = 3n^2 - 5$;
 (e) $m = \dfrac{(n - 5)^2}{3}$.

*6 Give flow charts equivalent to the following formulae and use your calculator to help you find the values of y when $x = 1.96$.
 (a) $y = (x - 1.74)^2$;
 (b) $y = x^2 - 1.74$;
 (c) $y = 2x^2 - 1.74$;
 (d) $y = 2(x - 1.74)^2$;
 (e) $y = \dfrac{x^2 - 1.74}{2}$;
 (f) $y = \frac{1}{2}(x - 1.74)^2$.

7 Give flow charts equivalent to the following formulae and use your calculator to help you find the values of q when $p = 0.25$.
 (a) $q = (p + 0.35)^2$;
 (b) $q = p^2 + 0.35$;
 (c) $q = 5p^2 + 0.35$;
 (d) $q = 5(p + 0.35)^2$;
 (e) $q = \dfrac{p^2 + 0.35}{5}$;
 (f) $q = \frac{1}{5}(p + 0.35)^2$.

8 Freda Livingstone, exploring the country of Zambania (imaginary), decides to build a square house in the corner of a square garden (see Figure 1).

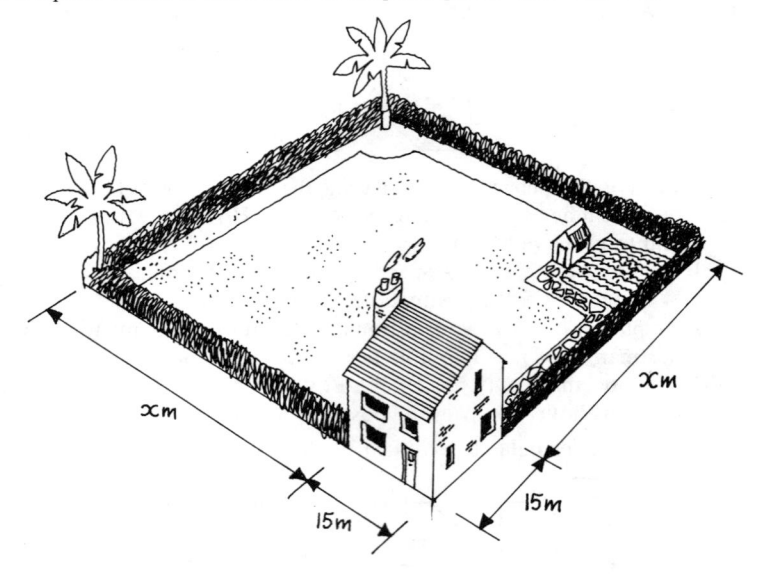

Figure 1

The ruler of that region demands tax (to be paid in cowrie shells) at the rate of one shell per square metre of the land taken up by her house and garden.
  (a) One wall of the house is to be 15 m long. If the extra length of garden is x m as shown, give a flow chart for working out the whole area of her square of land with the house in one corner.
  (b) Give a formula for the number of shells, N, Freda must pay in tax.
  (c) How many shells must she supply if $x = 25$?
  (d) If she has 900 cowrie shells, what length, x m, can she afford? What is then the area of garden, not including the house?

3. FORMULAE USING SEVERAL LETTERS

So far, our formulae have used two letters, for example:

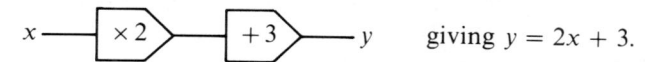

$$x \longrightarrow \boxed{\times 2} \longrightarrow \boxed{+3} \longrightarrow y \qquad \text{giving } y = 2x + 3.$$

x is the number we put in (the input), y is the result (the output).
Here are some examples of formulae with more than one input.

Example 8
The area of the rectangle shown is found by multiplying the length by the breadth.

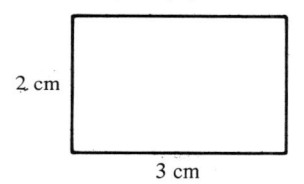

Figure 2

$3 \times 2 = 6.$ Area $= 6$ cm^2.

We could think in terms of a flow chart, for instance:

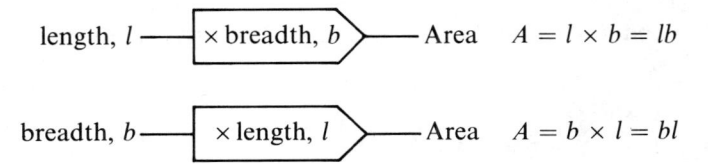

length, $l \longrightarrow \boxed{\times \text{breadth, } b} \longrightarrow$ Area $A = l \times b = lb$

or   breadth, $b \longrightarrow \boxed{\times \text{length, } l} \longrightarrow$ Area $A = b \times l = bl$

Of course 3×2 is the same as 2×3 and the formula could be written

$$A = lb \quad \text{or} \quad A = bl.$$

When there is more than one variable (letter), a flow chart is no longer particularly helpful and so will not be used.

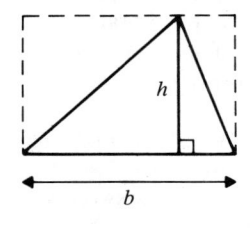

Figure 3

Example 9
The area, A, of the triangle shown is half the area of the rectangle containing it, that is $A = \frac{1}{2} \times b \times h$, which may be written $\frac{1}{2}bh$.

Notice that all the following versions of the formula come to the same thing:

$$A = \tfrac{1}{2}bh; \quad A = \tfrac{1}{2}hb; \quad A = \frac{bh}{2}; \quad A = \frac{hb}{2}; \quad A = bh/2; \quad A = hb/2.$$

If, for instance, $b = 5$ and $h = 6$, we can work out the area in any of these ways:

$A = \tfrac{1}{2}bh = \tfrac{1}{2} \times 5 \times 6 = (\tfrac{1}{2} \times 5) \times 6 = 2.5 \times 6 = 15$

$A = \tfrac{1}{2}bh = \tfrac{1}{2} \times 5 \times 6 = \tfrac{1}{2} \times (5 \times 6) = \tfrac{1}{2} \times 30 = 15$

$A = \tfrac{1}{2}hb = \tfrac{1}{2} \times 6 \times 5 = (\tfrac{1}{2} \times 6) \times 5 = 3 \times 5 = 15$

$A = \tfrac{1}{2}hb = \tfrac{1}{2} \times 6 \times 5 = \tfrac{1}{2} \times (6 \times 5) = \tfrac{1}{2} \times 30 = 15$

$A = \dfrac{bh}{2} = \dfrac{5 \times 6}{2} = \dfrac{30}{2} = 15$

$A = \dfrac{hb}{2} = \dfrac{6 \times 5}{2} = \dfrac{30}{2} = 15$

$A = bh/2 = b \times (h/2) = 5 \times (6/2) = 5 \times 3 = 15$

$A = hb/2 = h \times (b/2) = 6 \times (5/2) = 6 \times 2.5 = 15$

Example 11
If $c = 3$ and $d = 5$, calculate the values of $2cd$; cd^2; c^2d.

$2cd = 2 \times c \times d = 2 \times 3 \times 5 = 30;$
$cd^2 = c \times d \times d = 3 \times 5 \times 5 = 75;$
$c^2d = c \times c \times d = 3 \times 3 \times 5 = 45.$

Exercise C

*1 If I buy 7 oranges at 5p each, the bill is $7 \times 5p = 35p$.
   (a) Give a formula, as in Example 8, for working out the total bill B pence, if I buy n oranges at c pence each.
   (b) Calculate the total cost of 13 oranges costing 9p each.

2 If I have 6 gold coins each of mass 20 g, the total mass of gold is $6 \times 20\,\text{g} = 120\,\text{g}$.
   (a) Give a formula for working out the total mass of n gold coins each of mass m grams.
   (b) Calculate the total mass of 213 gold coins each of mass 37.5 g.

*3 The total bill for a bag of sweets was 75p. If there are 25 sweets in the bag, how much does each cost, assuming every sweet costs the same?
   Give a formula for working out the cost, c pence, of each sweet if the total bill is B pence and there are n sweets altogether.

4 5 friends share a Chinese meal, the total cost of which is £21. If the cost is divided equally, how much must each friend pay? Give a formula for working out the share, £s, that each person must pay if n people share a meal costing £p.

***5** In each of these formulae, work out the value of F, using your calculator to help you if you wish.
(a) $F = ab$ if $a = 5$ and $b = 7$;
(b) $F = cd$ if $c = 2.1$ and $d = 3.7$;
(c) $F = \dfrac{e}{f}$ if $e = 20$ and $f = 4$;
(d) $F = g/h$ if $g = 12.1$ and $h = 1.1$;
(e) $F = jkl$ if $j = 0.1$, $k = 10$, $l = 2$;
(f) $F = m^2n$ if $m = 5$ and $n = 3$;
(g) $F = mn^2$ if $m = 5$ and $n = 3$;
(h) $F = p^2/q$ if $p = 4$ and $q = 2$;
(i) $F = 3xy$ if $x = 2$ and $y = 4$;
(j) $F = \tfrac{1}{3}xy$ if $x = 6$ and $y = 9$;
(k) $F = 2s^2t$ if $s = 3$ and $t = 5$;
(l) $F = 2st^2$ if $s = 3$ and $t = 5$.

6 In each of the following formulae, work out the value of t, using your calculator to help you if you wish, where $p = 3.5$, $q = 0.7$ and $r = 0.5$.
(a) $t = pq$; (b) $t = p/q$;
(c) $t = p^2q$; (d) $t = pq^2$;
(e) $t = 2pq$; (f) $t = 2p^2q$;
(g) $t = 2pq^2$; (h) $t = 2p/q$;
(i) $t = \tfrac{1}{2}pq$; (j) $t = pqr$;
(k) $t = pq/r$; (l) $t = pq + qr + pr$.

SUMMARY

Here are examples of flow charts for formulae involving squares:

(a) p ⟶ [SQ] ⟶ [+2] ⟶ q

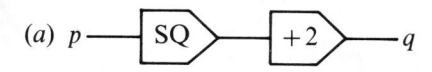

is written as a formula:

$q = p^2 + 2.$

(b) p ⟶ [+2] ⟶ [SQ] ⟶ q

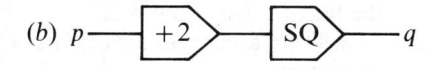

is written as a formula:

$q = (p + 2)^2.$

When several letters are involved in a formula, flow charts are no longer particularly helpful.

Formulae using squares

Summary exercise

1. In each part of this question start by writing a formula equivalent to the given flow chart.

   (a) $x \longrightarrow \boxed{-1.5} \longrightarrow \boxed{SQ} \longrightarrow y$ Calculate y if $x = 4.5$.

   (b) $y \longrightarrow \boxed{SQ} \longrightarrow \boxed{+2.4} \longrightarrow x$ Calculate x if $y = 3$.

2. Give flow charts for the following formulae.
   (a) $q = 3p^2 + 5$;
   (b) $q = 3(p + 5)^2$.
   For each formula, calculate q if $p = 2$.

3. For the formula $V = iR$ and $P = i^2R$, calculate V and P if $i = 3.2$ and $R = 1.5$.
4. If $V = \frac{1}{3}x^2y$, calculate V when $x = 4$ and $y = 6$.
5. Use the formula $A = \frac{1}{2}bh$ to find the area of a triangle of base 6.8 cm with height 10.7 cm.

Miscellaneous exercise

1. Write a flow chart for the formula
$$y = (3x - 2)^2 - 1.$$
Calculate y, (a) if $x = 3$; (b) if $x = 2$; (c) if $x = 1.5$.
Find a value of x which makes $y = 0$.

2. (a) If $p = (a + b)^2$, calculate p when $a = 5$ and $b = 3$.
   (b) If $q = (a - b)^2$, calculate q when $a = 5$ and $b = 3$.
   (c) If $r = 4ab$, calculate r when $a = 5$ and $b = 3$. Suggest a connection between p, q and r.
   Experiment with other values of a and b to check your idea.

3. If $s = ut + \frac{1}{2}at^2$, calculate s when $u = 3.5$, $t = 4$ and $a = 10$.
   With the values of u and a given, if $s > 200$, what can you say about t?

4. If $p = 3.5$ and $q = 5.3$ evaluate
$$pq; \quad p^2q; \quad pq^2; \quad p^2q + pq^2; \quad pq(p + q).$$
What do you notice about the last two results?
Try another pair of values of p and q.

5. The Highway Code gives braking distances for cars according to the formula
$$b = s + \frac{s^2}{20}$$
where s is the car's speed in m.p.h. and b is the braking distance in feet.
Calculate the braking distances where (a) $s = 30$ (in a built up area); (b) $s = 70$ (maximum speed on a dual carriageway or motorway).

25

Factors

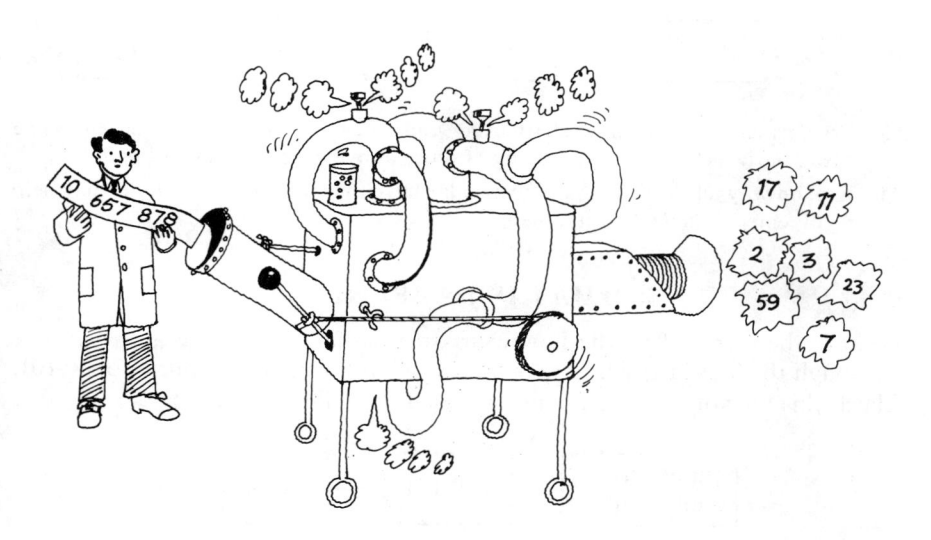

1. INTRODUCTION: A TRICK!

In this chapter we shall investigate breaking numbers down into their factors and, particularly, into prime factors. Most of the investigating will be found within the exercises. Start by working through this flow chart using your calculator. Remember that you should write down the output.

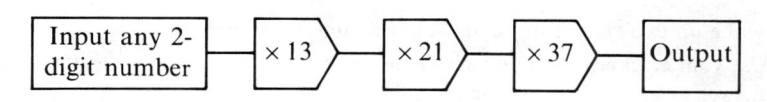

| Input any 2-digit number | → | ×13 | → | ×21 | → | ×37 | → | Output |

Now try it twice more, with different 2-digit numbers.
What output would it give if you started with 78,... or 26?
You can try this trick on your friends. The questions in Exercise A investigate this trick.

143

144   Factors   Ch. 25

Exercise A

*1   [Input any 2-digit number] → [× 259] → [× 39] → [Output]

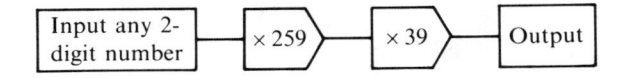

Work through this flow chart with two different inputs. Comment on your results. Guess the output for an input of 11.

*2   This flow chart is to have the same effect as that in question 1 but one of the boxes is incomplete. What number should replace the question mark?

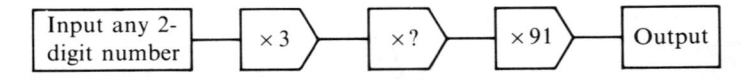

[Input any 2-digit number] → [× 3] → [× ?] → [× 91] → [Output]

*3   Try to make another flow chart using multiplications only, which has the same effect, but which is longer than any of those above. Is it the longest possible?

*4   Explain why all the flow charts met so far have the effect that they do. It may help if you enter a *single* digit number.

2. WHAT IS HAPPENING?

What is the secret of all the flow charts met so far? If you use an input of 1 (although the first instruction says otherwise) you will get an output of 10 101. Check this for yourself. You could write all these flow charts as

[Input any 2-digit number] → [× 10 101] → [Output]

But this is obviously a give-away!

Exercise B investigates a flow chart that will convert 253 into 253 253 and 927 into 927 927 etc.

Exercise B

*1   Use your calculator to work out:
$$127\,127 \div 127 \quad \text{and}$$
$$253\,253 \div 253.$$
Make up two similar divisions yourself, and work them out.

*2   Use your calculator to find two whole numbers which multiply together to give the answer to question 1. Now make a flow chart using these numbers which will convert 179 into 179 179 and 543 into 543 543

3   Investigate whether there are any flow charts different from the one you used in question 2 but which have the same effect.

4   Make a flow chart which will convert 132 into 264 264 and 413 into 826 826 etc. Find the output for an input of 613. Is the flow chart still working?

3. WHY IT WORKS

The secret of the flow charts in the introduction and Exercise A was in knowing which numbers you need to multiply together to give 10 101. For instance:

$$13 \times 21 \times 37 = 10\ 101$$

and

$$259 \times 39 = 10\ 101.$$

As you already know, each of the numbers 13, 21, 37, 39, 259 is called a factor of 10 101. This is because each of them divides into 10 101 a whole number of times:

$$10\ 101 \div 13 = 777$$
$$10\ 101 \div 21 = 481$$
$$10\ 101 \div 37 = 273$$
$$10\ 101 \div 39 = 259$$

and

$$10\ 101 \div 259 = 39$$

Check these on your calculator.

If you divide 10 101 by 53, say, you will get 190.584 905 7 (or something very near) displayed on your calculator. This means that 53 is *not* a factor of 10 101 because the result is *not* a whole number. You have only found a factor when your calculator gives you a whole number result.

Each time you find a factor, you automatically get another one at the same time. For instance, since

$$10\ 101 \div 13 = 777,$$

it follows that $10\ 101 \div 777 = 13.$

So $10\ 101 = 13 \times 777.$

13 and 777 are a *factor-pair* of 10 101. (777 and 13 are the same factor-pair.) This could be illustrated by a rectangle of dots with 13 along one side and 777 along the other.

Exercise C

*1 (a) Use your calculator to find which of the following are true.
    (i) 24 is a factor of 720;
    (ii) 13 is a factor of 5885;
    (iii) 21 is a factor of 365;
    (iv) 83 is a factor of 5146;
    (v) 27 is a factor of 629.
  (b) Write down the factor-pair for each true statement in (a).

2 Use your results from Exercise B to list the factors of 1001. For each factor write down the appropriate factor-pair.

*3 (a) Find a factor-pair for 777. Call this pair *i* and *j*.
  (b) Find a factor-pair for 13. Call this pair *k* and *l*.
  (c) Now find a factor-pair for each of *i*, *j*, *k*, *l*.
  (d) Is there any end to this process?

4 (a) Find a factor-pair for 259. Call this pair *m* and *n*.
  (b) Find a factor-pair for 39. Call this pair *p* and *q*.
  (c) Now find a factor pair for each of *m, n, p, q*.
  (d) Is there any end to this process?

*5 (a) Find all the factor-pairs of
   (i) 36; (ii) 48; (iii) 25; (iv) 52; (v) 57; (vi) 81; (vii) 64; (viii) 53;
   (ix) 96; (x) 47.
  (b) Which of the numbers in (a) have just one factor-pair?

6 Spot the number! Find:
  (a) a three-digit number less than 500 with factors of 17 and 21;
  (b) a two-digit number over 80 with factors of 3 and 8;
  (c) a three-digit number whose second digit is 1, with factors of 24 and 17.

*7 (a) A number has 4, 9 and 7 as factors. Which of the following must be true?
   (i)   2 is a factor;
   (ii) 8 is a factor;
   (iii) 36 is a factor;
   (iv) 63 is a factor;
   (v)   35 is a factor.
  (b) What is the smallest number with 4, 9 and 7 as factors?

8 A number has 3, 4, 8 and 9 as factors.
  (a) Give four other factors it must have.
  (b) What is the smallest number with these factors?

9 13, 21, 39 and 91 are all factors of 10 101.

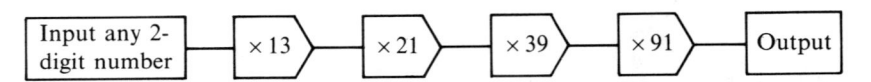

| Input any 2-digit number | × 13 | × 21 | × 39 | × 91 | Output |

Try this flow chart with some easy inputs. Try to explain what happens.

10 (a) Is 1 a factor of 10 101?
  (b) Is 1 a factor of (i) 53; (ii) 197; (iii) 217 549?
  (c) What is suggested by the results of (a) and (b)?

4. PRIME NUMBERS

We can only find one factor-pair for 19, namely 1 and 19. 19 is not a rectangle number and can only be represented by a single line of dots. You will remember from Chapter 21 that we call such numbers *prime* numbers. We do not call 1 itself a prime number. You will soon see why.

The first few prime numbers are 2, 3, 5, 7, 11. You can find all the prime numbers less than 100 using the 'Sieve of Eratosthenes'.

2 is the first prime number. Multiples of 2 (4, 6, 8, 10, . . .) cannot be prime. We can therefore delete them from Table 1.

Finding all the factors of a number

1	2	3	4	5	6	7	8	9	10
11	12	13	14	15	16	17	18	19	20
21	22	23	24	25	26	27	28	29	30
31	32	33	34	35	36	37	38	39	40
41	42	43	44	45	46	47	48	49	50
51	52	53	54	55	56	57	58	59	60
61	62	63	64	65	66	67	68	69	70
71	72	73	74	75	76	77	78	79	80
81	82	83	84	85	86	87	88	89	90
91	92	93	94	95	96	97	98	99	100

Table 1

Exercise D

Attempt all questions, in order.
1. Make a copy of Table 1, showing numbers from 1 to 100, or, to save time, place a piece of tracing paper over Table 1 in your textbook. Put a ring round 2, and delete 4, 6, 8, ... etc.
2. Move on to the first number which has not been deleted, i.e. 3. Now put a ring round 3, and delete all the multiples of 3. (Some will already be deleted.)
3. 4 has been deleted so move on to 5. Continue in this way until no further deletions are possible.
4. Use the resulting table to give a list of all the prime numbers less than 100.
5. If you had counted 1 as a prime number, and then deleted all the multiples of 1, what would have happened? Why, then, do we say that 1 is not a prime number?

5. FINDING ALL THE FACTORS OF A NUMBER

As we know, if a number greater than 1 is not a prime number, it is a rectangle number. Rectangle numbers are often called *composite* because they are composed of two or more factors.

Suppose we want to find all the factors of 42. We might start by noticing that 42 is even. This means that 42 has 2 as a factor and we have

$$42 = 2 \times 21.$$

So 21 is also a factor of 42.

Next we might recognise that 21 is in the 3 times table. In fact $21 = 3 \times 7$. So we can write

$$42 = 2 \times 3 \times 7.$$

We stop here, because 2, 3 and 7 are all prime numbers.

However 42 has factors which are not prime numbers, for example 21 which we found above. Once we have all the *prime* factors we can find all the other factors.

We can see that 6 is also a factor because

$$42 = \boxed{2 \times 3} \times 7 \quad \text{and} \quad 2 \times 3 = 6.$$

Also
$$42 = 2 \times \boxed{3 \times 7} \quad \text{and} \quad 3 \times 7 = 21$$

producing the factor 21 which we already knew.

We have not finished because 14 is a factor as well:

$$42 = \boxed{2 \times 3 \times 7} \quad \text{and} \quad 2 \times 7 = 14.$$

Finally, and obviously, 42 itself is a factor. So is 1!

$$42 = 1 \times 42$$

So if we can write a number as a product of prime numbers, it is easy to find all its factors. The set of factors of 42 is

$$\{1, 2, 3, 6, 7, 14, 21, 42\}$$

Exercise E

*1 Find the sets of factors of
    (a) 12; (b) 18; (c) 36; (d) 81.

*2 (a) $770 = 2 \times 5 \times 7 \times 11$ (check this!). So 2, 5, 7 and 11 are factors of 770. Find three other factors, and check them with your calculator. Is 154 a factor? How could you tell without a calculator?

    (b) Similarly, given that

$$255 = 3 \times 5 \times 17$$

find three factors of 255 (other than 3, 5 and 17!).

    (c) $128 = 2 \times 2 \times 2 \times 2 \times 2 \times 2 \times 2$. Find three factors of 128.

*3 Find a number which fits these clues:
   (a) 2 is a factor;
   (b) 8 is a factor;
   (c) 16 is not a factor;
   (d) 14 is a factor.
   What is the smallest number which fits these clues? Do you need all of the clues?

4 Here are some clues about a number:
   (a) it is less than 1000;
   (b) 91 is a factor;
   (c) 35 is a factor;
   (d) 65 is a factor.
   Can you find the number? Do you need to use all the clues? (Hint: find the factors of 91, 35 and 65 first.)

*5 The complete set of factors of 6 is 1, 2, 3 and 6. If we add them up (except for the 6) we get
$$1 + 2 + 3 = 6,$$
the number we started with.
   We call numbers which are the sum of all their factors (except the number itself) *perfect numbers*. So 6 is a perfect number.
   (a) Is 12 perfect?
   (b) Is 20 perfect?
   (c) There is another perfect number less than 30. Find it.

6 Choose any three consecutive numbers, and multiply them together.
   Is 3 a factor of the result?
   Is 6 a factor of the result?
   Is 12 a factor of the result?
   Repeat this four times and try to explain the answers. State a general rule.

*7 Choose any four consecutive numbers and multiply them together (e.g. $12 \times 13 \times 14 \times 15$). Are there any numbers which *must* be factors of the result? Find them.

Questions 8–10 concern divisibility by 3.

8 When we add up the digits of a number the result is called the *digit-sum* of that number. The process can be repeated until we get a single digit that we shall call the *final digit-sum* of the number we started with.
   For example, starting with 9586 we have
$$9 + 5 + 8 + 6 = 28 \quad \text{(first digit sum)}$$
   then 28 gives
$$2 + 8 = 10$$
$$1 + 0 = 1 \quad \text{(final digit-sum)}.$$
   (a) Find the final digit-sum of
      (i) 56; (ii) 151; (ii) 4128; (iv) 857; (v) 19 165.
   (b) Take each number in (a) and multiply it by 3. Find the final digit-sums of the results.
   (c) Make a general statement which seems to be true about the final digit-sums of numbers which have 3 as a factor.

*9 The results of question 8 form the basis of a test for divisibility by 3, in other words whether or not 3 is a factor of a number. If the final digit-sum is 3, 6 or 9 (i.e. is divisible by 3) then 3 is a factor of the original number.

For example, starting with 7825 we have
$$7 + 2 + 8 + 5 = 22$$
$$2 + 2 = 4.$$

Now 4 is not divisible by 3 so 3 is not a factor of 7825.

Test to see which of the following numbers have a factor of 3.

(a) 381; (b) 9072; (c) 1124; (d) 8 000 002;
(e) 111; (f) 6073; (g) 4472; (h) 92 220.

10 A simpler way to test whether or not 3 is a factor of a number is just to find the first digit sum and see whether this is divisible by 3.

For example, starting with 56 738.
$$5 + 6 + 7 + 3 + 8 = 29$$

Now 29 is not divisible by 3 so 56 738 is also not divisible by 3. Use this shorter test to see which of the following numbers have a factor of 3.

(a) 473; (b) 3975; (c) 4 000 001; (d) 222 222; (e) 33 333 333 332.

6. FACTOR TREES

One way to write 2145 as a product of prime factors is to proceed as follows. It is obvious that 2145 is a multiple of the prime number 5. By division we get

$$2145 \div 5 = 429.$$

We write this result in the form of a *factor-tree*.

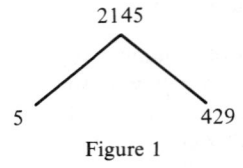

```
      2145
      /  \
     5    429
```

Figure 1

We now have to find the factors of 429. This number is odd and so the prime number 2 is not a factor. We test to see if the next prime number, 3, is a factor. Using the idea from question 10 in Exercise E we see that it is. By division we have

$$429 \div 3 = 143.$$

We now extend our tree.

```
        2145
       /    \
      5     429
           /   \
          3    143
```
Figure 2

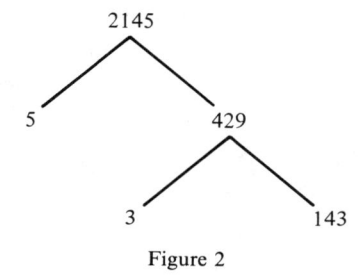

We now need to find the factors of 143. We can eliminate 2 and 5, also 3 by using the digit-sum again. By trial 7 is not a factor and we do not try 8 or 9 or 10. (Why not?) Dividing by 11, however, gives

$$143 = 11 \times 13.$$

As 13 is also prime we have finished and can write a final factor-tree.

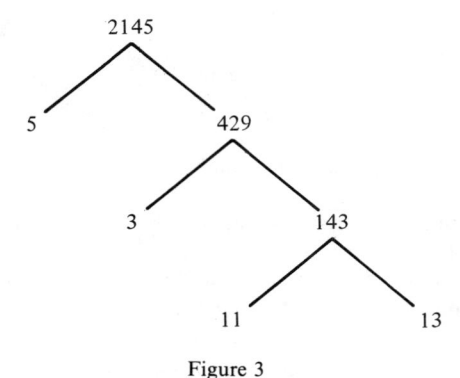

```
        2145
       /    \
      5     429
           /   \
          3    143
              /   \
             11   13
```
Figure 3

Using the factor-tree we can now write 2145 as a product of prime factors

$$2145 = 3 \times 5 \times 11 \times 13.$$

Notice that the prime factors are the numbers at the end of the branches.

Exercise F

*1 Use factor trees to write each of the following numbers as a product of prime factors.
   (a) 65; (b) 28; (c) 87; (d) 120; (e) 275.

152 Factors Ch. 25

2 Here are two ways of starting a tree for 350. Which one gives the quicker result?

```
      350                    350
     /   \                  /   \
   10     35               2    175
```
Figure 4

3 Here is part of a tree. Copy and complete it:

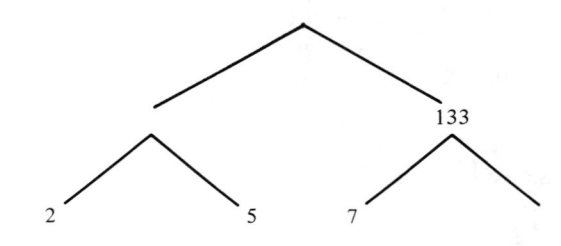

```
              /    \
             /      \
            /\      133
           /  \    /   \
          2    5  7
```
Figure 5

*4 (a) How can you tell that the number $2 \times 2 \times 3 \times 3 \times 11 \times 11$ is a square number?
  (b) What is the square root of the number in (a)? (If the square root of a number N is a then $a \times a = N$.)
  (c) Work out $3 \times 3 \times 5 \times 5 \times 5 \times 5$ on your calculator. What is the square root of the number? Check this on your calculator.

*5 (a) Give factor trees for (i) 676; (ii) 1089; (iii) 1764.
  (b) Write each number as a product of primes.
  (c) Use (b) to find the square root of each of the numbers in (a).
  (d) Check that your answers are correct using your calculator.

6 (a) Find the factor tree for 216.
  (b) What is the *cube root* of 216? (If the cube root is a, then $a \times a \times a = 216$.)

7 (a) The number $2 \times p \times q \times 7 \times 13 \times r$ is a square number. Suggest values for p, q and r.
  (b) Are there any other values of p, q and r which would work?

*8 (a) Write each of these numbers as a product of prime factors:
      (i) 10; (ii) 100; (iii) 1000; (iv) 10 000; (v) 100 000; (vi) 1 000 000.
      Which ones are square numbers and which are not?
  (b) Write 40 as a product of prime factors.
  (c) Use your answers to (a) and (b) to find r, where $40 \times r = 1000$.
  (d) The fraction $\frac{7}{40}$ is equivalent to the fraction $\frac{t}{1000}$. What is the value of t?
  (e) Work out $7 \div 40$ on your calculator.

9 (a) If $\dfrac{11}{20} = \dfrac{x}{100}$, find x.
   (b) Work out $11 \div 20$ on your calculator.
   (c) If $\dfrac{13}{125} = \dfrac{y}{1000}$, find y.
   (d) Work out $13 \div 125$ on your calculator.

SUMMARY

Since 72 can be divided exactly by 12, we say that 12 is a factor of 72. In general if a can be divided exactly by b, we say that b is a factor of a.

Since $72 = 6 \times 12$, we call 6 and 12 a factor-pair of 72. If the whole numbers a and b have product n, then a and b are a factor-pair of n.

If a number greater than one has just one factor-pair, then it is a prime number. Every whole number greater than one is either a prime number or a composite number.

The first few prime numbers are 2, 3, 5, 7, 11, 13, 17, 19.

We can test for factors using a calculator, but
– some factors can be found by inspection (e.g. 2, 5);
– a factor of 3 can be detected by a simple test on the digit sum of the number.

Summary exercise

1 Find the prime factors of 111. Use the result to make a flow chart which converts 5 into 555, 7 into 777 etc.

2 Find the prime factors of 111 111. Use the result to make a flow chart which converts 3 into 333 333 etc.

3 Which of the following are true?
   (a) 25 is a factor of 175.   (b) 37 is a factor of 8917.
   (c) 65 is a factor of 779.   (d) 7, 11 and 13 are factors of 9009.

4 (a) What is the smallest number with factors of 12, 15 and 10?
   (b) Why is the answer to (a) not $12 \times 15 \times 10$?

5 (a) Find the factor trees of
       (i) 2205;   (ii) 7436.
   (b) $2205 \times p$ and $7436 \times q$ are both square numbers and p and q are both prime. What are the values of p and q?

6 Find an equivalent fraction to $\frac{91}{625}$ whose denominator is 10 000.

Miscellaneous exercise

1. We call multiplying by 4 'quadrupling'. When you quadruple a square number you seem to get another square number; for instance

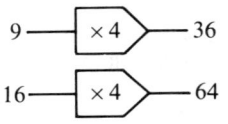

    $9 \longrightarrow \boxed{\times 4} \longrightarrow 36$

    $16 \longrightarrow \boxed{\times 4} \longrightarrow 64$

    and 36 and 64 are square numbers.
    - (a) Try some more examples. Does it still work?
    - (b) Try to explain why it works.
    - (c) Does multiplying a square number by 9 give another square number?
    - (d) Suggest other multipliers which always give square number results when you start with a square number.

2. $18 \times 8 = 144$. Neither 18 nor 8 is a square number, but 144 is. Can you find other examples. When does this work?

3. Can you find a square number which is exactly double another square number? Think about the prime factors. (25 and 49, 144 and 289 are near misses!)

4. Find the prime factors of
    (a) 111; (b) 1111; (c) 11 111; (d) 111 111; (e) 1 111 111.

5. Work out 142 857 × 7 on your calculator. Use the result and one of the results of question 4 to give the prime factors of 142 857.

6. (a) Choose a pair of consecutive single digit numbers, multiply them together, and then add 11. Find the factors of the result.
    (b) Repeat this a few times. What do you notice?
    (c) Does it work for 2-digit consecutive pairs?

7. (a) Choose a pair of consecutive numbers not too large, multiply them together and then add 41. Find the factors of the result.
    (b) Repeat four times (with different pairs of numbers!).
    (c) What do you notice about the numbers you get?
    (d) Why will it not always work?

8. Add up the first, third, fifth, ... etc. digits of a number and then add up the second, fourth ... etc. digits. Then find the difference between these two totals.
    The result in the case of 2381 is $(2 + 8) - (3 + 1)$, which is 6.
    (a) Find the result in the case of the following:
        (i) 5432; (ii) 2563; (iii) 687; (iv) 4112; (v) 7439; (vi) 824 629.
    (b) Take each number in (a), multiply it by 11, and find the result of applying the above technique to the answers you get.
    (c) Make a general statement about the digits of numbers which have 11 as a factor.

9. Find, without using your calculator, which of these numbers are divisible by 11:
    (a) 1221; (b) 4235; (c) 3795; (d) 19 327.
    Now test them on your calculator.

10. Use the digit-sum idea (used for testing whether 3 is a factor) to develop a test to see whether 9 is a factor of a number.

Quickies 8

CLOSED BOOK

Calculators must not be used.
1. Which number, when squared, gives 121?
2. What is 2.7 divided by 0.9?
3. What is the total area of the faces of a cube of edge 2 cm?
4. What is the value of $2p^2$ when $p = 3$?
5. Sandra spends one-third of her pocket money on a book and one-quarter of it on some biscuits. What fraction is left?
6. What is the value of $^-8 - {}^-2$?
7. I think of a number, x, square it and then subtract 3. Write down an expression for the result.
8. How many lines of symmetry has a rhombus?
9. A rectangle has a length of 16 cm and an area of 40 cm². What is its width?
10. What is my average speed if I walk 28 miles in 8 hours?

OPEN BOOK

Calculators must not be used.
1. Give the formula represented by the flow chart:

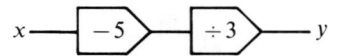

    $x \longrightarrow \boxed{-5} \longrightarrow \boxed{\div 3} \longrightarrow y$

2. With reference to Figure 1, what is the value of a?

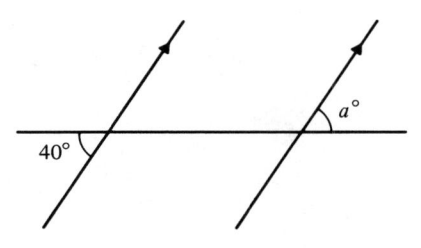

    Figure 1

3. The bearing of A from B is 120°. What is the bearing of B from A?

Quickies 8

4. Jason spends $\frac{1}{4}$ hour on his mathematics homework, $\frac{1}{2}$ hour on his English and then $\frac{1}{3}$ hour on his French. How many minutes does he spend altogether?
5. Arrange the following in order of size, smallest first:
$$0.51, \quad \tfrac{1}{2}, \quad \tfrac{2}{5}, \quad 0.498.$$
6. Remove the brackets from $5(m - 2n)$.
7. Estimate the value of 489×0.93 to the nearest ten.
8. State a fraction lying between $\frac{3}{4}$ and $\frac{5}{6}$.
9. A darts player scores 'treble 19' with each of his three darts. What is his total score?
10. Write down the next two terms in the sequence:
$$1, 2, 0, 3, {}^-1, 4, {}^-2, \ldots, \ldots$$

Revision exercises 8A, 8B

REVISION EXERCISE 8A

1 Without using a calculator, *estimate*:
   (a) the total cost of 4 dozen 'ocean sticks' at 18p each;
   (b) the price per gallon of petrol at a time when 23 gallons cost £40.89.
2 Find the angles indicated by letters in the diagrams of Figure 1

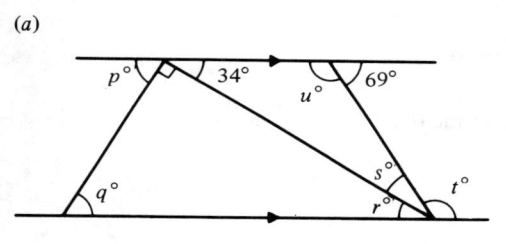

(a)

(b)

Figure 1

3 Write in their simplest form:

$$\frac{18}{27}, \frac{35}{40}, \frac{49}{56}, \frac{77}{121}, \frac{36}{84}$$

4 Give flow charts for the following formulae. In each case find the output for the given input.
   (a) $v = u^2 - 6$, input 7;
   (b) $v = (u - 6)^2$, input 7;
   (c) $v = 2u^2 - 6$, input 7;
   (d) $k = 5(h + 4)^2$, input 0.3;
   (e) $k = \frac{1}{5}(h + 4)^2$, input 0.3.
5 In each of the diagrams in Figure 2 give the bearing of P from Q.

(a)

(b)

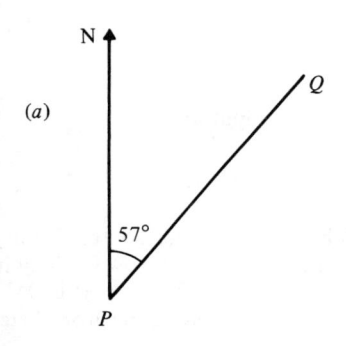

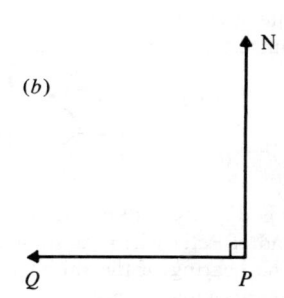

Figure 2

REVISION EXERCISE 8B

1 Find the areas of the quadrilaterals in the diagrams of Figure 3.

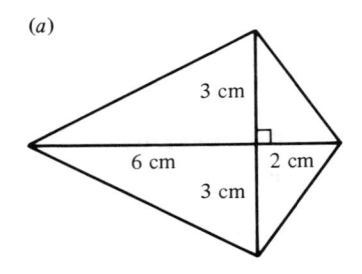

(a)

(b)

Figure 3

2 Find the angles indicated by letters in the diagrams of Figure 4.

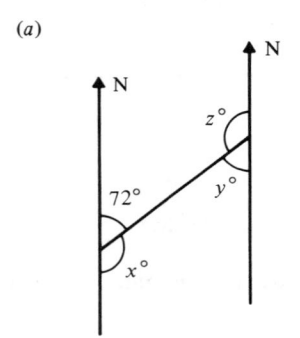

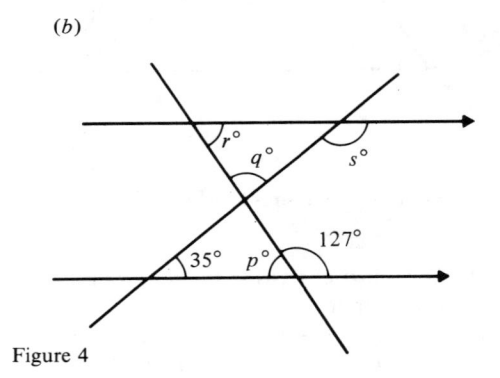

(a)

(b)

Figure 4

3 Copy and complete the two following lists of equivalent fractions.

(a) $\frac{1}{3} = \frac{2}{} = \frac{}{12} = \frac{5}{} = \frac{}{33}$;

(b) $\frac{3}{4} = \frac{}{12} = \frac{12}{} = \frac{}{24} = \frac{27}{}$.

4 For each of the flow charts (a) and (b) give:
   (i) an equivalent formula;
   (ii) the output for the given value of the input.

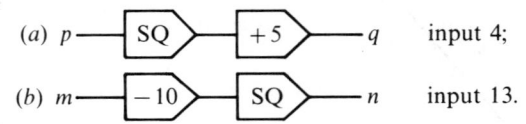

    (a) p ⟶ SQ ⟶ +5 ⟶ q input 4;

    (b) m ⟶ −10 ⟶ SQ ⟶ n input 13.

5 Peter and his dog are walking along a path which runs due north–south. The dog is 20 m ahead of Peter when she spots a rabbit sitting outside its burrow washing its whiskers. The bearing of the rabbit from the dog is 070° and from Peter is 042°. Make a scale drawing to show this and find the distances of the rabbit from Peter and from his dog.

26
Volume

A happy Boxoid
from the planet
Voluminus

1. INTRODUCTION

Figure 1 (below) shows some *nets* of a cube. These are formed by squares and should be drawn on some thick paper, or card, cut out and folded to form a cube. Some of the tabs required for glueing have been shown but many have been left out. One tab (only one) is needed where two edges join.

(a)

(b)

(c)

(d)

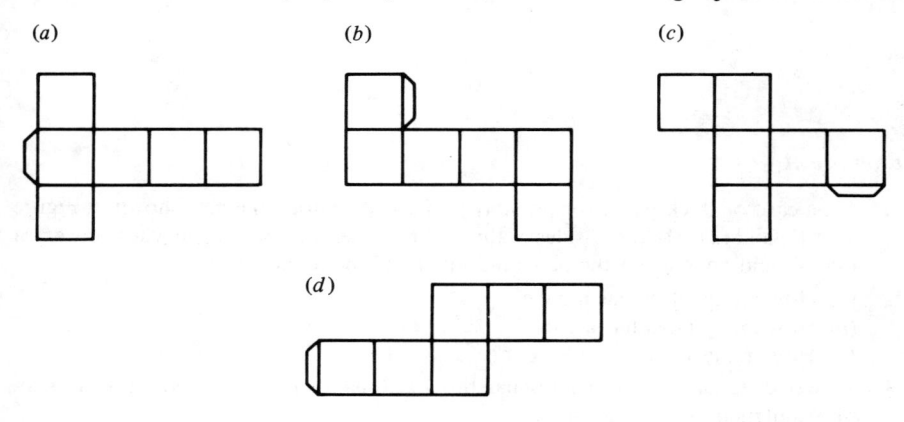

Figure 1

159

160   Volume   Ch. 26

Figure 2 shows how the net in Figure 1(a) can be folded up to form a cube.

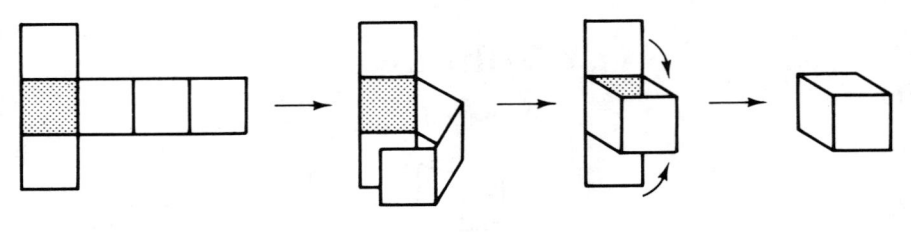

Figure 2

Strictly speaking, a cube is a solid object, whose faces are all squares. Figure 2 outlines the making of a cubical box and the card forms the *surface of a cube*. However, in practice, the word cube is often used to mean either the solid or the surface.

Figure 3

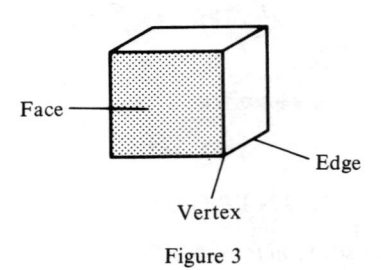

Figure 3 shows a cube and illustrates the use of the words *face*, *edge* and *vertex* in connection with the cube.

Exercise A

1   On a card or thick paper (or possibly graph paper) draw the nets shown in Figure 1(b), (c) and (d). Make the sides of the squares at least 2 cm. Decide where the extra tabs should go, cut out the nets (and tabs) and make the cubes.

*2 (a) How many edges has a cube?
    (b) How many faces has a cube?
    (c) How many vertices has a cube?

3   Answer question 2 for a rectangular box (such as a shoe box) where the faces are all rectangular rather than square.

4 On graph paper draw a net for a rectangular box which measures 4 cm long, 3 cm wide and 2 cm high.

2. VOLUME

In Chapter 22 area was said to be the amount of space taken up by a plane shape. Similarly *volume* is the amount of space taken up by a solid object. To indicate the size of a plane shape (typically a rectangle) we need two measurements, length and breadth. For this reason plane shapes are said to be *two-dimensional*. For a solid object (typically a rectangular block) we need a third measurement, the height, and, therefore, solid objects are said to be *three-dimensional*.

When discussing area it was decided to use a square as the basic unit of measurement, for example 1 cm². Similarly volume is measured in terms of a cube as a basic unit, for example 1 cm³ (or 1 cubic centimetre).

A cube with edges 1 cm in length is a unit cube with a volume of 1 cm³.

Two such cubes put together would have a volume of 2 cm³.

A rectangular box of size 2 cm × 1 cm × 1 cm has the same volume of 2 cm³.

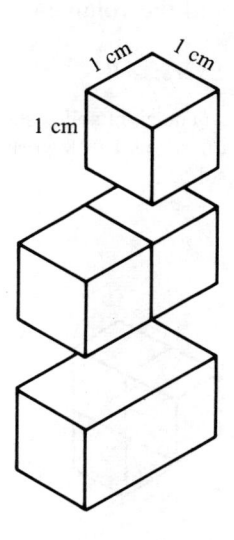

Figure 4

Example 1
Find the volume of a rectangular block of wood measuring 5 cm long, 3 cm wide and 2 cm high.

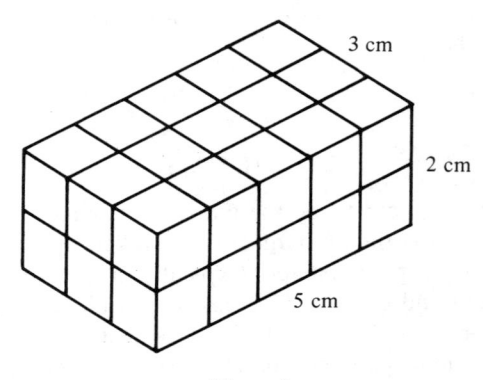

162   Volume   Ch. 26

Figure 5

Figure 5 shows the block of wood and divisions into unit cubes. The top layer contains 3 rows of 5 cubes. There are 2 layers. So the total number of cubes is

$$3 \times 5 \times 2 = 30$$

and the volume is therefore 30 cm^3.

Exercise B

The eight solids shown in Figure 6 are made up of unit cubes of side 1 cm. In each of questions 1 to 8 work out the number of unit cubes and write down the volume of each solid.

*1

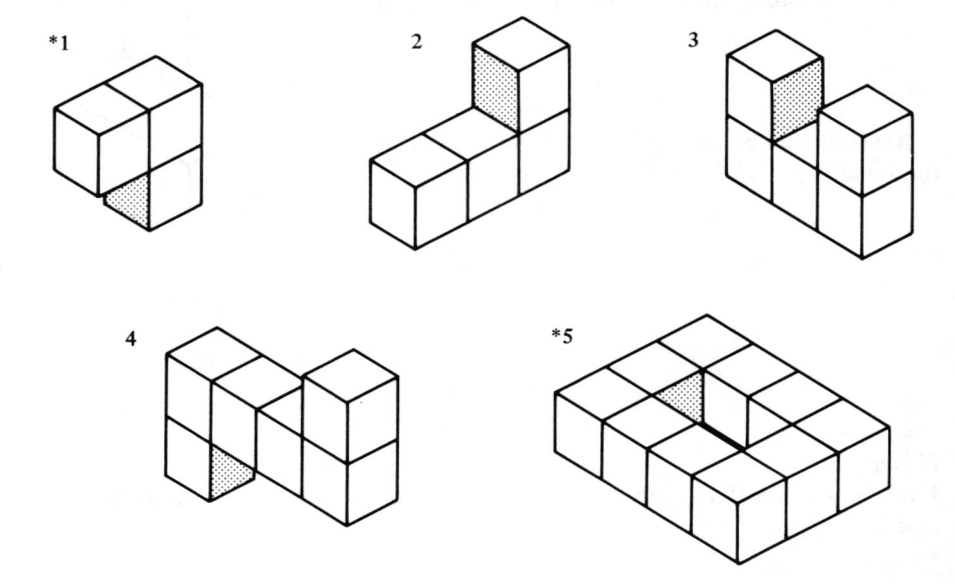

2

3

4

*5

6

7

*8

Figure 6

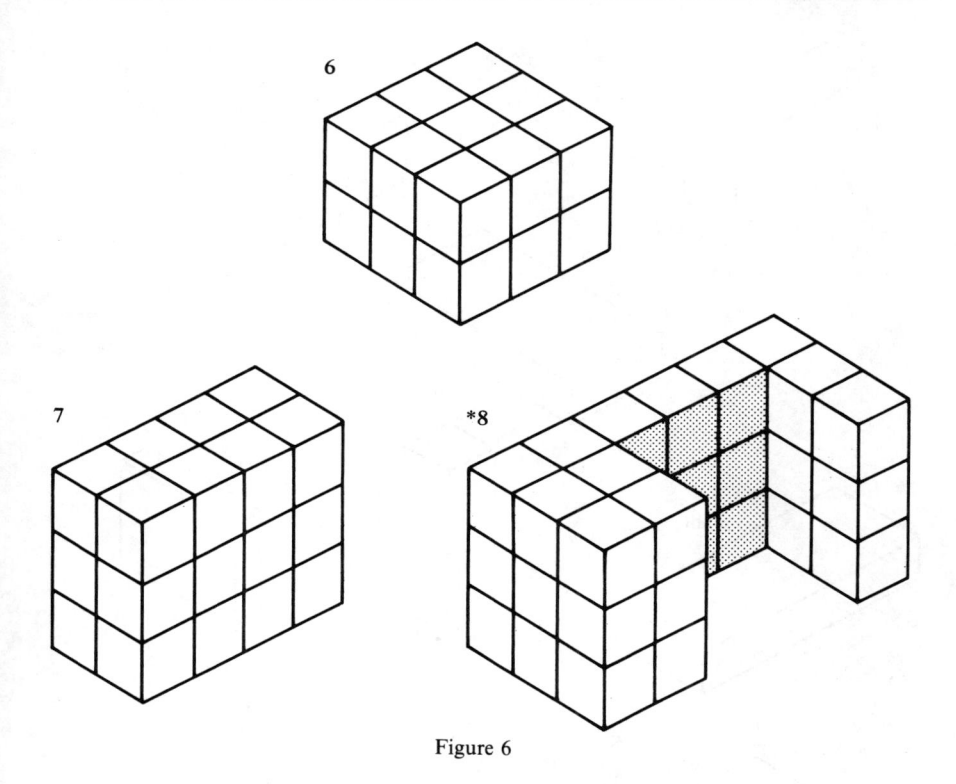

In questions 9 to 20 find the volumes of the solids shown in Figure 7.

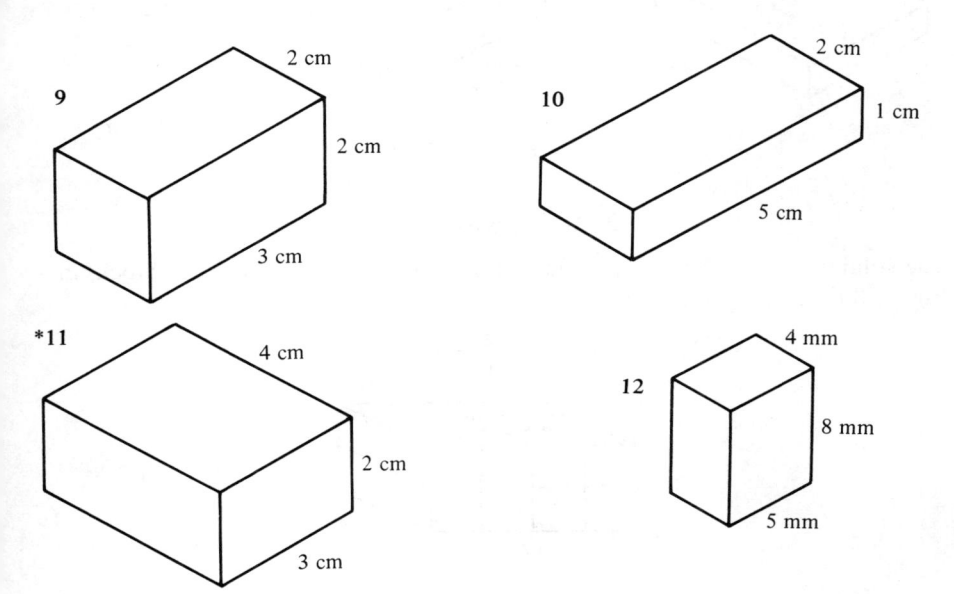

9   2 cm, 2 cm, 3 cm

10   2 cm, 1 cm, 5 cm

*11   4 cm, 2 cm, 3 cm

12   4 mm, 8 mm, 5 mm

164 Volume   Ch. 26

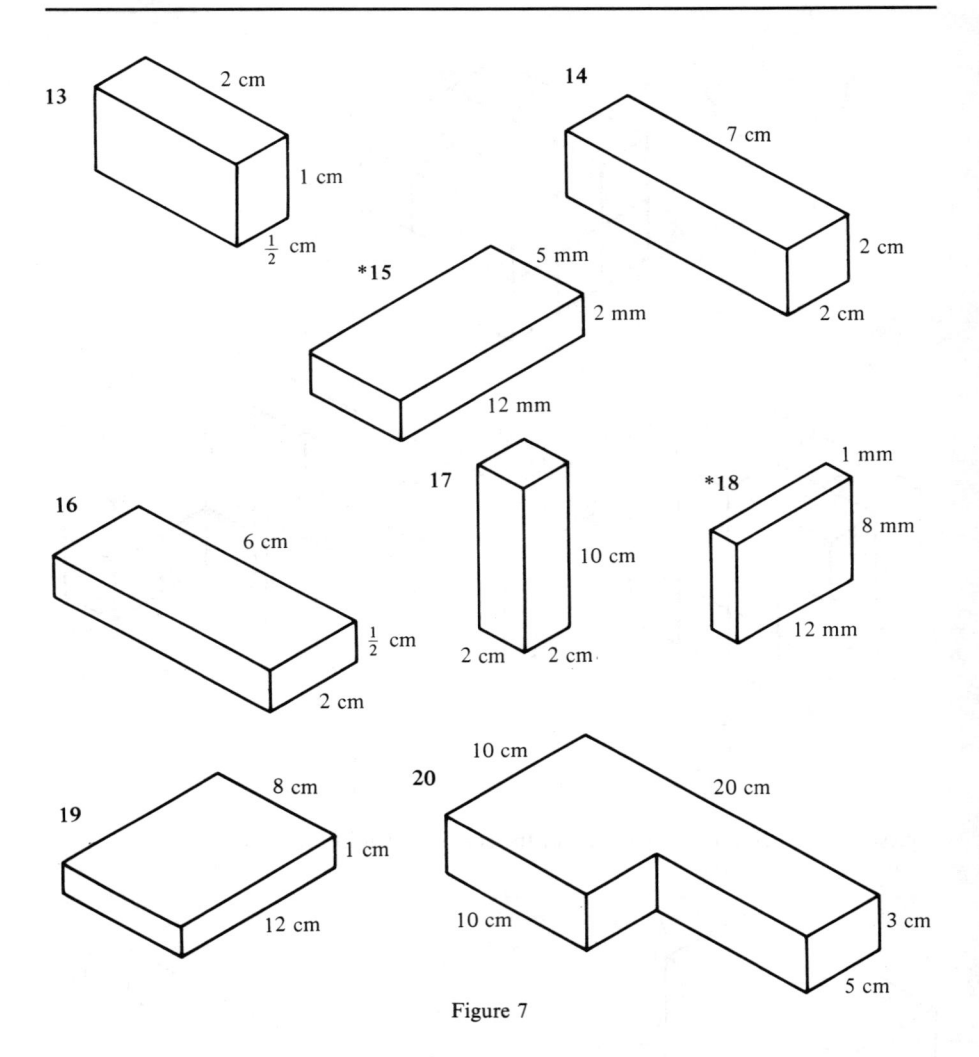

Figure 7

3. A FORMULA

The volume of the *cuboid* (mathematical name for a rectangular faced block) in Figure 8 can easily be seen to be

$$2 \times 4 \times 3 \text{ cm}^3 = 24 \text{ cm}^3.$$

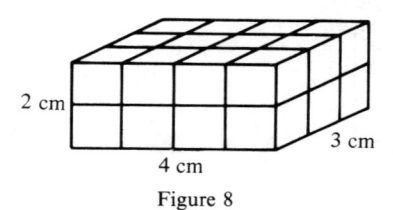

Figure 8

A formula 165

The volume is obtained by multiplying together the length, width and height of the cuboid. As a formula (see Figure 9)

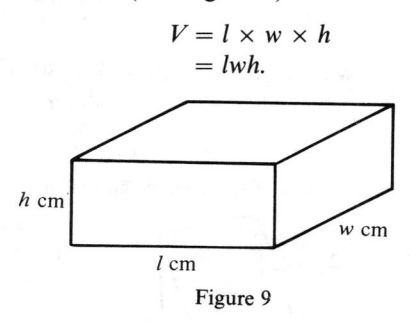

$$V = l \times w \times h$$
$$= lwh.$$

h cm
w cm
l cm
Figure 9

Example 2
Find the volume of a cuboid measuring 2 m × 3.5 m × 0.5 m.

Here the lengths are in metres and the volume will be measured in m³ (cubic metres).

$$V = lwh = 2 \times 3.5 \times 0.5$$
$$= 3.5.$$

The volume is 3.5 m³.

Example 3
Calculate the volume of the wedge shown in Figure 10.

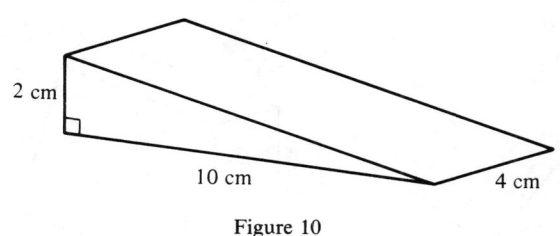

2 cm
10 cm
4 cm
Figure 10

The volume of the wedge is half that of the cuboid which encloses it, as indicated by broken lines in Figure 11.

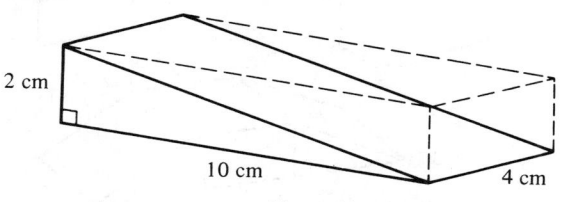

2 cm
10 cm
4 cm
Figure 11

166 Volume Ch. 26

$$\text{For the cuboid: } V = lwh$$
$$= 2 \times 10 \times 4$$
$$= 80$$

Thus, for the wedge, the volume $= \frac{1}{2} \times 80 \text{ cm}^3$
$= 40 \text{ cm}^3$.

Exercise C

In questions 1–5 calculate the volumes of the wedges shown in Figure 12. All lengths are in cm.

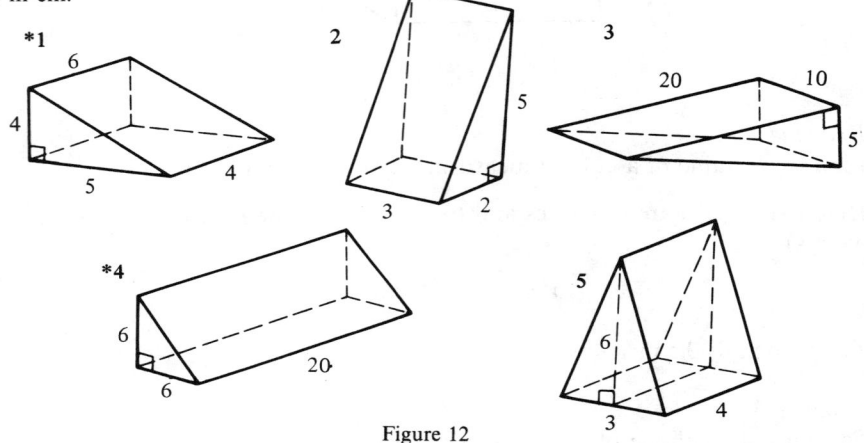

Figure 12

In questions 6–10 calculate the volumes of the solids shown in Figure 13. All lengths are in cm.

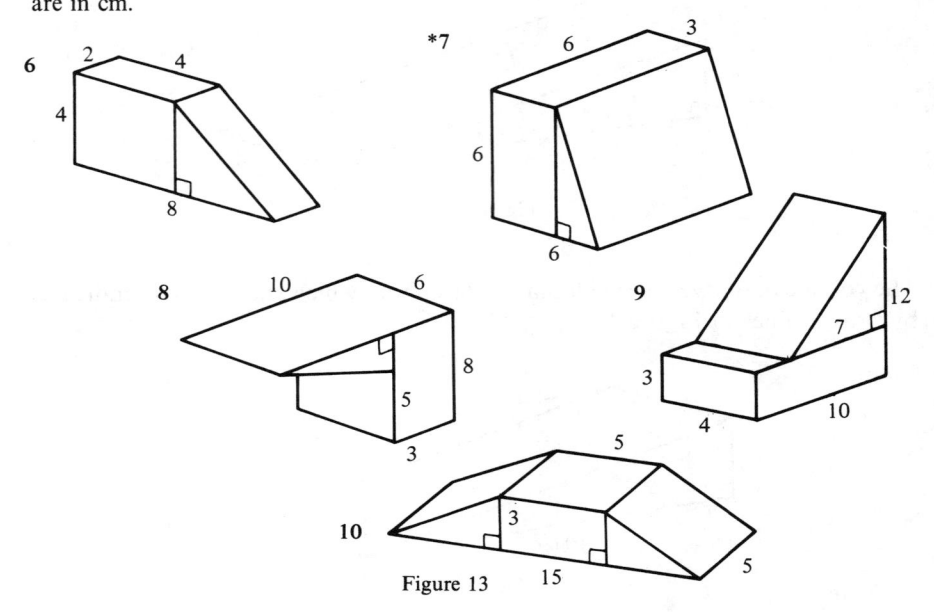

Figure 13

11 Figure 14 shows a house built on ground that is 2 m above the level of the road. A drive 3 m wide is constructed by removing the earth indicated by broken lines. Calculate the volume of earth to be moved.

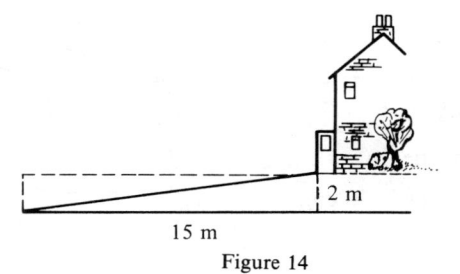

Figure 14

12 Calculate the volume of water in the paddling pool shown in Figure 15. The pool is full to the brim.

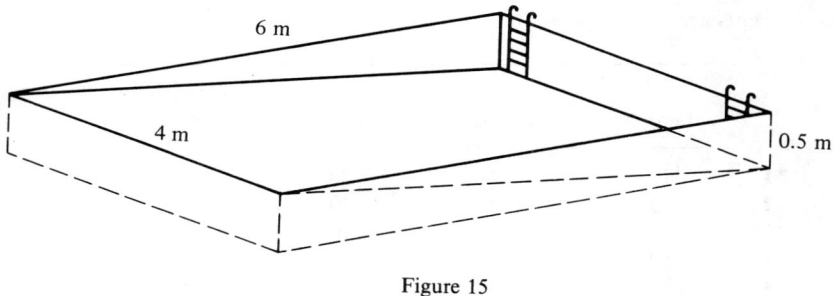

Figure 15

4. VOLUMES OF LIQUIDS

In Chapter 11 'Living metric' it was said that a *litre* of distilled water is almost exactly the volume of water that fills a cubical box of side 10 cm. It is usual to measure the volume of a liquid in terms of litres rather than cm^3 or m^3. Petrol, for example, is sold by the litre (or gallon) and the volume of petrol that can be taken by a car's tank is referred to as the *capacity* of the tank.

Example 4
Find the capacity of a rectangular petrol can measuring 10 cm by 10 cm by 15 cm (see Figure 16).

$$V = 10 \times 10 \times 15 = 1500$$
$$= 1500 \text{ cm}^3.$$
So capacity = 1500 ÷ 1000 litres
= 1.5 litres.

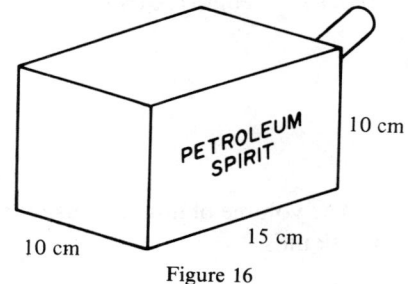

Figure 16

168 Volume   Ch. 26

Example 5

A goldfish tank has a base measuring 30 cm by 20 cm. What is the depth of the water if the tank contains 12 litres of water?

$$V = lwh$$
$$\text{so } 12\,000 = 30 \times 20 \times h$$
$$= 600h$$

h can easily be seen to be 20.

Hence the depth of water is 20 cm.

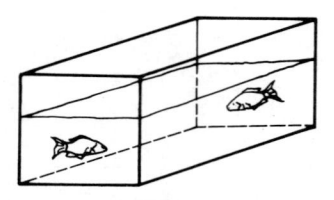

Figure 17

Exercise D

Find the capacity, or the missing measurement, of the following rectangular containers. Measurements are all in centimetres.

	Length	Width	Height	Capacity (litres)
*1	10	20	30	?
2	15	30	40	?
*3	5	50	50	?
3	7	12	20	?
5	8	9	22	?
*6	5	20	?	1
7	25	?	2	1
8	?	10	20	2
9	20	?	25	10
10	5	100	?	4

SUMMARY

The volume of an object is the amount of three-dimensional space it occupies. The main units of volume are cm³ and m³.

The volume of a cuboid (rectangular block) = (length) × (width) × (height).

$V = lwh$ cm³

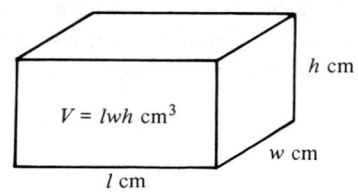

Figure 18

The volume of liquids is usually given in litres, as is the capacity of containers for liquids.

$$1000 \text{ cm}^3 = 1 \text{ litre.}$$

Summary exercise

1 The solids shown in Figure 19 are composed of small building bricks of side 1 cm. Find their volumes.

(a)

(b)

(c)

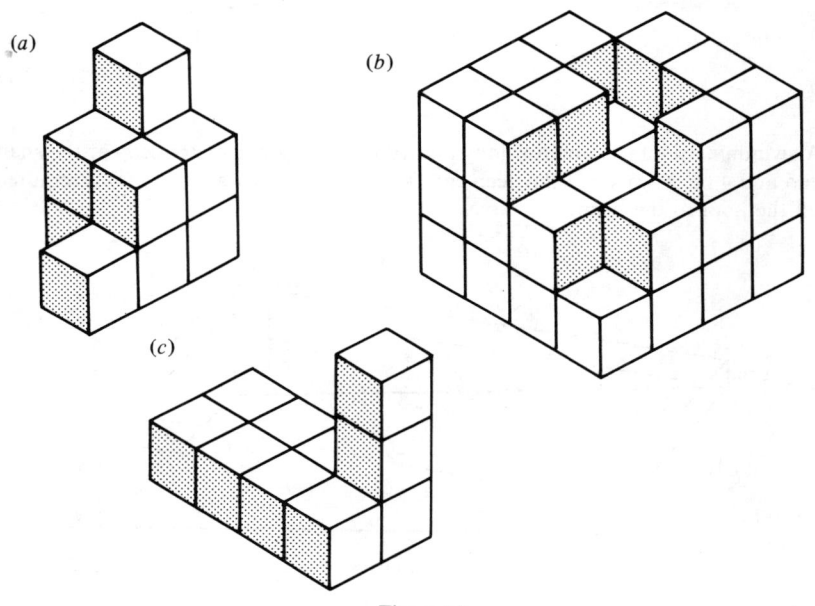

Figure 19

2 Calculate the volumes of the solids shown in Figure 20.

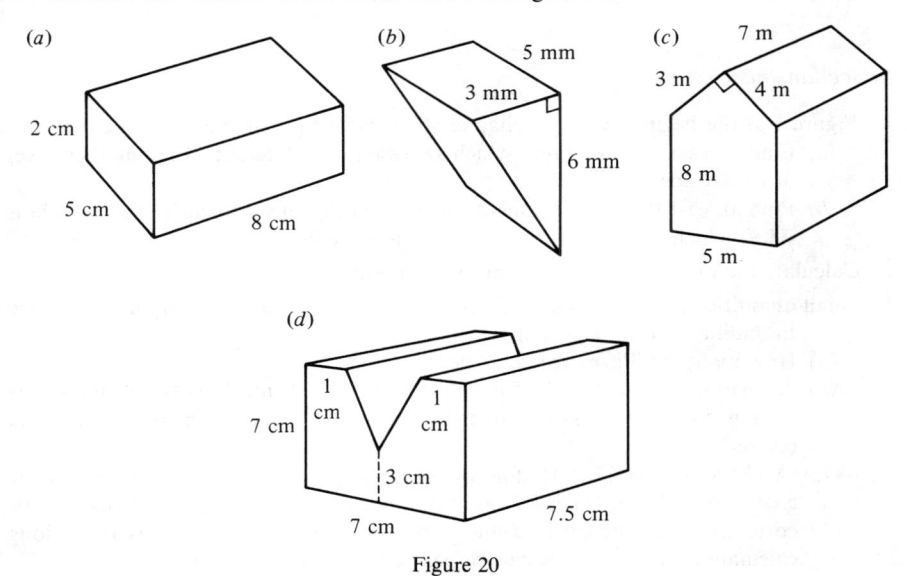

(a) 2 cm, 5 cm, 8 cm

(b) 5 mm, 3 mm, 6 mm

(c) 7 m, 3 m, 4 m, 8 m, 5 m

(d) 7 cm, 1 cm, 1 cm, 3 cm, 7 cm, 7.5 cm

Figure 20

170 Volume   Ch. 26

3 Figure 21 shows an ice-cream box for the freezer. What is its capacity in litres?

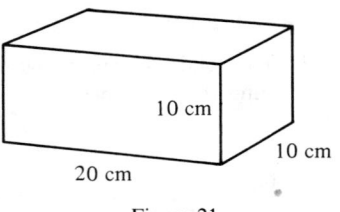

Figure 21

4 A swimming pool is 25 metres long and 10 metres wide, 1 metre deep at the shallow end and 4 metres deep at the deep end. What volume of water (in m^3) is required to fill the pool to the brim?

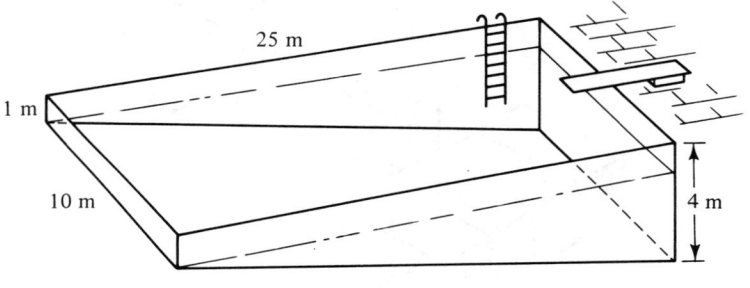

Figure 22

5 A long jump pit is to be constructed with length 8 m and width 1 m. If 4 m^3 of sand are available how deep will the sand in the pit be?

Miscellaneous exercise

1 Figure 1 at the beginning of the chapter showed four possible nets for a cube.
  (a) Find at least two other nets which are essentially different. (Turning them over or round doesn't count!)
  (b) Find at least three arrangements of six squares (joined to each other by whole sides) which cannot be folded up to make a cube.

2 Calculate the number of litres in one cubic metre.

3 Small quantities of liquids such as those used in medicine or chemistry are measured in millilitres. 1 ml = $\frac{1}{1000}$ litre.
  (a) How many millilitres are equivalent to 1 cm^3?
  (b) A carton of concentrated fruit juice contains 200 ml. It is to be diluted by adding 'four times its own quantity of water'. How much fruit juice drink results?
  (c) A bottle of PAINTOUT, for correcting mistakes, contains 20 ml of fluid. If a coat of PAINTOUT is 0.1 mm thick calculate the area of paper that can be corrected. If the height of a line of writing is 5 mm and a line is 16 cm long calculate how many lines can be painted out with one bottle.

4 Calculate the volume of a sheet of plasterboard which measures 3 m by 1.2 m by 1.5 cm.
5 Estimate the volume of air in your classroom.
6 1 gallon is approximately 4.5 litres. Which is the better buy:
petrol at £2.05 per gallon or
petrol at 46p per litre?
7 Chipboard which is 1 cm thick is used to make the open box (with a base) shown in Figure 23.
   Calculate (a) the capacity of the box;
            (b) the volume of wood used to make it.

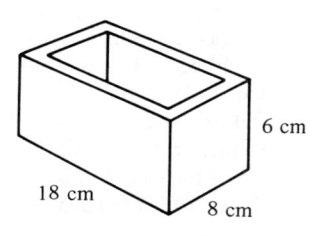

Figure 23

8 Bill answers questions on the volumes of objects like those in Figures 7 and 13. His answer to one question starts:
   '$V = 3 \times 3 \times 6 + 4 \times 2 \times 1 + 3 \times 8 + 1 \times 1 \times 4.$'
He got his answer wrong. What do you think he may have done wrong?
   His answer to another question starts:
   '$V = 2 \times 3 \times 4 + \frac{1}{2} \times 2 \times 1 \times 5.$'
Do you think he has made another slip? Explain.

9 Figure 24 shows a net for a wedge. Make a full-size accurate copy of this onto thin card. Cut it out and fold it up to make the wedge. Calculate the volume of the wedge. What are the measurements of the cuboid which has twice the volume of this wedge?

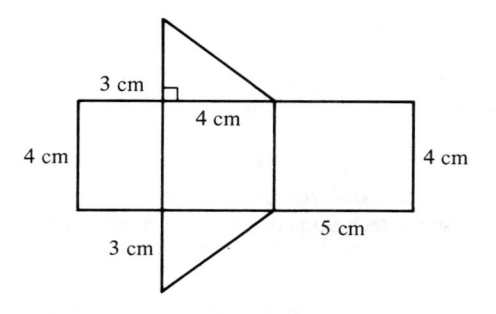

Figure 24

Try this

Try this 5: Constructions

A Draw a line PQ 6 cm long in the middle of your page. Set your compasses to radius 4 cm. Draw a circle with this radius with its centre at P and another with the same radius centred at Q.

The circles intersect twice. Join the points of intersection with a straight line. Describe the line you have drawn in relation to the points P and Q.

B Use the diagram you drew for part A. Set your compasses at any radius greater than 3 cm and draw two new circles, one centred at P, the other at Q. Again draw the line joining the points of intersection of the circles. What do you notice?

C The final line drawn in both parts A and B is known as the *mediator* (or *perpendicular bisector*) of the line PQ. It is perpendicular to PQ and is equidistant from P and Q.
  (a) Why, in part B, does the radius have to be greater than 3 cm?
  (b) Does it matter what radius is used (provided that it is greater than 3 cm)?
  (c) Do you have to draw complete circles in order to draw the mediator?
  (d) Why do you think this process produces a mediator?

D Draw any triangle XYZ. It should be fairly large and be placed in the centre of your page. Use the process outlined in parts A and B to draw the mediators of XY, YZ and ZX. (Do not draw complete circles, and make your construction lines lightly.)

The three mediators should intersect at a single point (provided you have been careful and accurate). This point is the centre of a circle which can be drawn to pass through X, Y and Z. Draw it. If you have not been very accurate you might like to try again.

E Make a full size copy of the diagram indicated in Figure 1. With centre X and radius 3 cm draw a circle. Label the intersections with XY and YZ as shown in Figure 2. Keep the same radius draw two more circles with P and Q as their centres. These two circles intersect at X and a new point R. Join XR.

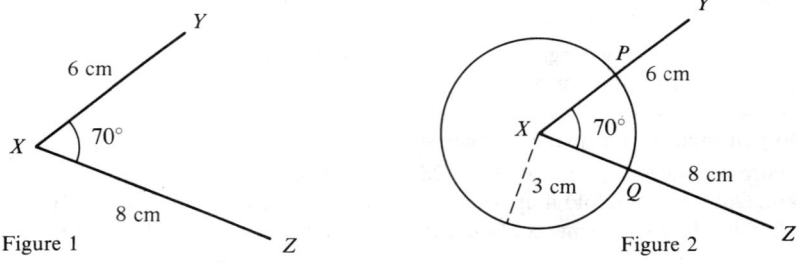

Figure 1

Figure 2

The line XR is the *angle bisector* of $\angle YXZ$.
Check this by measuring $\angle YXR$ and $\angle ZXR$.

F Copy Figure 1 again and repeat the process of part E but with circles of radius 4 cm.
  (a) Does a different radius affect the final result?
  (b) Is there any radius which you think might not work?
  (c) Do you have to draw complete circles in order to construct the angle bisector?
  (d) Why do you think this process bisects the angle?

G Draw any scalene triangle LMN. Again this should be fairly large and placed in the centre of the page. Use the technique of part E to construct the angle bisectors of all three angles of the triangle. (Draw your construction arcs lightly, and do not draw complete circles.)

The three angle bisectors should all meet at a single point. This point is the centre of a circle which just touches each side of the original triangle. Draw it.
(It takes a great deal of care to be able to draw this final circle accurately.)

27
Through the centre of enlargement

1. SOME REMINDERS

An enlargement of scale factor 3 with centre of enlargement at the origin is shown in Figure 1.

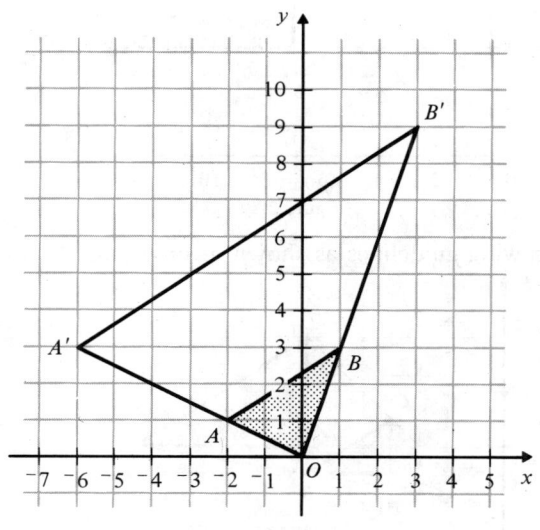

Figure 1

Note that: (a) Every object point and its image point are in a straight line with the centre of enlargement (e.g. O, A, A');

173

(b) object and image lines are parallel (e.g. AB and $A'B'$) or coincident (e.g. OA and OA');

(c) image lengths are 3 times the corresponding object lengths.

Since the origin is the centre of enlargement, it is possible to calculate the image coordinates using the rule:

(object coordinate) × (scale factor) = (image coordinate).

Here, for example, using the x-coordinate of A we have

$$^-2 \times 3 = {}^-6.$$

In Book 1, part 1, this result was put in the form

(negative coordinate) × (positive scale factor) = (negative coordinate)

but, of course, this is also just a fact about multiplying numbers.

We know that it does not matter in which order two numbers are written before multiplication so we also have the result

$$3 \times {}^-2 = {}^-6.$$

Figure 2 shows two triangles ABC and $A'B'C'$. It looks as if $A'BC'$ is an enlargement of ABC.

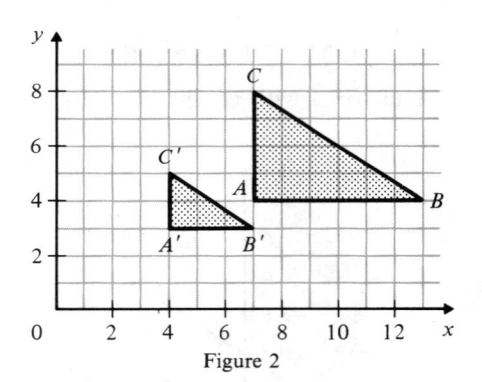

Figure 2

We can test by drawing guidelines as shown in Figure 3.

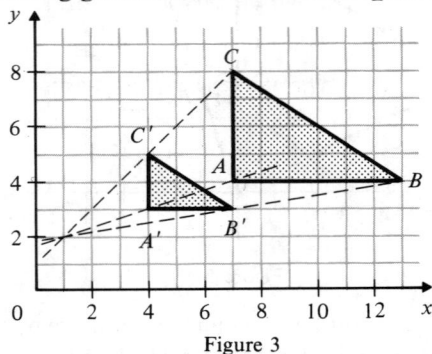

Figure 3

We note that the guidelines pass through (1, 2) which is therefore the centre. (We often say just 'centre' rather than 'centre of enlargement' provided there is no doubt about what is meant.)

In this case, as the centre is not the origin, there is no easy calculation with coordinates to help us find the scale factor. However $A'B' = 3$ units and $AB = 6$ units and we can find the scale factor by division.

$$(\text{object length}) \times (\text{scale factor}) = (\text{image length})$$
hence
$$6 \times (\text{scale factor}) = 3$$
and
$$\text{scale factor} = 3 \div 6 \quad (\text{or } \tfrac{3}{6})$$
$$= 0.5 \quad (\text{or } \tfrac{1}{2}).$$

Remember that: scale factors greater than 1 make objects larger; fractional scale factors make objects smaller.

Combining enlargements

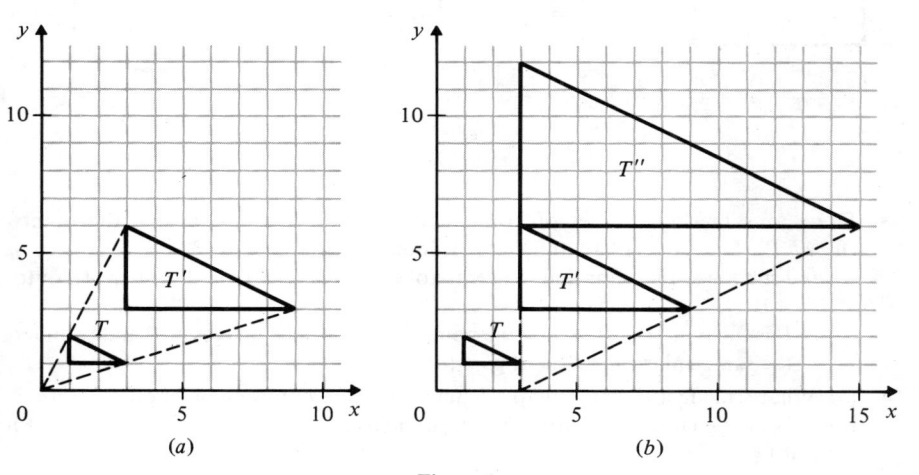

Figure 4

Figure 4(a) shows a triangle T and its image T' after an enlargement centre the origin with scale factor 3. Figure 4(b) shows also the *image of T'* after enlargement centre (3, 0) with scale factor 2.

As T'' is the same shape as T it is an enlargement of T. The horizontal side of T is 2 units and that of T'' is 12 units. From this we calculate that the scale factor of the single enlargement from T to T'' is $12 \div 2 = 6$.

Note that this single scale factor is the product of the two separate scale factors.

$$3 \times 2 = 6$$
(first scale factor) × (second scale factor) = (single scale factor).

Exercise A

*1 Give the coordinates of the images of the following points after enlargements, centre the origin, with the stated scale factors:
   (a) (3, ⁻2), scale factor 6;
   (b) (⁻2, 7), scale factor $\frac{1}{2}$;
   (c) (3.2, ⁻1.4), scale factor 1.5.

*2 State whether the diagrams in Figure 5 are enlargements of each other and if so state the scale factors. (Tracing paper may be helpful.)

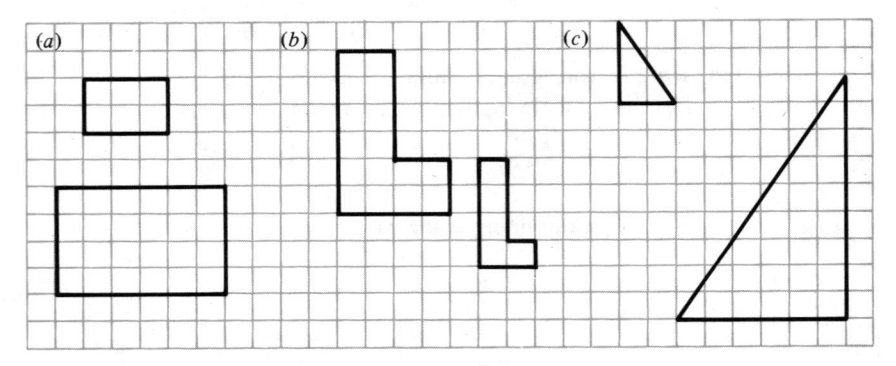

Figure 5

*3 Draw axes marking values of both x and y from ⁻10 to 10. Plot the points $A(^-4, ^-2)$, $B(^-1, 4)$ $A'(4, 0)$ and $B'(5, 2)$. Join A to B and A' to B'.
   (a) Find the scale factor and the centre of enlargement required to map AB onto $A'B'$.
   (b) P is the point (8, 10) and Q the point (2, 7). Find the images of P and Q under the same enlargement as in part (a).

*4 (a) What scale factor would map a length of 3.5 cm onto one of length 2.1 cm?
   (b) What scale factor of enlargement from the origin would map the point (12, ⁻8) onto (3, ⁻2)?

*5 (a) An enlargement scale factor 3 is followed by an enlargement with scale 4. What is the scale factor of the single enlargement mapping the object onto the final image?
   (b) Repeat part (a) for scale factors of (i) 2.5 and 6; (ii) 1.2 and 1.4.

2. UPSIDE-DOWN ENLARGEMENTS

Figure 6 shows two triangles PQR and $P'Q'R'$. These seem to be the same shape but one is 'upside-down' and reversed compared to the other. We investigate this situation by drawing guidelines, joining what seem to be corresponding vertices, as in the previous section. The result is shown in Figure 7.

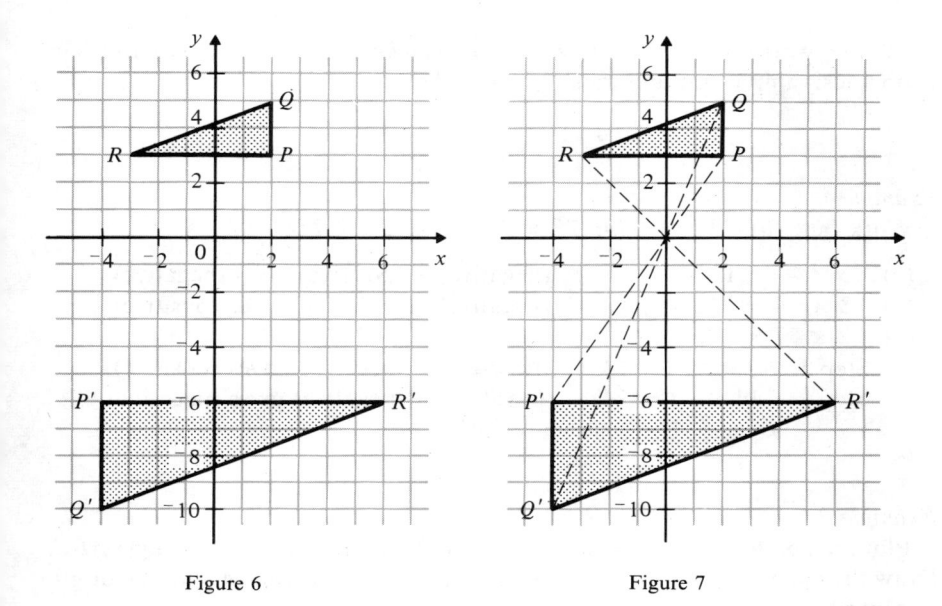

Upside-down enlargements 177

Figure 6

Figure 7

Notice that
(a) all the guidelines pass through the same point, in this case the origin;
(b) that each side in $P'Q'R'$ is twice the length of the corresponding side in PQR.

These two comments indicate an enlargement. But the scale factor cannot be 2 for then the image of $P(2, 3)$ would be at $(4, 6)$ instead of $(^-4, ^-6)$.

We look again at the result used in the previous section:

(object coordinate) × (scale factor) = (image coordinate)

For this enlargement, considering point P we must have:

$$2 \times \text{(scale factor)} = {}^-4$$
and
$$3 \times \text{(scale factor)} = {}^-6.$$

Both of these are true if we use $^-2$ as the scale factor.

This is the first time we have met a negative scale factor; the centre of enlargement is between the object and image, just like Alice through the centre of enlargement in the picture at the head of this chapter.

Check that the coordinates of Q and Q' also satisfy the relation:

(object coordinate) × (scale factor) = (image coordinate).

Consider now the x-coordinate of the point R. If the result is to hold we must have:

(object coordinate) × (scale factor) = (image coordinate) or, in this case,
$\quad\quad {}^-3 \quad\quad\quad \times\ {}^-2 \quad\quad = {}^+6$ (the + for emphasis).

In other words *the product of two negative numbers must be positive.* This result is obviously important and must be remembered.

Example 1
Work out: (a) ⁻3 × 4; (b) ⁻3 × ⁻4; (c) ⁻2 × ⁻7 × ⁻3.

(a) ⁻3 × 4 = ⁻12   (negative) × (positive) gives (negative).
(b) ⁻3 × ⁻4 = ⁺12   (negative) × (negative) gives (positive).
(c) ⁻2 × ⁻7 × ⁻3.
    Step 1. ⁻2 × ⁻7 = ⁺14   (negative) × (negative) gives (positive).
    Step 2. ⁺14 × ⁻3 = ⁻42   (positive) × (negative) gives (negative).
        Hence ⁻2 × ⁻7 × ⁻3 = ⁻42.

Example 2
Plot the points $A(0, 1)$, $B(2, 1)$, $C(2, ⁻1)$ and join them to form triangle ABC. Draw the image of ABC after an enlargement by scale factor ⁻4 with the origin as centre.

Remember that it is only when the centre of enlargement is the origin that we may obtain the image by multiplying the coordinates of the object by the scale factor. In this case:

$A(0, 1)$ maps onto $A'(0, ⁻4)$
$B(2, 1)$ maps onto $B'(⁻8, ⁻4)$
$C(2, ⁻1)$ maps onto $C'(⁻8, ⁺4)$.   (See Figure 8.)

(You should make sure that you understand the details of the multiplication and the signs of the image coordinates.)

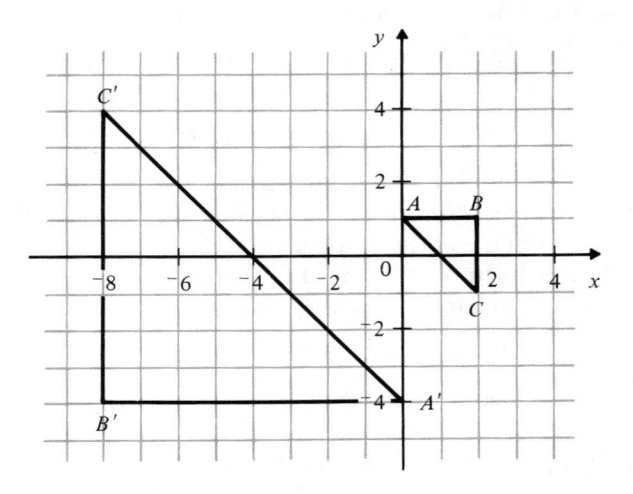

Figure 8

Upside-down enlargements 179

Example 3 (*Using guidelines*)
Enlarge triangle ABC by scale factor $^-3$ using X as the centre of enlargement. (See Figure 9.)

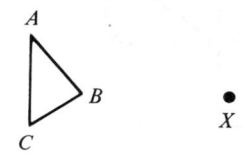

Figure 9

In this case, we must use the fact that the points on the image $A'B'C'$ will be 3 times as far away from X as the corresponding points of the object ABC and on the opposite side of X.

Draw guide lines from A, B and C through X.
Now mark off lengths XA', XB', XC' so that

$$XA' = 3AX, \quad XB' = 3BX \quad \text{and} \quad XC' = 3CX. \quad \text{(See Figure 10.)}$$

Figure 10

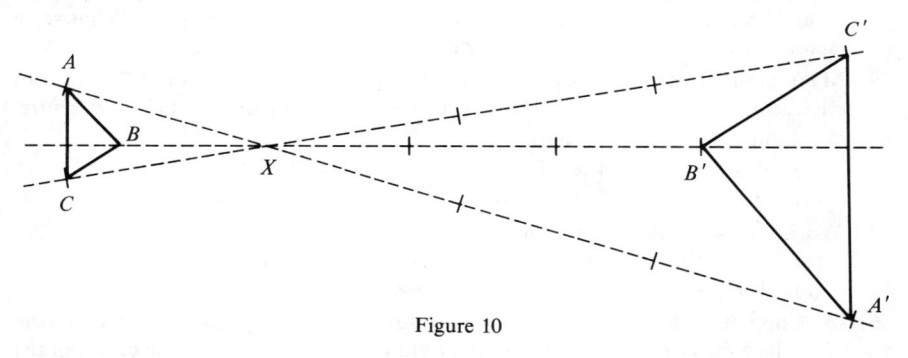

Exercise B

*1 Figure 11 shows a picture of a ROM chip for a computer and its enlargement from some centre. By making suitable measurements, find the scale factors which enlarge:
   (*a*) chip A onto chip B;
   (*b*) chip B onto chip A.

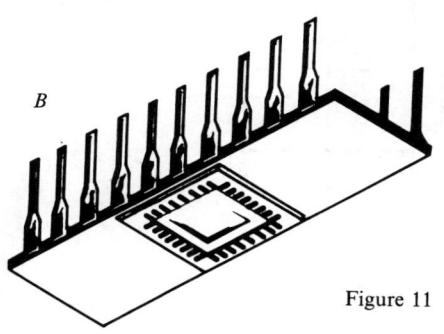

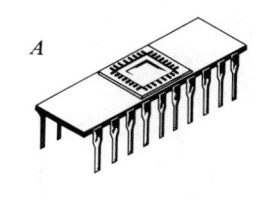

Figure 11

180   Through the centre of enlargement   Ch. 27

2

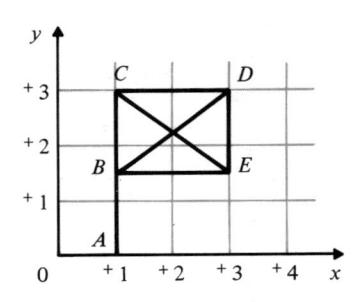

Figure 12

Write down the coordinates of A, B, C, D, E of the flag in Figure 12 and calculate the coordinates of an enlargement, centre O, with scale factor ⁻2. Draw axes marking values of both x and y from ⁻7 to ⁺7. Draw the two flags and check that the lines joining corresponding points all pass through O.
  Calculate the coordinates of another enlargement of the original flag with centre O, and scale factor ⁻0.5. Draw the new image on the same diagram. What scale factor of enlargement will map the smaller image on to the larger?

3 Make another copy of Figure 12 with axes the same as in question 2. Draw an enlargement of the flag ABCDE with scale factor ⁻2 using the point (2, 1) as centre.

*4 Work out, without a calculator:
   (a) ⁻5 × ⁻7;   (b) ⁻4 × ⁺5;   (c) ⁻3 × ⁺7;   (d) ⁺8 × ⁺6;
   (e) ⁺3 × ⁻8;   (f) ⁻7 × ⁻3;   (g) ⁺7 × ⁻3;   (h) ⁻2 × ⁻10.

5 Work out, without a calculator:
   (a) ⁺4 × ⁻10;   (b) ⁻3 × ⁻20;   (c) ⁻50 × 7;   (d) ⁺1.5 × ⁻2;
   (e) ⁻8 × ⁻4;   (f) ⁻20 × ⁺6;   (g) ⁻5 × ⁻5;   (h) ⁺8.5 × ⁺2.

6 (a) Copy the squares in Figure 13(a) onto squared paper and letter them as shown. (Place the larger square well to the right of your paper.) Find the centre of the of the enlargement which maps ABCD onto A'B'C'D' by drawing guide lines through corresponding points, extending the lines if necessary.

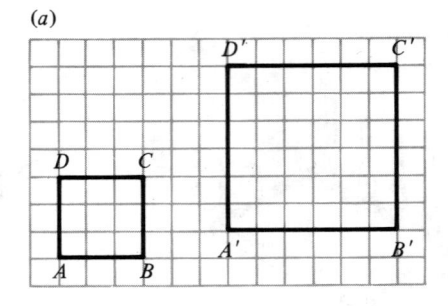

(a)

Upside-down enlargements 181

(b)

(c)

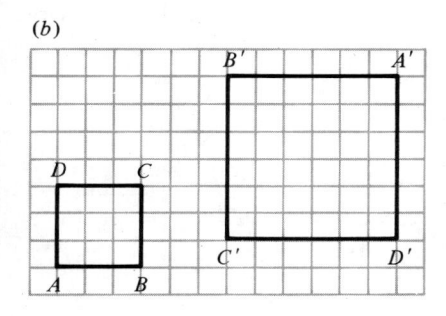

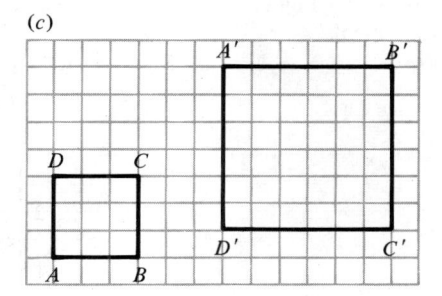

Figure 13

(b) Repeat part (a) for the squares in Figure 13(b).
(c) Repeat part (a) for the squares in Figure 13(c). What happens? Explain.

*7

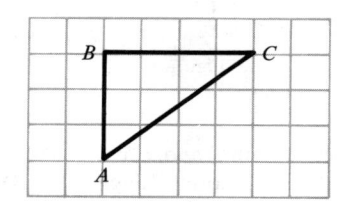

Figure 14

Copy the triangle ABC in Figure 14 onto squared paper towards the right hand side and about half way up the page.
    (a) Draw $A'BC'$ which is the enlargement of ABC with centre B and scale factor $^-2$.
    (b) Draw $AB''C''$ which is the enlargement of ABC with centre A and scale factor $^-3$.
    (c) What scale factor enlarges the image in (a) onto the image in (b)?

*8 What numbers should be used to fill the boxes to make the following true?
    (a) $^-3 \times \square = {}^-30$; (b) $8 \times \square = 24$; (c) $\square \times 12 = {}^-24$;
    (d) $\square \times {}^-15 = 30$; (e) $^-5 \times \square = 45$ (f) $\square \times {}^-11 = {}^-5.5$.

*9 Copy and complete the following flow charts.

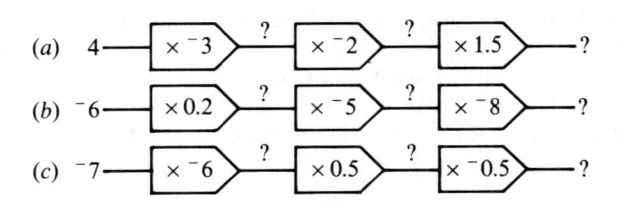

(a) $4 \longrightarrow [\times {}^-3] \xrightarrow{?} [\times {}^-2] \xrightarrow{?} [\times 1.5] \longrightarrow ?$

(b) $^-6 \longrightarrow [\times 0.2] \xrightarrow{?} [\times {}^-5] \xrightarrow{?} [\times {}^-8] \longrightarrow ?$

(c) $^-7 \longrightarrow [\times {}^-6] \xrightarrow{?} [\times 0.5] \xrightarrow{?} [\times {}^-0.5] \longrightarrow ?$

*10 Copy Figure 15 and find the centres and scale factors of the following enlargements.
(a) $S \to S_1$; (b) $S \to S_2$; (c) $S_2 \to S_1$.

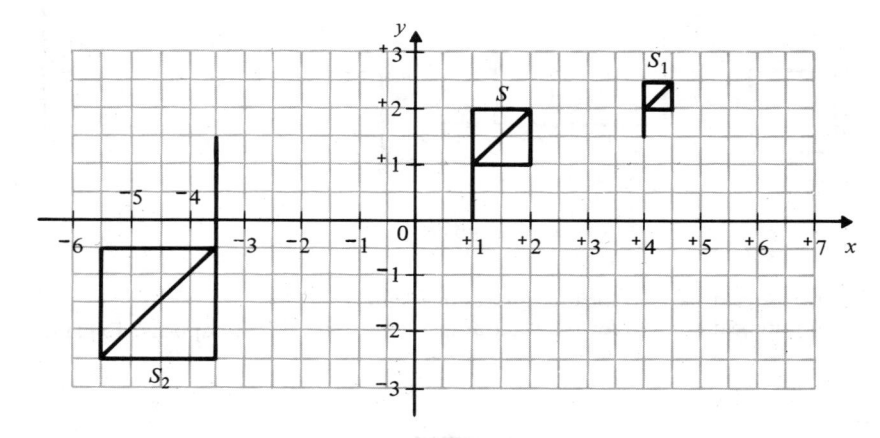

Figure 15

11 Draw axes marking values of both x and y from $^-6$ to $^+6$.
$P(^-1, 1)$, $Q(^-1, ^-2)$ and $R(^-3, ^-3)$ form triangle PQR. Draw this triangle.
(a) Calculate the coordinates for $P'Q'R'$ which is an enlargement of PQR by scale factor 2, centre the origin. Draw $P'Q'R'$.
(b) Calculate the coordinates for $P''Q''R''$ which is an enlargement of PQR by scale factor $^-2$, centre the origin. Draw $P''Q''R''$.
(c) Check the accuracy of your calculation by:
   (i) drawing guide lines;
   (ii) comparing the lengths of corresponding sides.

12 Draw axes marking values of both x and y from $^-12$ to $^+12$.
$A(^-2, ^-2)$, $B(2, ^-2)$ and $C(^-2, 1)$ form triangle ABC. Draw this triangle.
(a) By calculating coordinates draw $A'B'C'$ which is the image of ABC under an enlargement scale factor 2, centre the origin.
(b) By calculating coordinates draw $A''B''C''$, the image of $A'B'C'$, under an enlargement scale factor $^-3$, centre the origin. (Note it is $A'B'C'$ that is enlarged.)
(c) What scale factor of enlargement will map ABC directly onto $A''B''C''$?

*13 What single factor of enlargement would have the same effect as the two enlargements:
(a) first by scale factor 3 and then by scale factor $^-4$;
(b) first by scale factor $^-4$ and then by scale factor $^-2$;
(c) first by scale factor $^-3$ and then by scale factor 0.5?

14 Copy and complete the multiplication table.
Note the pattern formed by the signs in the blocks.

×	⁻4	⁻3	⁻2	⁻1	0	1	2	3	4
4									
3									
2									
1									
0									
⁻1									
⁻2									
⁻3									
⁻4									

Table 1

(a) What do you notice about the result of squaring numbers whether they are positive or negative?

(b) What number gives 9 when it is squared? Is there more than one such number?

(c) I think of a number; I square it. The answer is 64. What number did I think of? Can you be sure?

(d) Two whole numbers multiplied together equal ⁻4. List all the pairs you can think of which do this.

(e) Two whole numbers multiplied together equal 12. List all the pairs you can find which do this.

3. DIVISION WITH NEGATIVE NUMBERS

Example 3
Work out   (a) ⁻6 ÷ ⁻3;   (b) ⁺6 ÷ ⁻3;   (c) ⁻6 ÷ ⁺3.

Table 2 shows the multiplication table from question 14 of Exercise B. Since division is the reverse of multiplication we can use this to answer the above questions.

Through the centre of enlargement

×	$^-4$	$^-3$	$^-2$	$^-1$	0	1	2	3	4
4	$^-16$	$^-12$	$^-8$	$^-4$	0	4	8	12	16
3	$^-12$	$^-9$	$^-6$	$^-3$	0	3	6	9	12
2	$^-8$	$^-6$	$^-4$	$^-2$	0	2	4	6	8
1	$^-4$	$^-3$	$^-2$	$^-1$	0	1	2	3	4
0	0	0	0	0	0	0	0	0	0
$^-1$	4	3	2	1	0	$^-1$	$^-2$	$^-3$	$^-4$
$^-2$	8	6	4	2	0	$^-2$	$^-4$	$^-6$	$^-8$
$^-3$	12	9	6	3	0	$^-3$	$^-6$	$^-9$	$^-12$
$^-4$	16	12	8	4	0	$^-4$	$^-8$	$^-12$	$^-16$

Table 2

(a) What must we multiply $^-3$ by to get $^-6$? From the table, we can see that the answer is 2. Another way of saying this is $^-6 \div {}^-3 = 2$ or $\dfrac{^-6}{^-3} = 2$.

(b) What is $^+6 \div {}^-3$? From the table, $^-3 \times {}^-2 = 6$, so $6 \div {}^-3 = {}^-2$ or $\dfrac{6}{^-3} = {}^-2$.

(c) What is $^-6 \div {}^+3$ (or $^-6 \div 3$)? Since $3 \times {}^-2 = {}^-6$, $^-6 \div 3 = {}^-2$.

Summarising, we have:

$^-6 \div {}^-3 = {}^+2$ (negative) ÷ (negative) gives (positive)
$^+6 \div {}^-3 = {}^-2$ (positive) ÷ (negative) gives (negative)
$^-6 \div {}^+3 = {}^-2$ (negative) ÷ (positive) gives (negative)

and, of course, as

$6 \div 3 = 2$ (positive) ÷ (positive) gives (positive)

The results for multiplication and division are summarised in the following table.

Division with negative numbers 185

	second number	
× or ÷	positive	negative
first number positive	positive	negative
negative	negative	positive

Example 4
Calculate (a) $^-24 \div 4$; (b) $^-24 \div {}^-4$; (c) $25 \div {}^-5$.

Solutions:
(a) $^-24 \div 4 = {}^-6$ (negative divided by positive gives negative).
(b) $^-24 \div {}^-4 = 6$ (negative divided by negative gives positive).
(c) $25 \div {}^-5 = {}^-5$ (positive divided by negative gives negative).

Example 5
Under an enlargement with centre the origin the point $(7, {}^-5)$ maps onto $({}^-21, 15)$. What is the scale factor?

Looking at the *x*-coordinates of object and image we must have

$$7 \times (\text{scale factor}) = {}^-21$$

or
$$(\text{scale factor}) = {}^-21 \div 7 \quad \left(\text{or } \frac{-21}{7}\right)$$

$$= {}^-3.$$

It is a good idea to check that dividing the *y*-coordinates gives the same result:

$$15 \div {}^-5 = {}^-3.$$

Example 6
Use your calculator, but not the $\boxed{+/-}$ key to evaluate
(a) $^-7.2 \times 6.3$; (b) $^-4212 \div 12$.

(a) The answer will be negative. $7.2 \times 6.3 = 45.36$.   Answer $^-45.36$.
(b) The answer will be negative. $421.2 \div 12 = 35.1$.   Answer $^-35.1$.

Exercise C (Many questions may be answered orally.)

*1 Say what numbers should fill the boxes in each part (i) to make them true and give the answers to the divisions in each part (ii).
    (a) (i) $^-6 \times \square = {}^-24$,   (ii) $^-24 \div {}^-6 = $;
    (b) (i) $10 \times \square = {}^-30$,   (ii) $^-30 \div 10 = $;
    (c) (i) $^-3 \times \square = 33$,   (ii) $33 \div {}^-3 = $;
    (d) (i) $^-7 \times \square = {}^-42$,   (ii) $^-42 \div {}^-7 = $;
    (e) (i) $\square \times {}^-1.5 = {}^-6$,   (ii) $^-6 \div {}^-1.5 = $;
    (f) (i) $^-8 \times \square = 32$,   (ii) $32 \div {}^-8 = $;
    (g) (i) $^-12 \times \square = 36$,   (ii) $36 \div {}^-12 = $.

*2 Calculate (a) $^-30 \div 10$; (b) $^-30 \div {}^-3$; (c) $\dfrac{^-70}{^-10}$; (d) $36 \div {}^-4$; (e) $\dfrac{^-60}{6}$;
(f) $^-50 \div 10$; (g) $\dfrac{27}{^-9}$; (h) $^-28 \div {}^-7$; (i) $32 \div 8$.

*3 In this question the origin is the centre of enlargement. Find what scale factor, if any, will map
    (a) $(^-7, {}^-6)$ onto $(^-21, {}^-18)$;
    (b) $(6, {}^-2)$ onto $(^-12, 4)$;
    (c) $(3, 2)$ onto $(^-9, 6)$;
    (d) $(^-6, {}^-4)$ onto $(3, 2)$.

*4 Use your calculator, but not the $\boxed{+/-}$ key, to work out:
    (a) $^-7.2 \times {}^-6.3$; (b) $^-2.6 \times {}^+1.85$; (c) $^-7.1 \times {}^-2.4$;
    (d) $3.8 \times {}^-3.5$; (e) $^-3.24 \div {}^-1.8$; (f) $^-14.49 \div 2.07$;
    (g) $\dfrac{720}{^-4.5}$; (h) $\dfrac{^-5.6}{11.2}$.
Check your answers by entering negative numbers into your calculator using the $\boxed{+/-}$ key or an equivalent method.

5 *ABCD* is enlarged by scale factor $^-4$ with $(0, 0)$ as the centre of enlargement. $A'B'C'D'$ is the image with $A'(^-4, 6)$, $B'(^-8, 0)$, $C'(^-4, {}^-6)$, $D'(0, 0)$. Calculate the coordinate of A, B, C and D.

*6 What numbers should fill the boxes in the following to make them true?
    (a) $6 \times {}^-7 \times \square = {}^-84$; (b) $^-5 \times {}^-2 \times \square = {}^-30$;
    (c) $\square \times {}^-6 \div 2 = 30$; (d) $(16 \div {}^-8) \times 2 = \square$.

7 What numbers should fill the boxes in the following to make them true?
    (a) $^-3 \times {}^-7 \times \square = {}^-63$; (b) $\square \times 8 \times {}^-1.5 = {}^-24$.
    (c) $^-3 \times \square \times {}^-0.5 = 6$; (d) $8 \times (^-20 \div {}^-5) = \square$.

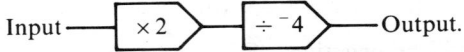

8   Input —[×2]—[÷ $^-4$]— Output.

    (a) Using the flow chart shown find the output when the input is (i) 8; (ii) $^-20$.
    (b) Draw a reverse flow chart to find the input when the output is (i) 1; (ii) $^-5$.

9   Input —[+6]—[× $^-3$]—[÷8]— Output.

Using the flow chart shown find
    (a) the output when the input is (i) 10; (ii) $^-14$;
    (b) the input when the output is (i) 24; (ii) $^-21$.

4. ADDITION AND SUBTRACTION – A REMINDER

The following examples remind you how to deal with the addition and subtraction of directed numbers (i.e. positive and negative numbers).

Example 7
　Work out　$^-7 + {}^-3$.

We start at $^-7$ on the number line; adding a negative number involves a shift to the left. The number line below shows that the answer is $^-10$.

$$^-7 + {}^-3 = {}^-10$$

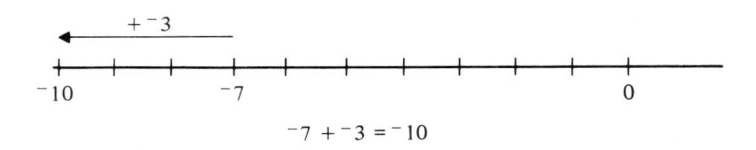

Example 8
　Work out　$5 - {}^+8$.

We start at 5, which of course means $^+5$, on the number line; subtracting a positive number involves a shift to the left. The number line below shows that the answer is $^-3$.

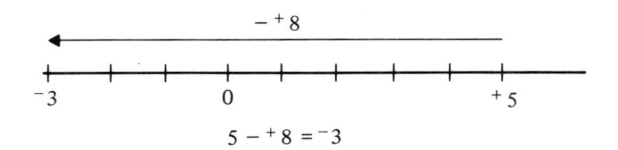

$$5 - {}^+8 = {}^-3$$

Example 9
　Work out　$^-3 - {}^-9$.

We start at $^-3$ on the number line; subtracting a negative number is equivalent to adding a positive number and thus involves a shift to the right. The number line below shows that the answer is $^+6$ (or just 6).

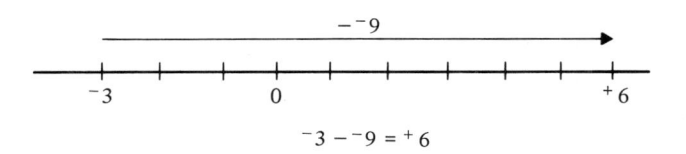

$$^-3 - {}^-9 = {}^+6$$

Through the centre of enlargement

Example 10 (Involving multiplication as well)
Work out $3 \times {}^-4 - {}^-2 \times {}^-5$.

Multiplication must be done first, thus we have:

$$3 \times {}^-4 - {}^-2 \times {}^-5 = {}^-12 - {}^+10$$
$$= {}^-22.$$

Exercise D

Calculators should not be used in this exercise.

*1 Work out
  (a) ${}^-5 + {}^-6$;   (b) ${}^+5 + {}^-1$;   (c) ${}^-2 + {}^+4$;
  (d) ${}^+3 + {}^-8$;   (e) ${}^+6 - {}^-2$;   (f) ${}^+3 - {}^+4$;
  (g) ${}^-5 - {}^+8$;   (h) ${}^-5 - {}^-7$.

2 Remembering that ${}^+7$ can also be written as 7, work out
  (a) $3 + 8$;   (b) ${}^-3 + 6$;   (c) $5 + {}^-8$;
  (d) $9 - 10$;   (e) ${}^-3 - 1$;   (f) ${}^-8 + 1$.

*3 Remember that calculations in brackets must be worked out first and that otherwise, multiplication and division have priority over addition and subtraction. Work out

  (a) ${}^-8 + (2 \times {}^-6)$;   (b) $({}^-3 \times {}^-7) + ({}^-2)$;   (c) $2 + 3 \times {}^-7$;
  (d) $3 + 2 \times {}^-4 + 1$;   (e) $({}^-3 + 2) \times ({}^-4 + 1)$;   (f) $20 - \dfrac{3}{1.5}$.

4 Work out
  (a) $4 \times 6 - {}^-3$;   (b) $4 \times (6 - {}^-3)$;   (c) $8 + 16 \div {}^-4 + {}^-2$;
  (d) $4 - 32 \div 4 \times 2$;   (e) $4 - 32 \div (4 \times 2)$;   (f) $4 - \dfrac{32}{4 \times {}^-2}$.

*5 What numbers should fill the gaps in the following flow diagrams?

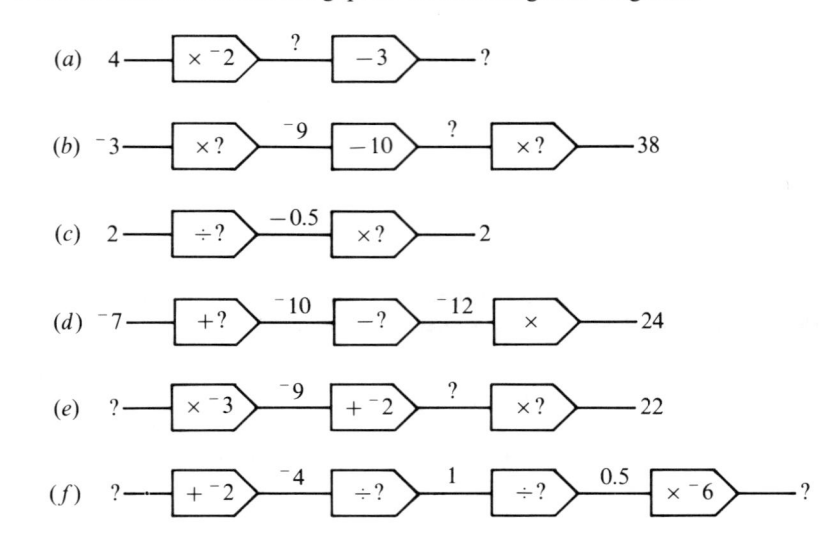

(a) $4 \longrightarrow \boxed{\times {}^-2} \xrightarrow{?} \boxed{-3} \longrightarrow ?$

(b) ${}^-3 \longrightarrow \boxed{\times ?} \xrightarrow{{}^-9} \boxed{-10} \xrightarrow{?} \boxed{\times ?} \longrightarrow 38$

(c) $2 \longrightarrow \boxed{\div ?} \xrightarrow{-0.5} \boxed{\times ?} \longrightarrow 2$

(d) ${}^-7 \longrightarrow \boxed{+?} \xrightarrow{{}^-10} \boxed{-?} \xrightarrow{{}^-12} \boxed{\times} \longrightarrow 24$

(e) $? \longrightarrow \boxed{\times {}^-3} \xrightarrow{{}^-9} \boxed{+{}^-2} \xrightarrow{?} \boxed{\times ?} \longrightarrow 22$

(f) $? \longrightarrow \boxed{+{}^-2} \xrightarrow{{}^-4} \boxed{\div ?} \xrightarrow{1} \boxed{\div ?} \xrightarrow{0.5} \boxed{\times {}^-6} \longrightarrow ?$

SUMMARY

Enlargement by a negative scale factor, say ⁻3, will give an image the same size as an enlargement obtained by scale factor 3. However with a negative scale factor the object and image are on opposite sides of the centre of enlargement.

In Figure 16, O is the centre of enlargement.

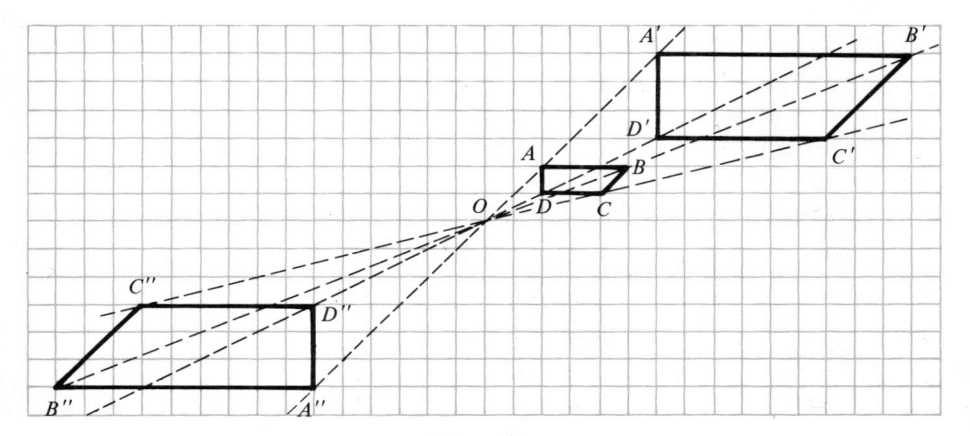

Figure 16

$ABCD$ is the object.
$A'B'C'D'$ is the image with scale factor 3.
$A''B''C''D''$ is the image with scale factor ⁻3.

Multiplication and division

		second number	
	× or ÷	positive	negative
first number	positive	positive	negative
	negative	negative	positive

Summary exercise

1 Draw axes marking values of both x and y from ⁻7 to ⁺7. Draw triangle ABC with $A(^-2, 0)$, $B(^-3, ^-2)$ and $C(2, ^-3)$.
   (a) With the point $(0, 0)$ as centre draw $A'B'C'$ which is the image of triangle ABC after enlargement by scale factor ⁻2.
   (b) With the point $(^-1, ^-1)$ as centre, draw $A''B''C''$ the image of ABC after enlargement by scale factor ⁻2.

2 Work out, without the use of a calculator:
(a) $6 \times {}^-5$; (b) ${}^-7 \times 6$; (c) ${}^-2 \times {}^-9$; (d) ${}^-4 \times {}^-20$.

3 Work out, without the use of a calculator:
(a) ${}^-16 \div 2$; (b) ${}^-12 \div {}^-4$; (c) $18 \div {}^-4$; (d) $\dfrac{{}^-25}{{}^-5}$.

4 Using your calculator, find:
(a) ${}^-8.9 \times {}^-5.3$; (b) $2.8 \times {}^-3.6$; (c) ${}^-5.4 \times 0.68$.

5 Calculate:
(a) $\dfrac{{}^-7.6}{2.5}$; (b) $\dfrac{33.6}{{}^-1.2}$; (c) ${}^-44.1 \div {}^-4.2$.

6 $ABCD$ is a rectangle with $A(2, {}^-1)$, $B(2, 6)$, $C({}^-4, {}^-1)$, $D({}^-4, 6)$, which is enlarged with $(0, 0)$ as the centre. Without making an accurate drawing, write down the co-ordinates of the images of the points A, B, C, D when

(a) the scale factor is ${}^-4$;
(b) the scale factor is 0.6;
(c) the scale factor is $\dfrac{{}^-1}{2}$.

7 Find the output for each of the following flow diagrams:

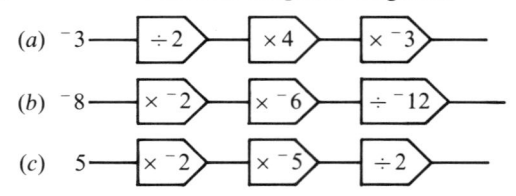

(a) ${}^-3 \longrightarrow \boxed{\div 2} \longrightarrow \boxed{\times 4} \longrightarrow \boxed{\times {}^-3} \longrightarrow$

(b) ${}^-8 \longrightarrow \boxed{\times {}^-2} \longrightarrow \boxed{\times {}^-6} \longrightarrow \boxed{\div {}^-12} \longrightarrow$

(c) $5 \longrightarrow \boxed{\times {}^-2} \longrightarrow \boxed{\times {}^-5} \longrightarrow \boxed{\div 2} \longrightarrow$

Miscellaneous exercise

1 You may have made a simple pin-hole camera in a physics lesson with a piece of tracing paper instead of film so that you can see the image as in Figure 17.

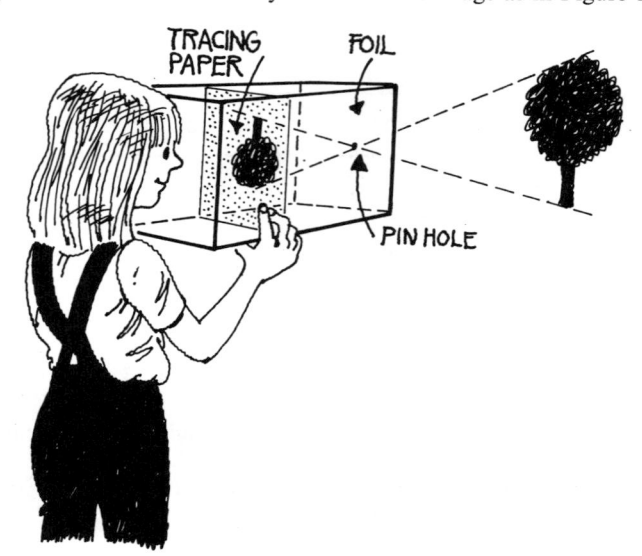

Summary

Suppose the distance of the object from the pin-hole is 2 m and the distance of the film from the hole is 4 cm. What scale factor of enlargement maps the object onto the image?

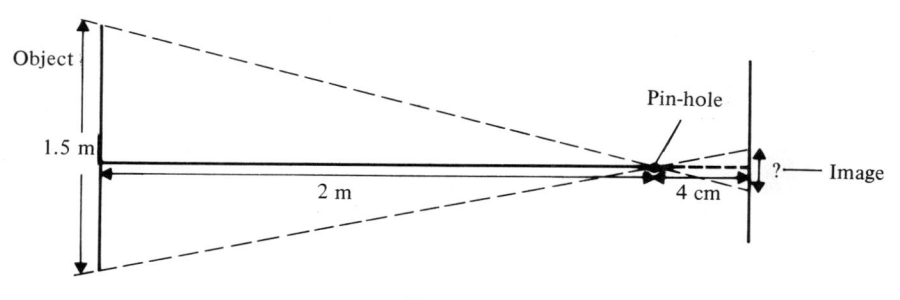

Figure 17

If the object to be viewed is 1.5 m high, what is the height of the image?
2   Copy Figure 18 and find two possible centres of enlargement to map one square onto the other.

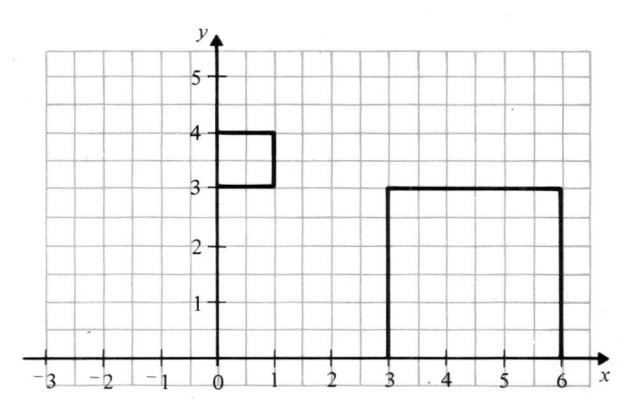

Figure 18

State two possible scale factors in each case.
3   (a) Multiply together
    (i) 2, 3, 4;   (ii) 2, ⁻5, 1;   (iii) 3, ⁻3, ⁻3;   (iv) ⁻5, ⁻6, ⁻2.
   (b) Three whose numbers (positive or negative) multiplied together equal ⁻6. What might they be? Write down as many sets as you can.
   (c) Three whole numbers (positive or negative) multiplied together equal 12. List as many sets as you can.

4 Figure 19 shows a picture of simple robot arm *A* which has been enlarged *twice* by the same factor to make the second image *C*.

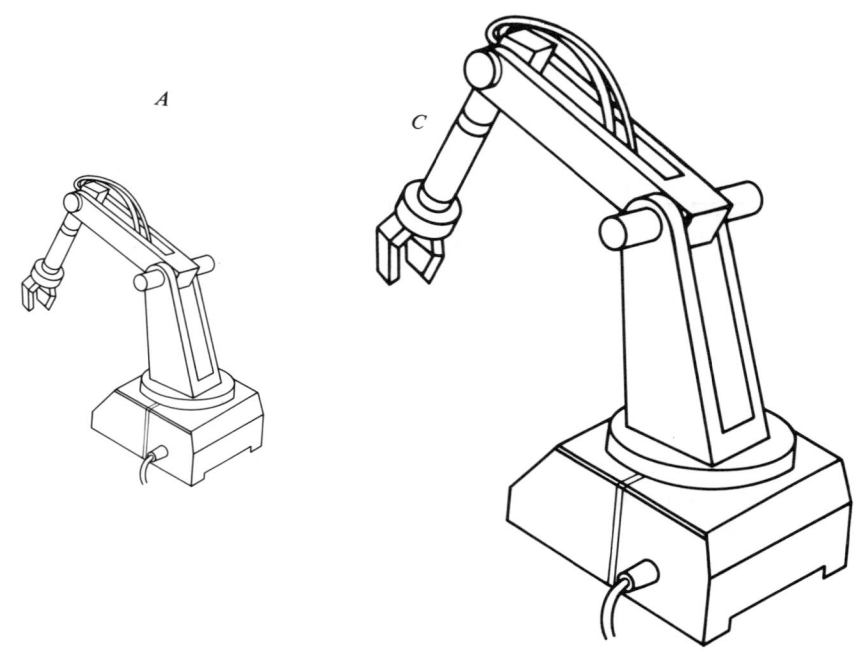

Figure 19

What scale factor has been used for each of the two enlargements? Illustrate with rough freehand sketches where the centres of enlargement might be.

5 The same two instructions are suitable for each of the following flow charts. Find them.

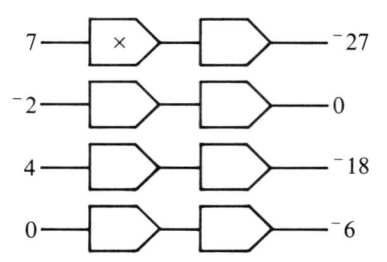

$7 \longrightarrow \boxed{\times} \longrightarrow \boxed{} \longrightarrow {}^-27$

${}^-2 \longrightarrow \boxed{} \longrightarrow \boxed{} \longrightarrow 0$

$4 \longrightarrow \boxed{} \longrightarrow \boxed{} \longrightarrow {}^-18$

$0 \longrightarrow \boxed{} \longrightarrow \boxed{} \longrightarrow {}^-6$

6 In this question, remember to deal with the brackets first. Work out
   (*a*) (i) $(2 \times {}^-4) \times {}^-3$, (ii) $2 \times ({}^-4 \times {}^-3)$;
   (*b*) (i) ${}^-3 \times (6 \times {}^-2)$, (ii) $({}^-3 \times 6) \times {}^-2$.
Does the position of the brackets make any difference to the results? Make up similar questions to include other operations $(+, -, \div)$ and investigate what happens.

7 Fill the boxes in the following with the numbers required to make the statements true.

(a) $\dfrac{-25}{4 + \square} = 5;$ (b) $28 \div \square - 6 = 2;$

(c) $\square \times {}^-3 + 4 = 28;$ (d) $\dfrac{-36}{\square - 2} + {}^-5 = {}^-8.$

8 Figure 20 shows five enlargements. Take suitable measurements from the diagrams and write down the scale factors involved.

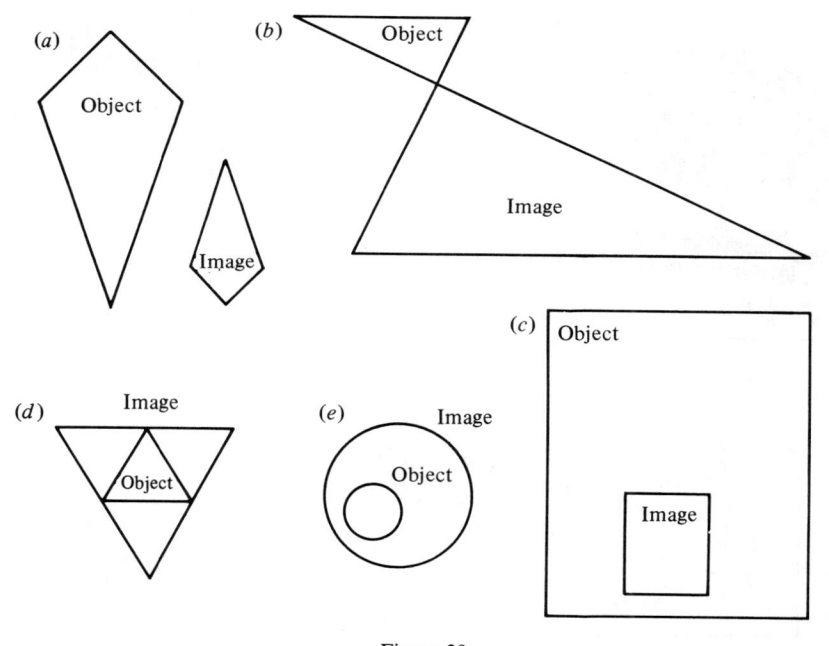

Figure 20

Discuss the positions of possible centres of enlargement illustrating your answer with sketches.

28

Fractions

We talk about fractions and meet them in different ways. School assembly may finish at a quarter past nine; a third of the class may have a cold today; Jane cycled half a mile to get to school; perhaps Bryan got nine tenths of the possible marks for last week's homework.

It is easy to understand simple statements about fractions like these, but we sometimes need to compare different fractions and to add, subtract, multiply and divide them too.

1. EQUIVALENT FRACTIONS

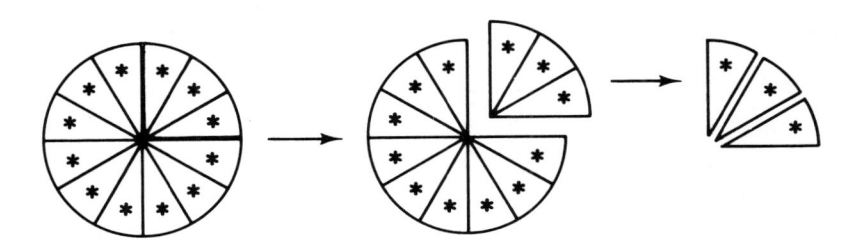

Figure 1

Some cakes can be bought with markings on them so that they break easily into fractions. It is easy to see from Figure 1 that one quarter is the same as three twelfths.

$$\tfrac{1}{4} = \tfrac{3}{12}$$

We say that $\tfrac{1}{4}$ and $\tfrac{3}{12}$ are equivalent fractions.

Notice that $\dfrac{1}{4} = \dfrac{1 \times 3}{4 \times 3} = \dfrac{3}{12}$.

The fact that $\dfrac{1}{4} = \dfrac{1 \times 3}{4 \times 3} = \dfrac{3}{12}$ shows how we can find other fractions equivalent to $\tfrac{1}{4}$.

For example $\dfrac{1}{4} = \dfrac{1 \times 5}{4 \times 5} = \dfrac{5}{20}$.

In general we have $\dfrac{1}{4} = \dfrac{1 \times x}{4 \times x}$ where x is any number but not 0. x does not have to be a whole number, but it will be in this chapter.

A fraction of the form $\dfrac{x}{x}$, for example $\dfrac{3}{3}$ or $\dfrac{5}{5}$ is of course equal to 1 and we are using the fact that

$$\tfrac{1}{4} = \tfrac{1}{4} \times 1.$$

(Strictly speaking we are using facts about multiplying fractions. If you do not remember these you will be reminded in a later chapter.)

Notation

The number in the top part of the fraction is the *numerator*, that on the bottom is the *denominator*. We usually write fractions in their *simplest form,* that is with the numerator and denominator as small as possible.

Fractions

Example 1
Find some fractions equivalent to $\frac{2}{3}$.

Multiplying both numerator and denominator by 5 we have:

$$\frac{2}{3} = \frac{2 \times 5}{3 \times 5} = \frac{10}{15}.$$ (x is 5)

Multiplying both numerator and denominator by 7 we have:

$$\frac{2}{3} = \frac{2 \times 7}{3 \times 7} = \frac{14}{21}.$$ (x is 7)

Example 2
Write $\frac{36}{48}$ in its simplest form.

Suppose we notice that 6 is a factor of both 36 and 48. We write:

$$\frac{36}{48} = \frac{6 \times 6}{8 \times 6} = \frac{6}{8}.$$

Now notice that 2 is a factor of both 6 and 8:

$$\frac{6}{8} = \frac{3 \times 2}{4 \times 2} = \frac{3}{4}.$$

If, of course, we had noticed that 12 is a factor of both 36 and 48 we would have saved a lot of work!

$$\frac{36}{48} = \frac{3 \times 12}{4 \times 12} = \frac{3}{4}.$$

Example 3
Copy and complete the following equivalent fractions:

$$\frac{2}{7} = \frac{6}{} = \frac{}{42}$$

To complete $\frac{2}{7} = \frac{6}{}$ notice that $6 = 2 \times 3$

so $$\frac{2}{7} = \frac{2 \times 3}{7 \times 3} = \frac{6}{21}.$$ (x is 3)

Now write $$\frac{2}{7} = \frac{}{42} = \frac{2 \times 6}{7 \times 6} = \frac{12}{42}.$$

Finally $$\frac{2}{7} = \frac{6}{21} = \frac{12}{42}.$$

Example 4
Write the fractions $\frac{5}{7}$ and $\frac{2}{3}$ in equivalent forms using the same denominator.

We could start $\quad \frac{5}{7} = \frac{10}{14} = \frac{15}{21} = \frac{20}{28} = \frac{25}{35} = \cdots$

and $\quad \frac{2}{3} = \frac{4}{6} = \frac{6}{9} = \frac{8}{12} = \frac{10}{15} = \frac{12}{18} = \frac{14}{21} = \frac{16}{24} = \cdots$

Equivalent fractions

We notice that the first denominator in common is 21 (obtained by multiplying together the two given denominators). 21 is the smallest number into which both 3 and 7 divide.

We have $\frac{5}{7} = \frac{15}{21}$ and $\frac{2}{3} = \frac{14}{21}$.

Example 5

Write the fractions $\frac{3}{4}$ and $\frac{2}{5}$ in equivalent forms with the same denominator.

Using our experience in Example 4, we choose a denominator of $4 \times 5 = 20$.

We have $\dfrac{3}{4} = \dfrac{3 \times 5}{4 \times 5} = \dfrac{15}{20}$ and $\dfrac{2}{5} = \dfrac{2 \times 4}{5 \times 4} = \dfrac{8}{20}$.

Example 6

Write the fractions $\frac{5}{8}$ and $\frac{11}{12}$ in equivalent forms with the same denominator.

In this case 8 and 12 have a factor in common so we do not choose $8 \times 12 = 96$. We see that $8 = 2 \times 4$ and $12 = 3 \times 4$. Thus the smallest number into which each will divide is $2 \times 4 \times 3 = 24$. We use 24 as the denominator and obtain

$$\frac{5}{8} = \frac{5 \times 3}{8 \times 3} = \frac{15}{24}$$

and

$$\frac{11}{12} = \frac{11 \times 2}{12 \times 2} = \frac{22}{24}.$$

Exercise A

*1 Express the shaded parts of each diagram in Figure 2 as fractions in two different ways. Hence write down pairs of equivalent fractions

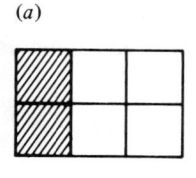

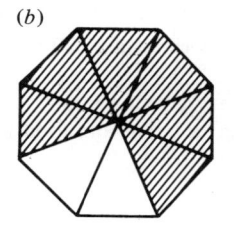

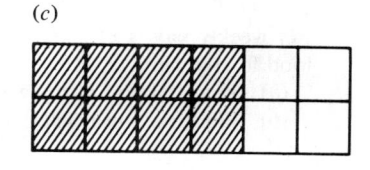

(a)   (b)   (c)

Figure 2

2 Write the following fractions in their simplest form:
(a) $\frac{35}{45}$; (b) $\frac{14}{18}$; (c) $\frac{28}{35}$; (d) $\frac{12}{16}$; (e) $\frac{39}{45}$;
(f) $\frac{16}{40}$; (g) $\frac{6}{21}$; (h) $\frac{12}{30}$; (i) $\frac{21}{49}$; (j) $\frac{40}{64}$.

In questions 3–7 complete the equivalent fractions:

3 $\frac{1}{4} = \frac{2}{} = \frac{}{20} = \frac{3}{} = \frac{}{96}$.   **4** $\frac{3}{5} = \frac{}{10} = \frac{12}{} = \frac{}{35} = \frac{24}{}$.

5 $\frac{2}{3} = \frac{6}{} = \frac{}{15} = \frac{16}{} = \frac{}{27}$.   **6** $\frac{5}{7} = \frac{}{14} = \frac{15}{} = \frac{}{35} = \frac{60}{}$.

7 $\frac{3}{8} = \frac{9}{} = \frac{}{32} = \frac{21}{} = \frac{}{72}$.

In questions 8–12 write down equivalent fractions with the same denominator for the two fractions given. Make sure you find the smallest possible denominator each time.

8 $\frac{2}{3}, \frac{4}{5}$.   **9** $\frac{5}{6}, \frac{11}{18}$.   **10** $\frac{2}{15}, \frac{7}{25}$.   **11** $\frac{7}{12}, \frac{3}{8}$.   **12** $\frac{3}{14}, \frac{5}{21}$.

In questions 13–16 give your answers as the simplest possible equivalent fractions.

13 Out of 488 people questioned in a survey, 366 said they watched 'Top of the Pops'. What fraction of those questioned watched the programme?

14 I set off for the station riding my bicycle. After going 320 metres the front tyre was punctured, so I then walked for 480 metres, but then I had to run the last 200 metres to catch the train.
(a) What fraction of the total distance did I run?
(b) What fraction of the total distance did I walk?

15 On checking his patients' records a dentist found that 618 of his patients were children under the age of 15, that 412 were between the ages of 15 and 18 and that the rest (206) were adults.
What fraction of his patients were (a) adults, (b) children under the age of 15?

16 My weekly pay is £120. Of this £35 goes in tax, £20 pays the rent and £30 buys food for the family.
(a) What fraction of my weekly pay goes on tax?
(b) What fraction is left over after tax, rent and food have been paid for?

2. COMPARING FRACTIONS

We can easily see that three quarters of a cake is more than half a cake, so we can write $\frac{3}{4} > \frac{1}{2}$.

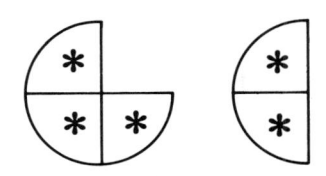

But suppose Alan has to walk $\frac{3}{4}$ of a mile to school and Betty has to walk $\frac{2}{3}$ of a mile? Who has the farthest to walk?

We can answer this question in the same way as we considered the fractions of cake. We find equivalent fractions for $\frac{3}{4}$ and $\frac{2}{3}$ with the same denominator. For $\frac{3}{4}$ and $\frac{2}{3}$ the obvious denominator to use is 12, since both 4 and 3 are factors of 12.

So we want to complete

$$\frac{3}{4} = \frac{}{12} \quad \text{and} \quad \frac{2}{3} = \frac{}{12}.$$

Basing our work on the method of Example 4 we have:

$$\frac{3}{4} = \frac{3 \times 3}{4 \times 3} = \frac{9}{12} \quad \text{and} \quad \frac{2}{3} = \frac{2 \times 4}{3 \times 4} = \frac{8}{12}.$$

As $\frac{9}{12} > \frac{8}{12}$ we have $\frac{3}{4} > \frac{2}{3}$.

So Alan has farther to walk to school.

Fractions Ch. 28

Example 7

Arrange the following in order of size, smallest on the left, using the symbol <.

$$\tfrac{4}{5}, \quad \tfrac{2}{3}, \quad \tfrac{5}{7}.$$

We need to find a suitable denominator which has 5, 3 and 7 as factors. 5, 3 and 7 have no factor in common and $5 \times 3 \times 7 = 105$. So we use 105.

$$\frac{4}{5} = \frac{}{105} \quad \text{requires} \quad \frac{4}{5} = \frac{4 \times 21}{5 \times 21} = \frac{84}{105};$$

$$\frac{2}{3} = \frac{}{105} \quad \text{requires} \quad \frac{2}{3} = \frac{2 \times 35}{3 \times 35} = \frac{70}{105};$$

$$\frac{5}{7} = \frac{}{105} \quad \text{requires} \quad \frac{5}{7} = \frac{5 \times 15}{7 \times 15} = \frac{75}{105}.$$

Now $\quad \tfrac{70}{105} < \tfrac{75}{105} < \tfrac{84}{105} \quad$ so $\quad \tfrac{2}{3} < \tfrac{5}{7} < \tfrac{4}{5}.$

Exercise B

Show your working and the equivalent fractions used.

In questions 1–10 place the correct symbol < or > between the fractions.

*1 $\tfrac{5}{8}$ $\tfrac{19}{32}$. 2 $\tfrac{2}{5}$ $\tfrac{3}{8}$. 3 $\tfrac{7}{10}$ $\tfrac{2}{3}$. 4 $\tfrac{5}{8}$ $\tfrac{7}{10}$. *5 $\tfrac{3}{5}$ $\tfrac{2}{3}$.
6 $\tfrac{7}{8}$ $\tfrac{8}{9}$. 7 $\tfrac{7}{13}$ $\tfrac{5}{9}$. 8 $\tfrac{5}{8}$ $\tfrac{9}{14}$. *9 $\tfrac{3}{5}$ $\tfrac{12}{19}$. 10 $\tfrac{5}{11}$ $\tfrac{4}{9}$.

In questions 11–14 arrange the fractions given in order of size with the largest on the left, using the symbol >.

*11 $\tfrac{5}{9}$ $\tfrac{11}{18}$ $\tfrac{25}{48}$.   12 $\tfrac{3}{5}$ $\tfrac{5}{11}$ $\tfrac{5}{8}$.   *13 $\tfrac{3}{8}$ $\tfrac{3}{10}$ $\tfrac{5}{8}$ $\tfrac{5}{10}$.   14 $\tfrac{4}{5}$ $\tfrac{5}{6}$ $\tfrac{6}{7}$ $\tfrac{7}{8}$.

15 Joan is looking for a piece of fabric to make a skirt. In a box of remnants in a shop she finds a piece which is 85 cm long, but the pattern says that she needs $\tfrac{7}{8}$ of a metre. Is the remnant long enough?

16 John wants to measure a length of balsa wood $\tfrac{5}{8}$ of an inch long, but he only has a ruler marked in tenths of an inch. Between which two marks on the ruler should he make the mark on the balsa wood?

3. ADDING AND SUBTRACTING FRACTIONS

Joe has bought a second-hand chair which needs to be re-covered. By measuring the old pieces of cloth he decides that he needs half a metre of cloth for the seat and a quarter of a metre for the back. How much does he need altogether?

Joe must buy $\tfrac{1}{2} + \tfrac{1}{4}$ metres of cloth.

We know that $\tfrac{1}{2} = \tfrac{2}{4}$ so Joe must buy $\tfrac{3}{4}$ metre altogether.

Adding and subtracting fractions 201

Joe goes to the shop to buy the cloth for the chair. The shopkeeper offers him a cheap remnant which is $\frac{7}{8}$ metre long. Is this enough for the chair and, if so, how much will Joe have left over?

Joe needs $\frac{3}{4}$ metre, which is $\frac{6}{8}$ metre, so if he buys the remnant which is $\frac{7}{8}$ metres long he will have

$$\frac{7}{8} - \frac{6}{8} = \frac{1}{8} \text{ metre left over.}$$

Notice how we have used equivalent fractions. When we have to add or subtract fractions we write them as equivalent fractions with the same denominator.

Example 8
Work out   (a) $\frac{1}{2} + \frac{3}{8}$;   (b) $\frac{7}{9} - \frac{1}{3}$;   (c) $\frac{3}{5} + \frac{2}{7}$.

(a) $\frac{1}{2} + \frac{3}{8} = \frac{4}{8} + \frac{3}{8} = \frac{7}{8}$.
(b) $\frac{7}{9} - \frac{1}{3} = \frac{7}{9} - \frac{3}{9} = \frac{4}{9}$.
(c) $\frac{3}{5} + \frac{2}{7} = \frac{21}{35} + \frac{10}{35} = \frac{31}{35}$.

Notice how, in (c), we had to use a new denominator.

Example 9
Charles is preparing the food for a party. He needs $\frac{3}{4}$ pint of milk for the pudding and $\frac{1}{2}$ pint for a cake. How much milk does he need and how much will be left over from two pint bottles?

Charles needs $\frac{3}{4} + \frac{1}{2}$ pint.

Now
$$\frac{3}{4} + \frac{1}{2} = \frac{3}{4} + \frac{2}{4} = \frac{5}{4} \text{ pints.}$$

But $\frac{5}{4}$ is more than 1, four of the quarters make one, so we can write $\frac{5}{4} = 1\frac{1}{4}$ and we see that Charles needs $1\frac{1}{4}$ pints of milk. Left over from 2 pints he will have $2 - 1\frac{1}{4}$ pints. You may be able to see what that comes to, but we can work it out by writing $2 = \frac{8}{4}$, so the amount left over is $\frac{8}{4} - \frac{5}{4} = \frac{3}{4}$ pint.

Exercise C

Work out:
- *1 (a) $\frac{1}{4} + \frac{2}{3}$; (b) $\frac{1}{6} + \frac{1}{3}$; (c) $\frac{1}{3} + \frac{5}{8}$.
- 2 (a) $\frac{3}{10} + \frac{2}{5}$; (b) $\frac{1}{3} + \frac{5}{12}$; (c) $\frac{3}{8} + \frac{1}{4}$.
- *3 (a) $\frac{2}{7} + \frac{5}{14}$; (b) $\frac{2}{9} + \frac{8}{27}$; (c) $\frac{5}{12} + \frac{1}{6}$.
- 4 (a) $\frac{5}{18} + \frac{8}{27}$; (b) $\frac{2}{21} + \frac{3}{14}$; (c) $\frac{3}{10} + \frac{4}{25}$.
- *5 (a) $\frac{4}{9} + \frac{1}{12} + \frac{1}{3}$; (b) $\frac{3}{10} + \frac{4}{15} + \frac{1}{6}$; (c) $\frac{7}{16} + \frac{5}{12} + \frac{2}{6}$.
- 6 (a) $\frac{9}{10} - \frac{2}{5}$; (b) $\frac{11}{12} - \frac{5}{6}$; (c) $\frac{13}{18} - \frac{1}{6}$.
- *7 (a) $\frac{2}{3} - \frac{5}{12}$; (b) $\frac{11}{20} - \frac{1}{4}$; (c) $\frac{17}{30} - \frac{3}{10}$.
- 8 (a) $\frac{11}{12} - \frac{3}{8}$; (b) $\frac{25}{27} - \frac{7}{18}$; (c) $\frac{21}{25} - \frac{7}{10}$.
- *9 (a) $\frac{3}{4} - \frac{1}{3}$; (b) $\frac{17}{25} - \frac{2}{15}$; (c) $\frac{11}{14} - \frac{4}{21}$.
- 10 Every morning Susheela walks $\frac{1}{8}$ mile to the bus stop, where she catches the bus to school, another $\frac{3}{4}$ mile away. How far from school does she live?
- *11 Each week Andrew spends half of his pocket money on sweets and one third on food for his pet rabbit. All the rest is put into savings. What fraction does he save?
- 12 Peter took his dog out for exercise. They walked for half an hour and spent $\frac{1}{4}$ hour on a training session. How long were they out? (Give your answer as a fraction of an hour.)
- *13 In a school $\frac{4}{25}$ of the pupils are in Form I, $\frac{1}{4}$ are in Form II, $\frac{3}{20}$ are in Form III and $\frac{1}{5}$ in Form IV. What fraction of the school is in these four forms?
- 14 Gwen is carrying a heavy basket and has to rest frequently. She carries it $\frac{2}{3}$ mile then rests; then she goes $\frac{1}{6}$ mile before the next rest, then $\frac{1}{8}$ of a mile, and the final part of her journey is $\frac{1}{24}$ mile. How far does she walk altogether?
- 15 To make toys I need the following lengths of felt; $\frac{1}{4}$ metre of red, $\frac{1}{3}$ metre of blue and $\frac{3}{8}$ metre of yellow. What is the total length of felt that I need? If the price of felt is 72p a metre how much shall I pay for all the felt?

4. MIXED NUMBERS

Jill is going to make a dress and sees that the pattern instructions say that she will need $3\frac{1}{4}$ metres of fabric. We call a number like $3\frac{1}{4}$, which is a whole number (3) and a fraction ($\frac{1}{4}$) added together a *mixed number*. You have already met a few mixed numbers; there is one in Example 9.

Calculations with mixed numbers can be done like calculations with fractions if we first of all change the mixed numbers into 'top-heavy' fractions where the numerator is larger than the denominator.

Example 10

Jill has a pattern for a jacket which requires $2\frac{1}{3}$ metres of fabric, a skirt which uses $\frac{7}{8}$ metre, a cape which requires 3 metres and a scarf which requires $1\frac{1}{4}$ metres. If she makes all four items from the same fabric, what length must she buy?

Fractions

Jill requires $2\frac{1}{3} + \frac{7}{8} + 3 + 1\frac{1}{4}$ metres of fabric.
So number of metres of fabric required

$$= 3 + 2\frac{1}{3} + \frac{7}{8} + 1\frac{1}{4}$$
$$= 3 + \frac{7}{3} + \frac{7}{8} + \frac{5}{4} \text{ (top heavy fractions)}$$
$$= 3 + \frac{56}{24} + \frac{21}{24} + \frac{30}{24} \text{ (equivalent fractions)}$$
$$= 3 + \frac{107}{24}$$
$$= 3 + 4\frac{11}{24}$$
$$= 7\frac{11}{24}.$$

Jill will need $7\frac{11}{24}$ metres of cloth; she will probably buy $7\frac{1}{2}$ metres.

There is another way to add mixed numbers; we can total up the whole numbers first. The calculation above can be done as follows:

$$3 + 2\frac{1}{3} + \frac{7}{8} + 1\frac{1}{4} = 3 + 2 + 1 + \frac{1}{3} + \frac{1}{4} + \frac{7}{8}$$
$$= 6 + \frac{8}{24} + \frac{6}{24} + \frac{21}{24}$$
$$= 6 + \frac{35}{24}$$
$$= 6 + 1\frac{11}{24}$$
$$= 7\frac{11}{24}.$$

Exercise D

Work out:

*1 (a) $2\frac{1}{4} + 1\frac{1}{8}$; (b) $3\frac{2}{5} + 1\frac{3}{10}$; (c) $4\frac{1}{6} + 2\frac{2}{3}$.

2 (a) $3\frac{1}{2} + 2\frac{3}{4}$; (b) $2\frac{3}{8} + 3\frac{3}{4}$; (c) $2\frac{7}{12} + 1\frac{2}{3}$.

*3 (a) $3\frac{1}{4} + 4\frac{5}{6}$; (b) $2\frac{2}{7} + 1\frac{2}{3}$; (c) $4\frac{5}{6} + 2\frac{3}{5}$.

4 (a) $2\frac{1}{2} - 1\frac{1}{3}$; (b) $3\frac{3}{4} - 2\frac{1}{8}$; (c) $5\frac{7}{10} - 3\frac{2}{15}$.

*5 (a) $1\frac{1}{2} - \frac{2}{3}$; (b) $2\frac{1}{3} - 1\frac{1}{2}$; (c) $4\frac{1}{5} - 2\frac{7}{10}$.

6 (a) $4\frac{1}{3} - 2\frac{3}{4}$; (b) $3\frac{2}{5} - 2\frac{3}{10}$; (c) $15\frac{1}{12} - 3\frac{3}{8}$.

7 Driving along a main road I see a sign saying 'Newhaven $2\frac{1}{2}$'. I know that from Newhaven I have to go a further $\frac{3}{4}$ mile to Piddenhoe, and then a further $\frac{2}{3}$ mile after that to my friend's house. What is the total distance I have to travel when I see the sign?

8   A recipe for a pudding requires $\frac{1}{5}$ kg of flour, $\frac{1}{10}$ kg of breadcrumbs, $\frac{1}{8}$ kg of suet, $\frac{1}{8}$ kg of sugar. The rest of the ingredients weigh $\frac{1}{4}$ kg (mostly fruit). What is the total weight of the pudding mixture before baking?

9   Jane is going to make a set of sheets and pillow cases for her bedroom. She wants to make two sheets and four pillow cases. For each sheet she needs $2\frac{1}{4}$ metres of fabric and for each pillow case $\frac{2}{3}$ m. How much fabric must she buy altogether?

10 Nini has to pack a large number of parcels for posting. She knows that the times which the three jobs that have to be done for each parcel are approximately:

collating the sheets	$\frac{1}{4}$ hour
packing and labelling	$\frac{1}{6}$ hour
sealing and tying up	$\frac{1}{10}$ hour.

About how many parcels will Nini be able to pack in $5\frac{1}{2}$ hours?

SUMMARY

Equivalent fractions may be formed by multiplying numerator and denominator by the same number. For example:

$$\frac{2}{5} = \frac{2 \times 7}{5 \times 7} = \frac{14}{35}.$$

The process can be reversed to find the simplest equivalent fraction. For example:

$$\frac{16}{24} = \frac{2 \times 8}{3 \times 8} = \frac{2}{3} \quad \text{or} \quad \frac{16}{24} = \frac{16 \div 8}{24 \div 8} = \frac{2}{3}.$$

When adding or subtracting fractions we need to write them with the same denominator; this should be as small as possible. In the examples which follow the common denominator is 24 because this is the smallest number into which 12 and 8 both divide. (12 = 3 × 4, 8 = 2 × 4 so we need 3 × 4 × 2 = 24.)

$$\frac{5}{12} + \frac{3}{8} = \frac{10}{24} + \frac{9}{24} = \frac{19}{24},$$

$$\frac{5}{12} - \frac{3}{8} = \frac{10}{24} - \frac{9}{24} = \frac{1}{24}.$$

If dealing with mixed numbers one method is to convert into 'top-heavy' fractions first:

$$3\tfrac{17}{20} + 2\tfrac{3}{5} = \tfrac{77}{20} + \tfrac{13}{5} = \tfrac{77}{20} + \tfrac{52}{20} = \tfrac{129}{20} = 6\tfrac{9}{20}.$$

Summary exercise

1   Write in their simplest form:
    (a) $\frac{16}{24}$; (b) $\frac{42}{147}$.

2   Find equivalent fractions with the same denominator for $\frac{5}{11}, \frac{4}{9}$ and $\frac{16}{33}$.
    Use the symbol > to arrange the original fractions in order of size, largest on the left.

3 Work out
   (a) $\frac{3}{10} + \frac{2}{3}$; (b) $\frac{3}{5} - \frac{1}{8}$; (c) $\frac{9}{16} + \frac{7}{8}$;
   (d) $2\frac{3}{7} + 3\frac{1}{3}$; (e) $3\frac{7}{8} - 1\frac{1}{4}$; (f) $4\frac{1}{4} - 2\frac{2}{3}$.

4 Heather spends $\frac{1}{2}$ of her savings on a dress and another $\frac{1}{3}$ on a matching pair of shoes and disco bag. What fraction of her savings is left?
   If she has £6 left what were her original savings?

Miscellaneous exercise

1 Arrange the following fractions in order of size, smallest on the left.
   $$\frac{5}{8} \quad \frac{2}{5} \quad \frac{4}{7} \quad \frac{3}{6}$$
   What pattern do you notice? Can you add another two fractions to continue the pattern?

2 A boy worked some sums with fractions. He wrote
   $$\frac{1}{2} - \frac{1}{3} = \frac{1 \times 1}{2 \times 3} = \frac{1}{6} \qquad \frac{1}{4} - \frac{1}{5} = \frac{1 \times 1}{4 \times 5} = \frac{1}{20}$$
   and got both answers right!
   Discuss his 'method'. Can you find some more examples for which it 'works'?

3 In a later sum the boy in question 2 used 'cancelling'. He wrote
   $$\frac{26}{65} = \frac{2\cancel{6}}{\cancel{6}5} = \frac{2}{5} \qquad \frac{16}{64} = \frac{1\cancel{6}}{\cancel{6}4} = \frac{1}{4}$$
   Are his answers correct? Can you find another example where his 'method' works?

4 Here are two other examples from the boy's exercise book.
   $$\frac{1}{3} + \frac{1}{4} = \frac{2}{7} \qquad \frac{9}{88} + \frac{3}{11} = \frac{\cancel{9}^3}{\cancel{88}_8} \times \frac{\cancel{11}^1}{\cancel{3}_1} = \frac{3 \times 1}{8 \times 1} = \frac{3}{8}$$
   Are the 'answers' correct? If so, can you find similar results?

5 Work out:
   (a) $1 + \frac{1}{2}$;
   (b) $1 + \frac{1}{2} + \frac{1}{4}$;
   (c) $1 + \frac{1}{2} + \frac{1}{4} + \frac{1}{8}$;
   (d) $1 + \frac{1}{2} + \frac{1}{4} + \frac{1}{8} + \frac{1}{16}$.
   In each case subtract your answer from 2. What do you find?
      Write down the answer to:
   (e) $1 + \frac{1}{2} + \frac{1}{4} + \frac{1}{8} + \frac{1}{16} + \cdots + \frac{1}{128}$.
   Write down the answer if this series was continued to include a last term of $\frac{1}{4096}$.

6 Work out:
   (a) $1 + \frac{1}{2}$;
   (b) $1 + \frac{1}{2} + \frac{1}{3}$;
   (c) $1 + \frac{1}{2} + \frac{1}{3} + \frac{1}{4}$;
   (d) $1 + \frac{1}{2} + \frac{1}{3} + \frac{1}{4} + \frac{1}{5}$.
   Do you think that, in the long run, this series will behave in the same way as question 5?

7 Investigate questions 5 and 6 with a calculator using the reciprocal key to convert the fractions into decimals. If you have a programmable calculator or access to a computer you could write programs for these questions.

Quickies 9

CLOSED BOOK

Calculators must not be used.
1. How many square centimetres are there in 1 square metre?
2. How many edges does a cube have?
3. I think of a number, *p*, subtract 4 and then halve the result. Write down an expression for the final result.
4. I use one-quarter of a metre of tape from a roll which is 1.5 m long. How much tape is left on the roll?
5. An enlargement of scale factor 6 is followed by one of scale factor ⁻0.5. What is the scale factor of the single equivalent enlargement?
6. What is the value of 49 ÷ 0.7?
7. I start from (4, 2) and move NE. I arrive at (*x*, 5). State the value of *x*.
8. Write 30 as a product of prime numbers.
9. With the origin as centre of enlargement the point (⁻6, ⁻4) maps onto (12, 8). What is the scale factor?
10. Write down four capital letters each having one line of symmetry.

OPEN BOOK

Calculators must not be used.
1. Give the value of *y* if $\frac{7}{8} = \frac{49}{y}$.
2. 60 runners start a marathon race. $\frac{1}{5}$ have dropped out after 10 miles and $\frac{1}{4}$ of those left have dropped out after 20 miles. If no more drop out, how many finish the race?
3. Find the values of *x* and *y* in Figure 1.

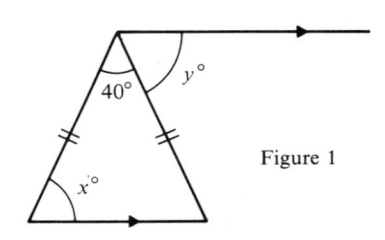

Figure 1

4 Find the output of the following flow chart given that the input is 10.

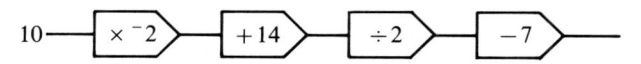

$$10 \longrightarrow \boxed{\times {-2}} \longrightarrow \boxed{+14} \longrightarrow \boxed{\div 2} \longrightarrow \boxed{-7} \longrightarrow$$

5 If $y = x^2 z$ give the value of y when $x = 2$ and $z = 3$.
6 The volume of a cuboid is 120 cm^3. If its length is 8 cm and its width is 5 cm what is its height?
7 List all the prime numbers which are factors of 28.
8 Give the value of $5\frac{1}{2} \div \frac{1}{2}$.
9 How many lines of symmetry has a parallelogram?
10 A monkey is at the bottom of a 30 foot deep well. Each day he manages to climb up 3 feet, only to slip back 2 feet at the end of the day. After how many days will he reach the top of the well? (Be careful!)

Revision exercises 9A, 9B

REVISION EXERCISE 9A

1 Take suitable measurements from the diagrams in Figure 1 and describe the journeys *ABC* and *PQRS* giving distances and bearings in each case.

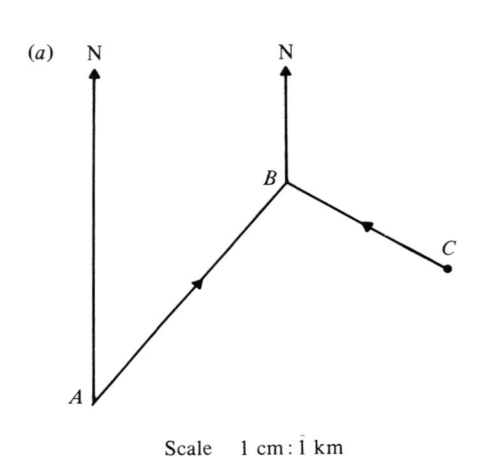

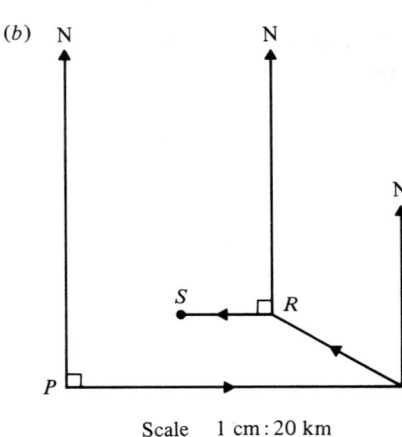

(a)   Scale   1 cm : 1 km

(b)   Scale   1 cm : 20 km

Figure 1

2 Work out:
(a) $\frac{3}{5} + \frac{1}{3}$; (b) $\frac{2}{5} - \frac{1}{7}$; (c) $\frac{11}{16} + \frac{5}{8}$; (d) $3\frac{2}{3} + 2\frac{1}{2}$; (e) $4\frac{1}{5} - 2\frac{1}{3}$.

3 Copy and complete the following table which shows measurements and volumes for a set of cuboids. (Lengths are in cm, volumes in cm^3.)

	Length	Width	Height	Volume
(a)	5	4	8	
(b)	3		8	120
(c)	10	5		150
(d)		8	2	144

4 Find the output for each of the following flow charts.

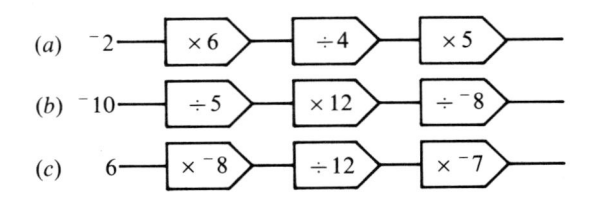

(a) $^-2$ → $\times 6$ → $\div 4$ → $\times 5$

(b) $^-10$ → $\div 5$ → $\times 12$ → $\div\ ^-8$

(c) 6 → $\times\ ^-8$ → $\div 12$ → $\times\ ^-7$

210

5 $P(^-3, 3)$, $Q(0, 3)$, $R(6, ^-3)$ form a triangle. Copy and complete the table to show images of P, Q and R after enlargements, centre the origin, with scale factors (a) 0.8; (b) $^-\frac{1}{3}$.

Scale factor	P	P'	Q	Q'	R	R'
0.8	$(^-3, 3)$		$(0, 3)$		$(6, ^-3)$	
$^-\frac{1}{3}$	$(^-3, 3)$		$(0, 3)$		$(6, ^-3)$	

REVISION EXERCISE 9B

1 Place the correct symbol $>$, $=$ or $<$ between each of the following pairs of fractions:
 (a) $\frac{6}{7}$ $\frac{7}{8}$; (b) $\frac{7}{10}$ $\frac{8}{9}$; (c) $\frac{5}{9}$ $\frac{6}{11}$; (d) $\frac{2}{5}$ $\frac{7}{17}$; (e) $\frac{3}{9}$ $\frac{4}{12}$.

2 Give flow charts for the following formulae. In each case use your calculator to find the output if the input is 0.75.
 (a) $y = (x - 0.25)^2$; (b) $y = x^2 - 0.25$; (c) $y = 4x^2 - 0.25$;
 (d) $y = 4(x^2 - 0.25)$; (e) $y = 4(x - 0.25)^2$.

3 The diagram in Figure 2 shows a piece of cardboard, all measurements being in cm. Find:
 (a) its area;
 (b) the volume of the open box made by folding about the dotted lines.

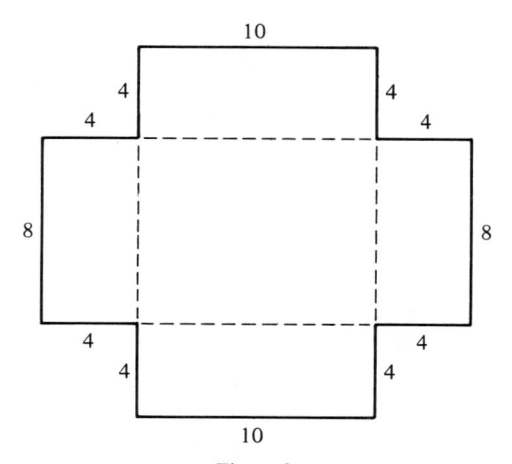

Figure 2

4 Without using a calculator, work out:
 (a) $5 \times {^-7}$; (b) 72×4; (c) $^-3 \times {^-8}$; (d) $28 \div {^-7}$; (e) $^-48 \div {^-12}$.

5 Draw axes marking values of both x and y from $^-9$ to $^+9$. Plot and join the points $A(^-4, 4)$, $B(4, 2)$, $C(3, ^-3)$ and $D(^-2, ^-4)$. What shape is $ABCD$? Draw the images of $ABCD$ after enlargements, centre the origin, with scale factors (a) $^-2$, (b) $^-\frac{1}{2}$. What scale factor enlarges the image in (a) onto the image in (b)?

29

Percentages

Figure 1

1. INTRODUCTION

All the displays in Figure 1 contain examples of percentages, numbers followed by the symbol %, for example 20%, 32%, 55%.

Percentages of a quantity

Try to find some examples for yourself by looking in newspapers, on food containers and medicine packets.

A percentage is so many hundredths and the symbol % is used to denote this. Remembering, for example, that 0.05 is 5 hundredths and 0.24 is 24 hundredths (2 tenths = 20 hundreths) we have:

$$0.05 = 5 \text{ hundredths} = 5\%,$$
$$0.24 = 24 \text{ hundredths} = 24\%.$$

Reversing this, for example:

$$32\% = 32 \text{ hundredths} = 0.32,$$
$$8\% = 8 \text{ hundredths} = 0.08,$$

so

'8% of' means '8 hundredths of' or × 0.08,
'32% of' means '32 hundredths of' or × 0.32.

2. PERCENTAGES OF A QUANTITY

Example 1
What is 23% of 40 kg?

23% means 23 hundredths

so '23% of' means × 0.23.

Working in kilograms,

$$23\% \text{ of } 40 = 40 \times 0.23 = 9.2$$

so 23% of 40 kg = 9.2 kg.

Therefore, to find a percentage of a quantity we use the following flow chart:

Original quantity ⟶ × percentage as a decimal ⟶ Final quantity

Example 2
If 10% of people are left-handed what percentage are right-handed?

Ignoring the very few who are truly ambidextrous we can say that everyone is either left-handed or right-handed. 'Everyone' means 100%. Therefore the percentage of right-handed people is 100 − 10 = 90.

90% of people are right-handed.

(Alternatively: 10% means 0.1 and 1 − 0.1 = 0.9 which means 90%.)

Some important percentages

'50% of' means '50 hundredths of' which is the same as 'half of'.
'100% of' means '100 hundredths of' which is the same as 'all of'.

What fractions, in words, do '25% of' and '75% of' represent?

These four percentages, 25%, 50%, 75%, 100% occur so frequently that they should be remembered in words.

Exercise A

*1 Write the following decimals as (i) hundredths, (ii) percentages.
  (a) 0.06; (b) 0.15; (c) 0.48; (d) 0.87; (e) 0.20; (f) 1.00.
*2 Write the following percentages as (i) hundredths, (ii) decimals.
  (a) 4%; (b) 12%; (c) 79%; (d) 1%; (e) 40%; (f) 100%.
*3 Calculate the following quantities, using a calculator where necessary
  (a) 17% of 20 kg; (b) 15% of 45 m; (c) 25% of 18 litres;
  (d) 10% of £25; (e) 63% of 700 g; (f) 20% of 55 km.
*4 Using sensible units, calculate the following quantities.
  (a) 1% of £1; (b) 10% of 1 km; (c) 35% of 2 m;
  (d) 45% of 3 litres; (e) 6% of £2.50; (f) 18% of 4 kg.

Questions 5 to 10 refer to the displays in Figure 1.

5 On the flour label what does the phrase 100% Wholewheat mean?
6 What percentage of the Parmesan cheese was not 'Fat in dry matter'?
*7 The R.A.P. (Ready Assembled Price) of a Supa kitchen was £560. How much will be saved?
8 If the normal retail price of a certain Drake bicycle was £95, at least how much could be saved?
9 The total mass of the Parmesan cheese is 40 g. What is the mass of the 'fat in dry matter'?
*10 (a) How much could be saved on a suite originally priced at £399?
   (b) What would the selling price be?
11 A sausage of mass 55g is said to contain 65% meat. What is the mass of the other substances in the sausage?
*12 Given that there are 360° in a whole turn how many degrees would there be in
   (a) 25%; (b) 10%; (c) 48%; (d) 77% of a whole turn?
13 The original price of a home computer is £150. In a sale, 20% is taken off this price.
   (a) How much is taken off?
   (b) What is the sale price?
   However, the shop found that in order to sell the computer, they had to deduct 5% of the sale price!
   (c) How much did the shop take off the sale price?
   (d) What is the final price?
   (e) If 25% were to be taken off the *original* price, what would be the selling price of the computer? Compare your answer with part (d).

3. PERCENTAGES OF SUMS OF MONEY

Figure 2

Percentages are very frequently used in connection with money. Because we have 100p in each £1 we often say '5p in the pound' for 5% and '15p in the pound' for 15%, etc. This leads to an alternative way of working out percentages of money, as shown in the following examples, which can often be done in the head.

Example 3
   Find 20% of £4.

   1% means one hundredth, so 1% of £1 is 1p.

So 20% of £1 = 20p
and 20% of £4 = 4 × 20p = 80p.

Example 4
   Find 17% of £6.50.

   Since few people remember their 17 times table this is better done on a calculator using the method of Section 2.

'17% of' means 'multiply by 0.17'.
0.17 × 6.50 = 1.105.

Our answer is £1.105 which means £1.10$\frac{1}{2}$. As the $\frac{1}{2}$p is no longer legal tender we must decide whether to give the answer as £1.11, by rounding up (as it most usual), or as £1.10.

Exercise B

*1 Work out the following sums of money *in your head* and write down the answers only.
 (a) 40% of £2;   (b) 25% of £3;   (c) 20% of £10;
 (d) 60% of £12; (e) 15% of £8;   (f) 30% of £40;
 (g) 12% of £4.50; (h) 8% of £10.50; (i) 16% of £6.25.

*2 Calculate the following to the nearest penny.
 (a) 12% of £6.40; (b) 23% of £17.50; (c) 18% of £32.50;
 (d) 35% of £600;   (e) 64% of £92.40.

3 I pay 6% of my salary into a pension fund. How much do I pay into the fund if my salary is £8450 per annum?

*4 In a sale, the price of the following electrical goods is reduced by 20%.

		Pre-sale price
(a)	Hi-fi	£200
(b)	Television	£320
(c)	Washing machine	£235
(d)	Video recorder	£495
(e)	Tumble drier	£84
(f)	Home computer	£129

Find (i) how much is taken off (discounted from) the prices, and
  (ii) the sale price of each article.

5 The price of a sewing machine is increased by 6%. If its original price was £150
 (a) by how much did it increase;
 (b) what is its new price?

*6 A paper boy is allowed to keep 5% of the money he takes for selling newspapers. If he sells £120 worth of newspapers in a week, how much money does he keep?

7 An ice cream salesman is allowed to keep 8% of the money he takes. If he sells £560 worth of ice cream in a week, how much money does he keep?

8 A door-to-door salesman receives commission of 2% of the value of the goods he sells. If he sells £750 worth of carpet at a certain house, how much commission does he receive on this sale?

9 A pop group receives royalties of 5% of the total value of their records sold. Their latest 'hit' sells 20 000 records at £1.25 each.
 (a) How much does the pop group receive in royalties?
 (b) If there are four people in the group, how much does each receive if the money is shared equally?

SUMMARY

'Percentage' means 'so many hundredths'.

 '15% of' means '15 hundredths of'.   15 hundredths = 0.15.
  15% of 24 m = 24 m × 0.15 = 3.6 m.

For money, $n\%$ of a sum of money means n pence in the pound.

so $n\%$ of £5 = 5 × n pence = $5n$ pence.

Summary

Summary exercise

1. Calculate 9% of £50 and 50% of £9 in your head.
2. The price of a cassette recorder is increased by 10%. The original price was £99.
   (a) By how much was it increased?
   (b) What is its new price?
3. 'Ripple' chocolate bars have a mass of 120 g. The manufacturers decide to increase the mass by 8%.
   (a) By how much is the mass increased?
   (b) What is the new mass?
4. A meat pie is said to contain 72% meat. If its total mass is 450 g, what is the mass of the other ingredients in the pie?
5. A coin of mass 12 g contains 30% zinc, 60% nickel with the rest being copper. What is the mass of each metal in the coin?
6. A school contains 720 pupils. If 15% are absent one day, how many are present?
7. A test is marked out of 140. If Elizabeth scores 75% in the test and Robert 70%, find how many marks each obtained.
8. In a sale 15% is discounted from a television which was originally priced at £250.
   (a) What is its sale price?
   (b) If another 5% is discounted from its sale price, what is its final price?
   (c) What would its final price be if 20% were discounted from its original price?

Miscellaneous exercise

1. In a 'closing down' sale, a shop reduces its prices at first by 40% and then a further 20% is taken from the discounted prices.
   (a) Find the first sale price of the items listed below.
   (b) Find the final sale price of the items.
   (c) Compare your answers to part (b) with a reduction of 60% on the original prices.

	Original price
(i) Refrigerator	£75
(ii) Freezer	£130
(iii) Music centre	£199

2. 'Venus' chocolate bars contain 22% sugar, 35% cocoa and 9% milk, together with other ingredients.
   (a) If the mass of a bar is 450 g find the mass of sugar, cocoa, milk and other ingredients in the bar.
   (b) The manufacturers decide to increase the mass of the bar by 6%, keeping the proportions of the ingredients the same. What will be the masses of these ingredients now?
3. A second-hand car is seen advertised at £3000 but with a 10% discount for a quick sale. Unfortunately, just before Jim decides to buy the car at the agreed discount, the government adds a new 10% tax on the agreed selling price of all second-hand cars. Nevertheless, Jim decides to buy. Does he pay £3000, less than £3000 or more than £3000?

4 Every year a car loses 15% of its value at the beginning of that year. If it was originally worth £5000, what will it be worth after 2 years? Compare your answer with a car worth £5000 losing 30% of its value after 2 years.

5 (a) Write the following percentages as decimals.
   (i) 12.5%; (ii) 6.5%; (iii) 17.25%; (iv) 4.75%; (v) 0.5%; (vi) 0.17%.
   (b) Write the following decimals as percentages.
   (i) 0.235; (ii) 0.075; (iii) 0.6275; (iv) 0.0325; (v) 0.004; (vi) 0.0092.

6 Daniel is offered a 15% increase in his pocket money this year followed by one of 20% next year. Annabelle is offered one of 20% this year but only 15% next year. Who has been given the better offer? Explain carefully.

7 A photograph measures 11 cm by 9 cm.
   (a) What is its area?
   (b) If it is enlarged so that its area is increased by 30% what is the area of the enlargement?
   (c) Instead, the photograph is enlarged so that its sides are each 30% longer. What is the area of this enlargement?
   (d) Comment on your answers to (b) and (c).

8 Under the 'Minotaur' Saving Scheme, children who put money into the Southern Bank receive 10.5% interest on the amount they have in their bank accounts at the end of each year. This interest is added to the amount in the account. If Enid puts £50 into her account, calculate:
   (a) how much interest she receives at the end of the first year;
   (b) what her account contains after one year;
   (c) what her account contains after two years if she gets interest on her first year's interest as well as the original £50 and she withdraws no money.

30

Conversion and travel graphs

1. CONVERSION GRAPHS

If you have been on a continental holiday by car you will have noticed that the distances between towns are indicated in kilometres. This can be a little confusing to start with until you learn to use a rough conversion rule that '5 miles is about the same as 8 kilometres'. In this section we are going to look at a graphical method of conversion between miles and kilometres.

The graph required is shown in Figure 1. The axes are labelled miles and kilometres (km) rather than x and y; it does not matter, here, which goes horizontally. The numbers on the axes indicate the scale being used. We mark two points, one using the fact that 5 miles $\approx$ 8 kilometres and the other using the fact that 0 miles = 0 kilometres.

219

220 Conversion and travel graphs Ch. 30

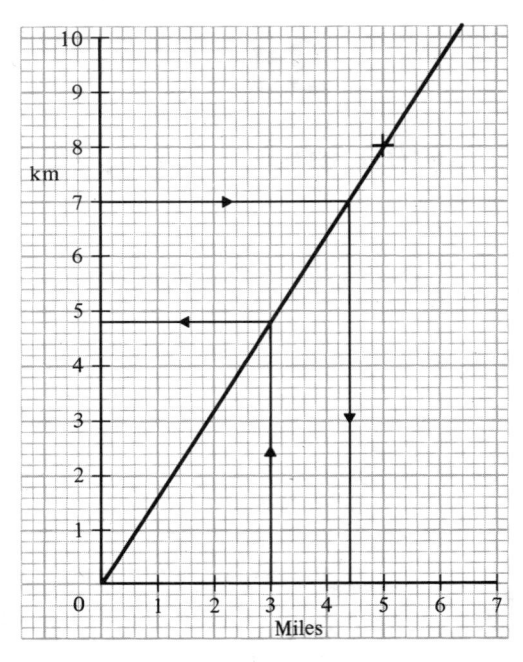

Figure 1

Example 1

Use the graph in Figure 1 to change
(a) 3 miles to kilometres;
(b) 7 kilometres to miles.

(a) We find the point 3 (miles) on the horizontal axis, follow a line up to the graph and read across onto the vertical axis to find 4.8 (km). The lines are shown in the diagram and when you draw your own graphs you should show the lines which you use.

Answer 3 miles ≈ 4.8 km.

(b) Reading across from 7 km on the vertical axis to 4.4 miles on the horizontal axis we find 7 km ≈ 4.4 miles.

Example 2

The label on a sauce bottle says 850 g (for grams) and 1.87 lb (for pounds). Use this information (together with the obvious fact that 0 g = 0 lb) to draw a conversion graph relating grams and pounds. Use the graph to find
(a) the mass in lb of a 600 g box of chocolates;
(b) the mass in grams of a $1\frac{1}{2}$ lb bag of carrots.

The conversion graph is shown in Figure 2. (Again it does not matter which quantity goes on which axis.) Care is needed in plotting the point (850, 1.87).

Conversion graphs 221

Along the grams axis each small square represents 20 units. 850 is therefore half way between 840 and 860. Along the other axis each small square shows 0.04 units. 1.87 is therefore shown between 1.84 and 1.88 at the three-quarter way point.

The lines needed to read off the answers to the questions are shown.

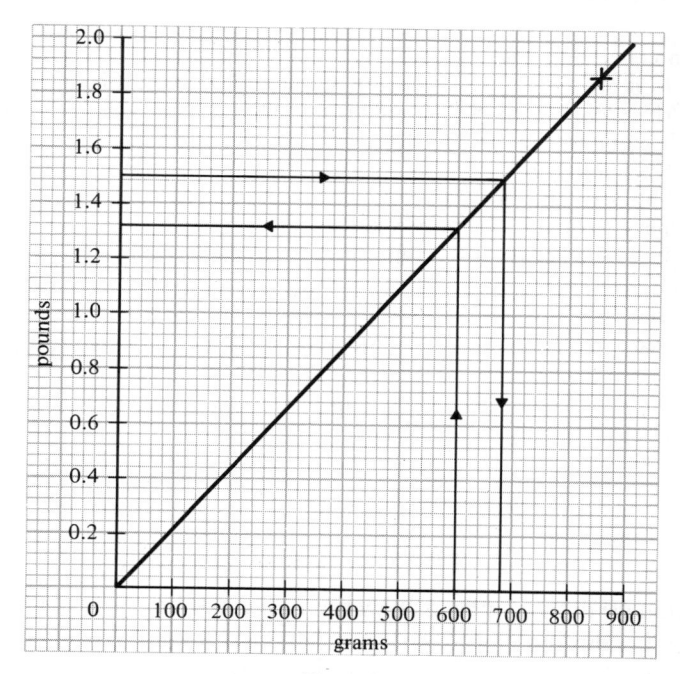

Figure 2

The answers are (a) 600 g ≈ 1.32 lb and (b) 1½ lb ≈ 680 g. Because of the difficulty in reading the graph and also because the original data are not exact both answers are, of course, approximate.

Exercise A

*1 Use Figures 1 and 2 to convert the following. (You should not mark your textbook but you may find it helpful to lay tracing paper over the graphs and to draw lines on it.)

    (a) 4 miles to km;   (b) 4.8 km to miles;   (c) 10 km to miles;
    (d) 1.6 miles to km;   (e) 0.8 lb to grams;   (f) 800 grams to lb;
    (g) 0.4 lb to grams;   (h) 1.64 lb to grams;   (i) 730 grams to lb.

2 Mini-investigation. When you get home or are next in a supermarket look at the label on a '1 lb' jar of jam or marmalade. You will probably find another pounds-to-grams conversion factor on the label. See if it agrees with the one on the sauce label used for Figure 2.

*3 A rule for relating lengths in centimetres to lengths in inches is 2.54 cm ≈ 1 inch. Multiplying by 10 gives 25.4 cm ≈ 10 inches. Use this fact, and the other obvious one, to draw a graph to relate lengths in centimetres to lengths in inches. Use a scale of 2 cm to represent a length of 5 centimetres and a scale of 1 cm to represent a length of 1 inch. Use your graph to convert:

    (a) 6 inches to cm;   (b) 20 cm to inches;
    (c) 1 foot to cm;   (d) 28.5 cm to inches.

*4 Petrol used to be priced by the gallon and is now more usually priced by the litre. A rough conversion guide is that 1 gallon ≈ 4.54 litres. Draw a graph to relate gallons to litres using this information and use it to answer the questions which follow. Make your scale sensible, and big enough to include 4 gallons and 20 litres. Use your graph to convert:

    (a) 2.5 gallons to litres;
    (b) 15 litres to gallons;
    (c) 6 pints to litres (1 gallon = 8 pints);
    (d) 1 litre to gallons and then give the answer also in pints.

*5 A speed of 60 miles per hour (m.p.h.) is roughly the same as one of 27 metres per second (m/s). Use this fact to draw a conversion graph for the systems of speed measurement. Allow for speeds up to 70 m.p.h. and 30 m/s. Use your graph to convert

    (a) 45 m.p.h. to m/s;   (b) 25 m/s to m.p.h.;
    (c) 18 m.p.h. to m/s;   (d) 30 m/s to m.p.h.

2. TRAVEL GRAPHS

In this section we draw graphs to show progress made on a journey. Consider a company of Guides hiking to their camp site: they leave the guide hut at 1000 (10.00 a.m.) and walk at 4 kilometres per hour (km/h) for one hour. They stop

Travel graphs

for half an hour for a drink and then continue their walk at 3 km/h for 2 hours. They have lunch and rest for an hour and then start the last part of their hike. They arrive at the camp at 1700 and, consulting their map, find they have walked a total distance of 16 km. The graph in Figure 3 shows all this information.

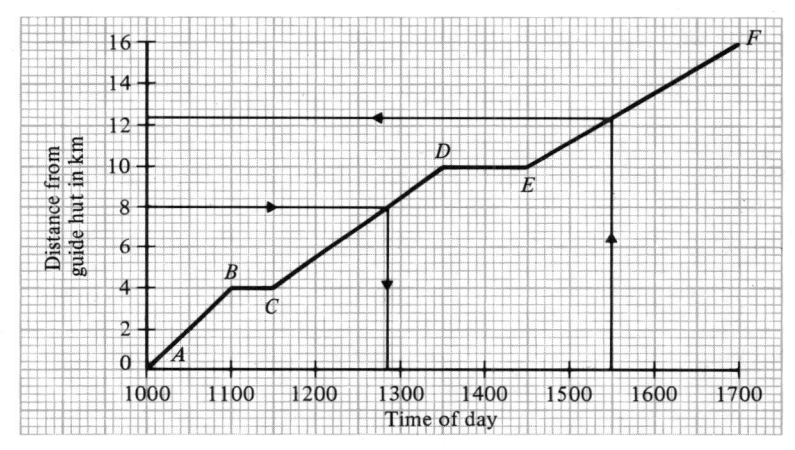

Figure 3

Notice that the vertical axis is labelled 'Distance *from* the guide hut'; this is preferred to just 'distance travelled' as you will see later. The section AB shows the first stage at 4 km/h for 1 hour. BC show the half hour interval for the first rest. The distance shown by the section CD is 6 km, this being the distance covered in 2 hours at 3 km/h. DE shows the lunch stop and EF the final stage.

Example 3

Use the graph in Figure 3 to find
(*a*) how far the Guides still had to travel at 1530;
(*b*) the time at which they saw a tramp asleep in a ditch (this was when they had walked 8 km).

As in the previous section the lines needed to answer these questions are drawn on the graph. The answers are:
(*a*) 3.6 km (they had already covered 12.4 km and had 16 km to go altogether);
(*b*) 1251 (each small square on the time axis represents 6 minutes).

Example 4

On the occasion of the Veteran Car Club Rally from London to Brighton (otherwise known as the Old Crocks' Race) one car 'Genevieve' covered the 80 km at a constant speed of 20 km/h. Another car 'Lionheart' started at the same time as 'Genevieve', 1000, at a cracking speed of 40 km/h. Sadly she broke down after an hour but recovered in time to finish the course at a constant speed of 30 km/h. The two cars arrived at the finishing line at exactly the same time.

Use a travel graph to find the times when:

(a) Genevieve overtook Lionheart;

(b) Lionheart started again after her breakdown.

The graph is shown in Figure 4.

It will take Genevieve 4 hours to cover 80 km at 20 km/h and the line AB shows this. AP shows the first stage of Lionheart's run. We do not know when Lionheart started up again and so have to draw the section BQ by using the fact that her final speed is 30 km/h. R is marked showing 30 km to go with an hour left, BR is extended to Q to meet the line from P which represents the breakdown.

By looking at the completed graph it can be seen that the answers are

(a) 1200 (where the graphs cross);

(b) approximately 1240 (indicated by point Q).

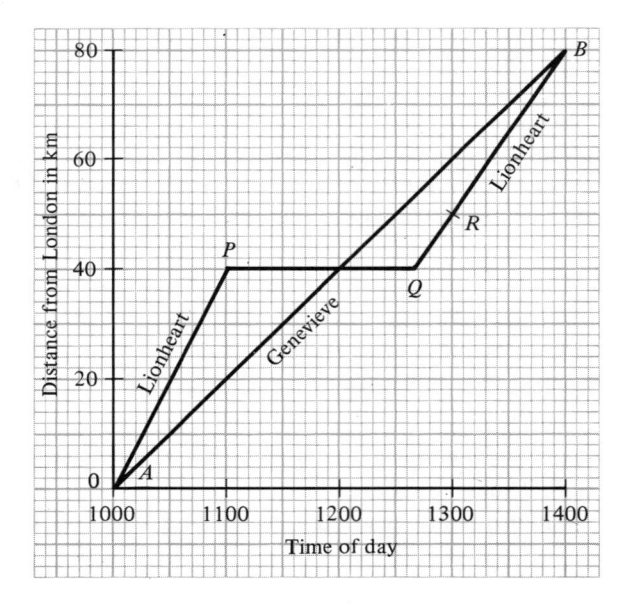

Figure 4

Exercise B

*1 Without drawing in your book use the graphs in Figures 3 and 4 to answer the questions which follow.
  (a) How long did the Guides take to cover the first 6 kilometres?
  (b) How far was it from their lunch place to their camp? How long did it take them to walk this last stretch?
  (c) Use your answers to (b) to work out their speed for this stage. (Use your calculator if you need to.)
  (d) How long had Lionheart been stopped when Genevieve passed her?
  (e) How far is Genevieve from London at (i) 1130; (ii) 1245?
  (f) If Lionheart had not broken down or had to reduce speed where would she have been at 1130?

2 Joe sets off from home to the seaside 20 kilometres away. He cycles at 10 km/h for $1\frac{1}{2}$ hours and then has a puncture which takes half an hour to mend. He then cycles on at the same speed. Draw a graph to represent his journey and use it to find how far from his destination he was after $2\frac{1}{4}$ hours.

3 Miss Avon reaches the M4 to drive to London. The traffic is heavy and she has driven 20 miles at 60 m.p.h. when her car's steering becomes faulty. She waits by an emergency phone for half an hour and then is towed at 30 m.p.h. to the nearest service area which is 15 miles further on. Draw a travel graph to show her journey.

4 Roy is exercising his Afghan hounds on the Downs and the dogs like to run to a large tree which is 180 m from the path. Sultan races off at 12 m/s, reaches the tree and waits there. Farrah runs at 10 m/s till she is 150 m from the path and sits down to wait for Roy who is walking steadily at 2 m/s. She then continues with Roy to the tree. Draw a graph to show their journeys. (Assume the paths of Roy and the dogs are all straight lines.) How long did Farrah sit waiting for Roy? How long did Sultan sit waiting for the others?

5 A cyclist travels at a steady 20 km/h from Salisbury to London, a distance of 140 km. How long will it take her? If she leaves Salisbury at 9.00 a.m. draw a graph to show her progress and show on your graph the point which represents her arrival in London.

A car leaves Salisbury at midday and travels towards London at 50 km/h. Show the graph representing its progress on the same diagram as for the cyclist. What can you say about the point where your two graphs cross?

3. HARDER TRAVEL GRAPHS

On the day the Guides were hiking to camp, a party of Scouts were returning from the camp site to their scout hut (next to the guide hut) and along the same path. However they had been on a light-weight cycle camp and left the camp at 1100 arriving at their hut at 1300.

226   Conversion and travel graphs   Ch. 30

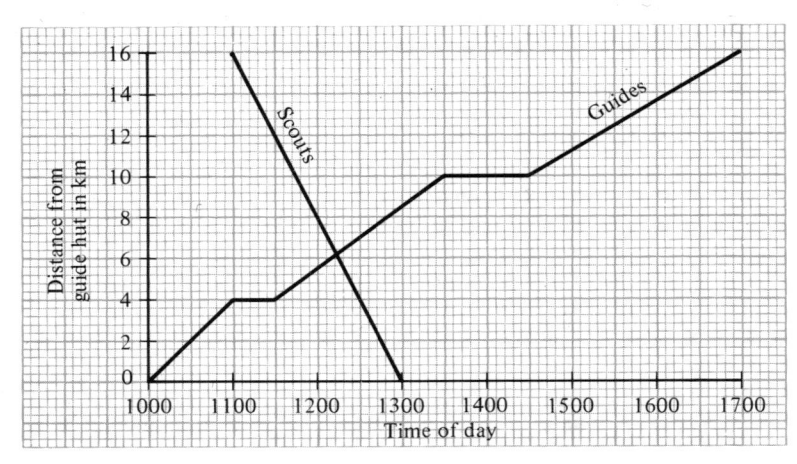

Figure 5

Figure 5 shows the original graph of the Guides' progress together with one showing the Scouts' journey. Notice carefully that the Scouts' graph 'slopes downwards'. This is because the vertical axis is labelled 'Distance *from* guide hut' and the scouts were 16 km from there at 1100, and 0 km from there at 1300. The point where the graphs cross indicates the time and the place where the Scouts and Guides passed each other, going in opposite directions.

Exercise C

*1 How far from the camp site is the place where the Scouts and Guides passed each other? At what time of day did they pass?

*2 Make a copy of the graph in Figure 4. On this draw another graph to show the progress of an ambulance which left Brighton at noon reaching London 1 hour 20 minutes later.
    (*a*) At what speed was the ambulance travelling?
    (*b*) At what time did the ambulance pass Genevieve?
    (*c*) When the ambulance passed Lionheart, was she repaired? If not, how much time was still required to complete the repair?

3 A cyclist leaves a town *A* at midday and cycles towards a town *B* 20 km away. For the first half hour she travels at 16 km/h and then, after a rest of 12 minutes, she continues at 10 km/h until she reaches *B*. She stays at *B* for 15 minutes and then cycles back to *A* at a steady speed of 15 km/h. Draw a graph to show her distance from *A* at any time.
    On her outward journey the cyclist passes a man walking at a steady speed from *B* to *A* at 1.30 p.m. and overtakes him on her return journey at 3.00 p.m. Plot two points to show the walker's position at these times. Use your graph to find the time at which he left *B*.

4 A High Speed Train leaves Bristol Parkway at 7.00 a.m. (0700) and reaches Swindon 40 miles away at 7.30 a.m. A section of the track between Swindon and Didcot is under repair and it takes another half an hour to cover the 20 miles to Didcot. The train then takes 15 minutes to reach Reading 20 miles further on. Draw a graph to

show the journey from Bristol to Reading. (Ignore stops at stations.) If a goods train leaves Reading at 7.45 a.m. and travels towards Swindon at a steady 30 m.p.h. how far from Reading will they meet?

5 Miss Avon leaves Bristol at 8.00 a.m. to drive to London which is 120 miles away. She is caught in rush hour traffic and it takes her half an hour to travel 10 miles to reach the motorway. She then drives at 70 m.p.h. until she reaches the services 35 miles away. She stays there for quarter of an hour and then continues her journey at 70 m.p.h.

Mr Billings leaves London at 9.00 a.m. and it takes him 20 minutes to drive the 10 miles to the motorway. He then drives at a steady speed of 70 m.p.h. towards Bristol. Draw travel graphs to represent their journeys and find at what time Miss Avon and Mr Billings will pass each other. How far from London are they then?

6 A High Speed train leaves Paddington at 1720 to travel to Bristol Parkway, non-stop. It is due at Bristol, 120 miles away, at 1826. At 1714 another train leaves Bristol Parkway and is due at Reading, 80 miles away, at 1805. This one travels the last 40 miles at a speed of 80 m.p.h. Draw a graph of the journeys of these two trains showing distance from Bristol on the axis up the page. Find how far they are from London Paddington when they pass.

SUMMARY

Conversion graphs are used to relate one measurement with another. They can be used either way, for example from gallons to litres or litres to gallons. Most conversion graphs pass through the origin (where the axes meet). They are drawn by using two facts, for example that 1 gallon ≈ 4.54 litres and that 0 gallons = 0 litres.

Travel Graphs show the progress of a moving object. The axis taken across the page show the time taken and the axis up the page shows the distance away from the starting point. The point where two travel graphs cross indicates where travellers meet, since they are then at the same place at the same time.

Summary exercise

1 You may have heard of areas of fields being measured in acres. An acre is the area enclosed by a length of 22 yards by 220 yards (or 1 cricket pitch by 10 cricket pitches!). In metric measure we use the hectare (the area enclosed by a square 100 m by 100 m.) The conversion fact required is that 10 acres = 4.05 hectares. Draw a graph to convert areas in acres to areas in hectares allowing for areas up to 10 acres. Use your graph to convert:
 (a) 2.5 acres to hectares; (b) 8.7 acres to hectares;
 (c) 3.6 hectares to acres; (d) 1 hectare to acres.

2 A car leaves town X at 10.00 a.m. to travel to Y which is 210 km away. It travels at 60 km/h for $1\frac{1}{2}$ hours, stops for $\frac{1}{2}$ hour and reaches Y at 3.00 p.m. Another car leaves Y at 11.00 a.m. and travels non-stop to X arriving at 2.00 p.m. Draw travel graphs to show these two journeys (use the 24-hour clock on the time-axis) and find:
 (a) the speed of the first car after the stop. (Hint: how far did it have to go and how long did it take?);
 (b) the time at which the cars passed each other;
 (c) how far from X they passed each other.

Miscellaneous exercise

1. Temperature is now usually measured in degrees Celsius whereas it often used to be measured in degrees Fahrenheit. To convert from one system to the other the following two facts are used.
    (*a*) the temperature of boiling water is 100 °C or 212 °F;
    (*b*) freezing point of water is 0 °C or 32 °F.
    Draw axes to show °C from 0 to 100 across the page and °F from 0 to 220 up the page. Plot points to show the information given in (*a*) and (*b*) and join them with a straight line. Note that this conversion graph does not pass through the origin. Try to find out why this is.
    Use your graph to convert
    (*a*) 30 °C to °F; (*b*) 87 °C to °F; (*c*) 180 °F to °C; (*d*) 50 °F to °C.
    Your normal blood temperature is well known to be 98.4 °F. Convert this to °C. Your doctor would possibly be concerned if your temperature rose above 100 °F. This is an easy number to remember as an obvious warning point. What is a suitable warning point in degrees Celsius?
    A really hot summer's day in England is 'into the eighties'; is this in degrees Fahrenheit or Celsius? What is the equivalent in the other system?

2. In 1985 the currency conversion rate for Greek drachmas into sterling was 150 drachmas to the £. Or, more simply, Dr 150 = £1. Obviously Dr 0 = £0 as well. Use this information to draw a graph to convert amounts up to £5 into drachmas. Take 2 cm across the page to represent £1. As the point showing Dr 150 = £1 is near the origin, use Dr 750 = £5 instead.
    Use your graph to convert
    (*a*) £3.80 to Dr; (*b*) £1.73 to Dr; (*c*) Dr 180 to £p; (*d*) Dr 624 to £p.
    When converting currency you must be careful to give a sensible answer. There is no such thing as a ½ drachma in regular use so your answers must always be to the nearest whole number of drachmas. The ½p coin in Britain was withdrawn in December 1984 and so amounts in British currency must also be given to the nearest whole number of pence.
    You may not have noticed this difficulty in answering (*a*) to (*d*) above. But now draw another graph showing values up to £1 (only) across the page and to Dr 150 (only) up the page. Use a scale of 1 cm = 10p and 1 cm = 10 drachmas.
    Use this graph to convert
    (*e*) 84p into Dr; (*f*) 35p into Dr; (*g*) Dr 71 into p; (*h*) Dr 100 into p.

3. Find out the up-to-date conversion rate of the £ into US dollars. Draw a graph to represent this conversion. Make a list of some articles on sale in this country, or the price of services (for example a haircut), and then work out the equivalent rate in dollars. Try and find out if these would be reasonable prices to pay if you were actually in the USA.

4. A car travels 16 miles from *A* to *B* at a steady speed of 32 m.p.h., waits for 6 minutes at *B* and then carries on its journey to *C*. *C* is 32 miles further on and for this stage the car's speed is increased to 48 m.p.h. After staying at *C* for only 10 minutes the driver has transacted his business and returns to *A* non-stop at 64 m.p.h. Draw a graph showing the car's distance from *A* at any time. A cyclist leaves *C* for *A* at the same time as the car started its journey and meets the car on its return journey 24 miles from *C*. Use your graph to find when this meeting takes place and the speed of the cyclist.

31
Illustrating data

1. A SURVEY

Let us imagine that a Headteacher wants to find out how pupils come to school and how many use each method of travel. Some will walk, some cycle, others come by train, and so on. The Headteacher must first decide how to group the pupils.

She might decide to try:

        Walk   Cycle   Bus   Train   Brought by car

Already there are difficulties. What about the boy who has a long walk from the bus stop? Does he come under the heading 'Walk' or 'Bus', or should the Headteacher make a new heading? What about the girl who cycles when it is fine weather but who is brought by car when it is raining?

The Headteacher will probably decide to put these 'awkward' cases into the group to which they most sensibly belong, although in many cases this might not be an easy decision to make.

This means that the results will not give a perfectly accurate picture of the situation. Two people faced with the same decision might decide differently.

Here are the results of a survey made on a group of first year boys and girls to find out how many are using each method.

        walk 13;   cycle 8;   bus 4;   train 9;   car 2.

230   Illustrating data   Ch. 31

We can just write out the results like this, or we could try to find a way to display them so that they were easier to understand or even to see at a glance. One method is a simple table:

Walk	Cycle	Bus	Train	Car	Total
13	8	4	9	2	36

The total has been included and this acts as a useful check.

However, particularly if there are a lot of data (numerical bits of information) it is useful to be able to illustrate them diagrammatically.

2. PICTOGRAMS

How the children travel to school

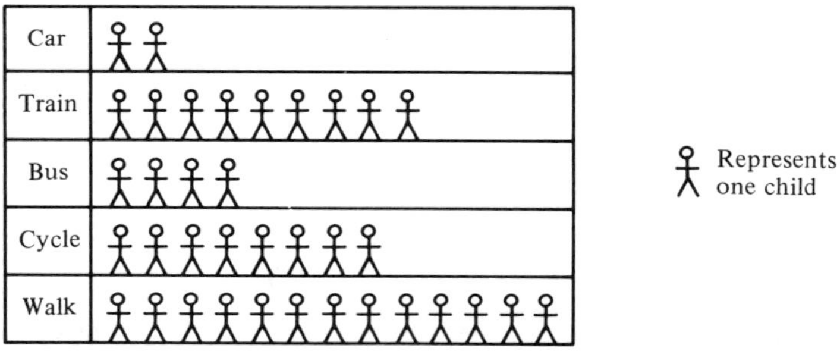

[Pictogram showing: Car - 2 figures; Train - 9 figures; Bus - 4 figures; Cycle - 8 figures; Walk - 13 figures. Key: Represents one child]

Figure 1

An attractive way of representing the information is a *pictogram*. See Figure 1. Little drawings are used to display the details. Note that
   (a) the diagram has a title;
   (b) all the symbols are the same size;
   (c) we give the 'scale' that is used ' 𝆢 represents one child'.

Exercise A

1 Make a survey of the ways in which the members of your class travel to school and draw a pictogram to illustrate the data.
2 Make a survey of the favourite pop-groups of the members of your class and illustrate with a pictogram.

Bar charts 231

[Pictogram showing rows of figures]
- BR (top row)
- LT Rail
- LT Bus

♦ Represents
10 000 commuters

Figure 2

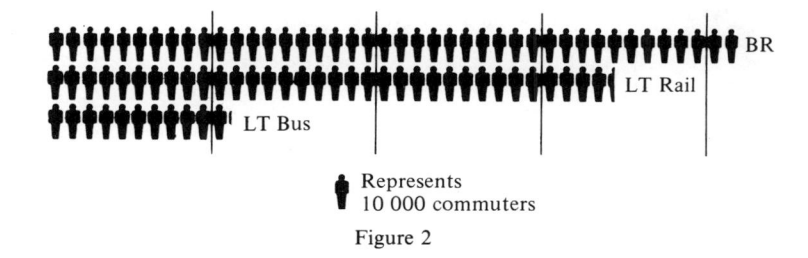

*3 Figure 2 illustrates the number of commuters arriving daily in central London, in 1979, by British Rail and by London Transport Bus and Rail (the Underground). Estimate how many commuters arrived by each means. Think carefully how to interpret the 'fractions of a man' in the London Transport rows.

3. BAR CHARTS

Another simple way to display the school transport data is a *bar chart*. Figure 3 shows the pictogram of Figure 1 in a slightly different form.

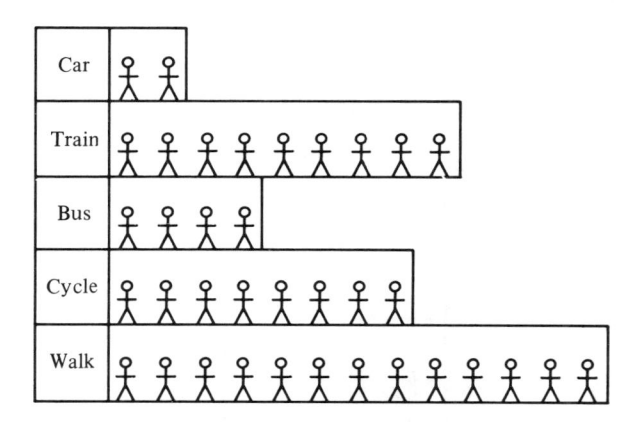

Figure 3

Figure 4 shows how this can be simplified as a bar chart.

232 Illustrating data Ch. 31

How children travel to school

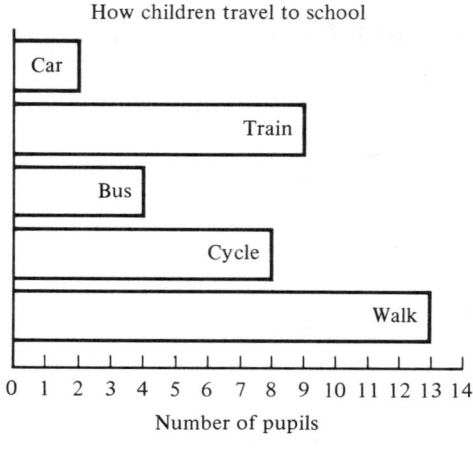

[Figure 4: Horizontal bar chart showing Car, Train, Bus, Cycle, Walk against Number of pupils, scale 0 to 14]

Figure 4

Note again that the chart has a heading. The words 'Number of pupils' show what the numbers stand for; they give the scale being used.

It is quite usual to draw a bar chart with the bars running vertically (up the page) rather than horizontally (across the page). Figure 5 shows the same information as Figure 4. Diagrams may be shaded or coloured if you wish.

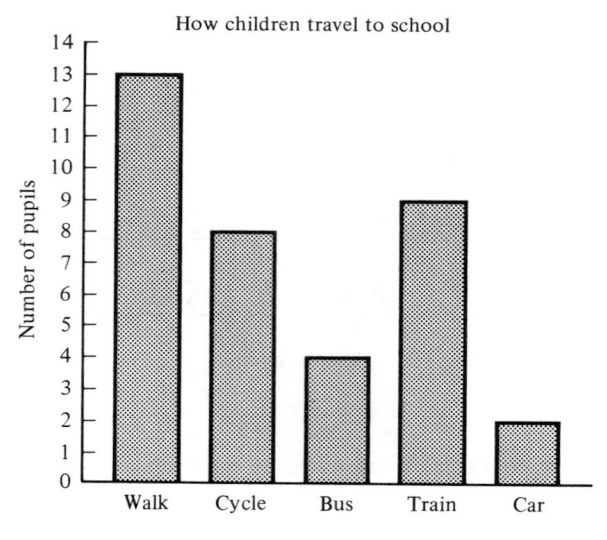

[Figure 5: Vertical bar chart showing Walk (13), Cycle (8), Bus (4), Train (9), Car (2) with Number of pupils on y-axis from 0 to 14]

Figure 5

Exercise B

1 The school referred to in the text also held a survey of how the Upper Sixth travelled to school. The results follow:

Walk	Cycle	Bus	Train	Car
6	10	3	7	10

Draw a bar chart to illustrate this information.

2 Draw bar charts to illustrate the data you collected for questions 1 and 2 in Exercise A.

3 Draw a bar chart to illustrate the transport information of Figure 2. Use a scale of 1 cm to represent 50 000 commuters.

4 Make a list of all the subjects on your timetable and the number of minutes spent on each in the course of the week. Display these results in the form of a bar chart.

*5 Daniel, Colin, Trudy and Annabelle drew a bar chart to illustrate their monthly pocket money. They forgot to give the scale but I know that Colin is given £5. How much do you think Daniel, Trudy and Annabelle were given?

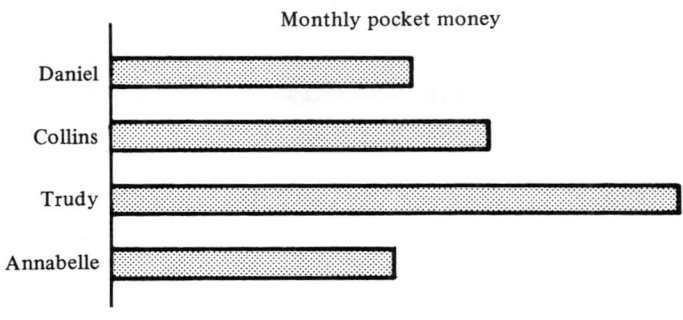

Figure 6

6 The numbers of the main farm animals in Great Britain were, in 1970, approximately:

12 million cattle;   30 million sheep;   6 million pigs.

(a) Draw a bar chart to illustrate the information.
(b) Obtain, if possible, up-to-date information. Draw a bar chart and compare with (a).

234 Illustrating data Ch. 31

Questions 7, 8 and 9 all refer to Figure 7 which is an extract from the brochure of a travel agent.

7 Draw a bar chart to illustrate the cost of dinner for two in the seven countries shown in the table.
8 Draw a bar chart to illustrate the cost of a bottle of wine in the seven countries.
9 Work out the total cost, in the seven countries, of dinner for two, a bottle of wine and coffee for *two*. Illustrate with a bar chart.

ITEMS	PORTUGAL £	BALEARIC ISLANDS £	SPANISH MAINLAND £	CANARY ISLANDS £	MALTA £	GREECE £	YUGOSLAVIA £
DINNER FOR TWO	4.54	6.55	6.43	8.72	9.00	6.07	5.73
WINE PER BOTTLE	1.02	0.92	0.80	1.72	2.25	1.02	1.40
CUP OF COFFEE	0.09	0.26	0.32	0.31	0.40	0.32	0.22

Figure 7

4. PIE CHARTS

Here again are the data on travel from the first section of this chapter.

Walk	Cycle	Bus	Train	Car	
13	8	4	9	2	Total 36

Table 1

Another simple way of displaying this information is by a *pie chart*. A circular 'pie' is drawn and slices are marked. Figure 8 shows a pie chart for the travel data from the table.

Pie chart to show
method of travel

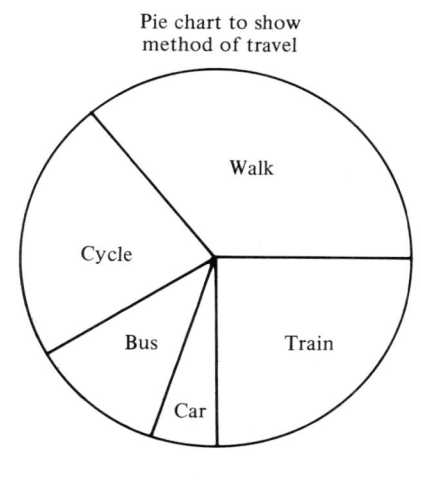

[Pie chart showing sectors labelled Walk, Cycle, Bus, Car, Train]

Figure 8

Note that the number of those who cycle is twice the number of those who travel by bus so that the angle for the cycle sector is twice that for the bus sector. We say that the angles are *proportional* to the numbers involved. (The mathematical name for a slice of a circle is a *sector*.)

To see how the angles are worked out we look again at the data of Table 1. These are put in a slightly different form in Table 2(*a*) and we have added the fact that the angles must total 360°.

	Number		Angle of sector in degrees
Walk	13		
Cycle	8		
Bus	4		
Train	9		
Car	2		
Total	36	× 10	360

Table 2(*a*)

We see that a scale factor of 10 is needed to map the number of children onto the total number of degrees. (This is because $360° \div 36 = 10°$.) We apply the same scale factor to the individual numbers in the table and get the results shown in Table 2(*b*).

	Number	Angle of sector in degrees
Walk	13	130
Cycle	8	80
Bus	4	40
Train	9	90
Car	2	20
Total	36	360

Table 2(b)

Notice that the totals have been included. Always check that the angles add up to 360°.

The angles may not always work out quite as easily as in the transport case. The following example shows, however, that the same method can be applied.

Example 1

In a survey to find out voting intentions at the next election the following results were obtained:

LBB (Let's Back Britain) 20; Conservative 60; Labour 50; Liberal 15; Don't know 5.

Calculate the angles required to illustrate these data in a pie chart.

Simple addition gives the fact that 150 people were surveyed.

A total of 150 people are represented by 360°. So the scale factor required is given by:

$$150 \longrightarrow \boxed{\times ?} \longrightarrow 360$$

As $360 \div 150 = 2.4$, this is the required scale factor. The working can then be completed as in Table 3.

	Number of voters		Angle of sector in degrees
LBB	20		48
Conservative	60		144
Labour	50		120
Liberal	15		36
Don't know	5		12
Total	150	× 2.4	360

Table 3

Pie charts

Exercise C

***1** In a small class of 20 pupils it was found that 9 prefer KOKOPOPS, 3 prefer CRACKFLAKES, 6 prefer RICESNAPS and 2 prefer BRANBITS. Draw a pie chart to illustrate their favourite breakfast cereals.

2 Tina estimates that, over a period of a fortnight, she spent 7 hours watching BBC 1, 6 hours watching ITV, 3 hours watching BBC 2 and 2 hours watching Channel 4 television. Draw a pie chart to show how she spent her viewing time.

***3** During one month a college student's expenditure was as follows:

	£		£
Rent	48	Food ⎫ Drink ⎭	52
Rates	8		
Heat ⎫ Light ⎭	24	Clothes	10
		Travel ⎫ Entertainment ⎭	38

(a) What was his total expenditure?
(b) Draw a pie chart to illustrate the information. Show how you calculate the various angles.

4 Of 100 pupils studying foreign languages, 35 prefer Spanish, 50 Russian and the rest Italian. Illustrate with a pie chart, showing how you calculate the various angles.

5 Work out how you spent your pocket money last month and draw a pie chart to illustrate.

*6 Draw a pie chart to illustrate the farm animal data of question 6 in Exercise B.

7 Draw a pie chart to illustrate the commuter data of question 3 in Exercise A.

8 Draw pie charts to illustrate the data you collected for questions 1 and 2 in Exercise A.

9 Figure 9 shows a pie chart to illustrate the popularity of certain brands of sun-tan cream. Nu-Glo received 21 votes. Work out how many votes were given to the other products and also how many people were interviewed.

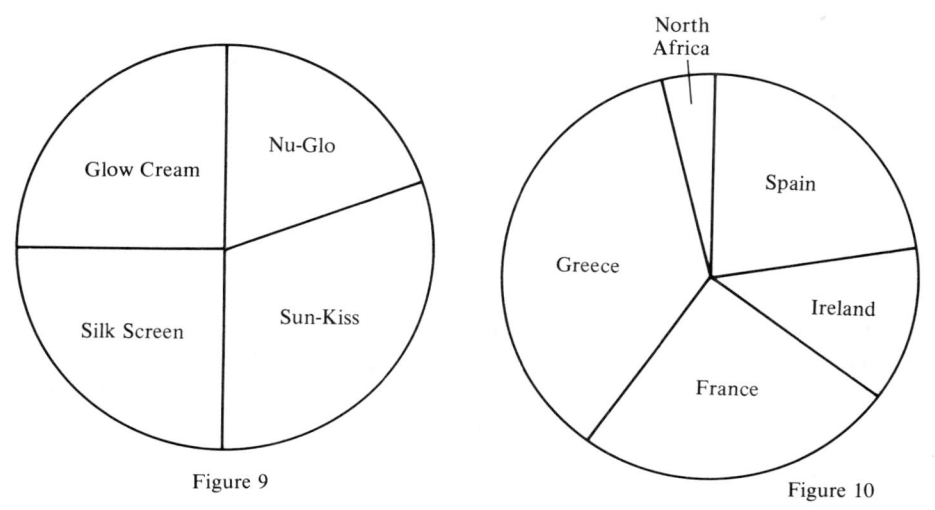

Figure 9

Figure 10

10 Figure 10 shows a pie chart to illustrate the places where 180 people spent their holidays in 1986. Work out how many went to each country.
Illustrate the information in a different way.

5. LINE GRAPHS

The table shown below gives the temperature in degrees Celsius at hourly intervals after midnight during the morning of a summer's day.

Time (hours after midnight)	1	2	3	4	5	6	7	8	9	10	11
Temperature (°C)	17.3	17.0	16.8	16.5	16.2	16.4	16.8	17.0	17.2	18.2	19.3

Table 4

This information is shown in Figure 11(a).

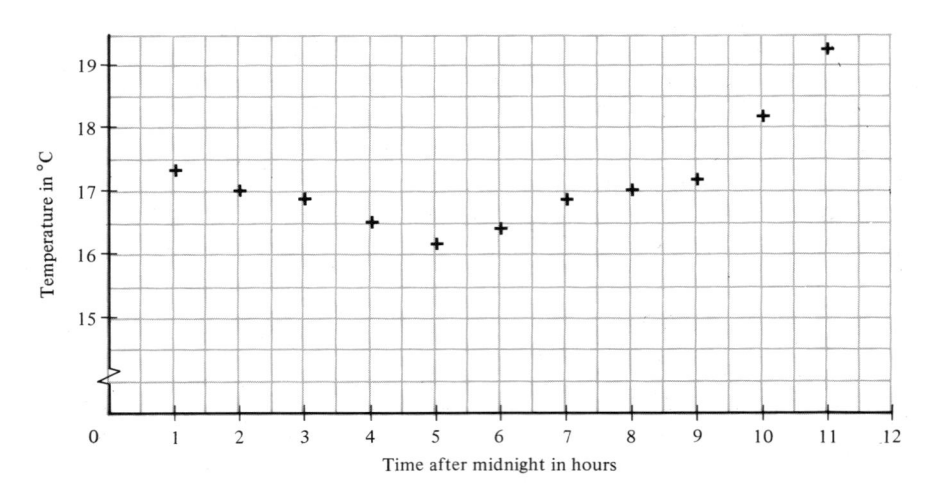

Figure 11(a)

This diagram is not particularly effective consisting, as it does, of a series of plotted points. We know the temperatures indicated by these points and between any two points we would assume a steady change. Accordingly we join the points with straight lines so that we can estimate temperatures at intermediate times, for example after $2\frac{1}{2}$ hours. Figure 11(b) illustrates this. (Note the zig-zag on the vertical axis. This is to draw attention to the fact that the temperature scale does not start at zero. Graphs without such indication can be very misleading.) Graphs like Figure 11(b) are called *line graphs* and are frequently used when time is involved.

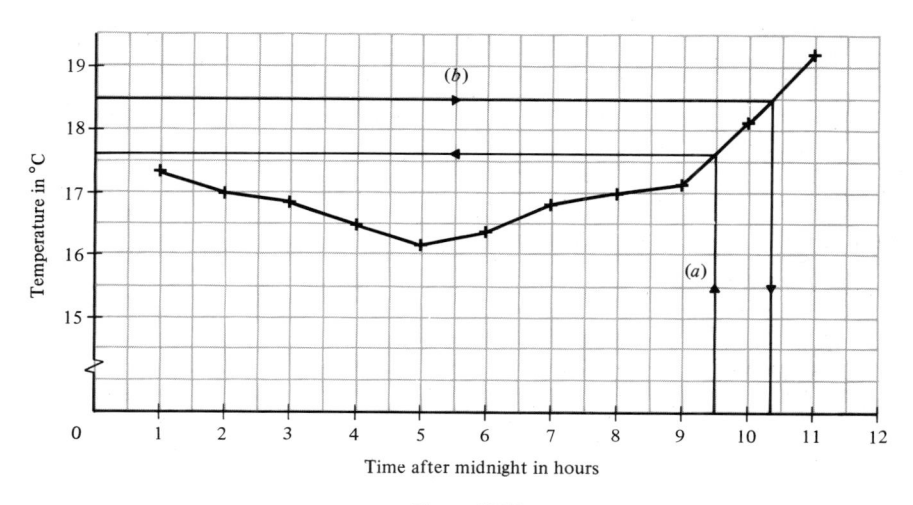

Figure 11(b)

We can use this graph to *estimate* temperatures at other times (within the limits of the graph). For instance the line marked (a) shows that the temperature at 9.30 a.m. was approximately 17.7 °C. The line marked (b) suggests that the temperature reached 18.5 °C at 10.20 a,m,

Trends

Table 5 shows the number of calculators possessed by the pupils of a large school during the years 1981 to 1986.

Year	1981	1982	1983	1984	1985	1986
Number of calculators	850	950	1040	1140	1260	1330

Table 5

This information is illustrated in Figure 12.

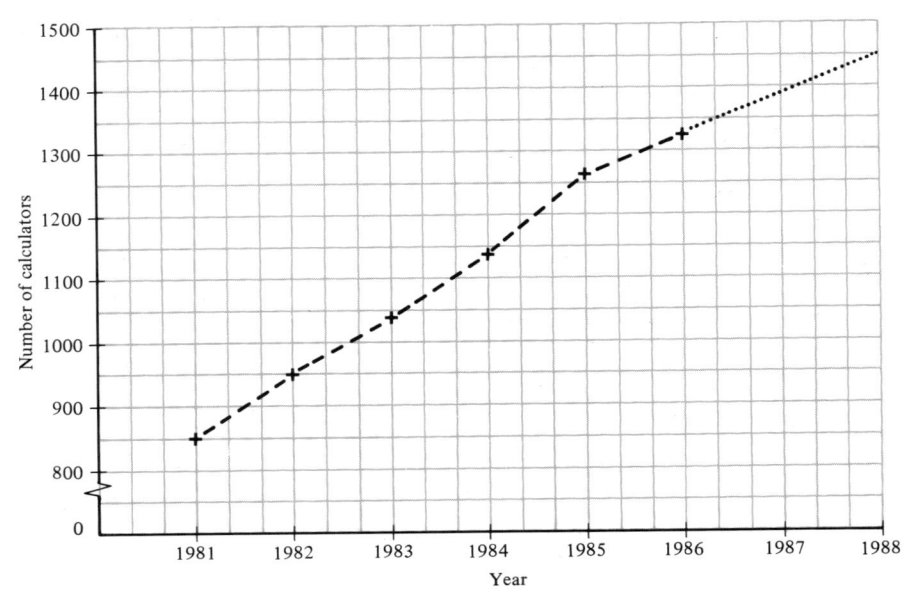

Figure 12

It does not make sense to take readings as we did from Figure 11(b). This is because it is nonsense to talk about the year $1983\frac{1}{2}$. However it makes the graph easier to read if the points are joined, but we use broken lines rather than full lines. It also makes sense to look at the *trend* of the results. The dotted line shows the extension of the graph to cover the years 1987 and 1988. Assuming that there is no reason why there should be a dramatic change we can estimate that there might be just under 1400 calculators in the school in 1987 and about 1450 in 1988. But there is no way of knowing this from the given data. The original steady upward trend may have returned; on the other hand there may have been a marked falling off in the possession of calculators.

Line graphs

Exercise D

*1 The graph in Figure 13 shows the 4-hourly temperature in °C of a patient suffering from 'flu. When was her temperature highest? When would you let her get up?

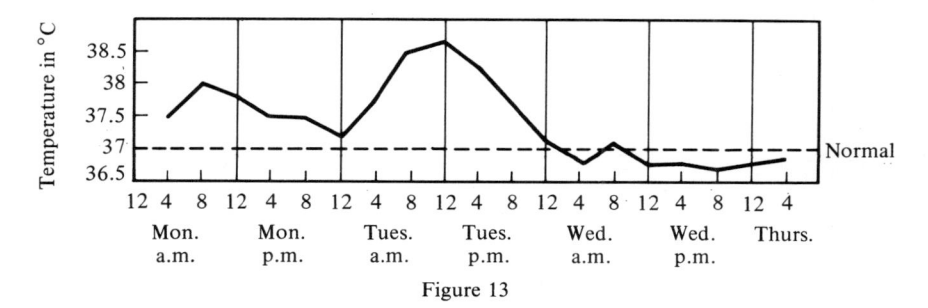

Figure 13

2 A survey was done to investigate the number of pairs of men's shoes sold of different sizes. The table shows the results.

Shoe size	7	$7\frac{1}{2}$	8	$8\frac{1}{2}$	9	$9\frac{1}{2}$
Number sold	20	23	32	38	48	58

Draw a graph to illustrate these data. It is suggested that you use your graph to predict the sales of shoes of sizes 10 and $10\frac{1}{2}$. Do you agree with this?

3 Table 6 gives information about cinema audiences for ten years.

Year	Cinema admissions (millions)	Year	Cinema admissions (millions)
1952	1312	1957	915
1953	1284	1958	756
1954	1276	1959	604
1955	1182	1960	530
1956	1101	1961	475

Table 6

Plot these data, and describe what is happening.
Try to find up-to-date information and compare the trend in the fifties and early sixties with the trend today.

6. MISLEADING DIAGRAMS

It is easy to mislead a casual reader by presenting information to him in diagrams that are deliberately inaccurate. For instance the money bags in Figure 14 are meant to represent a girl's weekly pay in 1980 and 1984.

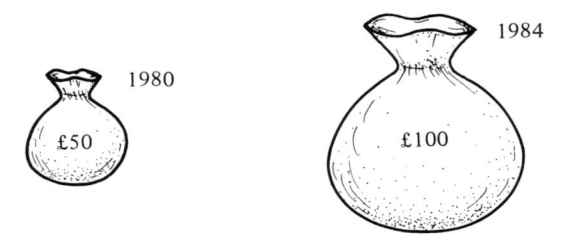

Figure 14

The second bag has been drawn twice as tall as the first because £100 is twice £50. But the reader's eye takes in the area of the figure making it look as if 1984's earnings are four times those in 1980. Or even it might be felt that the drawings look solid and that the larger could hold much more than four times the smaller. How many times?

Exercise E

Criticise the diagram in each of the following questions and, if it seems reasonable, draw a better one.

*1

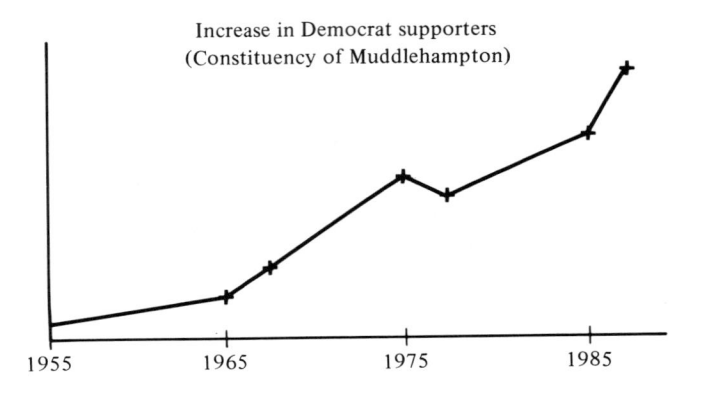

Figure 15

Misleading diagrams

2

Fluctuations in numbers at Dotheboys Hall

Present headmaster took over

Figure 16

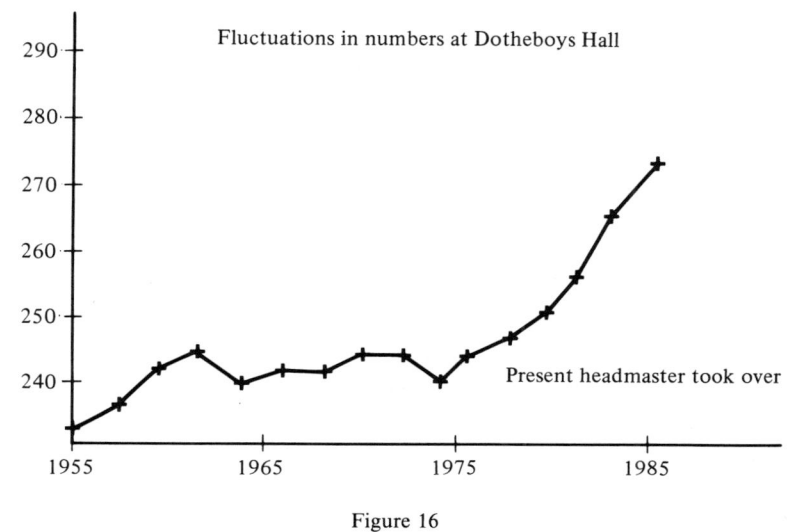

*3

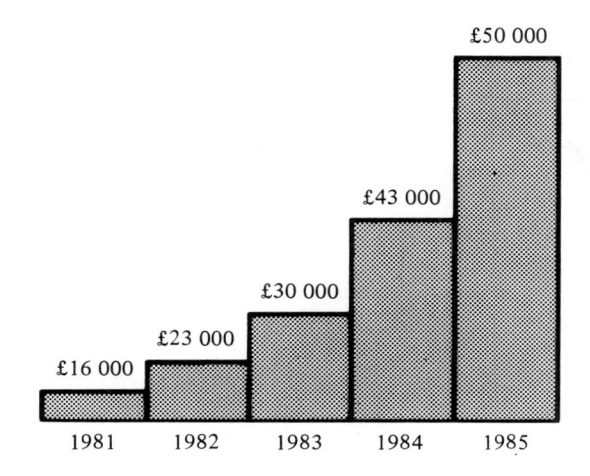

£50 000
£43 000
£30 000
£23 000
£16 000

1981 1982 1983 1984 1985

Profits of Skinner's Real Estate Company

Figure 17

4

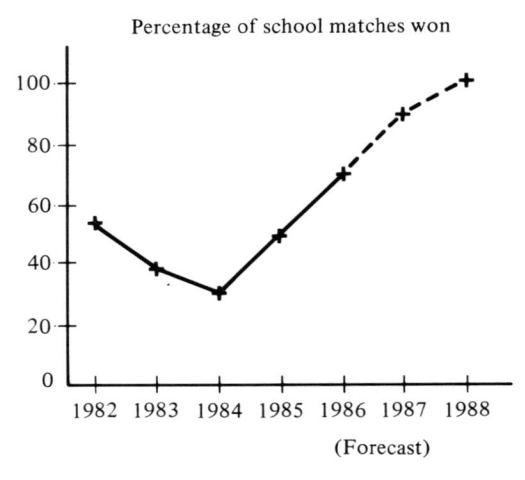

Percentage of school matches won

[Graph showing percentage from 1982 to 1988, with 1987 and 1988 marked as Forecast]

Figure 18

5

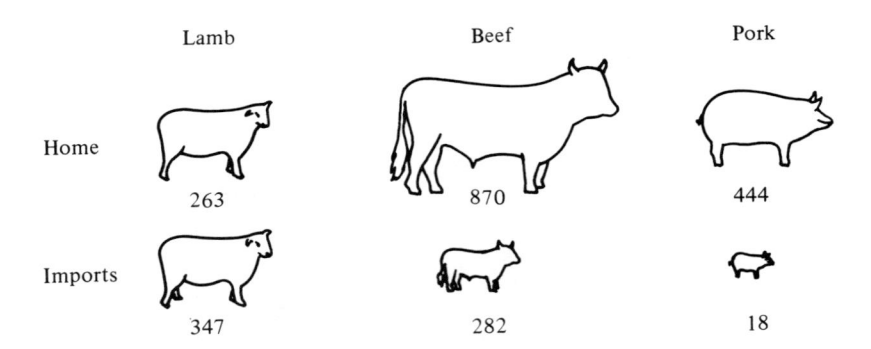

	Lamb	Beef	Pork
Home	263	870	444
Imports	347	282	18

Meat consumption in Northern Umboland 1985 (thousand tons)

Figure 19

7. PROJECTS

It is much more interesting to draw diagrams to illustrate data that you have collected yourself, or with others in a group. The following Exercise may give you some ideas. Perhaps you could do some large diagrams for display in your classroom.

Project exercise

1. Make a suitable diagram to show how your time is spent each day. How long sleeping, working, ...?
2. Roll a die 60 times and list the number of times each score is obtained. Illustrate with a diagram.
3. Make a survey of the shoe sizes of the members of your class. Illustrate with a diagram. If the class contains both boys and girls keep the data separate and do different diagrams. Is there any noticeable difference?
4. Make a survey of the colours of the cars passing the school gate or some other given point. Illustrate with a bar chart.
5. Use a Sunday paper to work out how many football league teams score no goals, how many 1 goal, how many 2 goals, etc. on a given Saturday. Illustrate by a diagram.
6. The most common letter
   Aim:
   To list the order of frequency of letters in an English book.
   Method:
   (a) Decide on a book which every member of the class has.
   (b) Assign a page to each pupil.
   (c) List the alphabet, read through the page putting a mark alongside each letter as it occurs. Count the marks to find how many times each letter has occurred. (These numbers are known as the *frequencies*.)
   (d) Put the results together.
   Results:
   (a) Display as a table from A to Z.
   (b) Rearrange the table and list the letters in order of frequency.
   (c) Display as a bar chart in order of frequency. Why is a pie chart unsuitable?
   Conclusions:
   What is the most common letter you have discovered? Would this have been the same if you had chosen any other book? Can these facts be put to use by anybody?

SUMMARY

Diagrams are useful to help present information in an attractive manner which is more easily understood than a list of figures. For example:

In 1956 the strengths of the British Armed Forces were

Royal Navy	116 100		
Army	393 000		
Royal Air Force	236 100	Total	745 200

The table gives the information very accurately but the following diagrams make it easier to follow.

246   Illustrating data   Ch. 31

(a)   Pictogram

RN

Army

RAF

1 figure to 50 000 men

Figure 20(a)

(b)   Bar Chart

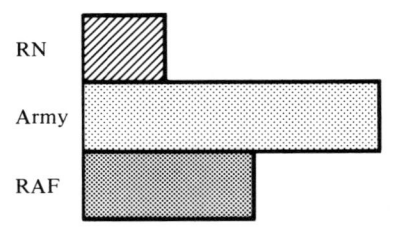

RN

Army

RAF

1 cm to 100 000 men

Figure 20(b)

(c)   Pie Chart

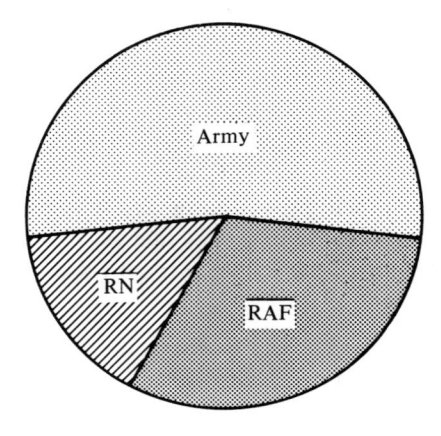

Army

RN

RAF

Figure 20(c)

The angle for the RAF sector (for example) has been calculated as follows:

Scale factor = 360 ÷ 745 200 = 0.000 483.
236 100 × 0.000 483 = 114 to nearest whole number.
Angle of sector = 114°.

Summary exercise

1 Draw a pictogram to illustrate the following data giving the values (in £100 000 units) of herring landed in England and Wales in the years shown.
    1952   15   1955   10
    1953   14½   1956   10
    1954   15   1957   9

2 Draw a bar chart to illustrate data from a survey of a school's staff.
    1 drove a Bentley
    5 drove Vauxhall cars
    7 drove Ford cars
    8 drove Austin Rover cars
    4 drove Foreign cars
    5 had no car.

3 Draw a pie chart to illustrate preferences in a school's science sixth form of 90 pupils.
    23 preferred Physics
    10 preferred Chemistry
    18 preferred Biology
    30 preferred Mathematics
    9 preferred Geology.

Miscellaneous exercise

1 A musical survey in form 2Z revealed the following facts about the popularity of certain groups:
    12 liked the Earwigs best of all
    9 liked the Caterwaulers
    4 liked the Crochet String Quartet
    3 liked the Popalongs
    2 liked the Squareboys.
   Illustrate this information by drawing:
    (a) a bar chart;
    (b) a pie chart;
   Devise some other method of showing the information.

2 Make a frequency table for the letters occurring in the following place-name.
    LLANFAIRPWLLGWYNGYLLGOGERYCHWYRNDROBWLL-
    LLANTYSILIOGOGOGOCH
   Which are the four most frequently appearing letters? Compare with the results from Project exercise, question 6. Comment on and explain any differences.

3 Criticise Figure 21 showing British Rail freight carried and draw a better one.

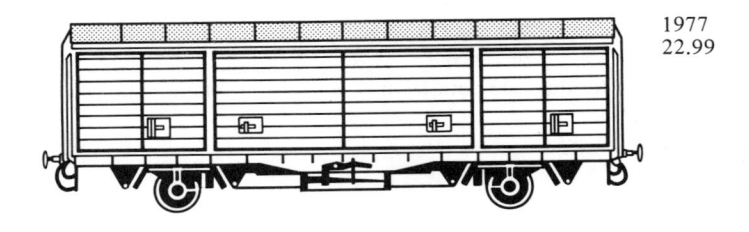

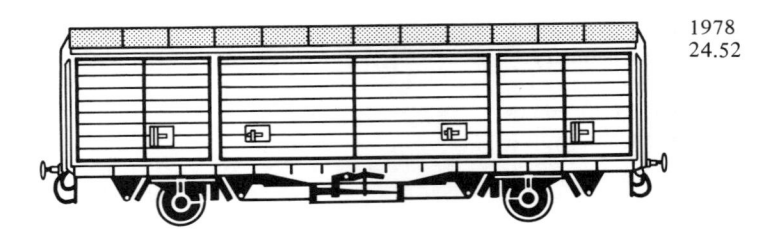

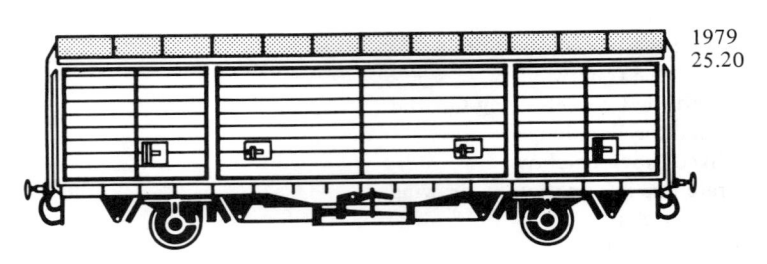

1967
14.12

1977
22.99

1978
24.52

1979
25.20

Figure 21 British Rail freight, average wagon load per journey (in tonnes).

4 Describe the data shown in Figure 22. How many families are involved? How many children.

Draw a similar chart for the families represented in your class. Discuss whether the same pattern of results would have been expected from a class of the same size 100 year ago.

Bar chart to show the number of children in a family

Number of children per family

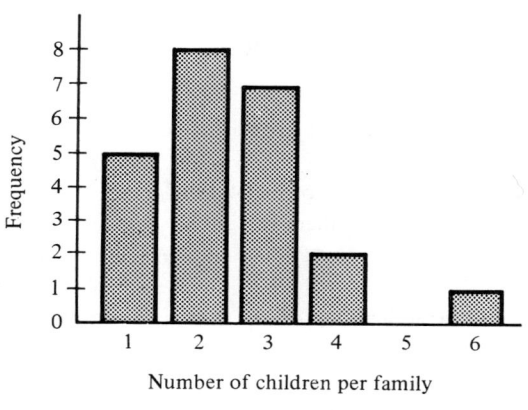

Figure 22

Quickies 10

CLOSED BOOK

Calculators must not be used.

1. If the Norwegian exchange rate is 11 kroner to the £, how many kroner will I get for £40?
2. How many grams are there in 20% of 1 kilogram?
3. How many cubic centimetres are there in 1 litre.
4. Find the image of the point (3, 7) after enlargement, centre the origin, scale factor ⁻4.
5. Give the bearing 045° as a direction on the mariner's compass.
6. I think of a number, square it and halve the result. My answer is 18. What number did I think of?
7. Ann and Lance share £36 so that Ann receives three times as much as Lance. How much does Lance get?
8. How long will it take to travel 130 km at an average speed of 40 km/h?
9. Find the area of a right-angled triangle with height 6 cm and base 5 cm.
10. Two circles have centres 17 cm apart. Their radii are 5 cm and 3 cm. What is the distance between the points that are furthest apart?

OPEN BOOK

Calculators must not be used.

1. After two enlargements, the first with scale factor ⁻3 and the second with scale factor ⁻9, a length of x cm maps onto one of 81 cm. What is the value of x?
2. Find x in Figure 1.

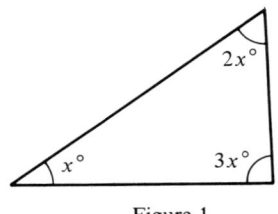

Figure 1

3 A chair costing £40 has its price increased by 5%. What is its new price?
4 In a survey of 90 people, 23 voted for the SNORY party. What angle would be used on a pie chart to represent this information?
5 I think of a number, add 4 and square the result. The answer is 49. What number did I think of?
6 $m = \frac{1}{2}(n - 5)^2$. What is the value of m if $n = 9$?
7 What is the exchange rate in dollars to the £ if I get 390 dollars for £300?
8 Calculate the area of Figure 2.

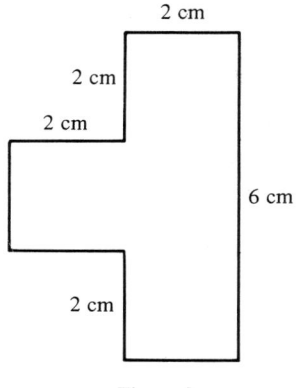

Figure 2

9 What is $^-2.7 - {}^-1.3$.
10 $\frac{3}{5}$ of a class are girls. If there are 14 boys in the class, how many pupils are there altogether?

Revision exercises 10A, 10B

REVISION EXERCISE 10A

1. Use your calculator to work out the following. Check mentally.
   (a) $2 \times 5 + {}^-3$;   (b) ${}^-7 + 3 \times {}^-4$;   (c) $(8 + {}^-3) \times ({}^-6 + 2)$;
   (d) $4 + {}^-2 \times 6$;   (e) $5 + 40 \times {}^-4$;   (f) $7 + \dfrac{60}{{}^-5 \times 3}$.

2. (a) Write the following decimals as (i) hundredths, (ii) percentages:
   0.07,   0.13,   0.565,   1.50.
   (b) Write the following percentages as (i) hundredths, (ii) decimals:
   15%,   9%,   95.3%,   200%.

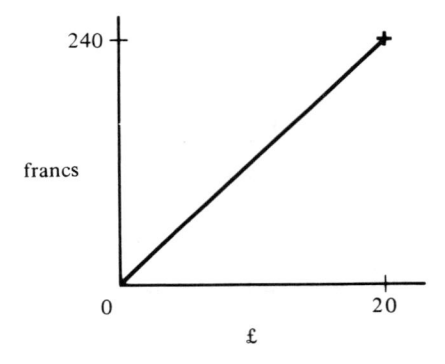

Figure 1

3. Form 1Z are getting ready for their day trip to France and have been told that £1 is worth about 12 francs. They have pinned a large copy of the graph sketched in Figure 1 to the classroom wall and are using it to answer some questions. Make your own copy and answer the following:
   (a) Joan has saved £7.50 for spending money. How many francs is this?
   (b) Dawn has saved £13.00. Will she be able to buy a jumper she sees advertised at 170 francs?
   (c) They have been told that a special outing will cost them 65 francs each. How much is this in English money?

4. A jar contains 720 sweets. If 15% of these are humbugs, how many sweets are not humbugs?

5. Moira conducted a survey of girls in the first year to find what flavour of MOG-GINOSH their cats preferred. Show the following results in a pictogram and in a bar chart.
   Liver 10,   Chicken 6,   Beef 8,   Cod 16,   Pilchard 10.

REVISION EXERCISE 10B

1. In a heavy storm 1.5 cm of rain fell in an afternoon. What volume of rain water fell on a flat roof measuring 4 m by 3 m? Give your answer in litres.
2. Calculate the following quantities.
    (a) 75% of 48 km; (b) 60% of 35 kg; (c) 7% of £150;
    (d) 9% of 1.5 m;   (e) 12% of £750;   (f) 18% of £1.72 (to nearest 1p).
3. Jill takes her small brother for a donkey ride at Easton-super-mare. The donkey walks at 2 m/s for 1 minute, then stops dead and refuses to move for 45 seconds. It then walks on very slowly and takes another a minute to go a further 30 m. It turns round and heads back to the start at 3 m/s. Draw a travel graph for the donkey ride.
4. An examination paper was marked out of 160 marks. If Saskia scored 35% and Catrina 80%, how many marks (out of 160) did each get?
5. Form 1Z kept a record of the main course at school lunch for the first eight weeks of term. Show the following results on (a) a bar chart; (b) a pie chart.

    sausages 12, shepherd's pie 10, fish fingers 8, chilli-con-carne 3, cottage pie 7.

Try this 6: A paper chase

A question in the Miscellaneous exercise to Chapter 12 (Scale factors) explored some of the mathematics of international paper sizes A4, A5, A6. The following investigation covers a little of the same ground and then extends the ideas.

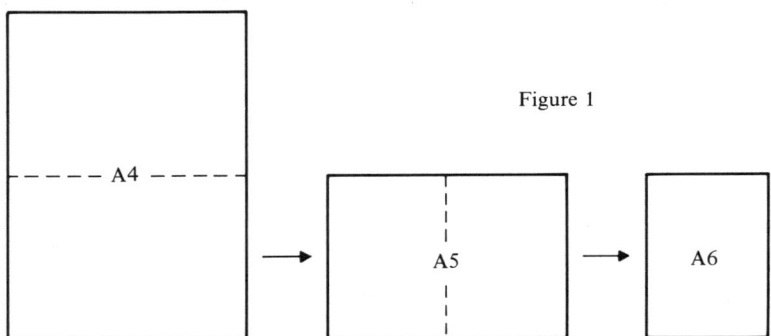

Figure 1

A Take two pieces of A4 paper. Label one 'A4' and cut the other in half as shown in Figure 1. Label one of the smaller pieces 'A5' and cut the other in half, labelling one of the resulting pieces 'A6'.

Continue this process to obtain pieces of size A7 and A8. You could, of course, go further if you wish!

B Measure the sides of your rectangles (in cm to the nearest mm). Copy and complete the first three columns of Table 1.

Paper	Longest side (cm)	Shortest side (cm)	(Longest) ÷ (shortest)	Area (cm^2)
A4				
A5				
○				
○				

Table 1

C Use your calculator to divide the length of the longest side by that of the shortest for each of your rectangles. Complete the fourth column of the table giving your answers rounded to the nearest hundredth. What do you notice about your answers? What does this tell you about the sheets of paper in the series?

D Sizes A4, A5, ..., A8 are only some of the range of international paper sizes each of which is obtained by halving a piece of the previous size in the series. A4 is obtained by halving A3 and A3 by halving A2. A3 and A2 and possibly A1 are to be found in your school's art department.

Make a new table, Table 2, with the same columns as Table 1. Enter paper sizes A4, A3, A2, A1 and A0. A0 is the largest paper size in the series. Look carefully at the pattern of lengths in Table 1 and hence complete the first four columns of Table 2.

E Working in cm^2, and giving as many figures as your calculator displays, complete the last column of the tables to give the area of each sheet from size A0 to A8.

F Your cutting and measuring is obviously not going to be 'spot on' accurate and any errors made will be exaggerated in your answers to the areas. However, look carefully at your results and write down that you think is the *exact* area of sheet A0. Give your answer in suitable units – and *think*!

Puzzle corner 2

1. It is possible to use all the digits from 1 to 9 once and once only to make three equivalent fractions. For example:
$$\tfrac{2}{4} = \tfrac{3}{6} = \tfrac{79}{158}.$$
Find another set of equivalent fractions using the digits 1 to 9 once and once only.

2. Work out:
$$9 \times 9 + 7 =$$
$$98 \times 9 + 6 =$$
$$987 \times 9 + 5 =$$
How does this pattern continue?

3. Two men play a card game and the stake is 1p per game. At the end Bill has won three games and Fred has won 3p. How many games did they play?

4. Draw a triangle with sides 10 cm, 8 cm and 7 cm. Divide it, by two cuts, into two triangles and a quadrilateral so that the pieces can be rearranged to make a rectangle.

5. Which is the smallest number which is the sum of the squares of 3 integers and also the sum of the squares of 4 integers and all 7 integers are different? (*Integer* is another name for a whole number.)

6. The number 15 can be written as the sum of consecutive integers in two ways,
$15 = 7 + 8 = 4 + 5 + 6$.
Write 105 as the sum of consecutive integers; it can be done in 5 ways.
Try this with 45, 48 and 64. Is there a pattern?

7. Given the seven integers from 0 to 6, how many different pairs can you make, including using the same number twice? (This, of course, gives the numbers used on a set of dominoes.)

8. One glass contains 10 cm^3 of wine, another glass 10 cm^3 of water. 1 cm^3 is removed from the first and mixed in the second and then 1 cm^3 is removed from the second and put in the first. Is there now more water in the first or wine in the second? What happens if this is done again?

9. Three glass tumblers are placed base down on a table. If you are allowed to turn over any pair at a time explain why you cannot arrange all three the wrong way up. What if there are four tumblers and you can turn over three, or there are five tumblers and you can turn over four?

10. An Egyptian fraction is one in which the numerator is 1 e.g. $\tfrac{1}{2}, \tfrac{1}{4}$. Other fractions can be written as the sum of these (with no denominator repeated). For example:
$$\tfrac{5}{6} = \tfrac{3}{6} + \tfrac{2}{6} = \tfrac{1}{2} + \tfrac{1}{3}.$$
Try the same with $\tfrac{17}{20}, \tfrac{23}{28}$ and $\tfrac{3}{7}$.

11. It is required to arrange four similar looking objects in order of weight. A simple balance is available so that objects, or pairs of objects can be compared. What is the minimum number of weighings necessary? What is the answer in the case of five objects?

Puzzle corner 2

12 Draw a square of side 10 cm and draw inside it a pentagon with sides all 5 cm as in Figure 1.

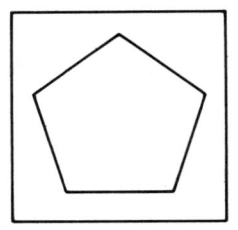

Figure 1

By drawing five lines each starting on the pentagon and ending on the square form five different irregular pentagons.

13 The ten digits are shuffled in some random order e.g. 3679421508. The object is to rearrange them in the order 0123456789 but each turn consists of taking a block of numbers always starting with the one on the left and reversing their order: in our example we could reverse the first four and write 9763421508. What is the least number of turns which will always succeed?

14 In Transylvania the coins are of value 1, 2, 4, 8, 16 and 32 dracs. 40 dracs make one vamp for which there are notes.

Show that with just these coins any sum of money can be paid (up to 1 vamp) using only one coin of any size in each sum. For example:
$$35 = 32 + 2 + 1.$$
Under a new government the 2, 4, 8, 16, 32 drac coins are to be scrapped and replaced by just 3 coins. It is still to be possible to pay for all items up to 1 vamp by just using one coin of each value, but it is allowed to give change. Find the values of the new coins.

Answers

CHAPTER 17 NEGATIVE NUMBERS

Exercise A (p. 4)
1 (a) (i) ⁻3, (ii) ⁺5;
   (b) (i) ⁻2, (ii) ⁺1;
   (c) (i) ⁺4, (ii) ⁻3.
2 (b) ⁻300.
3 (a) (i) ⁻13; (b) (i) 8.43 a.m.
4 (b) (i) 20, (ii) 24.
7 (a) ⁻16.
9 (a) ⁺1, ⁻1, ⁻3, ⁻5.

Exercise B (p. 9)
1 (a) (⁺5); (b) (⁻1); (c) (⁺1).
4 ⁺12.
7 ⁻12.
10 ⁻50.

Exercise C (p. 10)
1 ⁺38.
2 ⁻55.
6 ⁺9.
7 ⁺8.2.
11 ⁻18.

Exercise D (p. 13)
1 (a) ⁺3; (b) ⁺8; (c) ⁻2.
4 ⁻4.
7 ⁻10;
10 ⁻8.3.
16 (a) 4; (c) 16; (e) 8.

Exercise E (p. 16)
1 (a) (i) 22 degrees; (b) (i) Algiers and Barbados, (iii) Frankfurt and Montreal.
2 (a) (i) 20; (b) (i) 20.

CHAPTER 18 SYMMETRY

Exercise A (p. 25)
2 (a) One line of symmetry; (e) four lines of symmetry.
4 (a)   (c)

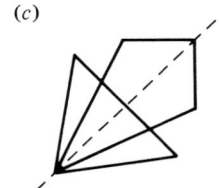

257

258 Answers

7

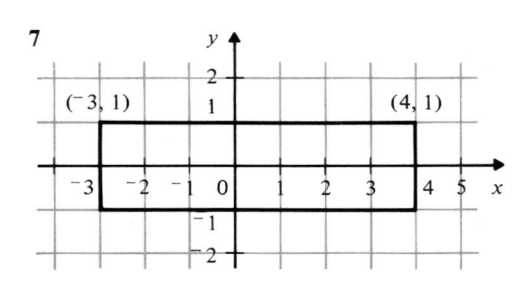

Other vertices are (4, ⁻1) and (⁻3, ⁻1).

Exercise B (p. 29)

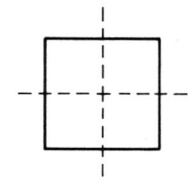

2 (*a*) Neither line of symmetry bisects an angle.

3 (*a*) For example:

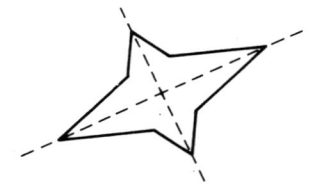

5 (*a*) 60°; (*b*) 30°.

Exercise C (p. 32)
1 (*a*) has rotational symmetry of order 3.
2 (*c*) order 2; (*e*) order 4.
4 (*a*) A C D E H I K M O T U V W X Y

CHAPTER 19   CALCULATIONS AND APPROXIMATIONS

Exercise A (p. 41)
1 35.   **4** 35.   **7** 0.35.   **10** 54.
13 0.2.   **16** 0.01.   **19** 600.   **22** 200.
28 (*a*) 9; (*c*) 80.
29 (*a*) 4; (*c*) 60; (*e*) 40.
30 (*a*) 6; (*c*) 0.06; (*e*) 200.
31 (*b*), (*c*), (*f*), (*h*), (*j*), (*k*).

Exercise B (p. 43)
1 (*a*) 2 cm.
5 360 km.

Exercise C (p. 44)
1 (*a*) 0.9;   (*c*) 0.009.
3 (*a*) 0.7;   (*c*) 0.7.
5 20.
8 2.
11 480.
14 0.07.
17 0.004.
21 £0.06.
24 0.06 mm.
25 (*a*) greater;   (*b*) less.
26 Smaller than 24.
31 Smaller than 240.

Exercise D (p. 46)
Possible answers are:
1 (*a*) 9 × 3 = 27.
3 (*a*) 0.9 × 0.4 = 0.36.
5 £9.
7 60 km.
10 (*a*) 6.
12 (*a*) 5.
14 50.

Exercise E (p. 48)
1 199 grams butter, 57 grams icing sugar.
2 193 cm.
3 175 cm;   170 cm.

Exercise F (p. 51)
1 8, 1, 5, 12, 8, 19, 6.
3 100, 100, 200, 800, 700, 800, 500, 1000.
6 (possible answers) (*a*) 8;   (*c*) 160;   (*e*) 5.
8 150 miles, 1 gallon every 2 miles, 75 gallons.
11 700 ÷ 25 = 28;   28 grams.

CHAPTER 20   BRACKETS IN FORMULAE

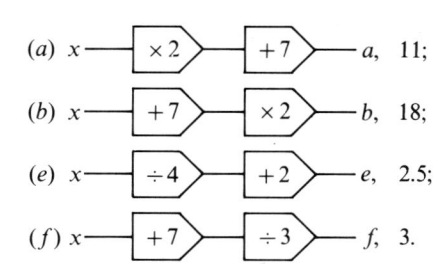

Exercise A (p. 61)
1 (*a*) 20;   (*c*) 6.
2
 (*a*) $x \to \times 2 \to +7 \to$ *a*, 11;
 (*b*) $x \to +7 \to \times 2 \to$ *b*, 18;
 (*e*) $x \to \div 4 \to +2 \to$ *e*, 2.5;
 (*f*) $x \to +7 \to \div 3 \to$ *f*, 3.

Exercise B (p. 64)
1 (*a*) $2x + 2y$;   (*c*) $7p + 7q + 7r$;   (*e*) $4a + 4b$.
3 (*a*) $15x - 6y$;   (*c*) $4p + 6q$;   (*e*) $15y - 20z$.
5 (*a*) $12(30 + 250) = 12 \times 280 = 3360$
    $12 \times 30 + 12 \times 250 = 360 + 3000 = 3360$ } 3360 g = 3.36 kg.

Answers

CHAPTER 21 LET'S LOOK AT NUMBER

Exercise A (p. 67)
1   13.
3   41.
5   40.

Exercise B (p. 69)
1   1, 2, 4, 8, 16, 32, 64, 128, 256, 512, 1024.
3   5, 12, 19, 26, 33, 40, 47.
5   10.

Exercise C (p. 70)
1   1, 2, 3, 4, 5, 6, 7, 8, 9, 10.
3   1, 3, 5, 7, 9, 11, 13, 15, 17, 19.
5   1, 4, 9, 16, 25, 36, 49, 64, 81, 100.

Exercise D (p. 78)
1   (*a*) Rectangle;   (*c*) prime.
3   64.
7   (*a*) 1, 2, 4, 8;   (*c*) 1, 2, 3, 5, 10, 15, 30.

CHAPTER 22 AREA

Exercise A (p. 83)
1   (*a*) 40 triangles.
2   108 triangles.
3   (*b*) 14 triangle units.

Exercise B (p. 85)
1   1.5 cm^2.
4   2 cm^2.
9   5.5 cm^2.
11 (*a*) 7.5 cm^2.

Exercise C (p. 89)
1   (*a*) m^2;   (*c*) cm^2;   (*g*) ha.
2   (*a*) 5 m^2;   (*c*) 1200 cm^2.

Exercise D (p. 93)
1   4 cm^2.
4   3 cm^2.
8   15 cm^2.
11 12 m^2.
17 13.5 m^2.

CHAPTER 23 ANGLES
Answers obtained by measurement must be treated as approxmate.

Exercise A (p. 110)
1   (*a*) 34°;   (*c*) 69°.   4   320°.   6   Barnes Farm is on a bearing of 302°.

Exercise B (p. 114)

1	560 m	5.6 cm	3	6 km	12 cm
	280 m	2.8 cm		2 km	4 cm
	1300 m	13 cm		7 km	14 cm
	1 km	10 cm		1.4 km	2.8 cm
	40 m	0.4 cm		4.5 km	9 cm

5   295°, 115°, 25 km apart.
8   (*a*) Distance 340 km, bearing 145°;
    (*d*) distance 520 km, bearing 255°, then
        distance 1035 km, bearing 188°.
10 270°, 135°;   97 km, 289°.

Exercise C (p. 122)
1 (a) $g = 61, f = 90$;
   (c) $j = 136, m = 44, l = 44, k = 44$;
   (e) $p = 73, q = 59$.
3 (a) 065°; (c) 310°.
5 (a) $g = 77, t = 77, m = 38$;
   (c) $f = 65, h = 65, n = 81$;
   (e) $v = 37, x = 143, u = 58, w = 122, y = 122$.
7 (a) 328°; (b) 237°.

Exercise D (p. 125)
1 (a) $q = 63, p = 117$;
   (c) $y = 75, x = 105$.
3 (a) (i) 7.8 km, (ii) 5 km, (iii) 7.8 km;
   (b) (i) 299°, (ii) 49°, (iii) 157°.
5 350 km.

CHAPTER 24 FORMULAE USING SQUARES

Exercise A (p. 134)
1 (a) $s = 5(t - 3)$, 20;
   (c) $y = \dfrac{x}{10} + 4$, 6.5.
2 (a) $g = 3.2x + 15.8$, 47.16;
   (c) $y = \dfrac{x - 5.3}{1.5}$, 3.
3 (a) $t \to [\times 2.5] \to [+1.5] \to s$;   24.
   (c) $t \to [\div 2.5] \to [-1.5] \to s$;   2.1.

Exercise B (p. 137)
1 (a) $5 \to [SQ] \to [+5] \to 30$; (b) $N = t^2 + 5$; (c) 69; (d) Yes.
2 (a) $q = p^2 - 3$, 22; (b) $q = (p - 3)^2$, 4.
4 (a) 14; (b) 144; (c) 288; (d) 18; (e) 72.
6 (a) $x \to [-1.74] \to [SQ] \to y$, 0.0484;
   (b) $x \to [SQ] \to [-1.74] \to y$, 2.1016;
   (c) $x \to [SQ] \to [\times 2] \to [-1.74] \to y$, 5.9432;
   (d) $x \to [-1.74] \to [SQ] \to [\times 2] \to y$, 0.0968;
   (e) $x \to [SQ] \to [-1.74] \to [\div 2] \to y$, 1.0508;
   (f) $x \to [-1.74] \to [SQ] \to [\div 2] \to y$, 0.0242.

Exercise C (p. 140)

1 $B = nc$; £1.17.
3 $3p$; $c = B/n$.
5 (a) 35; (b) 7.77; (c) 5; (d) 11; (e) 2; (f) 75; (g) 45; (h) 8; (i) 24; (j) 18; (k) 90; (l) 150.

CHAPTER 25 FACTORS

Exercise A (p. 144)

1 28, for example, gives 282 828.

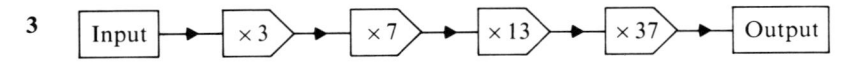

3 Input → ×3 → ×7 → ×13 → ×37 → Output

This is the longest.

Exercise B (p. 144)

1 1001.
2 7 × 143 is one possible answer.

Exercise C (p. 145)

1 (a) (i) true, (iii) false;
  (b) (i) 24 and 30.
3 (a) 7 and 111 is one possibility;
  (b) 1 and 13 is the only possibility.
5 (a) (i) 1 and 36, 2 and 18, 3 and 12, 4 and 9, 6 and 6; (iii) 1 and 25, 5 and 5; (iv) 1 and 52, 2 and 26; 4 and 13;
  (b) 53 has only one factor-pair, but there is another one to find.
7 (a) (i), (iii) and (iv) must be true.

Exercise E (p. 148)

1 (a) 1, 2, 3, 4, 6, 12; (b) 1, 2, 3, 6, 9, 18.
2 (a) 35, 70 and 110 are three possibilities.
3 168 is a possible answer but it is not the smallest.
5 (a) No.
7 2, 3, 4, 6, 8, 12, 24.
9 (a) has factor of 3; (c) does not have factor of 3; (e) has factor of 3.

Exercise F (p. 151)

1 (a) 5 × 13; (c) 3 × 29.
4 (b) 2 × 3 × 11 = 66.
5 (b) 676 = 2 × 2 × 13 × 13.
8 (a) (i) 2 × 5; (ii) 2 × 2 × 5 × 5; (iii) 2 × 2 × 2 × 5 × 5 × 5.
  (ii) is a square number, there are others.
  (d) $t = 175$.

Answers 263

CHAPTER 26 VOLUME

Exercise A (p. 160)
2 (*a*) 12; (*c*) 8.

Exercise B (p. 162)
1 3 cm³.
5 10 cm³.
8 36 cm³.
11 24 cm³.
15 120 mm³.
18 96 mm³.

Exercise C (p. 166)
1 60 cm³.
4 360 cm³.
7 162 cm³.

Exercise D (p. 168)
1 6 litres.
3 12.5 litres.
6 10 cm.

CHAPTER 27 THROUGH THE CENTRE OF ENLARGEMENT

Exercise A (p. 176)
1 (*a*) (18, ⁻12).
2 (*a*) Yes, 2 (or ½); (*b*) No.
3 (*a*) Centre (8, 1), scale factor ⅓.
4 (*a*) 0.6.
5 (*a*) 12.

Exercise B (p. 179)
1 (*a*) about 2; (*b*) about ⁻½.
4 (*a*) 35; (*c*) ⁻21; (*e*) ⁻24.
7 (*c*) 1.5.
8 (*a*) 10; (*c*) ⁻2; (*e*) ⁻9.
9 (*a*) ⁻12, ⁺24, ⁺36.
10 (*a*) ½, (7, 3).
13 (*a*) ⁻12.

Exercise C (p. 186)
1 (*a*) (i) and (ii) 4; (*c*) (i) and (ii) ⁻11; (*e*) (i) and (ii) 4.
2 (*a*) ⁻3; (*c*) 7; (*e*) ⁻10.
3 (*a*) 3.
4 (*a*) 45.36; (*c*) 17.04; (*e*) 1.8.
6 (*a*) 2; (*c*) ⁻10.
8 (*a*) (i) ⁻4; (*b*) (i) ⁻2.

Exercise D (p. 188)
1 (*a*) ⁻11; (*c*) ⁺2; (*e*) ⁺8.
3 (*a*) ⁻20; (*c*) ⁻19; (*e*) 3.
5 (*a*) ⁻8, ⁻11; (*c*) ⁻4, ⁻4; (*e*) 3, ⁻11, ⁻2.

CHAPTER 28 FRACTIONS

Exercise A (p. 197)
1 (*a*) $\frac{2}{6} = \frac{1}{3}$.
2 (*a*) $\frac{7}{9}$; (*c*) $\frac{4}{5}$; (*e*) $\frac{13}{15}$.
3 $\frac{1}{4} = \frac{2}{8} = \frac{5}{20} = \frac{3}{12} = \frac{24}{96}$.
5 $\frac{2}{3} = \frac{6}{9} = \frac{10}{15} = \frac{16}{24} = \frac{18}{27}$.
8 $\frac{10}{15}, \frac{12}{15}$.
11 $\frac{14}{24}, \frac{9}{24}$.
13 $\frac{366}{488} = \frac{3}{4}$.
15 (*a*) $\frac{1}{6}$.

Exercise B (p. 200)
1 $\frac{5}{8} > \frac{19}{32}$.
5 $\frac{3}{5} < \frac{2}{3}$.
9 $\frac{3}{5} < \frac{12}{19}$.
11 $\frac{11}{18} > \frac{5}{9} > \frac{25}{48}$.
13 $\frac{5}{8} > \frac{5}{10} > \frac{3}{8} > \frac{3}{10}$.

Exercise C (p. 202)
1 (*a*) $\frac{11}{12}$.
3 (*c*) $\frac{7}{12}$.
5 (*b*) $\frac{11}{15}$.
7 (*a*) $\frac{1}{4}$.
9 (*b*) $\frac{41}{75}$.
11 $\frac{1}{6}$.
13 $\frac{19}{25}$.

Exercise D (p. 204)
1 (*a*) 3⅜.   3 (*c*) 7$\frac{13}{30}$.   5 (*a*) ⅚.   8 ⅘ kg.

Answers

CHAPTER 29 PERCENTAGES

Exercise A (p. 214)

1. (*a*) (i) 6 hundredths, (ii) 6%;
   (*c*) (i) 48 hundredths, (ii) 48%.
2. (*a*) (i) 4 hundredths, (ii) 0.04;
   (*c*) (i) 79 hundredths, (ii) 0.79.
3. (*a*) 3.4 kg; (*c*) 4.5 litres.
4. (*a*) 1p; (*c*) 0.7 m or 70 cm.
7. £336.
10. (*a*) Up to £219.45.
12. (*a*) 90°; (*c*) 172.8°.

Exercise B (p. 216)

1. (*a*) 80p.
2. (*a*) 77p; (*c*) £5.85.
4. (*a*) Hi-fi: (i) £40, (ii) £160;
   (*d*) Video recorder: (i) £99, (ii) £396.
6. £6.

CHAPTER 30 CONVERSION AND TRAVEL GRAPHS

Most of the following answers are those that may reasonably be obtained from a graph.

Exercise A (p. 222)

1. (*a*) 6.4 km; (*c*) 6.2 or 6.3 m; (*e*) 360 or 370 g; (*f*) 1.76 lb.
3. (*a*) 15.2 or 15.3 cm; (*b*) 7.8 or 7.9 inches.
4. (*a*) 11.3 or 11.4 litres; (*b*) 3.3 gallons.
5. (*a*) 20 or 21 m/s; (*b*) 55.5 or 55.6 m.p.h.

Exercise B (p. 225)

1. (*a*) Approx. 2 hours 10 minutes; (*c*) 2.4 km/h; (*d*) 1 hour;
   (*f*) 60 km from London – 20 km from Brighton.

Exercise C (p. 226)

1. 9.8 km. Between 1212 and 1215 hrs.
2. (*a*) 60 km/h; (*c*) Just starting off again!
4. 12 miles.

CHAPTER 31 ILLUSTRATING DATA

Exercise A (p. 230)

3. BR 420 000.

Exercise B (p. 233)

5. Trudy £7.50.

Exercise C (p. 237)

1. Angle for KOKOPOPS is 162°.
3. (*a*) £180; (*b*) Angle for rent 96°, for clothes 20°.
6. Angle for cattle is 90°.
9. 108 people interviewed.

Exercise D (p. 241)

1. Temperature highest at 12 noon, Tuesday.

Exercise E (p. 242)

1. No label or scale on vertical axis.
3. £50 000 column is more than twice as high as the £30 000 column.

Index

accuracy 47
angles
  alternate 118
  bisector of 28
  corresponding 119
  interior 120
approximation 41ff
area 82
  of rectangle 90
  of triangle 92

bar chart 231
bearings 105
brackets 59
British units 81

calculator and negative numbers 9
capacity 167
composite numbers 147
constructions 172
conversion graphs 219

data 229
decision box 68
difference 13

edge 160
enlargement 173
  negative scale factor 177
equivalent fractions 195

face 160
factor 77, 143
factor-pair 145
factor tree 150
flow chart 66
formulae 132
fractions 194
  addition and subtraction 200
  equivalent 195

geoliner 25

hectare 88

line graphs 238

mediator 28
mixed numbers 203

negative numbers 3
  addition and subtraction 187
  on a calculator 9
  division 183
  multiplication 178
nets 159

parallel lines 117
percentage 212
perfect numbers 149
pictogram 230
pie chart 234
positive numbers 3
prime numbers 76, 146

rectangle numbers 76
removing brackets 62
rounding 50

scale drawing 111, 124
square numbers 72
symmetry 21
  line 22
  rotational 31

travel graphs 223
trends 239
triangle numbers 71

vertex 159
volume 160